THE CROSSING

ALSO BY RICHARD PARKER

Lone Star Nation

THE CROSSING

EL PASO, THE SOUTHWEST, AND AMERICA'S FORGOTTEN ORIGIN STORY

RICHARD PARKER

MARINER BOOKS
New York   Boston

FIRST EDITION

Designed by Emily Snyder

Library of Congress Cataloging-in-Publication Data has been applied for.

ISBN 978-0-06-316191-7

24 25 26 27 28 LBC 5 4 3 2 1

To my mother, Josefina Delgado Parker,
who bridged two families, two cultures,
and two worlds

Contents

CONTENTS

-------------- **Prologue** --------------

AUGUST 3, 2019, was just another hot summer Saturday in America, until startling news struck millions of people, coming from a place that few of them had given much thought to: El Paso, Texas. A gunman had massacred twenty-two people with an AK-47 while they shopped at Walmart because, as he later confessed, he "wanted to kill as many Mexicans as possible."

Patrick Crusius, age twenty-one, had driven six hundred miles from suburban Dallas to set a number of grisly records: the worst domestic terrorist attack since the 1995 Oklahoma City bombing, the deadliest assault on Latinos in US history, and the highest death toll of any mass shooting outside the 2017 killings on the Las Vegas strip. I had just arrived in El Paso to visit my mother and was taking a nap when my phone buzzed repeatedly with urgent emails and text messages, as my editor at the *New York Times* kept trying to hail me. He knew, after all, that this was my hometown.

Americans watched in horror as the body count mounted. The faces and names of the dead appeared on television screens and flickered on mobile phones while a vast makeshift memorial of flowers, candles, photos, and handwritten notes swelled at the site of the massacre. I roused myself out of bed, turned on the television, hurriedly packed a backpack, and headed out. "When Hate Came to El Paso" appeared in the *New York Times* the next day, August 4, 2019:

> If you want to know what a mass shooting is like in your hometown, it's like this: text alerts on your phone, a frantic woman on local television begging people to bring water to waiting families, 200 people lining up to give blood in the blistering heat, helicopters thundering overhead, the dead left lying inside the crime scene called "horrific" by the police chief. Those waiting on word of dead and lost stand calm and dignified as strangers pull up with truckloads of that bottled water. It's also like this: a stab in the heart not just to your hometown, but to your people, in my case Latinos. Mr. Crusius specifically came here to my town, to kill my people.

In the subsequent days, Latinos across the country felt "hunted," as one man put it. Most Americans felt that President Donald Trump, in his cruel treatment of Latino immigrants, had egged on dangerous white supremacists such as the killer. Nearly six in ten Americans called white nationalism a threat to the nation. Yet that young man, Crusius, didn't just murder Mexicans. In reality, he killed seven Mexican citizens, along with Anglos, Mexican Americans, a German, and others, while wounding another twenty.

Crusius had come some six hundred miles not just to kill people but to attack a unique feature of El Paso: this big, bustling city was a blend of Europeans, Americans, Native Americans, mestizos, and African Americans, all living side by side, intermarrying—a multicultural society that dated back for centuries. More than five hundred years earlier, the first person from the Old World to glimpse this part of the New World arrived. A Black man, he went by Esteban, the name his Spanish captors had given him. He was born in 1502 in Azemmour, Morocco, a bustling port city roughly three hundred miles from the Strait of Gibraltar that thrived on the pragmatism of diversity: Jews, Muslims, and some Christians lived, traded, and worshipped in relative peace. Then, in 1523, the Spanish raided the city and enslaved thousands, including Esteban, then twenty-one years old.

He was taken to Seville, another racially, ethnically, and culturally diverse city, which remained that way despite the Inquisition. There he was sold for a high price to Andres Dorantes de Carranza. One of the lowliest of Spanish nobles, known as hidalgos, or those without hereditary title, Dorantes would have to find fortune and reputation his own way. He needed a slave to make an impression in Spanish society, and he needed, indeed burned, to get to the Americas, where the future was being made. In compliance with Spanish law, Esteban was forced to convert to Catholicism. He learned to make the sign of the cross and pray the rosary and gave up the name of his birth, Mostafa.[1] Esteban was young and strong and a genius with languages. His health and skill would keep him alive when almost every other person around him fell dead.

On June 7, 1527, five ships laden with six hundred soldiers, sailors, and colonists sailed down the Guadalquivir on the high tide, stopped briefly at the beach town of Sanlúcar de Barrameda, then slipped out onto the broad swells of the Atlantic Ocean. Dorantes had managed to secure a place for himself and Esteban as part of the Narváez Expedition, which set out to explore Florida and ended up traversing much of the perimeter of the Gulf of Mexico and more.[2] It was a cursed voyage, with all but four members of the group succumbing to shipwreck, attack, disease, or starvation over the ensuing nine years.

As he wandered thousands of miles over many years, Esteban's acquisition of languages extended to those of the Native peoples, including Coahuiltecan, the lingua franca of the land. He became a skilled medicine man in his own right, sometimes adorning himself with a gourd decorated with owl feathers, which he took to be a symbol of death. His ability with languages and his size, certainly, gave him authority with Native peoples. But he was also quick to laugh and play with children, and girls and women, even the married ones—he frequently had sex with these girls and women, much to the rage of tribal leaders. Occasionally he was called Estevanico—Little Stephen or Stevie—either in irony or as an insult meant to cut him down to size.

Along with another survivor, he eventually found a settlement of the Jumano, a Puebloan people who lived in similar dwellings and grew corn and squash on the Upper Rio Grande, probably about seventy-five miles downriver from present-day El Paso, Texas. Alone, Esteban walked farther upriver, probably up the present-day Valley of Juárez. Esteban could not have known that he was now at nearly the exact same longitude on the globe as his hometown of Azemmour, 5,465 miles due west, at 31.8 degrees north and –106.4 degrees west. He was as little as twenty miles from what would become downtown El Paso and Juárez,[3] teeming five hundred years later with well over two million people, a metropolis on a stretch of land as big as Los Angeles County today and as populous as Houston.

"The first white man we ever saw," wrote the Puebloan historian Joe Sando, "was a black man."

Esteban was already one of the first foreigners to set foot in what would become the United States. The Rio Grande flowed from the north and then squeezed through desert mountains to turn sharply left or east-southeast. What stretched beyond it was a burning ocean of sand and desert that seemed to go on forever toward the setting sun. The Native people told him there was a sea, what we now know as the Pacific, beyond what lay ahead, but it was far away and the crossing was dangerous. He turned back, and all the castaways tiredly headed west into Mexico, and another year and five thousand miles of walking. They finally found the sea in February 1536, as they arrived at a Spanish outpost on the rocky shore of present-day Culiacán, Sinaloa. Not long after, they were safely in Mexico City.

Esteban and his fellow castaways had made history by walking off the very edge of the known world. Neither Walter Raleigh nor John Smith had yet been born. Nor was he some homegrown American hero of exploration, like Meriwether Lewis or William Clark, who wouldn't make it to the West for nearly three more centuries. No—he, Esteban, was an African.

It's not what most people think of as the heart of the American story. If they think of El Paso at all, perhaps most people imagine the city as a dusty West Texan outpost on the Mexican border. But the truth about my hometown is much more complex and important, though it took a massacre of global proportions for me to see it. El Paso is where Native, Spanish, European, African, Jewish, and Arab cultures fought, bled, died, and forged ties, including intermarriage: this vibrantly diverse culture paved the way for our melting-pot nation and serves as a model for an America ever torn over race, ethnicity, and religion. In fact, it's the unacknowledged cradle of American history, with beginnings stretching back before the Paleolithic period.

Simply put, the origin story of America, usually told as starting in the East, at Plymouth Rock, and extending to the West is wrong, erasing places and people between the coasts. The first known humans on the North American continent didn't cross the frozen seas of the Bering Strait fifteen thousand years ago; they were already here, living in the caves of present-day Oro Grande, New Mexico, just outside the city limits of El Paso. Two powerful Native empires were founded in or near this region: the Aztec and the Pueblo. The first significant encounter between Europeans and

Native Americans in what would become the United States did not take place in Virginia; it happened at a river crossing near modern El Paso.

American history did not begin in the Northeast. It began in the Southwest, and the first European colonies were not English, Dutch, or French: they were governed by the Spanish Empire. Jamestown was founded in 1607 and Plymouth Colony in 1620; the Spaniards and their allies made their homes in New Mexico in 1598. The first European Thanksgiving was not in Massachusetts; it took place on the banks of the Rio Grande twenty-two years earlier.

And the colonies weren't as white as the history books have told you. They were filled with Europeans from the Iberian Peninsula, the Netherlands, and the Italian states, certainly, but also Africans—including free men and women—as well as Native Americans from the length of North America. Before it was outlawed nationally, following the Civil War, chattel slavery was forbidden in what would become the American Southwest in 1811. Whereas Jews were persecuted in much of the world, including Spain, they experienced an evolving religious freedom in 1820 in the northern territories of the Mexican Republic. Those territories, in turn, figured into the American obsession known as manifest destiny—the quest to lay claim to land all the way to the Pacific Ocean. This idea dates back nearly to the founding of the United States.

In the ensuing decades, El Paso, as the nation's north-south and east-west portal, would become the most fought-over city in the world outside Jerusalem. The defeat of the Confederacy in the Southwest allowed in a flood of settlers, miners, and ruffians, bringing chaos and lawlessness. Most of the engagements of the Indian Wars were fought not on the Great Plains but in the Southwest, with a US scorched-earth strategy that went on for decades; the longest war in American history was not fought in Afghanistan, but in the Apacheria. Nor did the Apache Wars conclude with Geronimo's 1886 surrender involving only a few dozen people, south of Arizona in Mexican Sonora; they ended just south of El Paso in a huge battle at Tres Castillos, culminating in the death of the great Chiricahua chief Victorio. The first transcontinental railroad at Promontory Point, Utah, was so useless because of snowed-in mountain passes that it was quickly abandoned for the only other route, completed in 1881, across Texas to California—through El Paso.

In a rare instance of the rule of law supporting ethnic diversity, the people of the aptly named "Gunfighter Capital of the World" in the nineteenth century crushed the brothels, saloons, and gambling houses frequented by gunslingers to become a bustling port in the desert, where railroads crossed east to west and north to south, from Canada to Latin America. They fought a battle for one another and the Constitution ahead of the rest of the nation: A Mexican American soldier from El Paso destroyed two German machine-gun nests in World War I yet was refused the Medal of Honor. While the Ku Klux Klan rose in number across Texas and the South, El Paso ran the Klan out of town in 1920. In World War II a military unit from El Paso, made up entirely of Mexicans and Mexican Americans, suffered more casualties in a single battle against the Nazis than any other unit in that conflict but never received recognition. In the latter half of the twentieth century, college sports began to desegregate in El Paso, and the first Hispanic mayor of a major city was not voted into office in Miami or Los Angeles, but near the concrete channels of the Rio Grande.

Today El Paso is not a mere "town," as news reports often say. The population within its city limits is bigger than that of Boston or Detroit. What's more, it is a metropolitan megalopolis of 2.3 million people and the heart of a region that radiates outward, some sixty thousand square miles, into parts of three states and two nations. Nestled in one of the world's largest deserts, it's among America's five safest cities, largely spared the racial conflict experienced in other parts of the country.

For centuries, it has been a beacon for immigrants: more passed through El Paso than through Ellis Island. Migrants and émigrés came from the United States, Mexico, and Central America, certainly, but also from Europe and the Middle East of the old Ottoman Empire. Asian immigrants helped lay tracks of railroads headed to each point on the compass. African Americans came to serve at a sprawling army base, now the world's largest, and they stayed, bringing the first lawsuit against segregated education in the United States. Today West Africans, Cubans, Venezuelans, and Indians come to live in El Paso.

At this time in the twenty-first century, El Paso speaks to a great dilemma in the American story. A giant, globally consequential struggle is at hand concerning the preservation of democracy, but it is not rooted in differing constitutional principles. It is rooted in race, ethnicity, creed, and color. Half of the population of the world's longest-running democracy insists that it be governed by whites, for whites, and many of those fellow Americans say they will violently overthrow the government and the Constitution that has guided us since 1787. As a friend reminded me: This is nationalism that leads to dictatorship, despite the facade of parliamentary procedure. More aptly put, this is white nationalism; the shredding of the right to vote is not about mail-in ballots or polling locations, but about denying the Constitution's protections to Latinos, Blacks, Asians, Indians, Native Americans, women of all races and ethnicities, youth, LGBTQIA+ people . . . the list goes on.

El Paso provides the nation with a valuable contemporary lesson: American history started here, and it is very different from the beginnings of American history taught for centuries: thirteen little settlements, half of them steeped in slavery, that shivered and clung to the narrow coastal strip of the Atlantic. Yes, the lands of the Southwest and West are soaked in blood, but not for the reasons most Americans think. This is not merely an exercise in corrective academic fact-checking. El Paso, the historical capital of the Southwest, offers hope. For over a century, its various peoples have been at peace because they lived, fought, worked, married, and died alongside one another. They also believed in, and pushed hard to preserve and expand, the Constitution and its rule of liberty and justice for all. Diversity and democracy are, in fact, one and the same. They always have been.

I am an American. As the son of a Mexican immigrant mother and a white Southern American father, I consider Mexico my culture, but the United States is my country. I am not conflicted about being one versus the other, but many of my fellow countrypersons have been, so let me tell you who we *really* are. Americans have carved a unique chapter in the history of humankind. We are brilliant and kind, violent and dangerous. We lit a lamp for democracy and committed genocide against the Native peoples of North America. We massacred the Japanese with atomic weapons and fostered our own, sometimes shady, brand of democracy around the world. We are deeply conflicted, like orphans who have never known their fathers or mothers—capable of greatness, folly, and yes, evil.

When in 2019 the worst happened, a racist white gunman shooting dozens in an El Paso Walmart in the name of ethnic cleansing, it was no shock that the massacre was undertaken by an outsider: a white nationalist who murdered his victims for their races, beliefs, skin tones, and ethnicities. This too is part of the city's legacy. In one direction lie the lynchings, the Jim Crow laws, and the segregation of the past, and also today's Trumpism and desire for a dictatorship that will uphold a minority while granting only second-class citizenship to the majority. But overcoming hate and bloodshed is just as deeply ingrained. In the Southwest lies an increasingly democratic part of the republic, a productive and multicultural America, where Latinos alone will outnumber non-Hispanic whites in just ten years and exceed 100 million within thirty. It holds out hope for a future in which democracy is expanded and the Constitution is defended by and for all. But realizing that future will require absorbing and applying three powerful truths.

First, we are a nation of westerners. Most Americans now live west of the Mississippi River.

Second, the country was never really white, but always multi-hued: Native, Hispanic, European, Asian, and African. America is not slipping away from its white heritage and into an uncertain brown future. It is coming full circle, back to its origins.

And third, American history began not in the East, but here: at the crossing on the mighty Rio Grande known as El Paso.

—Richard Parker
El Paso, Texas
August 30, 2024

Part I

The phoenix hope, can wing her way through the desert skies, and still defying fortune's spite; revive from ashes and rise.

—MIGUEL DE CERVANTES SAAVEDRA

---------- **Chapter One** ----------

1598

T HE COLD SPRING wind roared unceasingly out of the north,
turning the sky a sickly beige and unleashing a blizzard of
sand that pelted the vague figures of hundreds of people and thousands of animals. The year was 1598, and this was the land that
would become El Paso.

On their knees, hunched over as if in prayer, women dug and
tore at the roots of the cactus and yucca with their bare hands,
desperate for any drop of moisture. Finding nothing, they rose,
wrapped coverings around their faces, and trudged onward, bent
into the wind. Cattle and sheep lost their way and scattered. Oxen
were plunged to their bellies in the fine sand, and wagons sank to
their axles.

The horses suffered the most, their eyes bulging and mouths
frothing at the bit, from being pulled through the dunes by their
rider, or from trailing behind with the remuda, or herd. They were
going blind from the flying sand that pelted their eyes; the tiny
grains of silica stung like needles. For nearly four days, 400 men,
130 women and children, and 6,000 head of livestock had circled
this blowing maze, and for just as long they had gone without water.
People and beasts alike foundered in the sand, going mad, delirious.

Descendants of Spanish colonists, they were far from home, a thousand miles north of Mexico City, the capital of New Spain. They were lost upon a giant sea of shifting sand: Los Médanos, also known as the Samalayuca Dunes, where the winds shaped millions of tons of pure silica, made of quartz of nearly equal purity, into waves that towered high over people and wagons alike. Cresting one dune, there was another, and another. It went on seemingly forever, for nearly eight hundred square miles, but it was impossible to tell, because people and animals could barely see a foot in front of them.

Before England landed a few men at Cape Henry, Virginia, in 1607 and fully twenty-two years prior to the Pilgrims' arrival at Plymouth Rock, these sons and daughters of Spain approached the frontiers of North America, until then inhabited by a tribe called Mansos, a name given by the Spaniards after first contact and now largely extinguished.[1] Theirs was an audacious plan, plunging off the edge of the known world to conquer and colonize a rich and mysterious land known only to them as El Norte, The North. No armed expedition had so dangerously stretched its supply lines since Hannibal crossed the Alps to invade Rome in 218 BCE. But the leader of this expedition, Juan de Oñate y Salazar, was ambitious and brash, and that was precisely why the expedition was now in danger of being lost altogether. In a hurry, he had chosen a shortcut in the desert—and he had chosen poorly.

One quarter of the wagons, twenty in all, broke down and were abandoned to the desert. There would be no resupply or rescue mission.

But Oñate pressed on.

EVEN AS A young man, Juan de Oñate y Salazar had worn a deep scowl etched upon his narrow, bearded face. With a strong, hooked nose and furrowed brow, he stared out at the world from underneath a dark, broad-brimmed hat. Oñate's expression revealed a private preoccupation: He had big shoes to fill. History would later label him the "last of the conquistadors," but history, it turned out, would be wrong.

That title was reserved for his father, Cristóbal de Oñate. As the Aztec Empire fell in 1519, two waves of Spanish conquistadors had come ashore in Mesoamerica. Hernán Cortés led the first, composed of soldiers, adventurers, and plunderers out for their own riches. Cristóbal de Oñate was in the second wave, dispatched by the crown in Madrid in 1524 to control the first wave, protect the monarchy's interests, and keep track of the plundered fortunes of gold and silver. This second wave was not here just to expand conquest, but to settle Mexico, now christened New Spain.

The Spanish were among the fiercest European warriors, not just from shaking off over five hundred years of Muslim occupation, but stretching at least as far back as the Roman Empire, when the province of Hispania was a vast training ground for generations of the Roman Legion. Born in the Basque country, Cristóbal de Oñate was descended from an ancient family whose lineage included Spain's last feudal lord. Just twenty-one years old, he arrived in Mexico to fulfill a seemingly dull role as auditor for Charles V, the Spanish king. But the job also entailed a certain amount of power and intrigue. The commander of all the conquistadors, Hernán Cortés, was a headstrong, even greedy man; while counting Aztec gold for the king, Oñate and his superior, Nuño Beltrán de Guzmán, kept their eyes on Cortés too.

In 1525, war and fortune beckoned as New Spain reached its zenith. It was a full viceroyalty of the empire and encompassed not just present-day Mexico, with Mexico City its beating heart, but Cuba and Florida to the east and the Philippines and Guam to the west. Yet this reach exceeded the Spaniards' grasp. Far closer to

their capital, western Mexico was still a wild country of highlands
and mountains. Though Cortés had claimed it, as had Spanish explorers along its Pacific coast, no one had settled this region; it was
still ruled by the indigenous Huichol and Cora peoples. So Beltrán
and Oñate went to crush them and prepare the way for colonists
and priests. Over three years, the two conquistadors and their army
waged a brutal war; Beltrán, in particular, became infamous as one
of the bloodiest conquerors of the Americas.

Renaming the new territory Nuevo Galicia, after the verdant
coastal northwest corner of Spain's Iberian Peninsula, the elder Oñate
founded four towns within it that would become cities in their
own right, including Guadalajara. Then he turned north toward
another wilderness, Zacatecas, where he found and took for himself
the richest silver mines discovered in Mexico up to that point. He
worked them with the labor of enslaved Native people, as he did
the vast fields and farms he established. Cristóbal de Oñate became
the richest man in all of Mexico, surpassing Cortés.

Despite his brutal history, Oñate mellowed as he aged, growing
into a patrician and even philanthropic figure. He donated money
to the cities he founded and Native villages alike and bought food
for the needy. He married Doña Catalina Salazar y de la Cadena,
a Spanish woman descended from a famous Jewish converso family that had converted to Catholicism during the Inquisition. One
of their six children would grow to emulate his father's zealous
younger self: Juan, born to the couple in 1550.

Zacatecas, in the north-central part of present-day Mexico, was
a hard and exacting place of lonesome beauty. The western Sierra
Madre rose jaggedly into the sky; alpine streams snaked down from
the peaks along deep-green meadows and drained into harsh high
desert; sparse shade was lent by paloverde, mesquite, and ironwood
trees, and towering yucca. As he grew, Juan followed his father
across these lands, inspecting their various holdings: mines, farms,

ranches, and more. His was a protected life, and he was later sent away to Mexico City for a formal education.

Yet upon reaching adulthood, Juan faced a challenge his father had never known. The son was not a *peninsulare*, a Spaniard born in Iberia, like his father; to the contrary, he had never even set eyes on Spain. Instead, he was a criollo native to Mexico—and at that time, the *peninsulares* ruled. They took the best positions in government, made the best marriages for their children, and were, like his father, the wealthiest. As the famous patriarch grew older, the pressure increased upon the son to make his mark in the world and find his own fortune. After all, the estate would be divided upon his father's death, and the glory of his life cast a long shadow.

Since the year of the younger Oñate's birth, conflict had been gathering like late-summer thunderheads over the Spanish occupiers and the native Chichimeca people, descendants of the early Aztecs, whose name meant "children of the wind." They were known for their long hair, their tattooed and painted bodies, their deep religious beliefs, their ability to live off the land, and their fierce raiding. Using short bows that shot obsidian-tipped arrows so sharp they could pierce Spanish armor, the Chichimeca raided supply trains nearly unopposed for years while the foreigners engulfed their ancestral lands and enslaved their people. Increasingly, those razor-sharp arrows fell on the Spanish troops and settlers, four thousand of whom had been killed by the time Oñate was eleven years old and his father seventy-six.

Led by a messianic leader, Temaxtle, who claimed to be descended from Moctezuma, the slain Aztec emperor, the Chichimeca forged an alliance with a dozen tribes in the 1560s. All were united in a singular mission—to drive the Spanish from Mexico once and for all.

The official Spanish response had been equally unequivocal: *fuego y sangre*, "fire and blood." The Spanish vowed enslavement for women and girls, mutilation for survivors of battle, and death to all men and boys of military age who resisted. The Chichimeca responded by becoming the first Native people in the Americas to thunder into battle mounted on horseback, destroying cattle and killing thousands more Spaniards and their Native allies. Leaders in Mexico City soon pleaded with the crown for more troops.

As the Chichimeca War swelled in the 1570s, the elder Oñate, despite his venerable age, gloriously went off to war—again. He led men into battle to defend Zacatecas and the family mines nearby. There, the Chichimeca and their allies, comprising just fifty warriors, killed two hundred Spanish troops. "No one can sustain the war. The cost is too big . . . The situation is very critical," Martín Enríquez de Almanza y Ulloa, viceroy of New Spain, wrote at the time. "We don't have weapons, squadrons or food."

But when the elder Oñate met his end in 1576, it was not in the beatification of war. He had left the battlefield to inspect one of his thirteen silver mines in the town of Panuco when he suddenly dropped dead at eighty-two years of age. It was the moment his son, Juan, who was now twenty-one and a grown man, had anticipated and perhaps feared. Fortune and glory called.

Oñate had been mesmerized by the tales of historic exploits his father brought home, an instructive—indeed, a formative— experience for the young scion. But at a safe distance, schooled by a private tutor, he wasn't privy to the sweaty desperation of battle. The war had been so vast, bloody, and cruel that in one significant battle, twelve thousand people (counting those on both sides) perished in a single day.

Increasingly, the church in Mexico pressed the crown in Spain for peace. The Spanish could not fight their way out of this war, so instead they bought their way out. They paid off the Chichimeca with safe Christian settlements, outright land grants, food, and freedom from taxation. The lesson of this devastating war would not blunt the Spanish desire for gold, silver, or a larger empire, but they would now pursue these through a mixture of negotiating, fighting, and settling as they pressed ever farther north. The Spanish authorities also arrested the worst of the slavers among their ranks, and finally, in 1590, the Chichimeca laid down those deadly bows.

In the final years of the Chichimeca War, the younger Oñate had not followed in his father's footsteps into battle. Instead, he married well. In a grand ceremony in Mexico City, he wed Isabel de Tolosa Cortés de Moctezuma, a woman of extraordinary beauty.[2] His new bride's father was a Basque silver magnate; her mother, Leonor Cortés Moctezuma, was the out-of-wedlock child of Cortés, the conqueror of Mexico, and Isabel Moctezuma, the last empress of the Aztec Empire. While her lineage was elevated by this lofty parentage (despite his initial denial, Cortés later acknowledged her as his daughter), the fact remained that Isabel de Tolosa Cortés de Moctezuma was a woman of mestizo, or "mixed," European and Native descent at a time when the *peninsulares* had all the power.

Like his wife, Oñate stood just outside that mighty circle. He was not the last conquistador, but rather, an original Mexican. After all, Mexico's cartographic borders were drawn by colonial conquerors, and lineages and cultures in the El Paso region—encompassing, as it does, both modern Mexico and the United States—have long interwoven. Oñate's marriage to Cortés de Moctezuma set the stage; it was one of the first formal marriages between a powerful European creole and a woman of Indigenous blood.

Back at the silver mines with his new wife, he led a comfortable life, as he had in his youth: educated, managing the fortune, never really exposed to the hardships of mining or ranching, as his father had been. Yet Oñate's privilege had spared him the glories of war—and a deep dissatisfaction set in, captured in his scowling portraits. "The mature Juan de Oñate's face belied his physique," a novelist would write five hundred years later. "It was delicate and somewhat sallow."[3]

By the time he was thirty-eight years old, in 1588, by the standards of his father and his time, Oñate had accomplished little. He began prospecting northward, seeking his own silver strikes, but found nothing.

Except for rumors of gold.

THE REPORTS CAME from travelers who straggled back to Mexico City from the north, shot full of arrows, half-naked, starving, and dying of thirst, carrying only astonishing tales. They were spread by a trio of lost shipwreck survivors from the Gulf of Mexico who wandered west speaking of the Seven Cities of Cibola, cities of gleaming gold, in 1534. A Franciscan friar staggered back in 1539 with still more stories of these cities, plus thirty uninhabited islands laden with shoals of pearl-bearing oysters. In 1540, an armed reconnaissance team returned, half-starved but seemingly affirming the wild tales of riches.

These were the accounts of Álvar Núñez Cabeza de Vaca, Friar Marcos de Niza, and Francisco Vázquez de Coronado, respectively. Each was entrusted by the Spanish crown and its viceroy, Antonio de Mendoza, to explore El Norte, the North. Mendoza loved these tales; they helped fuel the interest and loosen the coffers of Charles I in Madrid, head of the richest, biggest empire in the world at that time, financed by Mexican gold and silver. Galleons laden with the precious metals sailed west from Acapulco, bound for the Spanish treasury, but Charles needed more to keep fueling the project of extending his reach. Stories of more gold kept the king's ear conveniently to the mouth of his viceroy, whose explorers encountered total failure. But rather than admit it, they concocted ever-wilder claims.

No one had ever seen a city of gold, much less walked down

a street paved with ingots. Yet so alluring was the myth of the Seven Cities of Cibola that they were given individual names, such as Hawikuh and Kwakina, by the Spanish. In 1540, the explorer Francisco Vázquez de Coronado went north to find them; in a now-legendary expedition, he wandered as far as the Great Plains, where he discovered various Native peoples and their settlements, but no gold. He larded his reports with fanciful accounts, such as his discovery of a race of one-legged people who slept underwater and lived strictly on their sense of smell.

Unbeknownst to Mendoza or Charles I, the only thing Coronado had found was trouble. At a place called Shiewipag, "flint-kick-place" in the native Tiwa language[4] (the Spaniards called it Tiguex), Coronado's cattle ate the Isleta Pueblo people's cornstalks, a soldier raped a Pueblo woman, and war ensued. Coronado's men, along with Tlaxcalan troops from Mexico—Native people who had helped the Spanish destroy the Aztec Empire and remained their allies throughout the colonial period—killed hundreds and burned nearly everything to the ground.[5] Coronado returned to Mexico City bloodstained and empty-handed.

Still, the tales of gold made their way beyond the capital of New Spain to Madrid, where a new monarch, Philip II, became decidedly intrigued. The king didn't merely want gold for the royal coffers; he desperately needed it to finance his European wars. Subsequent expeditions fueled Spanish fascination with the north: a trio of Franciscans and a handful of soldiers set out in 1581,[6] retracing many of Cabeza de Vaca's steps as well as Coronado's; they returned only with reports that great riches and new Christian souls waited there to be harvested.[7] By their estimates, they found an incredible seventy-four pueblos, 230,000 inhabitants, a great river, and a rich territory on the shores of a great lake.

Oñate grew obsessed with the north. A creature of the age of exploration, he was driven by a complex and combustible mixture of greed, need, and outright curiosity. He thirsted to know what lay beyond that great river, on the other side of a harsh desert, which to the eager young men of his time marked the edge of the known world. He was thirsty for riches, yes, but also for the glory that those ever-elusive precious metals promised.

It was not only the Spanish who were obsessed by these cravings; nearly every European monarchy needed wealth if it was to become an empire. Spain was no more and no less greedy; it had simply gotten hold of the gold first, in Mexico, and later in Peru. The royal courts of the British, the French, the Portuguese, and the Belgians were also consumed with exploring, trading, and conquering the globe in search of riches: Europeans in the fifteenth century had been convinced, after all, that an island existed in the Atlantic Ocean with seven cities of gold. This tale arose when the bishop of Lisbon fled the Muslim invasion of Portugal by crossing the ocean with a stash of gold.[8] Antillia, as the island was called, even appeared on Spanish nautical charts. The Mercator Map of 1569 showed a shortcut from the Rio Salado—now known as the Pecos River, it runs from northern New Mexico south to Texas, emptying into the Rio Grande—to the Far East (a fantasy not unlike the dream of a Northwest Passage). As knowledge of the Atlantic and parts of North America grew, the tale of the seven cities simply, and conveniently, moved farther and farther inland: first to Florida, then westward to the uncharted north of Mexico.

In fact, almost nothing about these parts of the world was actually known. The men in New Spain had charts that put the Pacific Ocean in present-day Arizona. They believed a passage to China might lie off the coast of Alaska, not far from another shortcut to the Atlantic through Canada. It was maddening not to know what was out there while lust for gold was growing. These people were not far removed from medieval times, the men were bent on honor, glory, status, and power for their own sake. Despite the overwhelming absence of evidence, the Spanish could not be convinced they were looking at evidence of absence.

For his part, Oñate represented many of the worst impulses of his time. A wealthy man who had inherited his fortune from his father, he had no significant military training nor experience[9] and no track record in leading voyages. But that didn't stop an increasingly desperate Oñate from petitioning the king for permission to launch a royally chartered expedition to the fabled north. He pledged not only to bring home the gold but, doubling down, vowed to find a shortcut to China.

Oñate was champing at the bit, willing to personally finance the troops, supplies, and livestock for his expedition. He was hardly alone in this. In Mexico City, Mendoza stamped his seal of approval on Oñate's plans, then set off on his own voyage to Peru. But Oñate had one more hurdle to clear. The final decision on his expedition fell to Madrid. Philip II was desperate: his mighty armada had just been dashed upon the Irish and Scottish coasts in 1588, in the ill-fated invasion of England, and he needed money for a new fleet. So on August 24, 1595, he commissioned Oñate to go forth.

Go north.

Find the gold.

THE STORM OF stinging silica whirling through the Samalayuca Dunes continued to pelt the horde of humans and animals unmercifully as Oñate pressed them forward. Desperate and thirsty, the wayward explorers believed their cause was lost. Then suddenly four Native American men materialized out of the blinding sand like a mirage.

Naturally, the Spanish captured them, took them hostage, and threatened to kill them unless they revealed the way out of the desert. The Native men explained that the Spaniards were far off course, bound for a barren mountain range instead of the river crossing for which Oñate had aimed. They sent the Spaniards in the right direction.

At last, men, women, and livestock stumbled out of the shifting sands somewhere between present-day San Elizario and Tornillo, Texas,[10] and scrambled toward the river, which lay glistening in the sun, and the bright-green grass waving from its banks. Grateful, they collapsed into the water and gulped mightily.[11] Some horses and cattle drank so much, they drowned, but the people were overjoyed. Once they had their fill of water, they drove the oxen back into the dunes to haul out the broken wagons and carts.

Fittingly, it was Easter Sunday: April 20, 1598. On the verge of death, they had been delivered back to life.

When the spring winds finally abated, members of the expedition could see that there was no valley more beautiful than that of the Rio Grande. Ancient cottonwoods, predating Columbus, grew thick and reached to the sky, their leaves like silver in the breeze. Ducks and geese floated by on the current, their colors sparkling in the bright sun.

Gazing upon the scene, Oñate might have thought it was a miracle. He was mesmerized by the powerful river flowing past, muddy brown and rushing with the snowmelt of the faraway Rocky Mountains, writing:

> This river of the north is much bigger than the Conchos and with more water than the Nazas, although its bed is not very wide. It is muddy and rich with vegetation, abundant fish—*bagre* [catfish], *machete* and *robalo* [bass], and a great whitefish that looks like the *matalote* [sucker].

Oñate might have reflected too that his moment of glory had finally come. After all, no other settler had ever reached this point.

This expedition was his, and he had reason to smile; Spaniards, especially Basques, loved to strike a hard bargain. He had done so with the king, who agreed to make him not only the captain-general of the expedition, but also governor of all the land he conquered and colonized. Oñate would collect an annual salary and tribute from subjugated Native people while keeping 80 percent of the gold and silver he found, with cuts going to the members of his expedition. He would get ninety square miles of land—along with its Indigenous inhabitants, whom he'd enslave—and his family would keep title to the acreage for five generations. Finally, he would pay no royal tax on any working gold and silver mines he found. Philip II would get the rest.

Oñate's expedition stretched out in a luxurious encampment along the great, swift river, which the Spanish had named El Rio del Norte, "the River of the North." The group included four hundred cavalry and infantry, composed of Spanish, Europeans of various nations, mestizo, and Tlaxcalan warriors. Some 130 women tended camp, where a handful of Franciscans loafed. Sixty-three wagons survived, and more were being repaired. Most of the seven thousand head of livestock had somehow endured and now filled their bellies with the thick native grasses and wildflowers.[12] Slowly, the people started to gather around the friars to celebrate two miracles: the resurrection of their Christ and their own salvation from the desert.[13]

A full twenty-three years before the Pilgrims in Plymouth, the Franciscans traveling with Oñate's band organized the first Thanksgiving in America on the riverbanks near present-day San Elizario, Texas, just twenty miles south of modern El Paso.[14] Tattooed Manso and red-painted Suma entered the camp as guests. The new European arrivals called the Manso by that name because of their habit of calling out "manso, manso"—meaning "docile" or "peaceful"—when approaching the expedition's aggressive dogs.[15]

The Franciscans said mass, and together everyone feasted on

duck, geese, and fish. The first known performance of a play in the Americas formed part of the festivities. Written by one of the Spanish officers, it depicted the conversion of unwitting, yet willing, Native people to Christianity, a lighthearted foreshadowing of a cataclysm yet to come.

Giant mountains loomed across the bank, soaring thousands of feet into the sky. The foreigners named them the Sierra del Manso, after their painted Native American guests. Oñate stood and gave a speech forever known as "La Toma," "The Taking." He claimed for the king all he beheld to the north and west, including every rock, tree, and river both seen and unseen, stating in the audacious flourish—and redundancy—of sixteenth-century Spanish:

> I take and seize at this aforesaid River of the North, without excepting anything and without any limitation, with the meadows, pastures, and watering places. And I take this aforesaid possession, and I seize upon it, in the voice and name of the other lands, towns, cities, villas, castles, and strong houses and dwellings, which are now founded in the said kingdoms and provinces of New Mexico, and those neighboring to them, and shall in future time be founded in them, with their mountains, rivers, banks, waters, pastures, meadows, glens, watering places, and all its Indian natives . . . from the mountain to the rock and sands of the river to the leaf on the mountain.[16]

Having barely escaped the first part of his journey with his life and after putting his entire expedition at risk, he now issued a bold, perhaps naive, claim on behalf of his faraway king for a million square miles, stretching from the great river all the way west to the Pacific Ocean and as far north as present-day Oregon and Idaho.[17] As the festivities wound down, Oñate scoured the river for a place to cross into this vast, unknown, and tempting land at the edge of the European universe. Yet the roiling, muddy river showed little opportunity for a decent ford.

At last, Oñate found a shallow spot where the water pushed out of a pool over a beach of rocks. The ford linked two worlds: north and south, the rest of the North American continent with Latin America. As the only year-round, snow-free passage from east to west, it connected too the eastern half of the continent with the west.

After ten days of feasting and resting, the expedition gathered its belongings, lashed oxen to wooden-wheeled wagons and carts, and packed the camp. Cavalry and infantry moved to the front of the column. Then came wagons and carts, followed by women and families. Behind them, vaqueros—cattle drivers—formed up the thousands of heads of horses, cattle, sheep, and goats.

On May 4, 1598, the ambitious leader forded the river on horseback, his massive army of people and animals splashing behind him. He gave this place a name: El Paso del Rio del Norte.

The Crossing of the River of the North was born.[18]

Chapter Two

ANCESTORS, 38,000 BCE–1550 CE

T HE LUMBERING COLUMN of people, beasts, and ox-drawn vehicles splashed across the narrow ford and almost immediately climbed northeast onto the broad mesas that came down like fingers from the flanks of the desert mountains. Proceeding directly upriver along the north bank would have been impossible: rugged volcanic mountains rose, forming a deep gorge of cataracts, rapids, and rocky waterfalls. The Spanish called this dangerous passage Las Puertas, a forbidding portal to the unknown north.[1]

For two straight days, again without water, the expedition crawled northward. Along the route, Oñate glimpsed the wagon tracks of a previous, much smaller expedition of Catholic priests and a tree where a Spanish officer had hanged four Native Americans for horse theft.[2] He had every opportunity to return to the banks of the river, but instead demanded a beeline march northward. Finally, somewhere near present-day Mesilla, New Mexico, Oñate relented, and the expedition encamped, drank, and rested.

Presumably the weary travelers would've wanted to stay, and even settle, here in the river bottom. But after two more days, Oñate reassembled the mass of people and animals to proceed northward where the river shaped itself into a long westward bow: the Hatch

Valley, which was broken country and hard passage over hot, cracked earth. Still in a hurry, Oñate now cut a path away from the river entirely and went behind and east of the rugged massif known as Elephant Butte, stumbling into yet another barren, dry, and nearly lifeless desert.[3]

Among the thirsty were a soldier near the head of the column and his wife, trailing behind. He was one of nearly twenty Europeans who were not Spaniards, yet had enlisted in the Spanish army; he was Greek, born in the coastal city of Heraklion on the island of Crete, likely in 1556, not far from the ruins of Knossos. With his home city increasingly dominated by the occupying Venetians, who renamed it Candia, the soldier had set out for the Hapsburg Empire, arriving in Spain. The Spanish dubbed him simply "El Griego," the Greek,[4] and he adopted the first name Juan.[5] Oñate's motley crew also included about a hundred Tlaxcalan warriors from Mexico. Descended from a people never conquered by the Aztecs, their alliance with the Spanish was baptized by blood; they had originally resisted the occupiers and nearly defeated them before teaming up to turn on their common Aztec foe. As non-Europeans, the men received the lowest title of nobility, hidalgo. Like their fathers, the sons were superior warriors.[6]

El Griego's wife, Pascuala Bernal, was a Nahuatl-speaking Indigenous woman from the Valley of Mexico.[7] The two might have met in 1597, around the time that El Griego answered the expedition's initial call in Mexico for troops. Indeed, many of the women who walked behind the column in the choking dust were Indigenous, married to European men in the troops up ahead. Their children were, or would be, mestizos, part of a new and burgeoning group repopulating Mexico after its sixteenth-century apocalypse; by this time, the Spanish invasion, and its accompanying wave of disease, war, and famine, had killed all but two million of Mexico's fifteen to thirty million Native people within a mere two years.[8]

The expedition's massive train of eighty-odd wagons[9] and carts—likely carrying up to a hundred tons of cargo[10]—was pulled by all manner of straining livestock. Behind them trailed over a thousand animals in all, with cargo comprising everything from household items to weapons of war, including chain mail, body armor, and more than a hundred swords, plus an equal number of firearms.[11] Oñate himself rode at the head of the expedition with his selected officers, servants, and his young son Cristobal. His personal train certainly befitted a global conqueror: two coaches, additional carts, and over a dozen saddles; armor, coats of mail, weapons, and 119 of his personal horses.[12] His was a massive and ungainly expedition, striking out across a trackless, inhospitable desert, but it had been prudently planned. It was an invading force, after all—composed primarily of troops, with nearly everyone and everything else playing a supporting role.

For four days, the men, women, animals, and equipment drove northward, risking death and failure once more as wagons broke down, desperate animals wandered off, and thirst enveloped all. By branching away from the river, Oñate again added time to the journey to northern New Mexico, the source of the rumors of cities made of gold; on some days, the expedition covered fewer than three miles.[13] It was June now, and daily temperatures soared over 100 degrees Fahrenheit, with no respite. On the fifth day of what would become known as La Jornada del Muerto, The Dead Man's Journey, to the east of the Rio Grande, Oñate allowed his people to rejoin the banks of the Rio Grande near Bosque del Apache, a rich wetland teeming with waterfowl and other birds, shaded by tall cottonwoods and filled with the waters of the river. There, he gave them precisely one night of rest.

For years, popular literature claimed that the Journey was a shrewd military decision by Oñate, designed to avoid surprise encounters with the Apache in the river's woods. But none of the original records by Gaspar de Villagra nor secondary work such as that of the historian Marc Simmons suggest anything of the sort. Indeed, all of the brush rancherias, encampments of the Manso people or possibly the Apache, were abandoned; the Manso were well known for abandoning their camps as strangers approached, watching from a place of concealment. Yet unbeknownst to the expedition's leader, officers, and members, they had entered the earliest site of human life in North America. It has long been believed that humans arrived from Asia by walking the frozen ice bridge that once connected Russia and Alaska via the Bering Strait about fifteen thousand years ago. But in fact, people had lived on and walked the lands of El Paso far earlier, thirty-eight thousand years ago, making it the earliest known site of habitation on the continent.

While the Manso and Suma might have lived simply, their neighbors did not. The Pueblo people along the Rio Grande were the earliest, largest, and most successful Native American confederacy in what would become the United States. They preceded the eastern confederations of Algonquin, Mohawk, and Huron by centuries and employed more complex agriculture, technologies, and architecture. They were inheritors too of a powerful religion derived from deep inside Mexico. The Spaniards were not just wading into unknown territory, but into an advanced Indigenous culture skilled in yet another art: war.

A reconnaissance party went north and entered a village, despite strict orders not do so. Upon the party's return, Oñate wanted the commanding officer executed via strangulation, but the priests intervened and his anger waned. As a commander, he was gaining a reputation for bluffing when it came to discipline.

After the deadly five-day trek and fleeting wetland reprieve, the main wagon train lagged far behind Oñate, whose advance party encamped on the bank opposite a Pueblo village known as Qualacu, thereby blowing his cover.[14] On June 12, 1598, Oñate rode into the village, only to find it abandoned; the Piro-speaking inhabitants had apparently not been keen on meeting the new intruders. Oñate sent trinkets as gifts, and his people went about setting up an un-threatening encampment, clearly visible and without an attack posture. The Native people responded in kind, apparently provid-ing Oñate's men with much-needed corn; in return, they renamed the village Socorro, a Spanish word for "help." Once more, Native Americans had aided the armed newcomers.

The wagon train Oñate had long since left behind was strug-gling, still short of water as its officers began to dissent. Oñate rode back down the trail to straighten matters out, and on June 14, 1598, the entire expedition reassembled. As they continued north through June and then July, Oñate discovered just how much the Native people feared him. They fled as he approached; each pueblo, or settlement, he passed was abandoned, its food storage stripped.

Oñate finally encountered people at Kewa Pueblo, which the Spanish renamed Santo Domingo. The stop proved pivotal. Oñate did not make a humble gesture of coming in peace, despite all the Native help he had needed to get there, and the fact that his wagon train doggedly trailed in the distance, down 20 percent of its wag-ons and carts.[15] Instead, on July 7, he sent for every nearby Pueblo leader in all four directions, summoning them to a grand council;[16] whether insulted, curious, or cowed, they arrived. The would-be conqueror explained that he had come to save their souls through Christianity, the wish of both the Roman Holy Father and Philip II in Madrid. Then he demanded that they kneel, kiss the hand of Father Martinez, and render obedience as vassals to both Philip and himself.[17] Facing Oñate's fearsome reputation, manpower, and mechanized weaponry, depleted as it was, the Pueblo leaders had little choice but to acquiesce.

The way cleared, on July 11, 1598, Oñate finally reached his destination: a pueblo at the intersection of the big Rio Chama and the Rio Grande, its water frigid from spring snowmelt, known to the Native people there as Ohkay Owingeh, "the place of the strong people." In the rocks above the village were the ruins of the cliff. For the current inhabitants, the river bottom, shaded by huge cotton-woods, made for rich farmland.

Above rose the grand blue Sangre de Cristo Mountains, the southern terminus of the Rockies. To the east lay Chicoma, a peak soaring over eleven thousand feet, where the Pueblo gods resided. The Spanish promptly renamed the place San Juan. The typically impatient, scowling Oñate was exhilarated, surveying the land and securing allegiance from the local Pueblo people to him, the king, and the church. When his troops and colonists arrived, they imme-diately occupied the adobe apartments of the pueblo, whose people withdrew a few miles north. Oñate asked for volunteers to prepare his new capital; fifteen hundred Native people answered and began digging ditches for the acequias, or canals, for irrigation.

The colonists demanded robes and blankets for themselves and began levying the Pueblos' food, especially dried buffalo, venison, and corn. Some were dissatisfied: with their horrid journey, cer-tainly, but also with the dearth of gold ingots in the narrow paths of cities made not from gleaming metals, but of mud. Several dozen plotted to escape, snatch Pueblo people as slaves, and make their way back to Mexico City with whatever of value they could strip. After the plot was foiled, Oñate again wanted the ringleaders put to death by strangulation, but faltered once more, publicly forgiv-ing all the mutineers. Instead, he dedicated a new church, and a play, tilting matches, and bullfights ensued.[18]

Meanwhile, winter approached.

AT THE TIME of the Spanish encounter, the Pueblo people may have numbered as many as sixty thousand, though possibly as few as twenty thousand. (The Spanish accounts could be wildly exaggerated.) They were spread from the Upper Rio Grande to the west through the country of the Acoma, Zuni, and Hopi in present-day Arizona. There were likely more than nineteen different settlements and the people spoke five distinct languages—Tanoan, Tiwa, Towa, Keresan, and Zuni[19]—and were generally multilingual.

In a straight-up fight, their sheer numbers would have overwhelmed the smaller, if far better armed, invasive force. Yet the Pueblo people accepted the Spanish grudgingly for one main reason: they were starving. A pervasive drought had brought them to the point of desperation, and the acceptance of a new god, albeit one on a cross, might help mitigate their hunger. The Franciscans prayed and the rain fell, preserving the peace with the Pueblo, for now.

All around the peace was tenuous: from insolent officers to mutineers to deserters, Oñate's control was threatened. He had found no gold, and meat was still in short supply. As the ruddy colors of October descended, Oñate dispatched a hunting party to seek buffalo in the east while visiting still more pueblos to receive their people's submission.

Then, desperate for some sense of accomplishment, he struck west to find the fabled South Sea. At Sky City, the largest of the Acoma Pueblo settlements, set on a tabletop mesa, he had a tense encounter with the Pueblo leaders, as they quietly considered killing him and his whole party right there on the spot. They decided against it, and Oñate thought no further of the stiff, formal encounter. Crossing into present-day Arizona, his men excitedly found silver and brought some back to camp; then Oñate turned around, far short of any ocean.[20]

Back at San Juan, the frigid winter of the Little Ice Age gripped the main body of the expedition, as it did much of the Northern Hemisphere. Just as heavy snows fell on their native Europe, the Spaniards and their allies shivered in New Mexico.[21] Captain Don

Luis de Velasco wrote: "The cold is so intense that the rivers freeze over, and it snows most of the time during the winter, which lasts eight long months. After this there follows heat so oppressive it rivals burning fire. It has driven us from our houses and forced us to sleep outdoors. The country breeds an infinite number of bed bugs and other vermin. We burn no lights at night for lack of means. To keep warm in the winter, we have to go four or five leagues [more than ten miles] for firewood, and none is to be obtained except from cottonwood trees along the river."[22]

Velasco also described how the new arrivals demanded tributes of food from the Pueblo people, who too were struggling to survive: "The Indians fear us so much that, on seeing us approach from afar, they flee to the mountains with their women and children, abandoning their homes and so we take whatever we wish from them . . . The feelings of the natives against supplying it cannot be exaggerated, for I give your lordship my word that they weep and cry out as they and all their descendants were being killed."[23]

The Spanish not only took food but stole clothing and other valuables. At times they tortured Pueblo leaders and even hanged them to get the Pueblo to furnish food.[24]

One of Oñate's other captains and a nephew, Juan de Zaldivar, and his detachment had failed to catch up back in the fall, and now, on December 12, Oñate learned that his nephew and ten of his men were dead. The Acoma Pueblo had rebelled. The entire expedition was failing, both from within and without. His discovery of some silver visible at the surface of the earth had given Oñate some good news to report back to Mexico City, but that was little consolation. Despite being a miner by profession, he had actually unwittingly passed over three different gold fields on his journey northward in the spring. He rarely, if ever, employed his knowledge to look for the ore beneath the surface. Oñate's expedition was scattered and unfocused, and much time was spent scrounging for food on the plains and trying to Christianize the Native people.

NOW THAT A nephew had been killed, Oñate was fueled by a personal rage for revenge. But there were rules, even in the early Spanish Empire, and revenge alone could not justify war. So he turned to the priests to provide a legal basis for it: war, they ruled, could be waged in order to restore peace. Oñate publicly declared a war of "blood and fire," exactly as his father had done against the Chichimeca. After proclaiming that he wanted to personally lead the attack, he instead launched it in 1599 from a location 150 miles away: his capital, San Juan de los Caballeros, today known as Española, New Mexico. He dispatched the attacking force of seventy-two men under the command of his surviving nephew, Vicente de Zaldivar.

Nine days later, the nephew arrived at the mesa; its inhabitants looked down, unimpressed, from nearly four hundred feet above. Untested in war, the nephew demanded surrender, only to be met with a hail of rocks, ice, arrows, and spears. Failure, he intoned to his troops, would be a "serious blot upon our honor as Spaniards." That was his feeble call to battle.

But Zaldivar did have an idea: distract the defenders with a bold frontal attack, as a reserve force circled around to strike from behind. At precisely 3 p.m. on January 23, 1599, a dozen men breached the top of the seventy-acre mesa,[25] clambering up the 367-foot plateau. Zaldivar saw a man wearing the clothes of his dead brother, Juan; Zaldivar split that man's skull with his sword. Night fell, and gory hand-to-hand combat ensued in the cold winter dark. More soldiers arrived with daybreak on January 24, and the Spanish force laid a makeshift bridge across a deep split in the mesa to reach the more populated side.

The Spaniards were vastly outnumbered and no doubt wielded

as much courage as steel, but they also knew that they held a decisive technological advantage: guns. Their infantry carried the heavy arquebus, a long rifle steadied on a steel rod, up onto the mesa. With one rank kneeling and another standing behind, they fired dozens of volleys into the defending Native people, and they did so at a safer distance than that of their enemy while Spanish armor afforded some protection from deadly arrows. In contrast, the Acoma warriors wielded clubs, striking helmeted Spanish heads.

Zaldivar ordered two heavy, crude, long-barreled cannons to be hauled up by rope. His soldiers began firing it into the pueblo of four thousand people at point-blank range. The Spaniards then set fire to houses and kivas (ceremonial structures) alike; the people within died in the flames and smoke, refusing to surrender to captivity. Still more killed their own family members and then themselves to avoid capture. Hundreds leapt to their death, plunging off the cliffside to the desert floor below. The fabled Sky City of the Pueblo was turned into a slaughterhouse, consumed in flames and smoke, screaming and shouting, as the acrid smell of gunpowder billowed into the winter sky.

The Spaniards never counted the number of people killed and wounded at Acoma. Yet the attack and resulting massacre would frame Pueblo relations with these newcomer Europeans for at least a century. And it would lead to something just as disastrous for the Spaniards: Native American vengeance unlike anything North America had ever seen.

WHEN THE SPANISH encountered the Acoma Pueblo on their mesa in 1599, they came face to face with only the most recent human civilization to populate this ever-changing land. The Native denizens of the Rio Grande were among the oldest human cultures on earth, constantly adapting to survive.

Some scientists now suspect that a full 55,000 years before people crossed the Bering Strait from Asia, humans left footprints in the dunes of present-day White Sands, New Mexico, just north of El Paso. Thirty-five thousand years ago they left evidence of permanent inhabitation—animal bones, artifacts, and charcoal—at a cave in the low, saw-toothed mountains of Oro Grande, just north of the Texas state line near El Paso. Among the three hundred items discovered in 1991 by the archaeologist Richard MacNeish were the bones of saber-tooth cats, camels, and tapirs, stone tools for scraping hides and meat, and most important, forty-four specimens of human hair, carbon-dated to 39,500 years ago.[26] Humans brought most of the stone tools to the cave; over half were made of non-local rocks and materials. Nearby, human footprints were found. A human had been stalking a giant sloth.

Around 8000 BCE, not far from El Paso, a young Paleo-Indian woman strode across a vast savannah of tall grasses that waved like fields of grain. The giant peaks known today as the Fort Davis Mountains loomed to the southeast; the smaller cliffs of today's Puertocito ("Little Door") Mountains awaited due south, between her and the big river. Researchers nicknamed her "Effie" and learned from her remains that she had long, dark hair framing an oval face, a lean jaw, and a broad mouth; she bore strong Asian features and had curious eyes that peered out at the Paleolithic world. Effie was part of a small family band. Her ancestors had trekked from the Bering Strait land bridge between Asia and North America over twelve thousand years ago.[27]

Within two millennia, these Paleo-Indian people were living off prehistoric megafauna. They hunted the camel now known as camelops and the mastodon and its taller, bigger cousin, the giant shaggy mammoth—the largest of them stood thirteen feet tall and weighed six tons. In this moist climate, the mammoth browsed the basins around shallow lakes and forests of juniper and piñon. The now-extinct American horse, with the build of a zebra and the look of a mule, roamed there, as did the equally extinct more ancient version, which was three times the size of the modern buffalo.[28]

Effie's people were among the greatest hunters of the Stone Age, slaying these mighty prey at watering holes and driving them into arroyos and over cliffs.[29] They were part of the Clovis people of North America, the earliest and most advanced in what would become the United States. The most distinct traces they left behind were their clever spear points, fluted blades of pointed obsidian that drained the blood of game as it ran. A fertile alluvial valley grew along the great river's banks, giving way to the grassland steppes and forested mountains above, thick with fir and pine. An oasis arose, abundant with meltwater lakes, plants, and wildlife. Indeed, this was no ordinary spot on the map of prehistory; it was the cradle of early human life in North America.

Much later, Mexican anthropologists would call this place Oasisamerica. It became a bridge between the great Toltec, Mayan, and Aztec cultures of Mesoamerica to the south and the nomadic people on the plains of Aridoamerica to the north.

Nearly unimaginable now, this oasis occupied a sixty-thousand-mile radius within today's Chihuahuan Desert of West Texas, New Mexico, and northern Mexico. Today this area comprises one of the largest and harshest deserts on the planet. The oasis world centered on a shallow ford across the great river; this ford is now known as El Paso. Nomadic clans such as Effie's crossed back and forth here and elsewhere: meeting, mating, and communicating with clans far to the south.

Even in the oasis, life during Effie's time could be brutish and short. Her family would have arrived after trekking hundreds of miles yearly across harsh terrain in search of food. Injury was common. Disease was unchecked. And these early human hunters often became the quarry themselves, trailed by giant saber-tooth cats traveling in packs.

For the first time in the course of human life, climate change posed a threat. The region became noticeably warmer and drier as the Paleolithic age gave way to the Mesolithic. Lowland forests turned into grasslands.[30] Then even the great grasslands started to recede. The giant bison became scarcer and the meltwater lakes grew shallow. Between 4000 and 1500 BCE, the sun was setting on Effie's people, as it had on her.

Her remains were discovered by a Girl Scout troop camping during the summer of 1971. Hiking through a desert arroyo, the girls noticed human bones protruding from the layers of sand and rock. They phoned an amateur archaeologist, and eventually her fragile bones were examined at Texas Tech University, where she received her modern name.

She had died in her twenties, very young by today's standards. She didn't meet a violent end or break a bone. She may have fallen ill or simply starved because of the lack of game. Her people buried this slight figure, slipping her small feet into rough sandals knotted together from yucca fiber. Perhaps she would need these where she was going. They left no other signs of ritual. They simply moved on.

AS I WALKED along the trail, running deep in canyons four stories high, life stirred all around me. In the wet months, the fresh rains bring strings of toad eggs teeming with larvae; delicate desert fairy shrimp, which lie dormant for years in the sand, resurrect themselves as soon as raindrops fall. Hidden inside the rocks are springs, welling up generously with cool, clear water from underground, no matter the season.

Hueco Tanks was a "veritable oasis in the desert," the anthropologist Lula Kirkland wrote thousands of years later, in 1939. "These huge piles of rocks catch rain water in holes or crevices called tanks and keep it there clean and sweet for many months after the rain." The caves among the rocks were "like walking into an air-conditioned building from a hot street with temperatures over one hundred . . . icy cool and so refreshing."[31] The caves could also be a source of warmth in the cool months, and Paleo-Indians from about twelve thousand years ago would gather there to warm themselves, skinning the rabbits they'd snared or peeling the skinny ears of corn with multicolored kernels, which they grew just yards away.

Before the time of Christ, these people had built pit houses two feet into the earth; they could be as many as twelve feet wide. A millennium later, they surrounded the rocks with single-story, aboveground adobe homes. They fashioned clay jars from brown and red earth.

On cave roofs the Paleo-Indian people left messages that have endured for generations: pictographs painted in red, yellow, black, white, green, and blue. The long snake signified the great river, not far away. Elsewhere, in other caves, were hourglass-shaped hunters, abstract and wavy lines, and mountain sheep. The people were likely animists: for them, everything was alive, from human beings to the beasts to the desert itself. The hunter alone among the people had the power to transform the living into the dead and the dead into food.

This metamorphosis lay at the heart of the religion practiced by the people who came after Effie. As expressed in their cave art, hunter, weapon, and quarry, mountain sheep and deer, were fused in a spiritual kinship. Shamans, skilled and sensitive people who through trances and dreams entered the animals' world, transferred the quarry's spirit to the men and women who consumed it. The hunter risked death to bring home game; the shaman faced the possibility of dying in the trance that would bring the animal's spirit to the small group who clustered around the campfire in the evening to eat.[32]

At the time of death, human bodies were placed, lovingly and carefully, inside the smallest of caves, sometimes with trinkets of this life. Their spirits would join those of the departed and even the gods that arose in this new belief system. And the dead could intercede on behalf of the living, who often prayed simply for rain and the bounty it brought, enriching the physical bodies and the spirits of the living.

AS THE PALEO-INDIANS faded into prehistory, they left behind only faint traces of their existence, such as kill sites and spearpoints. The Archaic people took their place. These hunter-gatherers, encompassing multiple cultures, were among the earliest and most prominent ancestors of a people who would prevail into recorded history, and even into modernity: the Pueblo.

The Archaic people are among the least acknowledged and most important Native cultures in all of American history. Centuries before the Woodlands people arose in the American East and Midwest, they became America's first farmers, increasing both human longevity and population. In their development of agriculture, Archaic groups predated even the great mound-building cultures of the Ohio and Mississippi Valleys.

The Archaic people were different too from Effie and her clan: change, like a persistent desert wind wearing away a cliff's face, shaped them. Adapting to a millennium of shifts in climate and evolutionary history, they fashioned something new from the human species. By 5000 BCE, the mammalian megafauna were extinct, and so too were the long treks in pursuit of giant game. The Archaic people instead focused on smaller animals. These skilled hunters used traps, snares, and stone tools to subdue rabbits and the occasional deer, sheep, and buffalo. Traveling in small nomadic bands, they moved seasonally in pursuit of floral and faunal resources.

First they developed expertise with desert plants, prizing the big white blossoms of the yucca, as well as the sotol—an agave cooked and eaten like an artichoke leaf—and the sweet, purple fruit of the prickly pear. They turned seeds and stems into food, fashioned baskets of straw and grass, and made vessels out of gourds. Instead of living constantly on the move, they did so only seasonally and slept inside simple domed brush huts, always facing east toward the rising sun, with a fire near the center of the dirt floor.

Inside the dwelling, a man, a woman, and their children lived together; older children and grandparents stayed next door or nearby in another hut. Often, ten of these were clustered together to house a clan, which would join other clans to form bands. In the winter, different bands encamped in large villages along the river valley.[33]

In the autumn, hundreds would camp together to harvest desert plants and the handful of crops they introduced. "It was the gathering of the clans," said the archaeologist David Carmichael of the University of Texas at El Paso.[34] The human population was still tiny and stretched by vast expanse. Young men and women intermarrying expanded each clan's network for hunting, gathering, and information.

If the Paleo-Indian people were humanity's great hunters, the Archaic people who succeeded them were among the most tenaciously adaptive. As millennia passed, they concentrated along the big river, but not too near its banks. The deeply forested river valley was fine hunting ground but dangerous to inhabit yearlong. The river flooded without warning. The environment was unpredictable, marked not only by water and wind erosion, but also by periods of drought partially caused by a continually changing climate. As grasslands retreated, desert appeared and brought different, and meager, nourishment. The people gathered mesquite beans, yucca, agave, and sotol. The yucca and its cousins had thick, nutritious fibrous roots that could be baked in a pit. In the spring they tasted sweet enough to be enjoyed as a sort of desert sugarcane.[35]

With a little searching, water could still be found. At that giant rockpile visited by Effie's people, Hueco Tanks, deep pools were filled with tens of thousands of gallons of clear, cool water from natural springs, as the ancient waters of the old great lake bubbled up generously to the earth's parched surface. Indentations in the rock caught the rain that did fall, increasingly in the summer months instead of the winter and spring. The area also provided a wealth of caves to use for shelter and for storing food.

While the Celtic, Gaul, and Germanic tribes warred over Europe, at around 450 CE, in the American Southwest, a new culture arose from the Archaic clans: the early Mogollon, known as the Jornada Mogollon. They likely can be traced as far back as five thousand years, to the even older Cochise people,[36] an Archaic culture that had drifted down from the Pine Lawn area of southwestern New Mexico.[37] They also predated the better-known Pecos people farther east in Texas by some three millennia. The one thing that separated them from their ancestors was their turn to a technology unique to the Americas, a certain form of agriculture. They filled ceramic pots with water and hauled them out to the few hundred acres where they raised primitive crops, such as corn and squash, which they traded with far more advanced cultures that fueled the early Native American farming societies in Mesoamerica, namely, people in what is now Mexico and the highlands of Guatemala.[38] It would be centuries before the mound-building cultures of the Midwest learned agricultural techniques, even with the tutelage of

Mesoamerican people, most likely the Mayans, who traded up the coast of the Gulf of Mexico through the Mississippi River Basin.

This is where the story of America's most advanced Native culture began: over eight thousand years ago, in 6000 BCE, at that pile of rock that would be named Hueco Tanks, two dozen miles from the Rio Grande. As the millennia flew by, it formed a crossroads to other worlds, peoples, and continents. Groups from the Great Plains sometimes came and camped. The people who lived there took long walks to be among others in trips that brought knowledge that helped them learn, grow more food, and expand their numbers to survive and thrive, an increasingly larger population spreading across an increasingly sparse land.

NEAR THE HEADWATERS of the Casas Grandes River and the foothills of the Sierra Madre Occidental, the city of two thousand apartments, known by the Native name Paquimé, rose first in 700 CE, mirroring the temples and buildings of stone in the Yucatán and the Valley of Mexico. Composed of adobe, an untreated clay, the levels of each building were stacked one on top of the other, soaring several stories toward the blue desert sky in a blocky, pyramid-like fashion. Channels brought fresh water; wastewater flowed out. Fields in front of the city drew water from the river for crops of corn, squash, and beans. It held dwellings as well as stone pits, also a construct from far to the south, and was built not at random but on three axes: one was residential, another was made up of the public plazas, and the last was set aside for religious ceremonies.[39]

Life in the city was filled with ritual; religious pilgrims streamed in from suddenly arid regions, desperate to survive.[40] Rites administered by priests included sacrificing children to the god Tlaloc, a fearsome deity of Mexico, with what an archaeologist has described as "goggle eyes" and fangs: it was responsible for rains and fertility but also for thunder, lightning, and hail. In the Mexican pantheon Tlaloc dated at least as far back as the year 1 CE, if not further, to the Mayan pantheon, which featured a similar god, Chaac. In various spots, dismembered adults were buried alone and together in gruesome poses, all meant as appeals to the gods. By night, the city thrummed with the voices of chanting priests, the footfalls of religious dancers, and the beating of drums.

The society prioritized spectacle. Visitors like the Jornada Mogollon from the north would find earthen ceremonial mounds commemorating, among others, a horned snake: another ubiquitous god in Mexico, arising also from the Maya and representing Quetzacoatl, god of life, light, wisdom, and wind. The people imported another distinctly Mayan feature: huge T-shaped ball courts with seating for spectators who gambled; here, scores were settled as winners lived and losers died.[41]

Visitors came to pray and trade from all cardinal directions. From the west, they brought bags of seashells: conical Nassarius shells strung together in bracelets and anklets, some four million in all.[42] From the south, traders delivered macaw parrots, in their resplendent red, white, and blue plumage. From the east came finished copper, likely from the Maya themselves, who had a string of outposts far beyond their original home territory in the Yucatán and Guatemala, lining the Gulf Coast up to Veracruz. The Jornada Mogollon traded turquoise, which they increasingly picked out of the desert mountains around El Paso. Green and blue, this stone from the American Southwest was supplanting green jadeite in depictions of Mexican gods, making turquoise extremely valuable.[43] The Jornada Mogollon also harvested salt from the drying playas.

When the traders arrived home at Hueco Tanks, they brought with them the goods, culture, and technology that was filtering northward from southern Mexico. They unfurled their wares: macaw feathers, live turkeys, seashells, new varieties of corn and squash, and the first cultivated beans and chilis. But they had something more to share too: memory. They described what they had seen and how the people of Casas Grandes had gone beyond the dome-shaped brush huts their own people of Hueco Tanks now occupied.

Their earliest dabbling with farming was haphazard. They stuck a few seeds into the ground and returned to see if anything grew. To their surprise, it did, and plant food eased the need to travel, allowing young and old alike to live longer. But it also posed a new dilemma: they would need to grow still more food to nourish an ever-growing population.

Lying on his back, in a cave in what would become Mescalero Canyon, one of the traders painted the horned serpent Quetzacoatl. Another added a new figure altogether: a mask. Some believe that the Jornada Mogollon people had copied the Mexican gods,[44] but Carmichael, the archaeologist, said that they invented their own. By use of masks they would briefly transform themselves into gods. Their people, beginning in 450 CE, created a new religion. No longer part of an animist world, where everything was alive, the Jornada Mogollon were learning to take on the characteristics and powers of both living gods and their own dead relatives; still sub-servient to nature, they aimed to influence it through prayer and intercession. Like the Maya, they were devotees of Quetzacoatl and Tlaloc,[45] who granted rain to nourish the new croplands but also the violent flash floods that wiped them out and left the people starving.

BY ABOUT 800 CE, the Jornada Mogollon people had outgrown their settlement at Hueco Tanks. When the June monsoons came, they struck out for the Sacramento Mountains, over a hundred miles away; as the blue mountains arose over the clouds, they ascended a

canyon of old-growth pines and firs, some with trunks as wide as
four men standing hip to hip. After crossing the ridge nearly nine
thousand feet above sea level, with its cool air in the low fifties
Fahrenheit, they descended into a broad, green alpine valley. Some
stayed and made this land their home; others fanned out in all directions along the base of the big Sierra de los Mansos, which soared
seven thousand feet above sea level. The domain of the Mogollon
grew across the old Oasisamerica, from present-day Chihuahua into
central New Mexico, as well as westward into Arizona—and the
people who settled here, in what would become El Paso, planted
the very roots of the Pueblo civilization. No longer were these people merely scratching to survive. They grew crops in fields carefully
tended with digging sticks. The old and young shooed away birds
and snared opportunistic and persistent cottontails and jackrabbits. For housing, they made adobe for the first time, combining
clay and grass and using it to construct aboveground settlements
that spread into small communities. They began fashioning brown
pottery, swapping it as well as turquoise in Casas Grandes, where
trading networks now stretched not only as far as the jungles of
the Yucatán but along the coastlines of Central America. And they
developed new religious rituals, sending off their dead by covering
their eyes with broken pottery.

The people who settled west of the Sierra de los Mansos did so
in large numbers along a seasonal creek at the place now known
as Keystone, dropping the atlatl weapons of the Archaic period to
adopt far more accurate bows and arrows.[46] By 1000 CE, their architecture had become more deliberate and elaborate. They built
entire villages of multistory adobe buildings; doorways into their
structures were designed to require visitors to step up and in, keeping the elements out. Some sections of settlements were built for
lodging, while others stored food and grain for the next season.
The people even kept a burgeoning population of wild turkeys,

descended from those of Casas Grandes, penning them in at night and allowing them to roam the villages by day.

Their pottery became as artistic as it was functional, with a black-and-white style evolving alongside the signature brown. It was increasingly exchanged along north-south lines with the Casas Grandes people, as trade networks grew not just in reach but in abundance, with copper bells, bracelets adorned with seashells, red-and-white Mexican macaw feathers, and turquoise jewelry flowing northward.[47]

Religious rituals, such as funerary rites, grew more sophisticated; the sun and the moon became the basis of the culture, dictating not just seasonal change but times for hunting, travel, and settling in for the cool winters. New generations made pilgrimages to the rock pile of Hueco Tanks thirty miles away to pray, dance, and draw upon the cave walls. Burial sites too began to dot that jumbled landscape. But in El Paso and across the Southwest, there was one force people could not hold back: the climate, which was becoming relentlessly hotter and drier. As the twelfth century approached, the few remaining islands of grassland began to vanish. All that was left of the great lake were sandy alkaline flats, or playas, while forests retreated high into the mountains, where the land was too sloped and rugged to farm. Down where the people lived, the environment was turning into arid high desert: the Chihuahuan Desert, stretching from Texas to Arizona and hundreds of miles into New Mexico, was becoming the sixth largest in the world.

By around 1150 CE, the people of the Jornada Mogollon were living in settlements of one-story adobe apartment buildings, each one holding a family and often comprising seven rooms. These dwellings were arrayed around small plazas. There were reservoirs and ball courts. Some people made permanent settlements on the flanks of the Sacramento Mountains, settling at present-day Capitan, New Mexico, in 900 CE, at Three Rivers in 1100 CE, and around the San Andres Mountains beginning in 1200 CE.[48] Here they didn't simply paint their symbols on the rock, as they had at Hueco Tanks. Instead, they carved petroglyphs into it, likely creating symbols for the network of caves and natural tunnels found at their ancestral home.[49]

The various Mogollon peoples expanded, giving rise to new cultures. They built settlements such as Kinisba, a six-hundred-room great house, and had settled near present-day Flagstaff by 1100 CE. Some, the Mimbres, dwelled along the headwaters of the Gila River and made their way west and northwest to places like Canyon de Chelly in modern Arizona; the Ancestral Pueblo took up refuge in Chaco Canyon, New Mexico, and Mesa Verde, Colorado. Trading networks expanded as turquoise flowed south from Chaco Canyon and silver traveled north from Mexico, along with the influence of the god Quetzacoatl.[50] The Mimbres carved intricate ditch works, built towns of two hundred or so villagers, and harvested corn from along the river valley of the Numbers River. They painted their black-and-white pottery in fantastic detail, depicting insects, birds, animals, and geometric designs; the population swelled to five thousand people, with their culture peaking around the year 1250. From about 1300 onward, homes were always arrayed east to west, with four or five peeled logs holding up each room, walls carefully fashioned with five layers of adobe, and firepits inside. Doorways faced south.

The south, however, was lower, hotter, and drier, and between the years 1000 and 1500 CE, the Casas Grandes civilization frayed and the people began to leave.[51] It was a sign of things to come. On the heels of their great migration, war came to the Native people of Oasisamerica. The Apache—an Athabascan-speaking people originally from Canada—arrived from the Front Range of the Rocky Mountains and the wide-open plains to the east. Exposed in their broad valley, the Mimbres were vulnerable to attack—and attack the Apache did. In response, the Mimbres headed northwest into the narrower reaches of the Gila River,[52] where they merged with Jornada Mogollon people from the desert. Soon another group arrived from the Arizona lowlands of what is now Phoenix: the Hohokam, whose vast and intricate network of canals and farms had dried up.[53]

In their fortified cliff dwellings, their numbers grew and their culture spread. Clear water ran to sustain people and crops alike. There was also plenty of game, including turkey, deer, and elk. Most important, though, this narrow canyon country could be more easily defended. Scouts could keep a lookout on top; the people built their adobe dwellings within the cliffs, off the valley floor. In the event of an Apache raid, wooden ladders could be pulled up, rendering the village practically impregnable. A single dwelling contained up to forty-two rooms where eight to ten families could live.

Across the Southwest, Ancestral Pueblo and Mogollon peoples followed suit, building their own cliff dwellings. But there were disadvantages, namely a narrowing of their diet essentially to corn. Life under constant siege diminished hunting forays and, worse still, fewer and fewer trips to gather wild plants, for fear of an Apache raiding party.[54]

According to the oral history of the Pueblo people, their ancestors emerged in groups roughly tied to their various languages: the Tanoans settling around present-day Cortez, Colorado, and Mesa Verde; the Keresans at Chaco Canyon, Aztec, and Bloomfield, New Mexico; the Keresans with their Bear Cult and Corn Dance and the Hitsatsinom, or ancient Hopi, intermarrying with the others. A long and painful period of drought was recorded in the oral histories and by the modern study of tree rings, which grow thicker in rainy years and thinner in dry ones.[55] As the Pueblo historian Sando wrote, "Mother Earth was splitting apart. Thus they began to vacate the northwest area in favor of the Rio Grande and its tributaries."[56]

As hunter-gatherers, the newcomer Apache had to stay on the move. Those nearest to El Paso ranged widely in search of game, wandering with the seasons and staging raids deep into Mexico and Arizona. Around 1350, seasonal respites from their Apache foes allowed the expanding Mogollon people to breathe a sigh of relief and move down from the cold mountains and onto the broad, sunny mesas. Within a few decades, the last remaining people in the Tularosa and Hueco Bolson basins near present-day El Paso left for the mountains. The Mogollon had begun crossing the Plains of San Agustin in New Mexico, headed for the Rio Grande.[57] Yet a few remnant people had stayed behind after the great migration. They abandoned their adobe settlements, developed different languages, and formed new subsistence practices.

By 1450, the Suma and Manso peoples emerged along the banks of the great river. The Suma painted their faces with red clay. The Manso covered themselves in tattoos. Their societies were much simpler, less specialized, and more opportunistic. They did not build permanent dwellings, moving with the seasons and relying primarily on the deer, ducks, and doves of the cottonwoods that grew along the river. Indeed, they mostly did not bother to cook the game and birds they harvested; they just ate them raw. Not far away, in southern Arizona, another notable people claimed to live on an idyllic island on a lake from which they were then cast out, about the same time that climate change altered the earth of the American Southwest. First known as the Mexica and then as the Aztec, they may have inhabited the Colorado River Delta, a waterscape of reeds. Nevertheless, they abandoned it on a centuries-long journey south, spreading the Uto-Aztecan language down Mexico's western coast.[58]

Nature changed so much, it drove the ever-increasing number

of people away and reclaimed the heart of the oasis as its own. The climate dried in the mountains too. By the fifteenth century, even the mountain dwellers, the Mogollon in the south and the Ancestral Pueblo in the north, were barely surviving, this time because of agriculture and not in spite of it. The more food they grew, the more mouths there were to feed. They simply could not support their growing populations as decades of drought settled in. Both abandoned their mountain strongholds.

Thousands, possibly tens of thousands, of people streamed eastward from the Mogollon Rim, the Gila Mountains, Chaco, and Mesa Verde nearly overnight, taking little to nothing with them. The great Pueblo Diaspora had come, and no matter how much they prayed, the gods would not bring enough bounty. Entire cities were on the move toward the dependable waters of the great river, the Rio Grande, and survival itself.

Often in popular literature, on National Forest and Park signs, and even in texts written by historians, it has been claimed that many of these great cultures and their peoples simply vanished. But that's incorrect. Nobody just vanishes.

The hard-bitten survivors walked across the high desert and mountains to form the Pueblo, with villages from nearby Colorado to 250 miles to the south, well below present-day Albuquerque toward El Paso. Speaking seven different languages, they were united by their kachina religion and included pueblos as far as Arizona.

Exactly as their religion promised, the ancients had gone to join the gods, and in doing so, provided bounty to the new and increasingly powerful Native nation that arose from the ashes of diaspora.

Chapter Three

THE GREAT REVOLT, 1680–1700

I N HIS CAPITAL at San Juan, now known as San Juan de los Caballeros, Oñate anxiously awaited news of the expedition. Never lacking for visions of grandeur, he seemed to imagine a glorious parallel between his troops and the Knights Templar, who had conquered Jerusalem in 1099 during the Crusades. He had renamed his adobe quarters for them.

Matters at Sky City were less auspicious. Of the thousands of people who called this place home in 1599, only five hundred—mostly women and children—had surrendered.[1] The rest had died, killed themselves, or escaped the mesa. These surviving prisoners were marched a hundred miles across the high, sage-covered desert in winter. However, the expedition was so terrified of retribution at San Juan for the carnage at Sky City that women guarded the rooftops, led by Doña Eufemia, wife of Francisco de Sosa Peñalosa, who personally chastised the men for even discussing desertion.[2] Deep inside the shocked and increasingly seething Pueblo confederation, all the Spaniards had blood on their hands, were outnumbered, and were fourteen hundred miles from Mexico City.

The news of the slaughter spread like wildfire among the Pueblo; some prepared even to attack the understrength garrison at the capital, and Oñate himself learned the news from a Pueblo woman. On February 9, 1599, his nephew Vicente de Zaldivar arrived at Kewa Pueblo, which the Spanish called Santo Domingo, and Oñate rushed to meet him. On the very next day, all five hundred prisoners faced trial for refusing to surrender and killing the attacking Spanish troops. The "trial" was over in just three days; all but the children were declared guilty, which was practically a foregone conclusion.

Oñate had grown up with his father's stories about the grisly consequences of war fighting the native Chichemeca in Mexico. Those types of wars were a direct result of the astonishingly cruel nature of the wars fought by Spain against the Moors on the Iberian Peninsula.

Oñate spared the lives of his prisoners but ordered a horrific punishment. Each male over twenty-five years of age had one foot chopped off, then those twenty-four young men were sold into twenty years of servitude. Outright chattel slavery for Indigenous people was generally illegal by then, but captives of war were another case. Males older than age twelve but younger than twenty-five were sold into two decades of slavery, as were females over twelve years old. All of the children under twelve were torn from their parents and handed over to the priests for a Christian upbringing. Sixty small girls were shipped across the arduous overland route to Mexico City, distributed to convents there, and never returned.

Oñate held the trial in a large village in the heart of Pueblo country to demonstrate his resolve and ordered the punishments carried out there for the same reason. Screaming and wailing filled the air as feet were lopped off, along with the hands of two Moquis visiting Sky City. The captives, slaves for all intents and purposes, were then marched to San Juan de los Caballeros to be handed out to the colonists as their personal property. Oñate had certainly demonstrated his machismo, but he had also once more endangered his entire expedition. The few hundred colonists had relied for their survival on good relations with as many as twenty thousand Pueblo people, who had provided shelter and food to them, even when food was scarce.[3]

Now that goodwill was covered in Pueblo blood and bondage. Oñate was failing. His letters to the viceroy in Mexico City were filled with exaggerated prospects based on the few minerals he'd found lying around, which had yielded silver, not gold; hearsay of pearls from a distant sea; news about salt lake beds; and the few buffalo that his men had killed. "First, the great wealth which the mines have begun to reveal and the great number of them in this land, whence proceed the royal fifths and profits," he enumerated in a letter dated March 2, 1599. "Second, the certainty of the proximity of the South Sea, whose trade with . . . New Spain and China is not to be depreciated, for it will give birth in time to advantageous and continuous duties, because of its close proximity, particularly to China and to that land."[4]

Oñate's promises always ended in pleas for more help, more men, and more money. The savagery he and his men had displayed with the Acoma people was the beginning of the end for him, and in reality, for his entire colony. He clung to power as governor; traveled to the reeds of the Colorado River Delta and claimed that it was a rich harbor of the Pacific Ocean; he installed his family in power and moved the capital to Santa Fe. Some colonists left. Many complained to Mexico City of their leader's ineptitude and cruelty toward them. Soldiers deserted, and winter starvation became a common specter as the conquering Spaniards demanded everything, even blankets, from the people they encountered.

Oñate's expedition was not really ever about establishing a colony. It was an invasion, supported by a civilian workforce that relied upon enslaved Native Americans, whose mission was to seize gold and find a shortcut to China, the fabled Strait of Anián (which was, in reality, the Bering Strait, and a shortcut not to China but to Russia, over three thousand miles to the northwest). When the Seven Cities of Cibola turned out to be the adobe apartments of the Pueblo people, the Spaniards grew angry. Eventually the Spanish monarchy got tired of Oñate's excuses and pleas, while the viceroyalty got tired of all the complaints from his people.

Historians have generally defended Oñate, and even Coronado, for blazing a trail into what became the United States and leaving behind a Hispanic colony, and for not being as abusive as, say, other conquistadors in Mexico, Guatemala, and Peru. The latter seems an awfully low standard. The former accomplishments were important, but they were inadvertent byproducts of blundering misadventure. Oñate did not accomplish the chief objectives: getting the gold and finding the shortcut to China. He was a bad leader who prevaricated when disciplining his troops and treated his colonists, such as they were, poorly. He risked the entire expedition over and over again, and his own methods of governing were his downfall. In reality, the mighty conqueror was an abject failure.[5]

In April, Oñate passed by the giant sandstone bluff in New Mexico called El Morro and paused to engrave these words: "Paso por aquí el adelantado Don Juan de Oñate,"[6] "Don Juan de Oñate passed by here." He claimed to have passed by on his way back from the South Sea, or the Pacific Ocean, which he had never reached. The conqueror may not have been adept at fulfilling his mission for the king, but he was proficient at burnishing his legacy.[7]

By June 17, 1606, Philip III had enough: he ordered Oñate recalled to Mexico City, where he would stand trial for a slew of crimes. Oñate resigned as governor and installed his son. Three years later, a royally appointed governor took office. The crown considered pulling the plug on the colony entirely; it was a drain on the royal treasury, with little to no prospect of a return on investment.

In Spain, the Council of the Indies, which advised the king on everything in the Western Hemisphere, recommended abandoning New Mexico altogether.

However, the church objected, because now it had Christian souls it couldn't leave to the wolves. Indeed, the Franciscans in New Mexico started baptizing thousands of Pueblo people to box the monarchy into keeping the vast territory. Eventually, New Mexico was deemed such a mess that it was removed as a potentially profitable colony and funded by the king on behalf of the Catholic Church, a ward of the empire for Rome.

The baptism of Pueblo people was rarely a choice made freely by the catechumens themselves. At the now-destroyed Piro Pueblo settlement at Sevilleta, Little Seville, Franciscans practiced forced baptism: the sacrament, or death. Even the king objected to this. A letter dated to 1621 from the crown essentially said, according to the archaeologist and theologian Lynn Southard, "'Stop killing the Indians.' It was absolutely tragic and finding that letter broke my heart."[8]

The church could play politics, but the religious character of both the Pueblo and the Spaniards should not be underestimated. The latter were the products of medieval Europe. Just over two hundred years earlier, the Muslims had ruled Iberia, the Mongol Empire had peaked on the banks of the Danube, and the Black Death had claimed lives everywhere; as a result, some seventy-five million Europeans had died ugly, terrible, and tragic deaths in the fourteenth century.[9] The sheer fear that these calamities fueled—and the faith they inspired—persisted for generations.

After the destruction of Sky City in 1610, the Spanish soldiers claimed to see Saint James, urging them onward after their victory. The Franciscans imported their Mexican church architecture into Santa Fe as wagon trains lumberingly retraced the Jornada del

Muerto—now the royal road—carrying religious artwork and the means to make it, including a statue of Our Lady of the Assumption from Spain, renamed La Conquistadora. The wagons brought a stream of woodworking tools, pottery, oil paintings in gilded frames, crucifixes, and carved images of Jesus Christ. The Franciscans skillfully adapted to the frontier too, using the Pueblo people's tanned deer hides to paint religious images for catechism and, ultimately, their conversion.[10]

Whatever the state of his soul, Oñate, for his part, was hardly as financially bereft as he claimed.[11] En route to the capital, the old governor stopped off at the family mines in Zacatecas to shore up their operations. His whole expedition had been terribly costly and needless; after all, the mines produced over 137 marks of silver a year, worth millions of dollars in today's currency, before taxes. He went to face trial in Mexico City. He was acquitted on seventeen charges but found guilty of twelve, including illegally executing Native people, excessive force in Acoma, executing his own soldiers, and, for good measure during the Inquisition, adultery. On May 13, 1613, he was ordered into perpetual exile from the New Mexico territories he had once claimed, and exile from his native Mexico for four years.

So he left Mexico City for Spain, a country he had never seen. There, his children married; one daughter entered a convent. His wife, Isabela, died. Ever prideful, Oñate pleaded with the crown for a pardon and demanded the restoration of his various titles; he was turned down again and again. He was instead given the unpaid post of mining inspector to keep him busy, as the country needed every resource possible for the Thirty Years' War, which it was now fighting. In the end, the younger Oñate met his fate much like his late father had, minus the glory. To fulfill his duty to the crown, Oñate went into a flooded mine near Guadalcanal in southern Spain on June 3, 1626. The mine collapsed and killed him. He was seventy-six years old.[12]

BACK IN NORTH America, the Pueblo people seethed at the butchery that had taken place in the wake of the Sky City battle, as the Spanish expanded northward into southern Colorado in the 1620s.[13] It was clear the expedition could not be trusted, and though the Pueblo clearly outnumbered its seven-hundred-odd members, the invaders' firepower was daunting. The ensuing decades remained tense, filled with plots by both the Native people and the Spanish. The colony continued to sink into poverty—a child of the church nurtured grudgingly by the crown, no longer the promising new frontier of the empire. Even the morality of the colony came under question in 1626 or 1627 by a Franciscan, Father Geronimo de Zarate y Salmeron, a missionary to Jemez Pueblo. He quoted a prophecy of Fray Diego Mercado in Mexico, but was clearly referencing New Mexico:

> God certainly does have great riches in these remote parts of New Mexico, but the present settlers are not to enjoy them, for God is not keeping these for them; and so it has been, for all the first people have died without enjoying them, and amidst great suffering, because they have always come with these desires and greediness for riches, which is the reason they went there to settle, and they spent their fortunes.[14]

Spain's colonial enterprise in what would become the United States was far different, and indeed less cruel, than the English chattel slavery inflicted on Africans; the Catholic Church often, though not always, intervened against the viciousness of those representing the monarchy. Yet the system of taxation was brutal in its own way. The feudal system of the *encomienda* required every head of household in each pueblo to pay an annual tribute of gold, produce, or blankets to support the defense of the expedition. If the tax was not paid, the men were forced into labor. The tax was paid to the colonists, who, in turn, paid 10 percent to the lowest rank of nobility, the hidalgos, who in turn paid it further up the food chain.[15] In return, the Spanish provided almost nothing, not even protection from other tribes. It was a plantation system of sorts, keeping Native people in servitude so the occupying population could benefit,[16] yoking them with chains of debt as they struggled to feed themselves and their new occupiers.

In 1630, on the banks of the cool waters near the mouth of the yawning Rio Grande Gorge, a child known as Po'Pay was born in a pueblo called Ohkay Owingeh. The people had accommodated Oñate by giving up their dwellings when his expedition first arrived and moving a few miles upriver. The river bottom yielded rich farmland, while the rugged gorge, made of sharp, black volcanic rock, made for good hunting and a defensible retreat from the Spanish, should things come to that. But in the 1660s and 1670s, drought and disease gripped the Spanish, and slavers began raiding the pueblos, dragging captives off to Mexico. Starvation stalked Europeans, Mexicans, and Native Americans alike. Po'Pay grew up to become a religious zealot, believing he was commanded by ancestral spirits, the kachinas, to restore the old Pueblo way of life. His embrace of the kachina tradition quickly found a following.[17] After all, the Christian god was apparently failing: the rain hadn't fallen, the cornfields withered, and the people were hungry. In 1670, it appears from tree-ring studies, not a drop of rain leached from the sky.[18] In 1675, Governor Juan Francisco Treviño ordered the arrest of forty-seven Pueblo leaders, known as caciques, for plotting rebellion; one was Po'Pay, now age forty-five.

Some seventy warriors descended on Santa Fe, the capital of

New Mexico, to demand the prisoners' release, knowing full well the Spanish garrison was understaffed; most troops were off fighting the Apache. Po'Pay was among those released. He had become known to his fellow caciques as dynamic and fierce; those who dealt with him described themselves as bordering on fearful. As a free man, Po'Pay made his way to Taos Pueblo, perhaps the most fiercely independent of the Pueblo confederation. From the sweeping vistas of this seven-thousand-foot plateau, he planned a rebellion that would defeat the Spanish once and for all, driving them from this land. He secretly traveled to forty-five Pueblo settlements over the next five years, gaining the support of a broad coalition, including those who spoke different languages and lived in a variety of conditions. He even enlisted the Apache and the Diné (Navajo), peoples with whom the Pueblo were often at war.

In 1680, Po'Pay dispatched runners across the land, each one carrying a cord of knots. Leaders were to untie one knot each day; the day when they undid the last knot was to be the day of the rebellion: August 11, 1680.[19]

THAT PO'PAY, HIS Pueblo allies, and their co-conspirators maintained secrecy for five years was a remarkable feat of operational security, underscoring just how adept the Pueblo hierarchy was at the art of war. But the new Spanish governor, Antonio Otermín, appointed in 1678, was no slouch.[20] Though he had comparatively few resources, he was certainly cannier than Oñate. He was also probably better attuned to the precarity of the colony's security position. Even so, the governor was almost certainly caught by surprise by the uprising, his survival down mostly to luck.[21]

Two of Po'Pay's couriers, Catua and Omtua, had brought news of the pending uprising to other Pueblo leaders. But two days before the revolt, the governor ordered the two arrested and brought to him. By some accounts, they were tortured. By others, they were sworn to tell the truth and complied, spilling all they knew about the plot: the two remaining knots in the cords meant just two days remained before the assault.[22] Beyond that, the two knew nothing; they had not been privy to the years of planning. The dilemma the governor faced was clear: he and his people were completely outnumbered and overmatched. The Spanish and their allies comprised just twenty-five hundred against more than fifteen thousand Pueblo people, and their troops were spread out. Even advance warning could help only so much.

The conspirators, learning that their cover was blown, launched the rebellion one day early; the Acoma, Hopi, and Zuni didn't get the message about launching early but joined the fighting on the original date.[23] On August 10, 1680, all the rest of the pueblos, aided by the Apache and now the Diné, struck with precise and devastating effect. They razed Catholic missions and killed nearly every priest in New Mexico. The Pueblo people of Taos and their allies the Apache fell on settlements just below them, at the mouth of the Rio Grande Gorge. To the east, in Picuris, not a single colonist remained after the church was burned, the farm plots were destroyed, and the homes were razed.[24] Warriors from both pueblos then converged on Santa Fe. In Tesuque, a Catholic priest named Father Piro found an armed war party and begged them to stop: "What does this mean, my children? Are you crazy?"[25]

Slaughtering Spaniards and other Europeans, mestizos, and Native Mexicans, the Pueblo warriors succeeded in destroying every Spanish settlement in New Mexico in just three days. The Spaniards narrowly escaped death at La Cañada and Los Cerrillos. Demonstrating remarkable discipline, the noncombatant Pueblo civilians on the Upper Rio Grande formed two divisions and barricaded themselves inside the now-fortified settlements at Santa Clara and Tesuque.[26] The Acoma, having borne their own massacre decades before, killed every Spaniard they could find. And at Santo Domingo, the site of earlier butchery against the Pueblo, warriors killed all three priests, then started stacking dead civilians behind the church.[27]

Meanwhile, the warriors' frightened quarry took refuge at Santa Fe, but the Pueblo fighters simply laid siege to the town, cutting off its water supply during the hottest month of the summer. Nearly a thousand people desperately sought protection inside the long, narrow governor's palace at the plaza. Food ran out. Over twenty-five hundred Pueblo warriors massed outside the capital and the stage was set for another massacre, this time with the Spanish and their allies cast as the victims.[28]

Another thousand refugees made their way to Isleta, seventy miles to the south. Finally, on August 17, the few Spanish troops at Santa Fe broke through the Pueblo lines, and four days later, the besieged civilians rode or ran off, fleeing for their lives. The Pueblo killed over four hundred of the desperate colonists. Throughout September, the remaining two thousand survivors, along with a few hundred Pueblo slaves,[29] hostages, and defectors,[30] streamed headlong south, across the desert. In the confusion of war, neither column of refugees was aware of the other.

On October 9, 1680, the combined mass of exhausted refugees finally encamped safely where their stormy journey had begun, nearly a century earlier: El Paso.[31]

THE LAND BURNED, the haciendas and homes wrecked, the stench of the dead gathering in the warm fall air—almost nothing was left of the Spanish. The few churches not destroyed had been stripped of every ornament, crucifix, and sacramental vessel.

The violence and death of the Great Pueblo Revolt was as historic as it was grisly. It was the only time in the history of the Western Hemisphere that a European colonial power had been ejected by the Native people. From Canada to Peru, many Native peoples had tried to do this, but only the Pueblo succeeded. For his vision, leadership, and cunning, Po'Pay became one of the leaders of the restored Pueblo confederation.

The Pueblo people had proven themselves as brilliant at secrecy as at war. In fewer than two months, and mostly over three days, they had killed in action one-third as many people as the subsequent, and much longer, eighteenth-century French and Indian War in the American East.[32]

For their part, the Spanish considered the entire territory lost, at least for the time being, and they named El Paso the new capital of New Mexico. The little settlement that was now the emergency seat of government had been attached to the commercially successful province of Nueva Vizcaya, the present-day Mexican states of Chihuahua and Durango. But now it swelled with new migrants seeking shelter, food, and help in recovering from the trauma—and God. It was a role El Paso would play many times over in the centuries to come.

While chaos had ensued to the north, El Paso had rather quietly grown into a profitable, peaceable settlement that was already a gathering point for Native Americans from many backgrounds—Apache, Jumano, Suma, and others—whom the church was trying to convert into Christians and workers. These Native people were starving too; drought had caused the failure of crops upon which they depended more and more as the supply of wild game—cottontails, jackrabbits, mule deer, and pronghorn—grew thin. The rich, broad Rio Grande bottomland at El Paso was painstakingly converted into some of the most valuable and productive vineyards in North America. The wine the Franciscans produced there was so popular, it would eventually be shipped back across the world to Spain.

Just as important, and contrary to what most Americans know, El Paso would also become one of the oldest continuously inhabited settlements in the United States—behind St. Augustine, Florida, founded by the Spanish in 1565, and Santa Fe, New Mexico, founded in 1610. In 1659, Father García de San Francisco y Zúñiga built a church from mud and branches and a monastery with a straw-thatched roof, naming it Nuestra Señora de los Mansos—Our Lady of the Gentle—to minister to the local Native Americans.[33] By 1660, settlers began farming with the help of acequias, networks of interconnected, communally owned ditches and canals: common in upper New Mexico, this technology was imported from Spain, a holdover from its Muslim occupation. In Arabic, the ditches were known more elegantly as *as-sāqiya,* or conduits of water. In 1662, the church began work on a permanent mission dedicated to the Virgin of Guadalupe, complete by 1668. In 1678, its first Catholic wedding took place.[34] Once the refugees of the New Mexico war arrived, they celebrated with a Catholic mass on October 12, 1680. It was the first mass said in the Ysleta area[35] in what would eventually become the state of Texas, making this the oldest continuously settled area of the Lone Star State.[36]

Meanwhile, elsewhere in North America, better-known European settlements were taking root, with varying success. Quebec was founded by France in 1608, but had to be moved down the St. Lawrence River from its original location. Farther south, the Plymouth Colony in Massachusetts was founded in 1620 and survived for decades. Sir Walter Raleigh[37] established a colony at Roanoke, North Carolina, on the windswept Outer Banks in 1585 that was abandoned, reestablished two years later, and found entirely abandoned again in 1590. The English settlement at Jamestown, Virginia, was nearly as unfortunate: repeatedly moved, abandoned, and resettled.

Regardless, all these places arose more than a century after El

Paso had already spread its roots across the alluvial soil of the Middle Rio Grande Valley. With the arrival of the refugees, the population swelled to over three thousand people: up and down the river in El Paso and to towns such as San Lorenzo, Senecú, Socorro, and Ysleta, all longingly named for the lost villages of New Mexico. Those who fled were descendants of those who came to conquer; most of them knew no other world than the high deserts and soaring mountains of the Southwest.[38]

By now, people of many different walks of life sought refuge in El Paso, which became important to the crown in Madrid. El Paso was now the largest settlement in New Mexico. Indeed, it was the de facto capital of all the lands claimed by Spain in what would become the American Southwest and the Rockies—from California to Utah, Wyoming, Arizona, and New Mexico—and it would remain the capital, in most ways, for centuries to come.

The city didn't just fill with the Spanish and other Europeans. After the collapse of the Casas Grandes culture, a remnant people stirred in Chihuahua: a branch of the Jumano people who were already known along the Middle Rio Grande to the Spanish as the Suma, the very same people who had greeted Esteban and the Cabeza de Vaca survivors and feasted with Oñate's expedition. This branch journeyed east and north to El Paso, about a six-day journey,[39] where they camped alongside some bands of Apache who had laid down their warring and raiding ways, all of them seeking food, which they received as they were baptized by the Catholic missionary priests. By 1680, as more refugees arrived from the north, the priests had already recorded baptizing sixty-two Piro, seventeen Suma, ten Tano, five Apache and Jumano.[40]

The same hunger that helped spur the Great Pueblo Revolt gnawed at people across the region: the rain simply would not fall, and the crops, however desperately tended, did not survive to harvest. People of all races sought refuge in El Paso. It was a lively, if still rough, settlement. Jumano people from Chihuahua arrived with meager goods strapped to their dogs; there were few horses, and most Native Americans who had seen them thought they were just big dogs; they had not yet learned to master the strange equine beasts. Jumano people came from various points on the compass and among them was an entire clan who, just like Juan Griego, adopted a Hispanicized name, from the Galician people and language in northwestern Spain: the men of the Roybal, as they were called, were high-ranking caciques who settled in with the runaway Isleta Puebloans. Indeed, among the refugees from the north were numbered descendants of the old Greek soldier Juan Griego himself and his Nahuatl-speaking wife.

The local Manso, possibly remnant descendants of the Jornada Mogollon, fished in the Rio Grande.[41] Spanish slavers passed through, with their strings of human captives. Aztec *pocheta* traders arrived from the south, with goods strapped to the backs of their own slaves.[42] Even the Piro people, Puebloans who had survived the Apaches' destruction of their settlement at Senecu, settled in alongside their enemies.[43]

The defeated governor, Otermín, had all of his ragged colonists pass by him, one by one, so he could inspect them. Most men, even the soldiers, were left at best with wives and children, a few weapons, and perhaps four skinny horses. "Felipe Montoya, married, passed muster on foot, naked, very poor, with one tired horse and four sons," read one entry in the muster rolls.[44] The devastated colonists began to scatter and Otermín had to restrain them by threat of arrest. Otermín had been personally humiliated by the Great Pueblo Revolt; no other governor serving the Spanish crown had ever lost an entire territory. He vowed to recapture the north, but on October 2, 1680, he bowed to reality: no expedition would be mounted to achieve reconquest now. Otermín too camped on the north bank of the Rio Grande at what is now El Paso, Texas.

The new capital needed protection, of which it had precious little, and early in the coming year work would begin on a new presidio, or fort, chiefly to stop the warring Native Americans from reaching settlements in Sonora and Chihuahua.[45] As the refugees settled at three spots in El Paso, alongside the pueblos the native people built, they had come full circle in their cultures' long journey.[46]

El Paso was not just the capital of New Mexico now. It was the de facto capital of all the Southwest, from Chihuahua in the south to the Pueblo territory in the north, westward to the Pacific, and northward into the Rockies. It was the capital of what would become the border between the United States and Mexico, the portal to every direction on the map. For the people now huddled along the Rio Grande, El Paso was a refuge, their island in that blazing sea of sand and rocky desert. It was home.

THE SHORT, MUSCLED chestnut stud stood still in the stand of red Ponderosa pines, then started to twitch his tail and lift his head, taking in the mountain air and sifting scents for threats.[1] Behind him, nearly a dozen mares in his harem—black, chestnut, and bay, all with white snips, stars, or stripes between their eyes—looked up, ears alert. None of them liked being watched. The stallion shook his black, shaggy mane and shook out his long black tail.

The horses, sorted into harems by stallion, called these mountains home. In the spring, foals on their wobbly legs trailed their mothers. But now, by summer, they were colts, bolting here and there behind the safety of the others. This group was part of a larger herd easily numbering in the thousands. In the evenings they would gather in the high meadows of the Sacramento Mountains, in the shadow of twelve thousand peaks, which still bore snow. After resting at midday, they roamed the pines, munching on tall shoots of grass and slowly making their way down to the meadow.

These were feral horses that had escaped human captivity and care over the course of the seventeenth century, slipping away from their Spanish owners in the night or being traded to Pueblo people for food and blankets. Their genes shared a common microscopic stamp: each of these creatures descended from the remuda of a thousand horses that had splashed across the Rio Grande at El Paso with the Spanish in 1598, on their journey northward.

For all the things he did wrong, Oñate left behind a few fascinating legacies, though he did so accidentally. The mustang, the very symbol of the American West, was one of them. Today nearly every mustang in America can trace its heritage to the Oñate expedition over half a millennium ago.

These short, powerful, and hardy Spanish mustangs[2] were descended from the Colonial Spanish horse, itself a product of mixed breeding between the storied and purebred Iberian horse, also known as the Lusitano, and the North African Barb:[3] upon their invasion of Spain in the eighth century the Muslims crossed the two. The ensuing animal was just as sure-footed, fast, and equipped for long-endurance treks across the desert as its North African parent, but it had the strong intelligence of its European one.

The new offspring stood about fourteen hands high, often weighing no more than eight hundred pounds, with a fine head and muzzle. Viewed from the front, its legs looked slightly splayed instead of straight up and down, its hooves narrow instead of broad. Its hips were its tallest feature, making for a somewhat slouched look but offering an easy seat for a rider. Yet these animals, with their coats of chestnut, black, and bay, were more than the sum of their parents' DNA; their genes met the environment and created a new adaptive phenotype. Once introduced into the Americas, they grew bigger, up to fifteen or sixteen hands. A large stallion might weigh a thousand pounds. In turn, they spawned Appaloosas and paints, in buckskin, palomino, cremello, isabella, roan, and perino.

Even before the Great Pueblo Revolt they had been sold, bartered, and traded to the Pueblo, who first ate them but later learned to ride them. With time, they in turn traded these horses to other Native American peoples across New Mexico and Arizona—namely the Apache, and then on to the Kiowa and Comanche of the Great Plains. Within a century, the mustang gave rise to the great Native American horse cultures, revolutionizing the people's ability to move with the seasons and to wage war against longtime enemies and new intruders alike. But these horses lived without humans now too, roaming wild in every direction, even north into Canada.

THE HISTORY OF the horse's ancestry is a global one. With their invasion of the Iberian Peninsula in the eighth century, the Moors taught Europeans the importance of not just feeding horses but also breeding them. After Christopher Columbus arrived in the Western Hemisphere, horses quickly followed, with royal stables set up in Puerto Rico and Cuba; but after 1507, Spain banned the shipment of more horses to the New World for fear of draining its best stock. Cortés landed in Mexico with just sixteen horses, enough to throw fear into the native Aztec and other groups; they had never seen a domesticated animal bigger than a dog. Yet Cortés returned with all the surviving stock, leaving none in Mexico. While Coronado's armed expedition brought horses to the American Southwest and some undoubtedly escaped, their numbers were too small—and the odds against survival too tall—to establish a lasting, breeding population. Only Oñate's remuda could, and did, take root.[4] Now the horses could breed and grow in number and even escape, becoming creatures entirely of the New World.

The introduction of the horse did more than just change the Southwest and the West. For better and for worse, it changed America.

As the horses passed from Spaniard to Pueblo to Apache hands, at first certain traditions were passed along with them. They were mounted from the right, in the Spanish style adopted from the Moors. The Apache fashioned bits, bridles, and saddles. Their hunting range increased vastly, and by the 1650s, Spanish reports carried news of mounted Apache raids.[5] The new Native American horse culture slowed the penetration of the West by Europeans and later, Americans of European descent.[6] By 1664, the Apache had relieved hapless Spanish colonists of some hundred thousand horses. The Plains people acquired them and mastered ways of using this marvelous creature for hunting, war, and migration. By 1700, all the Native tribes of Texas had horses. By 1750, the First Nations of Canada were firing arrows as they galloped on horseback, to take down buffalo.[7]

Nearly a century later, a little-known US Army lieutenant, Ulysses S. Grant, would report from Texas that "horses were visible from horizon to horizon." By then, at least a million wild mustangs roamed Texas alone.[8] In some tribes, families owned as many as fifteen horses. A source of great pride, this animal became an icon, a symbol of a way of life.

- - - - - - - - -

DOWN IN THE Middle Rio Grande Valley, after 1680 and into the eighteenth century, as the settlement in El Paso grew, so did its horse population. The crown sent several thousand stallions and mares to the colonists.[9]

Because the Apache, and the Comanche after them, were little interested in working in a stable to care for and feed these animals, they stole some too; they preferred raiding to breeding. Horses had value; they could be traded to other tribes for captives and slaves. The colonists, in turn, went out onto the desert range each year to round up mustangs in order to replenish their own dwindling stock.[10] The people actually hunted these animals at times— sometimes taking them down as a nuisance for raiding crops and sometimes as meat when colonists faced starvation.

This was no easy task. Mustangs were skilled at hiding in the brush, picking up scents at long distances, and disappearing from the exact spot where they had just been seen. When cornered, mustangs were dangerous; filled with adrenaline, they could muster unbelievable strength. Mares, stallions, and colts alike could kick with power and precise aim, which could maim or kill. At the end of a lasso, they could bite hard; their giant, hard teeth could rip out a chunk of human flesh. As the American author Sinclair Ross later wrote of a particularly savage mare: "She was beautiful but dangerous. She had thrown one man and killed him, thrown another and broken his collarbone."[11]

Not just anybody was up to the task of capturing a mustang. No, this was a job for the vaqueros, the forefathers of the American cowboy. The cowboy's history can be traced to Texas, and in turn, back to the Mexican vaquero and his European predecessor. But in the eighteenth century, Texas did not exist in any meaningful sense; it would not be settled by Spaniards for a century, when the first vaqueros went to work in and around the burgeoning settlement at El Paso, whose population at this point was similar in size to those of New York and Boston, two British colonies on the Atlantic seaboard.[12]

The word *vaquero* comes from the name of the Native people of the Plains who rode valorously into stampeding buffalo, or bison, to fire their arrows. The Spanish had never seen these animals, so they just called them cows, and the men who rode with them were in turn called cowboys, or cattle drivers: vaqueros. On the ranches of El Paso, vaqueros might be European, but they might be Native as well, as they were on the giant estancias of Mexico.[13]

Their gear was nearly all the same: rawhide reatas, a term later anglicized as *lariats*. Many of their customs were directly inherited from the Spanish light cavalry known as the Jinete horsemen, who had played a crucial role in recapturing the Iberian Peninsula from its Muslim occupiers.[14]

But the people on this high desert frontier were quickly leaving behind their medieval European customs and a new civilization altogether was evolving. Out here, they did not enjoy the bounty of Mexico and the scale of its farming and ranching. Eking out a living was a hardscrabble affair. Isolated, they made do with their own hands to create and fix their gear, instead of relying on far-flung craftsmen. The vaqueros saved their fancy leather-trimmed saddles for the yearly rodeos, where they flashed their bravado and finery. But mostly they carved simple saddles from the nearest hardwood tree and covered them with the stretched hide of a recently killed steer. Gone were the giant stirrups of metal, the leather decorated skillfully and heavily.

A new culture was developing. Women, for their part, altered not only their appearance, but their role in colonial society. Here, with the men actually working instead of just chasing gold, women began to wield enormous power—albeit behind the scenes. Their families were highly selective in whom they married and the dowry they gave to a husband. In turn, wives frequently and fiercely controlled the finances and, therefore, the household; Spanish law dictated that a man could use the dowry only in his wife's interest, and frequently, he did so only with her consent, despite the old macho traditions of Spain.

Besides, this society was no longer, strictly speaking, a Spanish one. Yes, the burgundy cross of Spain[15] still flapped in the powerful winds, but the colony had become something more. There were at least as many men from other European nations, including the Netherlands, France, and Germany, as there were from Spain. Some married Spanish women; others wed those of Native descent. And the collection of Native people around the missions was large and complex: Pueblo, for certain, but also Manso, Jumano, and Apache. And just as the Manso and Jumano increasingly melted into the Apache, so did the Spanish and European into the newest race in the world: the mestizo, that uniquely Mexican fusion of Native and European (namely, Iberian) bloodlines. The culture that developed here, in the harsh environment of the high Chihuahuan Desert, would be decidedly different from its predecessors.

THE HELLISH SUMMERS and freezing winters at some three thousand feet above sea level brought a trinity of cruel forces to the growing settlement: drought, famine, and war. Like a new *potrillo*, a colt, El Paso struggled to its feet.

The people of El Paso fought nature itself to stay alive in the early eighteenth century. The Spanish first invaded the Americas on the heels of the worst known drought in history, almost forty years long, from 1450 to 1489; it engulfed both Mexico and the American Southwest. The settlers who entered both of these territories in the sixteenth century got, by contrast, a rosy picture of a fertile land, certainly hot but blessed with bountiful water, yet that vision was a mirage. The twenty driest years in history, as recorded by tree rings, took place exactly as El Paso struggled to emerge, from 1697 to 1717.[16] This was a harbinger of things to come.

Meanwhile, the Great Pueblo Revolt had faded into history, but the Pueblo people most certainly had not. Po'Pay and his junta fell from favor after twenty years, and the Spanish reentered northern New Mexico. While they proclaimed this action a *reconquista*, like the retaking of Iberia from the Muslims, in reality it was nothing of the sort. Yes, the Spanish flexed their muscle in Santa Fe after a few particularly harsh raids. But they reentered the north not as occupiers bent on gold, but with a specific royal mission: converting the Native people to Catholicism. The fever dream of fortune had finally been vanquished; there was far less stick and far more carrot this time—and northern New Mexico, while culturally significant, faded from historical importance. Even Albuquerque, to the north, was established as a mere outpost in 1706, primarily intended for farming and shepherding to feed and supply colonists, with a small troop garrison for protection. To the south, a settlement at Chihuahua grew out of the silver mines of the surrounding Santa Barbara region in 1709. Both were satellites of far bigger El Paso. Even the Catholic churches of El Paso predated the other Texas missions by a half century and those in California by a full hundred years.[17]

In contrast, El Paso prospered as the chief way station along the Camino Real: bustling with annual and then twice-annual wagon trains, lumbering in with finished goods from Mexico City moving northward and farm goods, hides, and wool heading south. But El Paso's rising prosperity also made it a target for warring Native people, chiefly the Apache.

The people of El Paso and the Apache quickly locked horns in a desperate battle for primacy and survival that would stretch over nearly two centuries—with a calamitous outcome for the Apache. As a result of this and ensuing wars, El Paso would become, and still remains, the most fought-over city in America. All the area tribes rose up in war from 1683 to 1684, just after the settlement grew with the New Mexico diaspora, and the Spanish rearranged *presidios*, or forts, to better defend the place. The Manso revolted in 1684, while smallpox decimated the Native people at the end of the seventeenth century.

The church established a mission specifically for the conversion of the Suma people in 1707. The Suma revolted in 1710 and then retreated into the rocky Organ Mountains, near present-day Las Cruces, to join the Apache. The Spanish kept building missions to tame the Suma, who would not be tamed. In 1745, the Suma killed a Spaniard at one of the missions, then destroyed it four years later; eventually, they fled again into the mountains. Desperate settlers, their crops and livestock ravaged by drought and raiders alike, pleaded with the viceroyalty in Mexico City to abandon El

Paso—but repeatedly, upon orders from Madrid, they were told to stand and fight. The city's position on the trade route was too vital; abandoning it would mean forsaking every Spanish possession remaining north of the Rio Grande and west of the Mississippi. So the settlers and soldiers, of all races and ethnicities, did just that: they stood and fought, pressing the line of presidios farther and farther north.[18]

However, the colonists' chief sworn enemy, the Apache, grew only stronger as former Mission Indians joined their nation. With drought and famine pressing and corn in short supply in El Paso, the Apache attacks grew bolder. They raided livestock there year after year, especially after 1760. Increasingly, troops left behind their fortifications and defensive mission to hunt the Apache in the desert. The Spanish often lured them to settle around the presidios in exchange for food, but the Apache knew a trap when they saw one. Sometimes they would come in for the food, then slip out to raid a different settlement. Socorro and San Elizario, just downriver from present-day El Paso, were under nearly constant attack even as their populations grew.[19]

The settlers' perseverance finally paid off in 1780.[20] That summer, the heat was brief, fading in early July instead of ratcheting up. Giant thunderheads rolled in from the east and south each evening, towering into the sky and glowering over the earth. That summer and well into autumn, those clouds actually smiled.

The sky didn't just rain upon the parched earth of El Paso and its surrounding sea of sand. It poured. And in the desert, that water yielded wine.

FOR PEOPLE WHO don't know the desert, the monsoon (drawn from the Arabic language) rains that begin in late summer and stretch into autumn are overwhelming, if occasional. Normally the desert sky only grudgingly yields a spitting moisture, the drops themselves covered in airborne dust by the time they strike the ground. But when the currents of the Pacific, the alternating El Niño and La Niña cycles of the equator, change, or when the high-altitude jet stream shifts north, the warm, water-laden air of the Gulf of Mexico comes in, and cascades of rain fall from the sky. They rush off the high peaks of the barren Franklin Mountains, leaving fields of grass, flowers, and forest-green ocotillos. Sheets of water cover the mesas and shimmer. Dry gulches and arroyos overflow in raging streams. Small lakes form in the lower reaches; shallow playas refill, as ducks, frogs, and toads mate. The water floods the bosques of the floodplain and the Rio Grande itself brims over its banks: a rushing, fertile brown sweeping its way relentlessly to the sea, over a thousand miles away.

By the late eighteenth century, the people in El Paso—Native Americans, Spanish and other Europeans, and mestizos—had labored to build the first extensive irrigation system in what would become the United States. A rough weir dam, composed of mud, logs, and rocks, was strung across the Rio Grande upriver. Large ditches connecting the wild river to smaller ditches, known as acequias, crisscrossed the fertile valley. The first canals may have been dug as far back as 1668, but the system of dams, gates, and locks—modeled on the technology the Moors had brought with their invasion of Spain centuries earlier—came after the Great Pueblo Revolt, when there was enough manpower to build it. Farms and ranches alike became capable of cultivating corn, orchards, and wheat; people could now water crops far from the capricious, flood-prone river in time for the summer drying. At the onset of the heat, all that remained of the river to the naked eye was a thick bed of loamy, tan-colored sand. In 1752, a Prussian explorer and scientist, Alexander von Humboldt, wrote that the riverbed was dry a hundred miles upstream and seventy miles downstream.[21] Likely some water still ran—but far underground. When rain came with the monsoons, the river would rise again, and in the late eighteenth century, the acequias made gardens bloom in the desert. Spanish longhorns, goats, and sheep roamed the green landscape, now thick with a carpet of grass and the tender shoots of desert plants.

Wheat fields grew high, orchards filled with apples, peaches, and pears, and fields of chickpeas glowed green. But no crop bloomed amid this bounty of rain and river water quite like the grape. The mission friars needed wine for the sacrament; nearly every person in a population of now nearly five thousand was a practicing Catholic, and masses were performed three times a day during the week, not counting Saturdays and Sundays. That required a lot of wine—and it made the friars plenty of money. Soon the Middle Rio Grande Valley enjoyed a monopoly on not just wine, but also brandy and even vinegar and raisins; wagon trains hauled casks of wine north to the struggling Santa Fe colony and south to the new one at Chihuahua, some three hundred miles in either direction.[22]

Winemakers trampled the harvest grapes upon a hide, perforated it to allow the juice to drain into a sack also made of hide, then suspended that sack in a barn. From the sacks the juice was poured into wooden barrels, where it fermented for ten days; then it was drawn off, leaving just the sediment. The juice sat in other barrels for two months; then it was drained again. In another thirty days, it was ready.[23]

By 1760, 250,000 vines had been knitted across the valley in green and purple crosshatch. Visitors proclaimed the El Paso wines the best anywhere in New Spain. Von Humboldt wrote later:

> The environs of El Paso are delicious and resemble the finest parts of Andalusia. The fields are cultivated with maize [corn] and wheat; and the vineyards produce such excellent sweet wines

that they are even preferred to the wines of Parras in New Biscay. The gardens contain in abundance all the fruits of Europe, figs, peaches, apples and pears.[24]

Shrewdly, the Franciscan friars also controlled the wagon trains[25]—at first. But these proved too lucrative for commercial teamsters to let a bunch of priests run the business. The wagons lumbered south from northern New Mexico in the fall, escorted by troops to El Paso. Another convoy transferred the cargo there for the journey to Chihuahua, also under armed escort. From there, they proceeded south to Mexico City. El Paso was not only the main weigh station where taxes were collected, but also the armed bulwark of northern Mexico, Nueva Vizcaya, against the Apache on the frontier, as the settlements in northern New Mexico were both sparse and weak.[26]

In 1766, Madrid dispatched an investigation to New Spain to review the government and the military. Captain Nicolas de Lafora, a royal engineer, went to the borderlands. In his judgment, Texas was of little value, so a single presidio each would be allocated to San Antonio and Santa Fe. They were simply too far from the most valued assets that lay on or below the thirtieth parallel, today's border between Mexico and the United States.

His opinion of El Paso, home to five thousand people, more populous than Britain's Massachusetts Bay Colony in 1780, was much higher: "All this stretch of land is very well cultivated, producing everything that is planted, particularly very good grapes which are in no way inferior to those of Spain."

There was so much fruit, orchards were left unharvested. The captain worried that colonists spent so much time on their vineyards for wine to drink that they weren't growing enough corn to eat.

Throughout the late 1690s and into the next century and

beyond, the descendants of Oñate too settled in El Paso. Men and women of the clan lived at the presidio, married at Guadalupe de El Paso del Norte, the primary church of the community where the Native people had once gathered for baptism, food, or both. Some dispersed back north to Santa Fe, and a good many settled in Nuevo Leon in northeastern Mexico. One of Oñate's great-granddaughters, Bernadilla de Salas y Trujillo, married Andrés Hurtado in Santa Fe; they had a daughter, Mariana. She, in turn, married Manuel Gonzales Vallejo at the presidio, and they had a son, Andrés Hurtado de Salas. Zacatecas was still the clan's ancestral home, but they radiated back to the northern Mexico of their dead scion[27] and stayed for centuries to come.[28]

El Paso had grown so big and bountiful that it was transferred out of New Mexico in 1772 and back to Nueva Vizcaya, now the Mexican states of Chihuahua and Durango. It was also big enough to provide for its own defense. Beginning in 1773, under the Royal Regulations of the previous year, all men between eighteen and sixty years of age became members of the local militia, supplying their own firearms and drawing lots for their respective companies. Failure to comply meant prison. Blacks, Native Americans, and those of mixed blood would also get fifty lashes for avoiding service. Four companies of militia grudgingly fell into formation.

Most important, it was during this period that distinctions between races began to fall away. The Belgians, Germans, and other Europeans, for example, melted into the thousands of other Spanish subjects. They learned the languages and customs of their ruler and fellow settlers alike. The Native people often spoke Spanish now. White European men frequently married and settled down with Native women, Pueblo and Manso, and many of the newest generation of adults and leaders were known as coyotes, mestizos, and ladinos.[29] *Coyote* was just another word for "half-breed"; a mestizo had a mix of European and Native blood; and the word *ladino* was adopted from faraway Spain, where it was employed to label Spanish Jews. Some Black men, slaves freed to become soldiers, married into the Pueblo culture or took Tlaxcalan wives: women descended from the original Indigenous Mexican troops who helped conquer New Mexico. In these marriages women were yoked to a culture characterized by machismo.

This budding tradition of intermarriage was, of course, inherited from the Native American people—who would marry into other bands and tribes—as well as the Spanish, who had intermarried with Jews and even their greatest enemy, the Moors, at least between wars. El Paso represented a turning point in American history, a sharp contrast to the British colonies of the East Coast: here and throughout the Southwest, color and creed were not obstacles to toiling together, fighting together for survival, or even joining in the holy sacrament of marriage.

In the British colonies that would come to dominate the American story, such intermarriages were rare and taboo. From Massachusetts southward, the British tradition of dividing whites from everyone else—especially Black people—was a norm that ruled the day. The East Coast was enmeshed in the original sin of chattel slavery from 1619 onward, deepening its commitment for centuries and cultivating a tradition of segregation and hatred. Intermarriage, with Native Americans too, was rare and roundly scorned. As the historian Jennifer Agee Jones wrote of these colonies:

> While settlers may have had the opportunity, very few such unions took place in the colonial era. Powerful psychological barriers prevented most Europeans from marrying Indians. That the Indians were "wild" people without knowledge of Christianity convinced many that marrying them was dangerous to one's soul. Other newcomers felt less constrained by cultural boundaries and easily shed the trappings of their culture to marry the

native way. To colonial officials, such actions provided evidence that the wild land and its inhabitants were a temptation to those struggling to maintain godly communities on the frontier. Such renegades served as a symbol of religious and cultural degeneration that could ultimately undermine colonial endeavors.

Because intermarriage would have proven a means of assimilation between the two groups, its absence underscores the most irreconcilable divisions between Europeans and Indians. The attitudes that prevented Europeans from marrying the natives were the same attitudes that governed most interactions between the two peoples in the seventeenth century. The failure of the two groups to marry one another was one component of a larger failure to cohabit peacefully in seventeenth-century North America.[30]

By 1776, of course, those racially divided colonies rebelled against Britain, and the American Revolution erupted. Seeing an opportunity to regain its Gulf Coast possessions, Spain too went to war against Great Britain in 1779, destroying a British force at Mobile Bay and another at Pensacola in 1781, the same year the Americans defeated the British army at Yorktown. And while it would have no impact on what is now the Southwest, the ideals of the breakaway colonists in the East would seize the imagination of the elite in Mexico City, in particular. Increasingly, the Spanish Empire could do little for its faraway colonies. El Paso was besieged by both smallpox and the Apache; Santa Fe and Albuquerque became walled cities to defend against the latter. But eventually, a new administration came to El Paso and defused, if temporarily, the Apache threat by breaking that people's alliance with the Diné people. Once again the Apache were lured to the presidios with supplies of food. This time, however, when things went wrong, the Spanish craftily laid the blame on other tribes, encouraging Native

Americans to fight among themselves and not against the Spanish; for a while, this deceptive disinformation strategy worked.

By 1800, a vaccine for smallpox had become widely available and the population grew again, with nearly seven thousand people inhabiting the valley. Homes clustered around the churches in Ysleta and upriver. In 1681, a band of Pueblo migrated up the Rio Grande toward present-day Las Cruces. Led by the Roybal family, they were known as the Tortugas, or turtles, because of their slow travel with the elderly and children in tow. They were also known for having great teeth and for the men's tradition of cutting their hair only once a year—with an ax.[31] Public schools sprang up and a royal postal system brought regular mail. El Camino Real now connected not just Mexico City, Chihuahua, El Paso, and Santa Fe, but linked New Spain to that nascent power: the United States.

Americans on the East Coast hungered for the vast Louisiana Territory on New Spain's periphery; after negotiations with Napoleon, Spain traded Louisiana back to France. As early as 1787, the man who would next purchase Louisiana, Thomas Jefferson, had grown interested in Mexico. From his home in Monticello, Virginia, the future American president wrote to the future secretary of state, John Jay, speculating about a Mexican revolt and the possibility of independence from Spain. He grew curious about the theory that the Aztec had once built great monuments out west; well before the Louisiana Purchase, his words foreshadowed the ideas that underlay manifest destiny. He wrote in 1803 of his desire for the "mines of Mexico."[32]

So a new people—this time coming from that very different, restless, and divided land of the East—cut a trail to St. Louis and then onward to Santa Fe. From there they turned south, into a strange land of mustangs and mestizos and toward that great gateway in the desert, El Paso.

Chapter Five

THE AMERICANS, 1800–1820

I N THE FALL of 1805, a small party of seventeen soldiers traced the Arkansas River upstream, leaving behind the Pawnee and Osage villages on the Great Plains. The country was a tabula rasa, an empty slate, to the young American mind. Members of the American Pike expedition lived off deer, buffalo, and elk while miraculously avoiding death in a territory of giant rattlesnakes.[1] Their commanding officer, an ambitious and dashing young lieutenant, was fixated on a distant spot on the horizon, which he kept referring to as a "blue cloud."

Over the plains of present-day eastern Colorado, the blue cloud grew in size each day as the expedition marched west. By mid-November, it became clear that this was no cloud. It never moved, remaining alluringly distant day after day. Before too long, a range of snow-capped mountains loomed. Following on the heels of Meriwether Lewis and William Clark (and on a more southerly course), the young lieutenant, Zebulon Pike, was at least as ambitious as his predecessors. Pike too rode the wave of nationalism that rose high during the Jeffersonian age. The boisterous young American republic had just expanded two years earlier, with the Louisiana Purchase.

There was nothing for it but to summit a particular mountain. Climbing out of the river drainage, the men saw it more clearly; Pike christened it Grand Peak. With three men, he set out to climb it, boldly predicting they could summit it and be back in time for dinner. He was wrong.

They quickly began to learn a lesson of the Southwest: everything is farther away than it seems. The going was rough; Pike turned the team around for lack of supplies before they could reach the top. Resuming the expedition up the Arkansas River, though, didn't go much better; the higher they climbed, the more difficult the terrain grew. The Arkansas is a wide, deep river close to its headwaters, with steep, boulder-strewn banks. Its waters are frigid, overpowering, and unfathomable in places, making river crossings difficult and time-consuming. The farther west the expedition went, the more the men tried to locate another important waterway, the Red River. Horses and men alike plunged through ice and lived off snowmelt and a pint of dried corn a day. Near present-day Buena Vista, they found, to their great frustration, that they were still in the vast drainage of the Arkansas River. By now, winter had set in with a wolflike bite. Leaving behind five men and horses, Pike took the rest over the Sangre de Cristo Mountains and into the San Luis Valley. All of this was Spanish territory.

Long after his death, the mountain would be renamed Pike's Peak, and his expedition would lose its luster in comparison to Lewis and Clark's. But Pike's entry into the American Southwest was notable because it wasn't just about exploration; it was an armed, illegal reconnaissance deep into a foreign sovereign territory, namely, New Spain. And it was based on the design of certain Founding Fathers of the United States: Thomas Jefferson, James Madison, and Aaron Burr. Decades before its war against Mexico, the young American republic was sniffing out the Southwest's riches and preparing to forcibly take them.

It appears Pike had a public set of orders—to explore the Louisiana Territory—along with a secret set of orders from the army: to perform a reconnaissance of Spanish territory as close as possible to Santa Fe. As Elliott Coues, an army surgeon, historian, and author, wrote in the second edition of Pike's personal papers: "Without going into any particulars here, it is to be said simply that Pike may have been ordered to proceed to Santa Fe—or as near that capital of Spanish New Mexico as he could go with the force at his command—without being informed of whatever ulterior designs the general of the army may have entertained."[2]

Pike had argued with Native Americans on the Plains, demanding that they put away their Spanish flags and fly only the new American one. Now, he increasingly encountered signs of Spanish roads and encampments. Pike sent a few troops back to get the men left behind with the horses and moved down the Rio Grande to set up winter camp on the smaller, gentler Conejo River, a tributary about 130 miles north of Santa Fe. On February 5, 1807, Pike wrote: "The great and lofty mountains, covered with eternal snows, seemed to surround the luxuriant vale, crowned with perennial flowers, like a terrestrial paradise shut out from the view of man."

However spectacular the surroundings, his expedition still needed help, and their surgeon walked to Santa Fe to try to find it. With most of his men either left behind in the southern Rockies or on their way to evacuate them now, Pike and a handful of troops stayed in camp. The men felled giant old cottonwoods to build a winter stockade. Pike hunted to keep them fed. Before any of his troops could arrive, ghost figures appeared out of the February snow, stalking Pike: mounted Spanish dragoons armed with muskets.

Pike asked a Spanish officer if they were not encamped near the Red River, in the newly American territory. They were not, the Spanish officer replied in French; they were near the Rio Grande.

Although proud of his new nation's colors in this frontier, Pike acted cautiously. "I immediately ordered my flag to be taken down and rolled up, feeling how sensibly I had committed myself in entering their territory, and conscious that they must have positive orders to take me in," he wrote on February 26, 1807.[3]

> I was induced to consent to this measure by the conviction that the officer had positive orders to bring me in; and as I had no orders to commit hostilities, and indeed had committed myself, although innocently, by violating their territory, I conceived it would appear better to show a will to come to an explanation than to be in any way constrained . . . it was with great reluctance I suffered all our labor to be lost without once trying the efficacy of it. My compliance seemed to spread general joy through their party, as soon as it was communicated; but it appeared to be different with my men, who wished to have "a little dust," as they expressed themselves, and were likewise fearful of treachery.

Pike and the Americans were taken prisoner but treated well, given blankets and fed—and told nearly nothing about where they were, though the Spanish inquired about the numbers and whereabouts of their troops. Pike made note that many of his captors were neither white nor of pure Spanish blood, a phenomenon he had noticed in various encounters throughout the territory. Pike was struck by the fact that people of different races and cultures worked and resided side by side—so wildly different from the culture back east, with its strict demarcation between free whites and enslaved Blacks. He recorded how well his men were treated by "Creols and Metifs," meaning creole Spaniards from Mexico and mestizos of mixed European and Native ancestry, who were a rarity back home.

Nevertheless, this was a serious matter. They were spies, caught red-handed in foreign territory, doing exactly as the Spanish had feared the Americans would after the Louisiana Purchase. Pike's commanding officer, General James Wilkinson, concluded in the early nineteenth century that war with Spain was inevitable; he was so convinced, in fact, that he was himself spying for the Spanish.[4]

But, on a larger scale, more than a few of the Founding Fathers, occupying the upper tiers of American government, were apparently engaged in espionage for European powers. Time and again, Wilkinson and Pike turn up in the papers of Aaron Burr, James Madison, and even President Thomas Jefferson himself.[5]

The young Pike was ordered to stand trial, so his captors led him down Oñate's old Camino Real with an armed escort of a hundred Spanish, mestizo, and Native troops. His first stop was the newly founded village at Albuquerque, where he met up with Don Facundo Malgare, a Spanish officer with whom he'd once crossed paths and who had been trying to locate the American's rumored reconnaissance team. As old spies tend to do, the two men remained fast friends to the end of their lives. Malgare accompanied Pike southward on the Camino Real. In his writings, Pike marveled at the exotic world he had entered: the Spanish churches, rich vineyards, and Native children.

He became the first US citizen to pass through that gateway between continents, empires, and cultures, this time from north to south, at El Paso. Treated more as a visitor than a prisoner suspected of espionage, he dined there with Don Francisco Garcia, a rich merchant and planter. Pike admired the canals, which made him think of Egypt, along with the vineyards and what he called "the industry of the inhabitants." He scribbled down details of the enormous flow of trade up and down the Camino Real: sheep, gold, silver, flour, wine, fine cloth, cigars, and cotton. Garcia alone owned tens of thousands of cattle and sheep. Pike carefully noted too the disposition of Native Americans, especially the Comanche and

Apache, and the relatively thin Spanish defenses, relying on just a thousand dragoons and perhaps five thousand militia in the whole region.[6] Somehow Pike managed to write in extensive, almost excruciating detail about the disposition of Spanish military forces in all of Mexico, as he learned of a rising restlessness among Mexicans under Spanish rule. A single locked wooden trunk carried all of Pike's notes, sketches, maps, and diaries.

In Chihuahua, on April 2, 1807, Pike was led to General Nemesio Salcedo, the highest-ranking official in northern Mexico. Pike could not help but notice that his Spanish officer's friend and escort, Malgare, became increasingly nervous as they approached Salcedo. A stern man in his mid-thirties, Salcedo did not rise from behind his desk, but instead motioned for the American to sit across from him. Salcedo had already decided to house this prisoner with Juan Pedro Walker, a cartographer who was now enlisted as a translator. "You have given us and yourself a great deal of trouble," Salcedo said of Walker's mapmaking. To Pike, Walker must have appeared exotic in his own way, the son of a British immigrant and a Creole woman from Spanish New Orleans.[7] What was in that trunk of Pike's was of profound interest. Spain had much to fear: Mexican independence, the Americans, democracy, even Protestantism. Was Pike capable of pushing it all to the brink?

Pike would not give up the contents of that trunk, knowing that if it were taken he'd have to store his most crucial information in his head, to write up upon his return. His detailed description of the disposition and organization of military forces was practically a blueprint for the Mexican-American War of 1848. Though Pike wouldn't surrender the trunk, he did allow Walker, a loyal Spaniard, to have copies of a few items.

The Mexicans were gauging the Americans, through the art of spycraft, as much as the Americans were gauging them. The Spanish never seized Pike's trunk and finally released him. It is entirely possible that they did so based on deliberate plans of their own; after all, their elite were considering their own rebellion against their European masters, and, fortified with Pike's knowledge, the Americans might just intervene against Spain, on the side of revolutionary brothers to the south. But to do this, the Americans would need detailed knowledge of the Spanish military presence in Mexico.

QUITE SUDDENLY, TWO worlds collided. Here was the restless young American nation, forging ambitiously west and riven by the racial divide of white versus Black, not to mention red. And there was the New World manifestation of the centuries-old Spanish Empire, a polyglot successor to Rome rife with Iberians, Native peoples speaking dozens of languages, Belgians, Germans, and Austrians— all united by the Hapsburg crown, the Catholic Church, and the Spanish language. While the War of 1812 would secure the permanent separation of the American republic from Great Britain— and take young Pike's life, at the Battle of York (now Toronto) in 1813—it was this new conflict in the Southwest that would shape the American nation in the nineteenth, twentieth, and twenty-first centuries.

The Americans were eager to come to this far, exotic corner of the world—whether it was theirs or not. There was no denying its beauty. The Spanish had brought not just their technologies and religion but an enviable way of life, bathed obviously in the Bible but increasingly opening itself to new art and cuisine. The boring old egg tortilla was transformed by experience in Mexico City, yielding a tortilla made of corn; the chilis of Mexico changed the Spanish dishes. Spanish flamenco, inherited from the Arabs, influenced music, dance, and even sex. Among the native Pueblo and the surviving Manso and Suma surged, according to Spanish accounts, a fantastical, nearly otherworldly kind of beauty: women with long, raven hair and buckhorn knifes draped around their necks.

This was a strange land to the eyes of those accustomed to the nineteenth-century dystopia that enveloped the East. They abandoned the played-out farms of the Appalachians and the cabins of Tennessee, leaving the letters "GTT"—"Gone to Texas"—painted on barn doors and cabin walls. They fled mounting debts and the threat of prison, crossed westward through lands from which tearful Native Americans had been expelled on death marches, lands where whole forests had been felled and burned, turning the Midwestern sky black. These migrants raced across the Great Plains to keep from being scalped by the Sioux or, worse, burned alive by the Comanche, Native peoples who were fighting for their very existence.

Out in the creosote desert of burnt pink sunrise they found a land where slavery had long since been outlawed: Spain had steadily forbidden the practice of enslaving Indigenous people since the passage of the New Laws of 1542.[8] Meanwhile in New Mexico, Oñate's barbarous cruelty toward the captives of Acoma was among the last known acts of large-scale indentured servitude—essentially slavery—in colonial Spanish America. Spain's use of human slaves from Africa had gradually diminished, partially due to its own interests; because of these interests, the Catholic Church provided a protective cloak to Native Americans in the Spanish Americas.

Some sixteen million people formed the Aztec Empire when Cortés arrived in 1519. Within two years, nearly half the people of Tenochtitlàn, present-day Mexico City, were dead—not at the receiving end of advanced Spanish weaponry, but from smallpox, carried by the alien invaders.[9] Perhaps the Spanish would wage the equivalent of nuclear war at Acoma, but first they would wage the equivalent of biological war against the original inhabitants of the Americas. This, in turn, had created the possibility of a massive labor shortage up and down the continents, from Colorado to Patagonia. The church pleaded—no, demanded—that Spanish kings protect the Native people; otherwise there would be no subjects, workers, or converts left. Seeing its economic future written on the wall, the monarchy gave in.

Of course, there were exceptions: the Native Americans who waged war on the Spanish, like the Acoma, most notable among them. There were illegal slavers capturing Native people and marching them across the deserts of northern Mexico like so many cattle, and cruel mining barons who worked people literally to death while digging their gold and silver fortunes from deep inside the earth. Many of the landed Spanish *peninsulares* and Creoles gave a royal fig about what the king ordered and the church wanted, when it came to their own profiteering on human misery. Yet the Catholic Church spelled the difference between colonial Spain and colonial England when it came to treatment of the Native people and the question of slavery in general. In 1619, the first African slaves were herded ashore to the British colonies, then chained and marched into the slave market near the docks of Annapolis, Maryland. By then, Spain had outlawed enslaving Native peoples. And so, with the exception of Veracruz, much of New Spain, Mexico, especially in the north, stood in stark contrast to the empire's voracious appetite for African slaves in the Caribbean, especially Cuba, Puerto Rico, and the colonies in and around the Caribbean Sea. There, the Spanish, with Portuguese help, fed over one million African souls into its hellish sugar plantations. Yet in Mexico, what really burned the angry *peninsulare* and Creole colonists was that the encomienda economic system, along the lines of medieval serfdom, had been banned as well. This fueled resentment among the wealthy—not toward the classes beneath them, but toward the king, the court, and Madrid.

The world into which the English-speaking Americans streamed, particularly from the American South, could not have been more different from their own. The land teemed with wild creatures: mustangs, elk, jaguars, striped-tailed and masked coatis, their families marching single file down desert arroyos; even buffalo, grown shaggy and dusty, adapted to the desert on the nearby Janos Plain. The Americans entered a universe in which Native Americans wandered the streets of places like El Paso; entire tribes, including the Apache, came in from the desert throughout the year, seeking food and trading their faith in, say, the Apache god Ussen to faith in Jesus Christ. Just as important, the American traders and teamsters likely marveled at the movement of free Blacks. Though still few in number, they enjoyed all the rights and responsibilities of any Dutchman or Belgian who was a Spanish subject. They dug the acequias and built the dams, served in the militias and married Native and mestizo women in numbers almost too large to count. The Naranjo family of New Mexico descended from a free Black man and a Pueblo woman; they chose to become leaders in the uprising of 1620 and also to live among the Pueblo. They remain influential to this day in the history of the state whose capital was El Paso. The first recorded Catholic interracial marriage in what would become the United States took place in Spanish Florida between a Spanish man and an African woman.

Something else, somewhat less obvious, was different too: the Jewish presence. The Mexican Inquisition differed from the Spanish Inquisition in Europe because it focused mainly on the persecution of women for alleged witchcraft. In doing so, the Mexican Inquisition was a cruel scalpel, precisely wielded while the church publicly insisted on protecting the Indigenous people. Charges of witchcraft weeded out Native women and struck the literal fear of God into whole clans and tribes. Most of the cases prosecuted by the church in Mexico were aimed first at witches, second at heretics—usually scholars within their own ranks—and finally at Jews. The most infamous case involved the persecution and execution of a Coahuila family of Jews, the Carvajal family. The brief union of Spain and

Portugal in the late sixteenth and early seventeenth centuries allowed Jews from Portugal to escape their own country's inquisition
by migrating to the Spanish Americas, and many did. Tens of thousands flocked to Mexican settlements such as Acapulco and Guadalajara and northward into Monterrey and what would become
the state of Coahuila, across from Texas. But Maria de Carvajal, the
wife of a rich and powerful settler in the city of Monterrey, insisted
on practicing her Sephardic Judaism privately in her own home.
This was not terribly uncommon. Sephardic Jews had been present
throughout Spanish history. Even Oñate, that pious soldier of the
Inquisition, was of Sephardic Jewish blood; his grandmother's family had converted to Catholicism in the fourteenth century. But in
1492, the same year Columbus arrived in the New World, Queen
Isabella and King Ferdinand had banned Judaism, forcing Jews to
convert or leave Spanish territory. Those suspected of or caught for
practicing Judaism were subjected to insults, such as being called
Marranos—pigs—or even imprisonment, torture, and in some cases,
execution. Maria Carvajal would be among them, burned at the
stake in Mexico City in 1601. Immediately after, her entire family
was put to death.

But in many cases, Jews escaped successfully into the New
World, whether they were conversos, accepting Christianity either
voluntarily or by force, or among the crypto-Jews of the Anusim.
This Hebrew term denotes the people of the great Spanish diaspora.
In the American Southwest, namely, in New Mexican El Paso, they
quietly closed the curtains and lit candles on Fridays to keep the
Sabbath. Likewise they preserved fragments of Hebrew Bibles in
small wooden boxes, hidden even from relatives, and observed the
Jewish High Holy Days for reasons they almost never confided.
As many as one in every twenty people in the El Paso region was,
secretly or even unwittingly, Jewish, part of a tribe that refused to

die and had kindled a new life in the New World.[10] In 1821, Mexican independence from Spain brought the centuries-long Mexican Inquisition to an end. Catholicism was still the official religion, certainly, but being a Jew no longer came under the penalty of death.[11] Jews could openly worship in Mexico.[12]

Early nineteenth-century Spain was a study in chaos. Napoleon had invaded, only to be ousted during a costly war that left behind monarchists and liberals who were deeply divided. The sprawling empire needed money, but the coffers in Madrid were increasingly barren. In Spain's final bid to retain its colonies, it began to grant royal lands. Some grants were absolutely massive. One, made to a friar, Fray Joaquín de Hinojosa, was the largest ever in the history of Texas, totaling more than 177,000 acres around El Paso; the priest was able to pass it on to a nephew, a captain of the Spanish army. At this point, the king had far more land than cash.[13] Another grant had gone to Juan Ponce de León for the area that would become downtown El Paso. Yet another went to a Spanish army captain near the present-day community of Santa Teresa, New Mexico, just across the Rio Grande. And still a fourth went to a colony of two hundred Missourians after Mexico became independent. Madrid was desperate to buy loyalty.

Critically low on settlers on its northern frontier, Mexico needed people, even if they were Americans—and the Americans just kept on coming. James Purcell came all the way from Illinois to El Paso in 1806 to work as a carpenter. Then came Pike. The Spanish and the Mexicans were always suspicious of spies and scouting parties. Three traders from Missouri entered illegally and found themselves in prison in Durango, Mexico. One of these traders, James Baird, returned after his release, but this time as a trapper, harvesting beaver from the Rio Grande. Robert McKnight bought and mined the rich copper veins of Santa Rita, near present-day Silver City.[14] The new Mexican nation made a deal with the devil, insisting that all new immigrants become loyal Mexican citizens and at least nominal Catholics. It would, of course, turn out to be a losing bet. Many newcomers would not comply. Even Baird, now a Mexican citizen, grew indignant, accusing new American trappers of "arrogance and haughtiness that they have openly said in spite of the Mexicans, they will hunt beaver wherever they please."[15]

Still, it was a period of relative peace. The Spanish system of providing food to Native Americans both exposed the Native people to Christianity and tempered their need to go on raids for supplies, especially reducing those of the Apache. The Pueblo people grew so much tobacco—the men particularly liked to smoke when they went out scouting for Apache—that the governor told them to dial it back. Rich with vineyards, corn, tomatoes, chickpeas, tall wheat fields, and apple orchards, the Middle Rio Grande Valley stretched out before the invariably rough and uncultured Americans as if ripe for the picking.[16] The new arrivals would encounter far more resistance than they imagined. As the historian C. L. Sonnichsen wrote: "The American newcomers, for their own part, were apt to underestimate the Mexicans. They did not understand the caste system or the rules which kept women in the background and, ideally, out of sight. They underestimated the courage of the Mexican men, many of them great Indian fighters and not accustomed to or sympathetic with the eye-gouging and fisticuffs of their northern neighbors. The two groups had much to learn before they could appreciate and understand each other."[17]

By the early nineteenth century, what was most notable about El Paso was its role as a crossroads. The Santa Fe Trail, running between Mexico City and northern New Mexico, boasted wagonloads of goods, increasingly brought from the United States via the Missouri Trail, the American drivers and mule skinners, old and landed Spanish families, and through intermarriage. As the old tribes, such as the Manso, dwindled, their members married mestizo and Apache alike. A multi-ethnic, multiracial and multi-religious society arose, slowly but surely.

Beginning in the early twentieth century, as Mexico fought a pitched war for independence against Spain, about thirty Americans made their homes among the thousands of Mexicans. All the Americans who succeeded changed their ways, adopting Mexican customs and Spanish names, but most of the Missourians, frankly, would not last. The Apache raids and depredations proved too much, and within a couple of years many simply abandoned their desert land grant on the east bank of the Rio Grande. Among the remaining Americans, one in particular was notable: Hugh Stephenson, an orphaned Kentuckian raised in Concordia, Missouri.[18] In August 1824, he arrived near what is now Las Cruces, New Mexico, thirty-seven miles upriver from El Paso, seemingly out of nowhere. He was just twenty-six years old; with no trade or profession, he was just another dusty, erstwhile trader—but he quickly gobbled up the land that the Spanish, and now the Mexicans, were busily handing out. The young Missourian bought twenty-three thousand acres of the Brazito tract in nearby New Mexico and, glimpsing the future, nine hundred acres of land just south of Ponce's old ranch in the very heart of downtown El Paso, Texas. In today's dollars, that land became worth billions.

This young Missourian was not quite alone on this rich frontier, new to the Americans, that sparkled in the desert sun. Not long after, a man named Simeon Hart, also out of Missouri, would follow.[19] In turn, he was followed by another American, James Wiley Magoffin, who had considerable experience in northern Mexico and tremendous business savvy. All three men followed the same path: to Santa Fe or Chihuahua, then to the banks of the Rio

Grande, where they settled. They married rich Mexican women, melding—not melting—their culture into the richly mixed prevailing one. These women, in turn, would play important and powerful roles. Their successful husbands now took Spanish names; Stephenson would go by the name Don Hugo. Their children would be influential Americans and Mexicans, settling on both sides of the Rio Grande. These men were friends, allies, and rivals.

Yet they would divide—as would their families' future—over the very things they thought they had left behind: slavery and empire.

Part II

All is fair in love and war.

—FRANCIS EDWARD SMEDLEY, 1857

Chapter Six

CONCORDIA, 1821–46

B Y ANY ACCOUNT, she was out of his league.[1]

Juana María Ascárate was a raven-haired aristocrat, born on February 8, 1809, to a wealthy landed family with holdings that spanned some two hundred miles, from El Paso to Chihuahua. Much of her family wealth stemmed from deep inside the earth, a lucrative Chihuahuan silver mine.[2] She was devoutly Catholic, and anyone marrying into this family, with its silver, cattle, and land, its role in the founding of both El Paso and San Antonio, had to prove worthy.[3] There would be no exceptions; Juana was the only daughter of Juan and Eugenia Ascárate.

Juana's father, Juan Ascárate, had arrived in Chihuahua in the eighteenth century straight from Spain, having been granted land by the crown. Her mother, Eugenia, came from a family no less successful and related to the land baron Ponce de León. The main homestead spread from the headquarters at Corralitos across the buffalo grounds of the Janos Plain to Casas Grandes, where many of the pre-Puebloan people had their roots in ancient times. The main house at Corralitos, known as Casa Grande del Amo, was a sprawling, graceful, single-story hacienda of white adobe walls up to six feet thick, for insulation and protection. Half of the thirteen bedrooms faced the mighty Sierra Madre and the Casas Grandes River. Half looked out toward San Pedro Peak and the mines at Candelaria. Six Ascárate children, five boys and Juana, ran up and down the halls of the hacienda. As they reached adulthood, three of the boys went off into the world. Two, Cristobal and Jacinto, stayed on as grown men to run the mines. So did Juana.

The dusty young Hugh Stephenson was less impressive, but not without his wiles. He had come via Missouri from Kentucky and knew how to play the part of the Kentucky gentleman.[4] Tall, brave, and as responsible as he was industrious, Stephenson had "keen, indomitable eyes, a firm chin and a tight, determined mouth,"[5] wrote C. L. Sonnichsen. He became a close student of the strictures of Mexican class politics, learning Spanish and converting to Catholicism. Interested in silver mining himself, Stephenson rustled up a job working for Juan Ascárate at the mine. With mesquite-fueled furnaces burning day and night, the mine also smelted the raw silver and was the first mint in this part of the world.[6]

Despite his rough arrival as just another woolly trader, as his fortune grew, Stephenson displayed a modest interest in the finer things in life. By the summer of 1828, he had earned both the notice of Juana—who was nineteen and so his junior by eleven years—and the approval of her family. That August, he married Juana in the first recorded marriage between an American and a Mexican.[7] Together they grew their fortunes. Stephenson opened a store and managed the silver mine in Chihuahua. He bought raw silver from his in-laws and smelted it, stamping his own name on the product. El Paso had gone from a barter economy to a cash and even credit economy. The value of locally mined silver rose. When the young couple was ready to make their own home on the river in the late 1830s, Juana's father sold the old Corralitos ranch to them. The whole clan now resided in El Paso.[8]

While most of El Paso lay on the south bank of the river, people increasingly ventured north. A wealthy merchant by this time, Ponce de León acquired over two hundred acres in 1827. He may have dug an irrigation ditch; planted corn, grapes, and wheat; and built several adobe roundhouses.[9] It's also possible that Ponce de León never made improvements beyond corrals for livestock and a shack or two for tired cow hands and goat herders. Nevertheless, in 1830, Juana's family, the Ascárates, granted the couple a vast tract north of the Rio Grande that they had used for livestock grazing.

For a decade they built their own little hamlet. Vineyards and crops grew. Cattle grazed. Juana insisted on a personal chapel, and Hugh, though busy with business and striking his own silver at a mine in the Organ Mountains, obliged.[10] Hugh brought home a lost fawn and Juana tended to it like a baby; then they had children of their own. Juana grew roses in the garden. They christened this personal paradise of theirs San José de Concordia el Alto, "Harmony on High," as the chapel and home now occupied the high ground overlooking the river.[11] For Hugh, Concordia was the Missouri town he'd left behind. In Juana's native Spanish, the blended name embodied the era itself in northern Mexico. The Americans who made it here had learned to let themselves be absorbed into the language and customs of the Mexicans, who, in turn, rewarded industriousness, honesty, and bravery.

The ranch headquarters, their home, was known as La Casa Grande del Alto; ranch hands, servants, and other workers dwelled at the eastern end. The Stephensons raised seven children and their home burst with family and servants, eighteen in all. Altogether, nearly two hundred people lived and worked on the nine hundred acres of Concordia. Hugh and Juana lived like aristocrats, which didn't just mean living well; it also meant doing good. Hugh's "greatest zeal was in personally helping, counseling, and befriending the poor, sick, and needy," his grandson later recalled. "These came to him from far and near, surely knowing that his house was always open to them and that they would not be disappointed."[12] This was the way of successful and pious *patróns* stretching back to Oñate's father and beyond. More than just a name, Concordia was a way of life here—even as the gringos in faraway Texas violated their oaths to Mexico and successfully rebelled in 1836. El Paso was not part of that, too far out in the burning desert for the new slave nation of Texas to care. At least, not yet.

Gradually, the gateway between the Americas revealed itself to swing not only north and south, but east and west too. Juana was known for her unfailing grace and kindness to strangers—especially worn-out traveling Americans, some headed as far away as Mexican California. They enjoyed the company not only of strangers and kin, but their fellow frontier aristocrats. Juana Marquez, the daughter of a Pueblo cacique, or chief, married Benjamin Shackett Dowell at the Concordia chapel on the ranch; the new couple settled nearby on Rancho Ponce, where Benjamin worked. He became proficient in Spanish, and she spoke three languages: Tewa, Spanish, and English.[13]

James Wiley Magoffin was another Kentuckian, like Stephenson, who had come by way of Missouri. Unlike Stephenson, he was already an experienced Mexico hand by the time he arrived, having spent years in Matamoros, over eight hundred miles downriver, where the same Rio Grande emptied into the Gulf of Mexico, then wandered through Saltillo to Chihuahua. In 1832 he took up with a married woman, living with María Gertrudis Valdez de Veramendi, a San Antonio native descended from the original Canary Island colonists in Texas and already mother to four children; her husband died in 1838, and the new couple married in 1839. From there, he made his way to Chihuahua and wrote home, stunned at the fortunes moving up and down the old, dust-choked Camino Real. There was so much silver to be made from mines and wagons that the men played high-stakes monte, a shell game of cards. "Oh

Lord," he wrote to his brother Samuel. "Chihuahua is a hell of a place as all the boys gamble like the devil."[14]

Magoffin was so at home in Mexico that for years already he had gone by the name Don Santiago.[15] Unlike Stephenson, Magoffin didn't stay in El Paso for years, but frequented the settlement, driving those bulging wagon trains up and down the old Camino Real, now known as the Chihuahua Trail. He moved María to Independence, Missouri, where she raised their seven children and he headquartered his business. But there was more wile to Magoffin than his middle name suggested. Mexican officials suspected him of spying for the United States and, more concretely, of dealing guns to the Comanche; for some curious reason, his wagon trains were never attacked, even as raids against settlements mounted.[16] Nevertheless, Mexicans assumed Magoffin was a citizen and even made him the municipal president—essentially the mayor—of Chihuahua, where he entertained lavishly.

Beyond the occasional double-dealing of some of these gringos, a new geopolitical reality unfolded. Mexico was losing its grip on its peripheries. Spain had combined its support for the church and taxation for the crown with settlers, soldiers, and humanitarian help in the way of food for Native American people, regardless of whether they converted to Christianity. Spanish authorities had also skillfully played one tribe against another. Yet, after achieving independence, in late 1821, Mexico's ruling classes simply turned on one another, establishing a short-lived empire, complete with an emperor and the trappings of a royal court, which lasted just two years. In 1824 they established a constitutional republic modeled after that of the United States, but lost control of Central America in the process. Rebellions broke out in Oaxaca, Guadalajara, Puebla, and Querétaro.[17] Yucátan broke away and became an independent republic. And the Napoleon of the West, Antonio López de Santa Anna Pérez de Lebrón, lurked through the chaos seeking his own dictatorship—losing Texas in 1836 in the process.[18] It would not be his last bumbling loss of Mexican territory.

In the north, namely the region around El Paso, people had no interest in independence. Indeed, they were widely known for being indifferent to government and politics in general, intent on making money off cattle, copper, goats, and trade.

But strung out across the nation, dousing rebellions, the Mexican army was of little use in protecting settlements from attacks, in particular from the Apache, who stepped up their raids when the Mexican army, for a period, stopped giving out food rations. Even Magoffin had to halt all of his trade for a full year because of the Apache attacks. In 1837 the state government in Chihuahua, nearly unprotected by the army, made a desperately drastic and cruel decision: to exterminate the Apache, paying hard cash for scalps of men, women, and children alike. Dead Apache adult males were worth two hundred pesos; women and children, less.

And the Mexicans enlisted Americans to do the grisly job. It turned out they had a taste for it.

MANGAS COLORADAS ("RED SLEEVES") stood tall, especially for an Apache. Born in the 1790s, he was not a young man anymore, but Mangas was a warrior through and through. His clothing—a cotton shirt, breechcloth, and buckskins—hung on him as if he were a wire hanger. His face was dark from the sun, etched by time and desert wind. Before Geronimo and even Cochise, who became more famous, Mangas was likely the greatest Apache leader who ever lived, the historian James Haley later wrote.

Mangas Coloradas "was a physical giant as well as a domineering personality. He was a truly striking figure with a hulking body and disproportionately large head," wrote Haley. "He possessed cunning as impenetrable as the thick mat of hair that hung down to his waist. His lips were thin and tightly drawn, his nose aquiline. Mangas Coloradas's following was large and exceptionally cohesive, and he commanded great respect."[19]

His people were the Mimbreño band of the Chiricahua, or Warm Springs, Apache, and he grew up and lived among the shady cottonwoods that sprang from the gentle Mimbres River of southwestern New Mexico, about 150 miles northwest of El Paso. A thousand years earlier, his people had driven the ancient Mimbres society into high cliff dwellings in the Gila Mountains, where they later forged the Pueblo culture. Mangas was from a line of people who had known war for most of a millennium. The Chiricahua had fought everyone: Diné, Pueblo, Papago, and of course, Spaniards and Mexicans. *Apache* means "my enemy," and the people— who called themselves Indé—were dubbed Apache by an opposing tribe, possibly the Zuni or Yavapai, a sign of their enduring enmities. With the Spanish, the name stuck. The Mexicans dubbed Mangas "El Fuerte," "the Strong One."[20]

Early in Mangas's life, there had been a tenuous peace under the Spanish. Most of the Chiricahua people, including his own, who called themselves Bedoonkohe, would make the trek to El Paso to encamp with other bands and even other tribes for food, especially in the hard, dry years when game was less plentiful. All along, the Apache knew that, other Native Americans aside, they faced formidable foes in the white men. Part of the Apache creation story involves God, known as Ussen, preparing to let his children into the world, deciding they will need weapons to survive. Ussen fashioned a rifle and a bow and arrow. The first child was Killer of Enemies, a white child who picked the rifle. The second child, Child of the Waters, became the Native people, left with the bow and arrow. So the Apache chose to make war and peace selectively, but they had always raided to steal food and supplies just to stay alive. There was a big difference for them between raiding and making war. Raiding was for survival. War was for revenge.

The Comanche, for one, signed the Treaty of El Paso del Norte in 1834 and promised to stop raiding. Mexican officers and troops then marched to present-day Silver City to commit the people of the Apacheria—the old Oasisamerica that was now Apache country—to do the same. Eyeballing a large Mexican presence, twenty-nine Apache leaders went ahead and signed their own pact with the Mexicans, the Treaty of Santa Rita del Cobre. The site was particularly important: the Santa Rita mines were, and remain, one of the world's richest and purest sources of copper. The Mexicans appointed three chiefs to three sectors of the Apacheria to be responsible for restoring stolen livestock and generally keeping the peace. Mangas got Santa Rita; it was rough, rocky, piñon-studded country, not far from the Mimbres River, where the vast Gila Mountains and the river itself melted into the flat playas of the Chihuahuan Desert. As they had done with the Comanche, the Mexican army was to deliver food rations to the Apache in exchange.

Hundreds of miles away, Central and South Texas were caught up in the Texans' 1836 rebellion against Mexico. Taken by surprise at first, the Mexican government found itself flat-footed. After all, every Texian colonist had promised not just loyalty to Mexico but fealty to the Catholic Church—only to break those promises and suffer the consequences at the Alamo in San Antonio and the massacre at Goliad. But breaking one's word was becoming commonplace. Back in the Southwest, at the peace gathering at Santa Rita, everyone broke that pact nearly immediately: Spaniard, Apache, and American.

The army didn't deliver the food, so the Apache started raiding again. With the new law, the state of Chihuahua issued letters of marque and reprisal. On the high seas, this was a license for piracy; on the high desert, it was a license for butchery. Not only would the killers get all the Apache loot they could carry, but also silver Mexican pesos for scalps. Soon twenty men, most of them Americans, were deep inside Mangas's territory, having spotted an Apache camp of fifty people. Led by the Kentuckian James Johnson, who had married a Mexican woman and lived in Sonora, the group was warned by the head man that the Apache would fight. Instead, in parley, Johnson proposed giving the Apache flour, coffee, and gunpowder in exchange for two guides. While the Apache were availing themselves of the flour, the Americans unveiled a small cannon—a swivel gun—and cut them to pieces with bits of glass, chain, and rifle balls. Then they killed those who fled with rifle fire.[21] In later tellings, the Americans were alleged to have killed as many as four hundred people; the real figure is unknowable. The surviving Apache, enraged, surrounded the Americans, killing nearly every last one of them as they fled south.

Then Mangas Coloradas strode into the picture. He and his warriors descended, hunting and killing white, American, European, and Mexican trappers wherever they could find them. He attacked the supply wagons to the vital mine at Santa Rita, burning wagon trains and making off with their goods. He starved the town of Santa Rita until the four hundred people who lived and worked there fled south for their lives to the Janos Plain. The mine shut down. Johnson himself barely escaped with his life and lost most of the Apache scalps he had taken for reward on a runaway mule. For his troubles he received a mere hundred pesos.

Nevertheless, the Mexicans pressed on with their policy of war and enlisted another American: James Kirker, an Irishman who also went by the name Santiago. Kirker was a trapper, hunter, mercenary, and an expert in treachery.[22] For the next two years, in exchange for the equivalent of $100,000, he killed an untold number of Apache people, taking as many as forty scalps at a time and bringing them to his paymasters in Chihuahua.[23]

All of Apacheria was now in flames. Much of it was united behind one of the deadliest enemies ever made: Mangas Coloradas. In all of the remaining years of his long life, he would never forget the butchery of the newcomers.

STEPHEN F. AUSTIN, the Missouri colonizer of Texas under Mexican rule, had declared flatly: "Texas must be a slave nation!" With independence, the Texans had their much-desired slaves. But this was a workforce that largely labored for a mighty and rich few on the cotton and sugar plantations of the Southeast. Beyond the blackland prairie, the economics of human misery simply didn't add up.

Compared to the rest of the Deep South, Texas had relatively few plantations. In fact, most Texans knew little firsthand about slavery and nothing about plantation farming; the land was too arid to support it.[24]

But Mirabeau Lamar, the first president of Texas, knew all too well that the breakaway nation he governed in the muddy settlement in Austin, on the banks of the Colorado River, was not only riddled with debt, but broke—its borders still not recognized by Mexico and effectively barred from joining the United States for rightful fear that the Lone Star Nation would upset the delicate balance of power between the slave South and the free North. Lamar didn't just want a piece of that lucrative trade on the Chihuahua Trail; he desperately needed it.

In 1840, a Kentuckian trader from Santa Fe named William Dryden visited with Lamar in Austin and agreed to be an agent for Texas in New Mexico, which to the Texans would include El Paso.

Also a captain of Mexican militia, Dryden was all but a double agent. He carried back a letter from Lamar to the citizens of Santa Fe, extolling the virtues of adding the seaport of Galveston to its trade route: to the east with the United States and to the south with El Paso, Chihuahua, and ultimately Mexico City.

Lamar then went about organizing an invasion. The Texas Congress refused to pay for it, so Lamar put out a call for volunteers. The column included $200,000 worth of trade goods loaded onto twenty-one ox-drawn wagons, but this was not exactly just a trading expedition; it was escorted by five infantry companies and an artillery company. Lamar arrogantly christened it the Santa Fe Pioneers—as if Santa Fe, settled by Spaniards in 1607 and the Pueblo people since time immemorial, needed Anglo pioneering. Lamar guessed the Texans would be welcomed with open arms, but that was only his first mistake. He also wrongly figured that Santa Fe was a mere five hundred miles away. Even by the most direct route across the Llano Estacado, the Staked Plains, he was still off by almost two hundred miles.

That mistake proved punishing for the Texans who pushed across the southern Great Plains. That part of Texas was rough, broken, and dry country, a sea of grass as tall as a man on horseback, alternating with empty gulches and jagged, parched canyons. The troops knew nothing about the terrain of West Texas. Wagons broke down; Comanches attacked the wagon train, triggering a stampede. The entire expedition followed the Wichita River, in the mistaken belief that it was the Red River; seven men died. Some thirteen hundred miles later, the expedition stumbled into eastern New Mexico, where it was promptly met by the Mexican army at Tucumcari, about three hundred miles northeast of El Paso— surrendering without ever firing a shot and thankful just to be alive. A good many would not live for long, though; they were marched thirteen hundred more miles to rot in a Mexico City prison.

When word reached Texas of the epic disaster, calls rang out for Lamar's impeachment. An anonymous letter published in the January 26, 1842, issue of the *Weekly Texian* recommended that the president be turned over to the Mexicans in exchange for the prisoners.[25] Although the survivors were released by April, Lamar's legacy was forever stained. Frustrated and humiliated, he challenged two of his political rivals to duels. Later he was talked out of one and settled the other, without a shot fired.[26] The ever-proud Texans were laid low and demoralized as their reach exceeded their grasp.

BY 1842, THE Mexicans threw in the towel with the Apache, ending the organized scalping and giving them food in exchange for some semblance of peace. The country was safe enough that settlements expanded to Socorro in the south and Doña Ana in the north. In Socorro, a statue of San Miguel had fallen off a wagon headed to Santa Fe; the locals took it as a sign and erected it safely inside their new church. In Doña Ana, a small group had dug an irrigation ditch, and within a year, three hundred people called the place home.[27]

But now, the gringos were the problem.

Whether Texans, Americans, or, like Magoffin the trader, presumed Mexican citizens, a good many of the gringos had treachery on their minds. In the lore of El Paso's history, the Magoffin name would become nearly sacred—a descendant would become mayor[28]—but Magoffin himself was a double-dealer, if not a traitor, to his adopted country. He opened his doors, providing food, water, and champagne to the survivors of the Texas expedition, and the Mexicans took note.[29] In 1843, they forbade any foreigners from engaging in overland trade and closed the border. But Magoffin, with his wife and seven children in tow, settled in Independence at the east end of the Santa Fe Trail. On his 258-acre farm, he bred mules and amassed wealth. Then in 1845, tragedy struck: María died.

It was here that Magoffin's course swung in a different, darker arc. He sold the farm to his brother Samuel and his new wife, Susan. Of Magoffin's children, the boys were shipped to boarding school in Kentucky, the girls farmed out to aunts and convents. With business interests and ties deep inside the Republic of Mexico and Texas—which became a state in 1845, severing ties between Washington and Mexico City—he was a valuable man, this time to the Americans.

So, in 1846, he received $20,000 from Washington and went to meet none other than the eleventh president, James K. Polk. Polk wanted northern Mexico—all of it, the five hundred thousand square miles that Oñate once claimed, all the way to the Pacific.[30] He had already used the break in diplomatic relations as an excuse to move US forces into disputed territory, the strip of land between the Rio Grande and the Nueces River in Texas. Then he'd sent an envoy to offer as much as $30 million for the far Mexican north, below the American Northwest. But the Mexican government knew full well that the Americans were planning to dismember their country. There would be no deal.

The Mexicans were already learning too that there was something in Mexican California that the Americans wanted and would, if necessary, take by force: gold.

Historians have tended to underestimate the lure of natural resources in America's invasion of Mexico, and focus instead on personalities or geopolitics. But greed has often guided American conduct abroad. Jefferson had expressed interest in Mexico's mines, and it is hard to believe that a man as cunning as Polk did not also learn that gold was turning up in California—lots and lots of it. In fact, the first big gold strike in California was not the rush on Sutter's Mill in 1849. It was actually found long before the Mexican-American War, on March 9, 1842, at Rancho San Francisco near Los Angeles. Francisco Lopez was out looking for some stray horses about three miles east of present-day Newhall when he found them grazing along a creek in Placerita Canyon. He stopped to pull up some wild onions from the bank, and caught in their root balls, there it was: gold. He dug and found more. He reported the find to the authorities, who confirmed its authenticity, so Lopez went back out; searching streambeds throughout Ventura County, he found still more. The news spread, and Mexican miners came up from Sonora.

Then Mexican officials made a deadly mistake: they sent some of the gold to be tested at the US Mint in November 1842. There was no way the Americans didn't know there was gold in California, though Polk himself would keep the secret well into 1848—after California was in American hands. The nearly $1 billion, in today's dollars, of California gold found in 1849 alone would finance the world's fastest-rising power.[31]

But in 1846 that fate was not yet sealed, and Chihuahua's new governor, Angel Trias, ordered every man, from teenagers to sixty-year-olds, into military service. Wanting for everything from money to equipment and weapons, northern Mexico teemed with excruciating fear and hurry.[32]

In Congress, a young Abraham Lincoln knew that Polk was cooking up a war with Mexico, even if he had to manufacture one, and in May 1846, Polk demanded a declaration of war. The cocky president predicted a short skirmish; his boastful allies said the boys would be home by Christmas. The House acquiesced to Polk over and above the objections of Northern Whigs like Lincoln, and the Senate passed the declaration, 40–2.[33] War was declared on May 13, and North America braced for conflict.

Standing just five feet, eight inches tall, Polk was a cunning man of outsized ambition,[34] and he recruited Magoffin as a spy; the president was impressed with him, and impressing a president causes no small swell of pride for a man. After all, Magoffin possessed more than knowledge of the terrain. He had relationships too: the governor of New Mexico in Santa Fe was the late María's cousin. Historians have politely called Magoffin a secret envoy, but his mission was to guide Colonel Stephen Watts Kearney;[35] in turn, Kearney and a force out of Fort Bent, Colorado, were meant to seize all of the New Mexico Territory at least to El Paso; grab Colorado, Arizona, Nevada, and Utah; and then take the ultimate prize: California.

The entire plan was right from the diaries, forty years earlier, of Zebulon Pike. Magoffin said yes, headed west to Santa Fe—and just like that, turned his back on his friends, his thirty years with María, and his adopted country. It would not be the last time. Samuel and Susan, his wife, headed west too, driving a huge wagon train of goods worth $300,000.

War or peace, hell or high water, the Magoffins were going to make some money.

Chapter Seven

MARS RETURNS, 1846–48

WITH THE ANNEXATION of Texas, the United States now claimed that the border with Mexico was on the Rio Grande rather than the Nueces River to its northeast. Because Texas also claimed everything east of the Rio Grande to the river's source in the San Juan Mountains of Colorado, where Pike had been caught, so did the United States. The Mexicans had told the Americans that annexation was casus belli, but the Americans did it anyway. When Mexico broke diplomatic relations, Polk moved the US Army into the disputed strip between the two rivers: another deliberately provocative move.

So General Anastasio Torrejón crossed the Rio Grande fourteen miles upstream of Matamoros, and Captain Seth B. Thornton, with two companies of American dragoons (about eighty men), ran smack into the sixteen-thousand-strong Mexican ambush. The Mexicans immediately killed fourteen and gravely wounded six more, but Torrejón was not done. He marched his force toward Port Isabel, where he leveled several Texas Rangers. From there, he covered the main force of the Mexican army moving north.

Despite Polk's estimations, the Mexican army was no bunch of bumblers. They were inheritors of Spain's military practice, experience, and training. After all, this had been Spanish territory only two decades earlier. Many of the officers were ex–Spanish officers who practiced not only conventional military tactics but also the brutal hunting, fighting, and killing learned from the Native peoples. The Mexican army knew too the practice of *deguëllo*, inherited from Arab armies via the Spanish: it was the black flag of no quarter, the dreadful sounding of the trumpet to mean that no prisoners would be taken—exactly what had befallen the Alamo just ten years earlier. They were disciplined officers—cavalry, infantry, artillery—and killers. Following battles at Resaca Palma and Palo Alto, Torrejón's forces captured the forlorn Thornton. The Mexican commanding general, Mariano Arista, agreed to a prisoner exchange with the commanding American general, Zachary Taylor; Thornton, among others, was returned. Thornton would surface again at the end of the war—one of the last casualties of the conflict.

Now sixty-two, Taylor did not exhibit the zeal he had once shown for earlier battles against the British army and the Black Hawk people. It was clear that the Mexicans, while gaining the tactical advantage, were sustaining massive losses: as many as a thousand dead at Resaca Palma and Palo Alto. Taylor effectively used the firepower of artillery to compensate for the Mexicans' deft use of infantry. His next move, he decided, would be to cross the Rio Grande and seize the Mexican port of Matamoros. This was no longer about enforcing the territorial claims of Texas or the United States; his mission was to move along Mexico's eastern half and plunge the dagger into the republic. But the Mexicans shrewdly withdrew, and when Taylor arrived, Matamoros was practically empty.[1]

What most Americans have never understood is how the Mexican-American War that commenced in 1846 was a complete and utter betrayal of the Mexican people—who had had great faith in the Americans. Each country was the product of rebellion against a colonial empire. The early Mexican government was admittedly imperfect, beginning as a copycat of Spain's, but its people had transformed it into a republic entirely modeled on the United States, down to its constitution. Mexicans revered George Washington, Thomas Jefferson, and Benjamin Franklin, naming streets for those American icons. Yet the Americans they so admired double-crossed them, from both within and without. Polk went so far as to employ one of the worst human beings Mexico ever produced: Antonio López de Santa Anna, the cadet, skilled soldier, and ruthless politician known as "the Napoleon of the West." Polk enlisted him to go back to Mexico and work out a territorial surrender by his native country, and, ever the opportunist, Santa Anna went.

Despite considerable disadvantage, the US Army found boats that carried six thousand men upstream on the Rio Grande to a point where they could strike the major northeastern city of Monterrey, once settled by Portuguese Jews. And strike they did, leaving their landing at Camargo in the heat of August 1846 to battle for three choking, dusty, blistering days, with as many as nine thousand Mexican defenders. Finally the Americans pushed the remaining Mexican troops into the colonial central plaza. Both sides were exhausted, with close to four hundred men on either side killed or wounded. The Mexicans offered to surrender Monterrey in exchange for safe passage of their surviving forces from the city, and Taylor agreed. When he learned the news in Washington, Polk flew into a rage. Taylor thought his mission was to thwart the Mexicans over the Texas border—but Polk wanted territory. Letting any Mexican forces go would only make conquest more difficult.

The American army got bogged down in northeastern Mexico. As for the Mexicans, after withdrawing, they slipped off their uniforms, a tactic the Iraqis would repeat precisely, over 150 years later. In civilian clothing, the Mexicans maintained their ranks and command structure, but now they struck out of the night, and by surprise. The Americans were further disadvantaged by their own filth. They were terrible about personal hygiene, and simply put, they shit where they ate. Brought low by cholera, more Americans died of disease than in combat.

Another army out of Texas, under General John E. Wool, wandered into Chihuahua, saw no action, and was attached to Taylor's force.[2] Meanwhile, Santa Anna did not press for peace after leaving Cuba for Mexico; instead, he double-crossed Polk and took command of the Mexican army again. The short war in the Mexican east stretched on and on, interminably.

THE WAR IN the west over the prized territory Polk *really* wanted— California—was an entirely different matter.

Newly commissioned as a colonel, Magoffin, at age forty-nine, raced to Bent's Fort, Colorado, just outside the Mexican border. On July 31, Kearney arrived with his Army of the West, a column of about twelve hundred infantry and mounted dragoons along with a motley crew of five thousand Missouri Volunteers: scallywags, rowdies, and ragamuffins. On August 2, Kearney ordered Magoffin and Captain Philip St. George Cook to ride ahead into Santa Fe with a dozen dragoons for protection, but under a white banner of truce. Behind them trailed a small force of seventeen hundred infantry, artillery, and cavalry. The men marveled at the beauty of the country as they descended; Cook was awestruck, he recorded, at the massive, ruined old Pueblo city at Pecos. Cook carried a tucked-away letter from the American commander to Manuel Armijo, the Mexican governor. It claimed the Americans wanted peace and all of New Mexico east of the Rio Grande, and that was all.

Which, of course, was a lie.

Now it was time for Magoffin to begin his treachery against his adopted country. He slipped into Santa Fe and visited the mayor; neighbors and friends gathered. On the night of August 12, he found the governor—his late wife's cousin, Manuel Armijo— conflicted. On the one hand, Armijo didn't think his forces could withstand the American invasion; it was simply too large for the undermanned Mexican force. On the other hand, he had a duty to fulfill on behalf of the nascent Mexican Republic. So, Magoffin led the governor on an all-night bender, even supplying the champagne.

Alas, Armijo was unconvinced. On August 14, he finally came down on one side—for the time being. The American claim to everything east of the Rio Grande was blatantly illegal, he said, and he pulled a hole card: he had mobilized as many as four thousand men at nearby Apache Canyon and deployed his regular forces to fight. Magoffin was botching the job; the whole point was for Kearney to enter Santa Fe without firing a shot and then depart west to California. For his part, Kearney moved another sixteen hundred men forward toward Apache Canyon and threw in sixteen artillery pieces for good measure.[3]

All signs pointed to a mighty clash on the golden plains south of Santa Fe. On August 16, Kearney issued a proclamation promising the defense of all people and property and no territorial designs past the east bank of the river. The hastily assembled militia at Apache Canyon started to melt away. Armijo led his regulars, mostly cavalry, out of the city—then turned and rode away. Kearney, his lie having succeeded, entered Santa Fe without firing a single shot. In the space of only a month, Kearney reorganized New Mexico and then went west with just three hundred dragoons, leaving behind his main force.

In September, Magoffin led his own wagon train toward El Paso, intending to keep on profiting. The Mexicans were furious: at

Brazito, just south of present-day Las Cruces, and practically on the new Stephenson farm, they arrested Magoffin and a handful of others, and threw them in jail in El Paso for treason. They also found Armijo and slammed him in a Mexico City prison to stand trial for "cowardice and desertion in the face of the enemy." The penalty for both crimes was death.[4]

After an exchange with a Native raiding party, the Mexicans made off with Magoffin's goods, impounding them. A judge deemed that the shrewd Magoffin was indeed a naturalized Mexican citizen and would stand trial for his life for treason. Just eighteen years old and sheltered in Santa Fe, Susan Magoffin wrote of her brother-in-law in her diary: "This makes him appear in their eyes as something of a spy though his intentions were of an entire different nature . . . Let us hope and pray, therefore, that our Almighty Father, The Just Judge, will be with him and deliver him from the hands of his enemies."[5]

The situation for Magoffin was indeed desperate. Susan, the first white, or Anglo, woman to travel the Santa Fe and Chihuahua Trails, added, "Brother James is on trial for his LIFE."[6]

As the December frost settled upon the western war, Kearney took control of California from the Mexicans, relieving a dangerous ragtag rebellion by the Americans there and a few stray officers violating their orders. With the Mexicans out of power, the Diné took quick advantage, kidnapping twenty Mexican families, killing sheepherders, and stealing two thousand sheep. Colonel Alexander Doniphan, yet another Kentuckian turned lawyer in Missouri, had spent months attacking the Diné and was on track to change the course of the war.

After turning west and ordering legalized reprisals—killings—against the Diné, Doniphan struck due south with a light force of Missouri volunteers. His invasion route was almost precisely the route taken north by Oñate over three hundred years earlier. Many now-familiar officers made themselves famous in combat against Mexico: Thomas J. "Stonewall" Jackson, George Gordon Meade, George McClellan, George Pickett, Joseph E. Johnston, Braxton Bragg, Henry Heth, Winfield Scott Hancock, and most famously, Robert E. Lee and Ulysses S. Grant. Kearney would do so as well, though he did not survive the war.[7] Cook would go on to become a principled opponent of the Apache. Theirs was a generation of officers who learned the value of speed and the power of massive artillery bombardments. Doniphan was a name most Americans would never know, and yet he was the commander who broke the stalemate—and the back of the Mexican army.

DONIPHAN'S FORCE PUSHED south to Socorro, retracing the route the Spaniards had used to extricate themselves from the Great Pueblo Revolt. Along the way, the Mexican people did not wish to be forcibly made residents or citizens of the United States. As Sonnichsen, the historian, wrote, "A fiercely patriotic people with a strong sense of national honor, [Mexicans] have died by the thousands during the last century for their country's welfare. They could not have been indifferent to this invasion."[8]

The Mexicans had barely begun to establish a national identity of their own—yet they deeply resented the Americans' taking so much of it as the war went on. The upper classes in the north viewed the Americans as dirty, rough drunks. Indeed, in 1847, New Mexicans rose up against the United States—starting with the January assassination of the new American governor, Charles Bent. A combined force of Hispanics and Native Americans, under Pablo Montoya and Tomas "Tomasito" Romero, broke into his house; they spared the women and children but shot Bent full of arrows and scalped him in front of his wife. Then the rebels killed and scalped American officials all over the place. The next day, five hundred rebels attacked an Anglo-owned mill and distillery. The American army was slow to respond to that and another attack, but intercepted fifteen hundred men just outside of Taos, their stronghold, at Santa Cruz de la Cañada and Embudo Pass. The remaining rebels reached the thick walls of the old adobe church in Taos and took shelter, but the army blasted a hole in the wall with a howitzer, killing 150 and capturing 400 more. A separate force lost a battle to the rebels in nearby Mora; at that point, the army razed the village.[9]

Mexicans and Native people alike were terrified by stories that filtered south about the Americans: they stole whatever they wanted, raped women, and then laughingly branded them on the cheek like they were mules.[10] The defense of El Paso that was being organized, if one could call it that, was chaotic at best. Governors changed by the month. Inconsistent orders arrived, were countermanded, and were replaced with still more inconsistent orders. Livestock were herded south as militia and regular troops prepared to harass the American force. The government planned a scorched-earth defense, destroying crops, supplies, and property—anything that could be of value to the Americans—but then that plan was abandoned. A force marched north to meet the Americans at Doña Ana, yet most of the men were on the verge of mutiny—so they all marched back to El Paso.

Finally, by mid-December, a defense of twelve hundred men was organized, most of them regular troops of the state guard and the rest volunteers. Yet they had just four artillery pieces. Leaders and civilians alike prayed. On December 23, various units of Doniphan's reunited at Doña Ana after the arduous ordeal of crossing the Jornada del Muerto, and on Christmas Day, 1846, the Americans called a halt just downriver of an arm of the Rio Grande known as Brazito, near present-day Vado. It was a ragged bunch; much of the unit was strung down the trail as loose horses, traders in a caravan, and just plain stragglers made their way.

Lieutenant Colonel Luis Vidal, now in charge of the Mexican defense of El Paso, decided against risking everything on a single battle. Keeping forces in reserve at the rough narrows of the Rio Grande, where the falls and cataracts churned, he sent another officer out with dragoons on horseback and militia on foot. The Americans seemed such a motley crew, Vidal thought, that "they could be lanced like rabbits."[11] The dragoons would conduct a reconnaissance in force and harass the Americans, enticing them to follow into the rough river canyon where the reserve force lay in wait. Given the desperate nature of the situation, Vidal's was a pretty good plan.

Yet as the Mexican dragoons approached on horseback, they kicked up a huge cloud of dust from the loose brown sand dunes around Vado, giving themselves away. This was a failure of leadership; they should have approached less directly, up the river valley, where they would not have revealed themselves. At 3 p.m. on December 25, Doniphan's unknowing troops relaxed in the warm winter sun. He was busy winning a game of Three-Trick Loo when a man hurried up and told him of the approaching Mexicans. Doniphan didn't buy it; Christmas Day in the Chihuahuan Desert is a glorious time of the year. And the Mexican forces would be at home in barracks, resting, or at home celebrating the Holy Days. But then he saw with his own eyes the colorful banners and uniforms of the Mexican cavalry in the distance. Jumping up, he told the other players: "Remember that I am ahead."

And with that he abandoned his card game.[12]

The bugler sounded assembly, and men came running in, grabbing weapons and lining up for battle. Having lost the element of surprise, the Mexican field commander spread his men to envelop the Americans. Militia approached with a single cannon. One officer held a small black flag: this would be another *deguëllo,* just like the Alamo. No prisoners would be taken. The Mexicans intended to kill every American, to the very last man. An American interpreter went forward to attempt a parley.

"We will not ask or give quarter," a Mexican officer told him.

"Charge and be damned" was the American response.

The Mexicans, imposing in appearance and number, advanced. But their infantry, armed with as few as four or five rounds each, fired their rifles high and above. Their brass howitzer twice fired two pounds of scrap metal. It sailed high and long. The five hundred or so Americans shrewdly held their fire and let the Mexicans advance farther. Then the order rang out: "Let them have it!" And the Americans opened up.

The Missourians blasted them at nearly point-blank range. Surviving riders veered still farther left to attack the American wagon train. But Doniphan had placed sharpshooters there, and they poured on the fire. The Mexican dragoons who weren't cut down suddenly turned away toward the mountains and beat a hasty and terrible retreat. Now, almost implausibly, the stragglers of Doniphan's force rushed toward the battle. They too kicked up a huge cloud of dust—and this time startled the rest of the Mexicans, who turned and fled.

The Americans captured ammunition, guns, supplies—and, most important, that fine El Paso wine. The Missouri Volunteers drank, hooted, and hollered into the night. They had killed or wounded a hundred defenders and not lost a single man. Upon his return to El Paso, the Mexican field commander, Antonio Ponce de León, took full responsibility for the rout and requested a full investigation. He promptly got it and was arrested, charged with cowardice, and hauled off to a Chihuahua prison for trial.[13] From there, the honest if incompetent officer disappears from the historical account;

it's not a stretch to conclude that he was executed. For their part, his men then stole everything they could carry, put it on horses—and abandoned El Paso. The people of the now-undefended city were disgusted.[14] The Battle of Brazito lasted but an hour. Historians have tended to dismiss it as unimportant, but in fact, it sealed the fate of New Mexico, Arizona, and West Texas, no less than Kearney had done in California.

Two days later, the Americans passed through the narrow gorge of the Rio Grande unopposed, precisely reversing the trek of Oñate's Spanish, Tlaxcalan, and European troops centuries earlier. The people of El Paso greeted them and said they had taken up arms against their will, an unlikely claim.

The Americans set up camp and tasted the fruits of nearly 250 years of careful cultivation: grapes, apples, pears, peaches, and gourds of wine, all gifts from the people of El Paso.[15] There was enough, it turned out, to go around for nearly every one of them. They learned Spanish, burned their mouths with chilis, and tried to date the local women. They raced horses and mules, and found the Mexicans were just as able gamblers as they were. The Missouri ruffians took to El Paso; they soaked up not just the fruit and wine but the climate, kindness, and hospitality. One, John T. Hughes, called El Paso "grand and picturesque beyond description."

Doniphan was strict with his rough-and-ready men, but there was one thing he could not do: get them to take a bath. George Ruxton, a traveling Englishman, passed through and noted that the Americans were the dirtiest, filthiest men he'd ever seen; they even relaxed near the butchered remains of cattle they'd used for meat.[16]

One soldier, Marcellus Ball Edwards, wrote, "Our hospital affairs are conducted scandalously. There is not a surgeon or steward who can much more than determine calomel from quinine and not one who would leave the card table to attend the deathbed of his patient." And George Rutledge Gibson, the quartermaster, re-marked: "The army was composed of men of a restless and roving disposition, and the little discipline which prevailed was totally insufficient to prevent rioting and dissipation." Indeed, on January 13, three Americans were court-martialed for rape.

Yet Doniphan himself was a good commander and, in fact, a decent man; a lesser mortal could not have effectively commanded this horde of ruffians. He took no reprisals, though he did order a house-to-house search for weapons. As Sonnichsen later recorded: "This first large-scale contact between Latin and Anglo did not turn out badly." In turn, Juan Ponce de León—now the richest man in El Paso—made sure Doniphan was both comfortable and reassured.

The American colonel had a new objective: the capital city of Chihuahua, even deeper inside the besieged republic.

ELSEWHERE, THE WAR in Mexico was in chaos.

President Polk in Washington lost faith in Taylor, bogged down in the Mexican northeast, and in late 1846, he ordered the top officer of the US Army, Winfield Scott, to get in the fight. Scott promptly sailed for the port of Veracruz on the Gulf of Mexico, making the first major amphibious landing in US history and then, taking most of Taylor's troops with him, retracing the route of Hernán Cortés to strike Mexico City. With the main prize—the seizure of the Southwest to the Pacific—secured, all the Americans needed was leverage to force the Mexicans to concede that the war was lost.

Santa Anna had by this point not only double-crossed Polk but also seized the presidency of Mexico; then, in a display of arrogance, he had personally taken to the field in command of the army. Taylor dutifully occupied Saltillo, only a short distance southwest of Monterrey, while Santa Anna massed his forces at San Luis Potosi in the very heart of Mexico. He knew Taylor's force was weak, now fewer than 5,000 men, with some 8,000 gone to Scott's command. Fifteen thousand Mexicans converged on nothing more than a bunch of sick and demoralized American volunteers under Taylor. On February 22, 1847, employing the French tactic of sending dense columns, the Mexicans were met with massed artillery and infantry fire by the Americans—who, frankly, slaughtered them. Once more, poor leadership by Mexican officers squandered a great advantage; they lost 2,000 men and withdrew to San Luis Potosi again to lick their wounds. The Americans too had taken a heavy toll, with over 750 casualties in their much smaller force.[17] Yet Scott landed over 13,000 troops at Veracruz, laid siege to the city, and took it with few casualties. Then he marched inland, a journey of some four hundred miles.

Once inside El Paso, Doniphan was initially unsure of his next order. He rounded up his men, and on February 8, 1847, he headed down the old Chihuahua Trail toward the capital city of the state, Chihuahua. Despite encountering a force of Mexican troops that far outnumbered his own, he prevailed and took the city.

Deep inside Mexico, the American army was getting its first baptism by fire outside of its country's rebellion against Great Britain and the Indian wars. It was learning to strike hard and fast and use ruthless, massed firepower, a lesson that would last well into the twenty-first century. As Doniphan reflected, "The fire of our battery was so effective as to completely silence theirs."

The Americans occupied Chihuahua, the high desert capital city of the Mexican state, on March 2, and raised the American flag over the place where the Spanish had executed the Mexican patriot priest Miguel Hidalgo, not far from where entire Native civilizations had arisen in prehistory. Mexico was now divided: the far northwest had fallen to Kearney and all of the near northern territory to Doniphan, despite the reassurances made at Santa Fe. Scott

marched to Mexico City, defeating Santa Anna in combat repeatedly: at Cerro Gordo, Contreras, Churubusco, and Chapultepec. En
route, he battled with Irish Americans who, aggrieved at how they
had been treated in America, had deserted the US Army to fight
in their own San Patricio Battalion in the Mexican army. But to
the Americans, the Irish were just deserters, so Scott destroyed the
battalion, captured seventy men—and executed every single one of
them.

Reaching the old stone fortress of Chapultepec, the final obsta-
cle, Scott laid siege, and the results were grisly. The Mexicans lost
two thousand men. Among them were young military cadets, the
Niños Héroes. Five were killed defending the old castle and their
country. A sixth, Juan Escutia, age twenty, wrapped himself in the
Mexican flag and jumped to his death.

Yet Scott really won the final stage of the war through sub-
terfuge. Once inside the Mexican capital, he simply bribed the
ever-willing and always squabbling elites. If they would drop their
support for the guerrilla war, he would guarantee the Americans
would leave. They did, and he did, with the Treaty of Guadalupe
Hidalgo: signed February 8, 1848, ratified by the legislatures of
both countries in March. Santa Anna, forever the double-crossing
bastard, abdicated the Mexican presidency and fled. Magoffin, the
trader turned traitor, avoided execution after two years in prison
by furnishing a massive bribe, which included six thousand bottles
of champagne. The last American soldier in what was left of a dismembered Mexico departed on August 1, 1848.[18]

As for the young Mexico, it gave up every inch of land Oñate
had ever claimed, more than five hundred thousand square miles,
the gold of California, and the dream of becoming the superpower
of the Americas.

After a hero's welcome in New Orleans, Doniphan made his
way back to New Mexico, where he had work to do. That great

big territory, which encompassed present-day Arizona, needed American laws and the rule of the Constitution. Kearney the soldier became Kearney the lawyer again. There, he drafted the first human rights bill in the United States—a cornerstone of law in the West—as well as the New Mexico Constitution. He understood the importance of protecting all Americans, including the Mexicans, who had been effectively forced to join the country against their will. He worked tirelessly at it, believing correctly that it would secure more than victory: peace itself.

In geopolitical terms, the war with Mexico had provided the US Army with its first combat experience abroad, as it seized the rest of the continent. The victor gained the long Pacific coast, a half-million square miles of territory, and the gold to finance still larger global ambitions. The loser spiraled into poverty, foreign invasion, and revolution.

But the Americans had made important mistakes in their frantic land grab. El Paso, for one, was on the Mexican side of the Rio Grande boundary; this was the very hub and most productive region of northern Mexico. The Mexicans had proposed during the treaty negotiations to draw the northern boundary at the thirty-seventh parallel—keeping for themselves most of New Mexico and Arizona, but giving the United States all of Colorado, Utah, most of Nevada, and the upper half of California.[19] Texas would not reach into New Mexico and remained at its present boundaries on the plains.[20]

But the Americans wanted three deep harbors—not just the two, Monterrey and San Francisco, that the Mexicans would concede. They called for the harbor at San Diego too. The Mexicans argued this was the northernmost point of Baja, California, and was not part of the deal. But a smart young lieutenant, Robert E. Lee, went rummaging through Mexican records and found that the mission there was labeled as part of Alta California, not Baja California.[21]

With some ten thousand US troops occupying Mexico City, the Mexicans had no leverage. They agreed to draw the northern boundary at the thirty-second parallel—giving up their part of Colorado and all of New Mexico, Arizona, Utah, Nevada, and present-day California.[22] Nations normally draw borders along geographical features that present natural barriers, but half of the nearly two-thousand-mile border with Mexico, as a result, was simply an imaginary line across the desert until it met the Rio Grande at Mexican El Paso. Later generations might fret about the border and migration from Latin America, but they should probably blame Lee.

Then there was the human cost. In the end, some thirteen thousand Americans, military and civilian, and twice that number of Mexicans lay dead from battle and disease.[23] Thousands more on both sides were wounded. Polk's so-called short war lasted two years and was the second costliest in American history; only the Civil War that followed had a higher casualty rate than the Mexican-American War's 17 percent.[24] Not even the world wars exceeded the deadliness of this war of territorial conquest.

The southern border neatly cleaved the most vibrant part of northern Mexico—the sixty thousand square miles around El Paso—into a no-man's land, inviting instability, opportunists, criminals, and foreign designs. The Americans got their West, but El Paso was about to become one of the most fought-over cities in the world.

Chapter Eight

WITH THE WAR over, Hugh Stephenson, now Don Hugo, was an American once again. He hadn't explicitly betrayed Mexico, and the Mexicans liked Don Hugo enough that before war broke out, the government granted him the old 23,000-acre Brazito tract, where Doniphan would later engage the Mexican force, abandoned by earlier if fainter-hearted Missourians. Stephenson labored hard to turn it into a profitable farm. At home, he and Juana took in American military officers, forty-niners—miners who partook in the 1849 California gold rush—and other travelers, nearly all headed still farther west. Stephenson also struck his own lode of silver amid the rocky spires of the Organ Mountains just to the north of El Paso; he was there when, in 1857, he got terrible news. Juana had been out in the rose garden with a deer she had fed by hand since he was a fawn. But he was no fawn now; he was a full-grown mule deer buck, standing over three feet tall at the shoulder and probably pushing two hundred pounds. His body had been coursing with testosterone, as the rut had come and gone. He reared up and gored her.

Stephenson hurried across the desert to Juana's bedside, but the infection was too much. Don Hugo held the funeral inside her beloved chapel, San José de Concordia el Alto. The gilded age of Concordia had briefly offered a hopeful glimpse of the future—but now it was over.

Stephenson was devastated without his Juana. Tall as ever, he was balding now, with white hair flowing around the bare crown of his head and down his beard. His eyes were big, dark, and serious, his mouth set in a frown.[1] Increasingly, and perhaps out of his grief, he spent more and more time at the farm at Brazito. The little town of La Mesa, named for a volcanic tabletop that nearly hung over the Rio Grande, sprung up under the nearby cottonwoods. After all, Concordia was in good hands: all the children were now adults, marrying and occupying prominent places in society, business, and government on both sides of the Rio Grande. In a sense, the fact that the river was now an international border didn't seem to matter in people's everyday lives.

At least, not at first.

The war the Americans had won got them their territory, but it unleashed over twenty years of chaos in the region. The Spanish had kept a tenuous sort of peace for most of two centuries. The Mexicans, weakened by internal strife and a collapsing economy, bobbled that peace, but the newcomer Americans smashed it to the ground. They took what they wanted, regardless of what Mexicans or Native Americans claimed, and fought the Mexicans, who were now American citizens, over their land. Sometimes the Americans just murdered them.

After a period filled with refugees and lawlessness, war came again. Between the Americans and the Apache, to be sure, but also at the hands of the Confederacy and the Union (and, surprisingly, the faraway Second French Empire). Claimed at least ten different times by warring nations, El Paso was about to become the most fought-over city in Latin America and the American West—and among the most disputed by foreign armies in all the world.[2]

IN AMERICAN HISTORY, the period after the invasion of Mexico was painted in the gold leaf of manifest destiny: the opening of the American West, covered wagons full of earnest women in bonnets and dresses and eager men in hats and overalls. Some of that was true, and the conflicts and cruelties with the tribes of the Great Plains are well documented. But in the Southwest, the newest territory, a sparse American army fought a grinding war of occupation for decades. It suppressed Americans who had once been Mexican and sought the destruction of many Native peoples: particularly the Diné, but especially the Apache.

As the summer heat reached its blistering peak, new American faces appeared in El Paso. One was not so new: James Wiley Magoffin, the trader-spy-traitor, came and decided to stay. Magoffin had billed the US government $37,000 dollars for his services, pain and suffering, and lost business. He accepted $30,000, then built a fine hacienda north of the river and called it Magoffinsville. He married right back into Mexican aristocracy: his new bride, Lolita, was his late wife's younger sister. He was forty-one years old at the time, and she was just seventeen.

A newer arrival was a former officer with the Missouri Volunteers: Simeon Hart, a short, dark-haired New Yorker and adjutant who took a liking to the place during the invasion. Spending much time at the family mill, just upriver from what is now downtown El Paso, he learned the business, returned to El Paso, and built a grist mill and home near the dam. Another newcomer arrived at Ponce's old Rancho: Sarah Bowman. She was well over six feet tall, and the men of her time characterized her as an Amazon. A famous prostitute nicknamed "The Great Western," after the largest steamship afloat, Bowman bought a hotel and restaurant nearby and ran a brothel out of them. As more Americans arrived, more sex workers were employed in El Paso, which became more unruly. Along with the prostitutes and parched cowboys, the wagonloads of goods and people, came thieves to prey upon them all.

And more Americans were indeed headed this way. Despite the arduous journey, they kept on coming. Probably in response to attacks by the Comanche, they abandoned some sixty wagon trains on the Pecos River and tried to continue on foot. Over sixteen hundred wagonloads of forty-niners left Austin for El Paso in this period.

Once more the Texans made trouble. They dispatched men to Santa Fe to argue that New Mexico east of the Rio Grande, including the settlements on the north bank of the river opposite El Paso, were part of Texas. They returned to Austin, yelling that New Mexico—which they'd never controlled—was in rebellion. Congress absorbed Texas's sizable debt from its republic days, to the tune of $10 million, in exchange for leaving New Mexico intact in the east, and the holders of Texas's otherwise worthless bonds lobbied hard.

Meanwhile, lawmakers were increasingly troubled by the division of the nation caused by slavery. Congress approved the Texas Compromise of 1850, the precursor to other measures like the Kansas-Nebraska Act, intended to maintain a precarious balance and to draw lines around slave states even as they sought to expand. Texas governor Peter Bell ordered the organization of El Paso County and dropped plans for other counties in New Mexico.

But the issue was still not settled. The Paseños, El Paso's citizens, needed to vote first.

ON FEBRUARY 18, 1850, the county of El Paso agreed to join Texas.

Somehow, just twenty people voted in a county of more than

twenty-five hundred on the US side of the river.[3] Paseños, who had shunned slavery for centuries, were now members of a slaveholding state. Despite the promises made with the Treaty of Guadalupe Hidalgo, Mexicans were not being granted their constitutional rights; in fact, they were often not even counted. Texas officially recorded no people living in El Paso in 1850 and only forty-three in 1860. Yet the Mexican census of 1840 recorded four thousand people on both sides of the river.[4] It is clear that the American census of 1850 undercounted the Mexican American population—not just in the El Paso region, but across the entire Mexican Cession, including California. Clearly, they were not to be treated as full citizens of the United States.[5]

Some eighty thousand Mexicans found themselves living in the United States now;[6] most were concentrated in New Mexico and, by extension, El Paso, but the rest were long since cut off from each other by territory. Academics have talked about the borderlands for decades, giving the impression that the United States–Mexico frontier is a cohesive region. But at that time, and up to the present day, there was little travel and communication there; it remains nearly impossible to traverse the north bank of the river even to Presidio, fewer than two hundred miles away. The same remains true of reaching Laredo and the Lower Rio Grande Valley. It is equally difficult to travel west and find large populations or livable conditions until reaching southern Arizona. The newly minted Mexican Americans of the Southwest were a people united by a shared language, but divided by mountains, deserts, Native peoples—and a new conqueror.[7] Across the Southwest, full citizenship was granted unconditionally only to Anglos.

Throughout the region, amid the political and economic turmoil, thousands of people were on the move. Most Mexicans now north of the international border elected to stay where they were; in turn, the United States pledged that they would become full citizens immediately, with all the rights of other Americans, and that their property would be respected. But others did not wish to stay in what was now a foreign land. The cash-strapped Mexican government paid for the resettlement of these refugees in the Mexican interior; some moved only a few hundred yards and simply started settlements on the Mexican side of the border.

The little settlements north of the river were flooded with forty-niners and others who were headed west, not all of them of good character. The gunfighter and confidence man Parker H. French arrived with two hundred forty-niners bound for California; he left behind hundreds of bad checks. Wagon trains were camped all over, from Ponce's rancho to Ysleta and up through the new settlement at Frontera, which consisted of a few shacks built by Frank White. Like locusts, these people on the move consumed everything. They bought up so much food that locals began price gouging or hoarding, for fear they would starve in the coming season.

Army Lieutenant Judson Van Horn, who commanded a garrison there, dispatched Companies A and C east to the Pecos River to escort a wagon train. Then he took a column up the river and west, patrolling for the Apache, who had resumed their raids, since the newly arrived American army—unlike the Mexicans and the Spanish before them—was not supplying rations. For the Apache, raiding was not a sport; it spelled the difference between survival and starvation, augmenting their own hunting and gathering. Apache people from varying bands wanted to see what was in store for them with the Americans, and in the fall of 1850, a group led by two Mescalero chiefs came down from the mountains and began to negotiate the beginnings of a peace treaty with Van Horn.[8]

At first, the US Army responded by mimicking the old Spanish strategy: Van Horn presented his visitors with gifts and requested orders from his commander, James S. Calhoun, the military governor and chief of relations with the Native people in the territory.

Calhoun responded with a peace offensive, offering Native people food in exchange; the Diné even sent a flock of sheep as a gift in return.[9] To his north, Calhoun made peace with the Plains Apache, the Jicarilla. His strategy was as shrewd as it was humane. After all, he had no more than fourteen hundred troops in the territory, from Colorado to El Paso and Texas to California.

Yet for the Native people, fighting with one hand and negotiating with the other was a common tactic. The theft of horses increased. Since the Americans still weren't providing food rations to supplement the Apache, they would ride, eat, trade, and sell stolen horses. In the spring of 1851 the Apache took off with horses and cattle at the village of Franklin, named for Benjamin Franklin Coons, a Missouri trader who had bought the ranch in what is now downtown El Paso from Juan María Ponce de León. They lifted eighty head of livestock from San Elizario in the south, then sawed through Magoffin's corral timbers and vanished with over forty more.

Americans throughout the area were stealing everything not nailed down, and even things that were—sometimes homesteads were wrested from the Mexican American population. At one end of the valley, several hundred people fled Doña Ana and the depredations committed by Americans, mostly Texans.[10] At the other end, the justice of the peace in Ysleta, Pedro Gonzalea, wrote Governor Bell in Austin that the people were "very much dissatisfied with the injuries and ravages they suffer from the Americans who live there."[11] The situation was so bad that the governor of the New Mexico Territory, which encompassed Arizona, wanted troops moved in to protect the Mesilla Valley from the Texans and Americans.[12]

The place was spinning out of control. Scalping for bounties had broken out on both sides of the border. The Apache got in on it too—for a while; the Mescalero in the Davis Mountains paid a bounty of $1,000 for any American or Mexican scalp. An army unit attacked a group of Mescalero in the winter of 1849–50 and took

250 scalps. The Mexicans paid for scalps in silver pesos too, but only fifty for those of children.[13]

The army post at Ponce's rancho was closed due to budget cuts, and the remaining troops were dispersed to San Elizario downriver and around Mesilla upriver. The ties between Mexicans and the old gringos frayed, but the new Anglo elite didn't seem to care all that much; they were reaping fortunes on top of fortunes. Magoffin went from trading to being a cattle and sheep baron. Great herds of both grazed upon the flanks of mountains, denuding much of their grasses; the last trees in the mountains were cut down in the 1850s.

In 1851, the Apache made off with forty of Magoffin's prized mules. Later, angry about the loss of his horses and cattle to the Apache, he convened Simeon Hart and others in 1852. They planned to press the army to safeguard their animals and ranches and take reprisals against the Native people. Nonetheless, within months, the Apache killed a herd of sheep a half-mile from Hart's house, then rustled horses out of Ysleta. The raids went on and on. Street violence rose; thirteen men were killed in just two months in 1852.[14] A string of murders in San Elizario prompted a posse to go out and arrest suspects. The army found four of its men among them, judged them guilty, and hanged them from a tree; the civilians stretched out the fourth one too.[15] Under American rule, El Paso had become an increasingly dangerous and violent place.

Yet El Paso was America's new frontier, and it faced unabashedly westward. The arrival of European Jewish, Syrian, and Lebanese immigrants would prove an important turning point. Syrian and Turkish cowboys wrangled for the US Army's so-called Camel Corps in the deserts of West Texas from 1857 until 1861, under the command of none other than Robert E. Lee, directed by War Secretary Jefferson Davis. None of the Texans or troopers could pronounce the name of one of the Syrians, Hali al-Ajaya, so they just called him "Hi Jolly." The odd-looking Egyptian camels survived in the desert more easily than mules did and appeared, along with their Syrian wranglers, at posts up into New Mexico. Jews practiced their faith openly too: the brothers Samuel and Joseph Schutz arrived from Westphalia in Germany to set up shop as cloth merchants, teaching the trade to their nephew, Solomon.[16] As for the camels, they ate creosote, a bush that virtually no desert animal will consume, re-creating a link to prehistory, when the now-extinct American camel roamed here, and its wanderings in the desert added to the general diversity of nature in the region.[17]

Yet the Americans had a problem: they had forgotten to find a year-round, snow-free pass for the railroads that would connect El Paso to San Diego, the much-vaunted harbor. Embarrassingly, Washington contacted Mexico City for help: the Americans needed some land below the thirty-second parallel, left out of the treaty with Mexico, and asked to add a strip to the southern end of New Mexico, near the Chiricahua Mountains. It was rough wilderness, whose boulders stack into the sky to greet the winter flurries, but south of it was flat and nearly snow-free playa. The Americans offered another $15 million. Santa Anna had popped into the presidency again and promptly agreed, absconding with his take and vacating the office; on June 30, 1854, the Gadsden Purchase became part of the New Mexico Territory.

A good many Mexicans who had picked up and moved in order to stay in Mexico found themselves again in American territory. At the river town of Mesilla, whose people had fled the violence of the new regime, the Mexican flag was lowered once more at the bandstand in the little plaza—and the American flag was hoisted into the southwestern sky.

UP IN THE cool, piñon-studded hills along the Mimbres River, Mangas Coloradas was willing to give the Americans the benefit of the doubt. The Mexicans, after all, had ordered that scalping at Santa Rita, and the Mexicans had been the enemy. Meanwhile, New Mexico's military governor, Calhoun, had treated the Apache fairly; he even wanted peace with the Chiricahua.

The enemy of Calhoun's enemy was, logically speaking, his friend. Besides, the raids were about more than just survival; among the Chiricahua, they were cultural events, celebrated with an elaborate four-stage dance that lasted all night. Raiding was considered a right: this was, after all, the Apacheria, and the Mexicans and gringos had so much bounty, they could surely spare some, or so the Apache believed. As a Chiricahua leader, Daklugie, put it: "Why should the Chiricahua go hungry with abundance of food on their own land?"[18]

Raids went easier, in a sense, on ranches and farms that did not retaliate; in these cases, the Apache left behind livestock, for example, so the Mexicans and gringos could keep breeding them. The Apache "did not consider it grand policy to destroy a people who so largely ministered to his support," the *Daily Arizonan* noted.[19] But making war on the Americans and engaging the US Army, which the Apache had watched from a distance, was another proposition altogether. After all, the Mimbres band of the Chiricahua numbered between only 450 and 750 during this period.[20] Both emboldened and starving, the Apache stepped up their raids.

Truth be told, the raiding was getting out of hand across much of the Apacheria, not just among the Chiricahua. An attack on a wagon train by Mescalero raiders wound up with numerous casualties on both sides, after a vicious battle in the dead end of Dog Canyon in the Sacramento Mountains. Another raid on a wagon train left more than thirty dead on both sides; the raiding party made off with nothing but mules for its trouble. Often enough, the raids turned deadly when the Americans fought back, usually with superior firepower and their own brand of aggression. Sometimes the raids were simply botched, and warriors were wounded or killed; the Apache, increasingly outnumbered by the civilians and the army, could ill afford such losses.

There was also a new territorial governor: General Edwin "Bullhead" Sumner. The nickname refers to a bullet ball that was said to have bounced off his head. Sumner had different orders, and a different attitude, than his predecessor; when Calhoun departed, he asked his replacement for an escort to the Mimbres country to entreat with Mangas. The answer was no.

The two increasingly opposed forces, the US Army and the Apache, could not have been more different. Both wielded distinct advantages and faced profound disadvantages. The troopers of the cavalry had good horses; most chose mustangs over thoroughbreds from the American East. But they were bogged down in heavy, wool uniforms and mountains of even heavier steel gear.[21] The Apache were lightning-fast when mounted—by one estimate, three times as fast as an American trooper on foot. At that point in history, the American soldier was given no formal physical training regimen, but an Apache warrior had been running, climbing, and scrambling all his life in the thin air of the high desert and mountains.[22] Raiding was, indeed, practice for war; the American troops in garrison were, by contrast, used to manual labor like digging ditches or improving officers' quarters, jobs their superiors wouldn't deign to do. The Ninth Cavalry was often short of horses, with mounts for only half to three-quarters of the men. Armed with their wild mulberry and chokeberry arrows, in contrast, the Apaches could strike fast— but they could not sustain long-distance campaigns.[23] They needed to return home to rest, replenish themselves, and regroup, given their small numbers: usually fewer than thirty and only rarely one to two hundred, under Mangas or Cochise, his counterpart in Arizona.

Under pressure from the locals, the army ultimately came to

consider raiding, even just the theft of livestock, an act of war. In the 1850s, the first stagecoaches crossed the desert sporadically, transporting passengers and mail from San Antonio to El Paso. The Butterfield Overland Mail Company took over the route in September 1858, regularly continuing west to Mesilla, Tucson, Yuma, and Los Angeles, a journey of twenty-one days. These stages presented a valuable asset and, to the Chiricahua, a fat target, along with the nearby Santa Rita copper mines, the site of the mass scalping and fighting in the 1830s where, also in the 1850s, the army established a fort. The Chiricahua approached in 1852, seeking to parley for rations, but were turned back and told they would be shot. Though the Native Americans retreated, the troops nevertheless opened fire. Many were wounded, but the Chiricahua managed to steal the fort's herd of livestock. When a party came out to get the animals, the Apache killed three soldiers. They also mutilated and scalped one trooper, who survived—when he stumbled past the gate, a frantic fear grabbed the rest by the throat.

A cycle of escalation ensued. The Americans regarded the destruction of property a call to war, while the Apache reserved war for vengeance; they did not understand each other's ethos. The army mounted a larger campaign while the Chiricahua tried to make peace again. Mangas signed a treaty acknowledging US military authority, promising to stay out of Mexico—part of the Treaty of Guadalupe Hidalgo—and to return captives. The United States would provide corn, beef, sheep, cattle, and other goods. Meanwhile, the army opened a new post in El Paso, at Magoffinsville, in 1854, naming it Fort Bliss, after a Mexican-American War veteran. Four companies of the Eighth Infantry Regiment occupied it.

Magoffin himself had become an influential and powerful man. Not only had he gotten the army back to El Paso, nearly in his own backyard, but he controlled the county sheriff. In 1853, Magoffin laid claim to salt deposits on the east slope of the San Andres

Mountains, north of the jagged Organ Mountains. He knew this was a clear violation of previous Mexican tradition and common frontier policy. Salt was precious, no mere table seasoning; it preserved meats, and it provided a valuable mineral for humans and livestock alike. In the dry desert air, it replenished the body's constant loss of salt through perspiration. Salt belonged to everyone and anyone, whether Native, Spanish, Mexican, or American, and it always had. People came from far away to procure it. Yet Magoffin, acting the part of feudal warlord, claimed it and slapped a tax on it.

On a frigid January morning in early 1854, when over a hundred *salineros* with their carts from New Mexico headed for the deposits, Magoffin's twenty-eight guns-for-hire, with their mortar, lay in ambush. After being served by the sheriff, the *salineros* refused to pay a tax to Magoffin. The gunmen opened fire with rifles, and the howitzer bellowed. The New Mexicans ran, and the posse made off with the livestock they had abandoned. It was an act of piracy, a seizure of booty on the high desert.[24]

During this period everything seemed in flux, up for grabs. Overstretched, the army closed Fort Webster at Santa Rita near the copper mine. Seeing this, the Apache rushed in to fill the vacuum. They burned the fort to the ground and reasserted themselves from the Mogollon Mountains to the Black Range. They abided by most of the Treaty of Guadalupe Hidalgo, which was intended to turn them into sedentary farmers on the Gila and Salt Rivers, but once more, the scheme failed: by 1855, the army had failed to keep delivering rations and supplies, so the Apache struck the stagecoaches. In 1856, Lieutenant Colonel Daniel Chandler, with troops from Fort Craig and Fort Thorn, retaliated by hitting Apache camps filled with the elderly, women, and children.

Like all wars of occupation, the ensuing Apache Wars were vicious and dirty. Mangas and the Mimbres and Ojo Caliente bands had disappeared into Mexico to the Janos Plain, leaving the Americans to kill innocent people. As Lieutenant John Van Deusen Du Bois, a West Point graduate, wrote, "Humanity, honor, a soldier's pride, every feeling of good in me was and is shocked by [Chandler's] act."[25]

The instability introduced by the Americans set off a wave of barbarous violence: not just summary executions, but more scalping, and worse. Torture and rape became a chilling feature of the landscape. Comancheros—Hispanics, often from New Mexico, along with a mixed bag of Comanche, Diné, or other Native peoples—took revenge on one another, just like the Anglos did. In return, the Mescalero grabbed a drummer boy who had wandered out of a cavalry camp. Outside Santa Fe, twenty-two Apache found a couple, Mr. and Mrs. White, traveling alone, and demanded the goods in their wagon. Mr. White refused, and they killed him in front of his wife. Then each man took turns raping her, as she watched them laughingly smash the teeth out of her dead husband's mouth, to make jewelry from them. The army mounted a frantic search for Mrs. White and, finding her in an Apache camp, recovered her and snatched up the young daughter of a leader as a hostage. Back in the troopers' camp, as they attended to the white woman, the Apache girl flew into a terrified rage, seized a knife, and began stabbing the mules; the troopers opened fire and killed her.[26]

The 1857 campaign was a terrible disaster. It not only sullied the army but instilled rage in the Apache, who hadn't been causing as much trouble as the Chiricahua had. On their return march to the forts, troops suffered for water and animals for grass. Uniforms came apart, and soldiers walked shoeless. They'd never even found Mangas and his Mimbres, nor any of the Chiricahua.

In 1858, the army returned to a policy of appeasement with the Apache. For the Chiricahua, this was a deal to take, as slipping into Mexico was increasingly hazardous.

In the end, in exchange for letting stagecoaches, mail, and

eastward-bound Americans cross their lands, the Chiricahua got their rations and their mountain strongholds. They had endured much for their mountain home, and so they were bent on keeping it.

AS THE NATION entered the 1860s, many of the gringos increasingly occupying the north bank of the Rio Grande were dealing yet again with a perennial scourge: treason. This time, the national wounds would be nearly fatal.

Men like James Wiley Magoffin, Simeon Hart, and, to a quieter and lesser extent, even Don Hugo Stephenson all crossed the line— these formerly loyal citizens of the United States became traitors to their country in the momentous year of 1861. Among the Americans, most in Texas supported the rebel Confederacy and its devotion to the economic profits derived from the misery of human chattel slavery. One notable newcomer, W. W. Mills, an engineer and surveyor from Indiana, stubbornly opposed it.[27] Mills and Magoffin became rivals, but Mills and Hart became enemies.[28] How the Mexican American people felt is unclear. They were, as Mills put it, divided, in part because some tried to follow the prevailing Anglo opinion. But as elsewhere in Texas, they were likely divided as much by class and money as they were over pure sentiments concerning war and slavery; those higher up the ladder tended to align with Anglos of the same ilk, while those lower on the ladder gauged how they themselves were treated by the Americans— which was often badly.

This corner of the world had been generally opposed to the chattel slavery of the American South. Mexico offered freedom to any Black slave who could reach it. New Mexico was militantly in the Union camp; it was a federal territory whose security, however shaky, relied upon Union troops. The American villages at El Paso made for a hazy, confused middle ground, where slaves were practically unknown too. Yet most of the influential Anglos were undoubtedly Southerners, and on the map, they were part of slave-holding Texas.

"We want more slaves," wrote Charles DeMorse of the Clarks-ville *Northern Standard*. "We need them." Slavery then spread north and west to the blackland prairie. By 1860, there were 182,000 slaves in Texas, an astounding forty-fold increase since independence.[29]

Large slaveholders were a decided minority, but a wealthy and powerful one. Out of a population of 600,000 people in 1860, just 20,000 white males owned slaves; of these, half owned fewer than three. Meanwhile, three men owned more than two hundred slaves, but this handful owned much of the wealth; still concentrated in the southeast, they were responsible for nine out of ten cotton bales bound for export. Texas may have been the West to the rest of the country, and much of its land might have been scrub grass, but the region that mattered—the east and the coast—was politically, culturally, and economically a part of the Deep South.

Texas became embroiled in the national politics of slavery from the beginning of its path to statehood. John C. Calhoun once planned to divide Texas into six states to magnify the power of slave states in the Senate; his plan failed. The Democratic Party, which controlled most of the state's political scene, pushed Texas further into the Deep South camp, and skepticism toward the Republicans and Washington grew intense. The Knights of the Golden Circle, a secret society established by Kentucky plantation owners to promote slavery in the West, spread quickly through the state, establishing "castles," or chapters, that encouraged talk of secession as the 1850s drew to a close and fear of a Republican win in 1860 rose.

Even Texans with little or no connection to slavery soured on the Union as Native American raids along the frontier in 1859 and 1860 drew a feckless response from the army. No strangers to revolution, Texans began to see secession as the route to expansion, particularly southward into Mexico and Central America. The Union would never allow such a thing—but, many believed, the Confederacy would.

In the summer of 1860, the balance of public opinion was finally tipped by hysteria when a series of mysterious fires broke out in Denton and Dallas. Charles R. Pryor, a Dallas newspaper editor, claimed that a slave rebellion was responsible and would soon eclipse the violence of Nat Turner's 1831 revolt in Virginia. Rumors of rape, murder, and poisoning consumed what was left of pro-Union sentiment. Vigilantes hanged as many as a hundred people, even though the fires were likely accidental, the result of storing the first phosphorus matches indoors in the withering Texas heat.

With Lincoln in office and the rest of the South in rebellion, it was only a matter of time before the powers-that-be in Texas pushed the state out of the Union. The decision finally came on February 1, 1861; as Governor Sam Houston sat in his office, the Secession Convention upstairs, led by the Supreme Court justice O. M. Roberts, demonstrated the full power of cotton and slavery interests. Each delegate had moved to Texas from a slaveholding state. Most were older and wealthier; many were lawyers, and 70 percent were slave owners. A large number were members of the Knights of the Golden Circle. Only eight Unionists took part in the convention, led by James W. Throckmorton, and their voices were drowned out.

At 11 a.m., the convention voted on the following ordinance, confined to a single sheet of paper: "To dissolve the union between the State of Texas and the other States, united under the compact styled 'The Constitution of the United States of America.'" Houston himself was in grudging attendance as the vote to secede was taken: 166 to 8.

The next day, the convention displayed the deep racism at work in secession, calling "the African race . . . an inferior and dependent race" for whom slavery is actually beneficial. Shrewdly, the convention called for a popular referendum, which was held on February 23. Though secession was deeply unpopular with the Germans of Central Texas, and eight northeast counties voted it down—amid threats to, in turn, secede from Texas itself—the gambit succeeded when a full three-quarters of Texans endorsed the convention vote. On March 1, the Confederacy accepted Texas as its seventh state. The Lone Star would now fly on the Confederate flag,[30] and that flag was hoisted over the Americans living on the north bank of the Rio Grande at El Paso.

A Georgia native who had logged forty-eight years in Union blues, General David Twiggs was in charge of federal troops in Texas. He had been in poor health and had so hoped to avoid participating in the looming Civil War that he put off returning to his post at the San Antonio arsenal the previous year. Once there, he became the constant target of secessionists who wanted to seize the arsenal; they feared that if the Union army escaped to New Mexico, Twiggs could open a western front against Texas.

To root him out, the secessionists dispatched the Texas Indian fighter Ben McCulloch. Throughout mid-February, inside the arsenal, Twiggs vacillated: he insisted he "would not be the first to shed blood," yet he ordered his troops to pack light baggage and to open fire if the secessionists tried to take their weapons. Meanwhile, McCulloch's force swelled to seven hundred armed, mounted men. He called for Twiggs's surrender on February 16, 1861, and entered San Antonio two days later.

Eventually the Unionists caved. In exchange for safe conduct to the coast, Twiggs, commander of the US Army in Texas, surrendered the arsenal and every federal military post in the state, ordering all 3,000 troops to evacuate to the coast. The scene on

February 18, 1861, was captured in a rare type of photograph, an ambrotype. In it, riflemen prowl the rooftops and McCulloch's horsemen line the street; under their gaze, the humiliated Union troops file out. Twiggs was summarily fired.

Things were going poorly for Unionists on the political front as well. Texas's secession ordinance went into effect on March 5, the day after Lincoln's inauguration; all government officials were required to swear an oath of allegiance to the Confederacy. In Austin, Governor Houston, a staunch Unionist who had fought secession throughout the crisis, told his wife, Margaret, "I will never do it." Ten days later, Houston received a final offer to take the oath, and declined. Fed up, the legislature unceremoniously fired him, appointing Lieutenant Governor Edward Clark to take his place.

Secession fever set in quickly. Militia companies were raised across the state; wealthy men funded them, and experienced soldiers and even Native American fighters led them. An assortment of units in colorful uniforms drilled in town squares: part of the First Texas Infantry in red stripes; some Fourth Texas Infantry troops in gray trimmed in blue. One cavalry commander even sported jaguar skins. There was no shortage of bravado. Private Ralph J. Smith, in Company K of the Second Texas Infantry, put it simply: "We knew no such words as fail."

Infantry and cavalry alike assembled in westerners' wide-brimmed hats; the volunteers from South Texas were partial to Mexican sombreros. They packed a frontiersman's arsenal of shotguns, swords, knives, spears, and carbines, along with Mississippi and Sharps rifles. Texans favored cavalry duty over infantry: twenty-five thousand Texans volunteered in 1861 and two-thirds formed cavalry units.

Most men were in their twenties, a mix of migrants from the Upper and Deep South. But sprinkled throughout were Europeans, Mexicans, Native Americans, and even former Unionists: Throckmorton, the most outspoken Unionist at the Secession Convention, donned a Confederate uniform and eventually rose in rank to general officer. General John Bell Hood's famed Texas Brigade, a favorite of General Robert E. Lee, included a mix of English, Welsh, Scottish, German, Irish, French, Jewish, and Dutch soldiers, at least twenty-five hundred Mexicans, and even a Native American. About twenty-five hundred Mexican Americans joined the Confederate Army, enlisting in the Eighth Texas Infantry out of San Antonio and General Hood's brigade—yet it appears that more joined the Union army. It paid better and offered the opportunity for payback against the oppressive, resented Anglos. The US Second Texas Cavalry fought in the Rio Grande Valley and later in Louisiana.[31]

Texans readied the beef too that the Confederacy needed to feed its new army. The short-legged English cattle from north Texas quickly proved ill-equipped for the long drive east—but the tough, nearly drought-proof Spanish longhorn was up to the task. Cowboys herded thousands of them in south and southeast Texas for the drive across Louisiana and the Mississippi River.

The Civil War set the Southwest afire. Back in El Paso, citizens crowded into Ben Dowell's saloon to vote on secession on February 23, 1861; Dowell himself opposed it, but his bar was where the ballot box was placed. Mexican Americans were in the crowd, with some undoubtedly taking their cues from the heated, impassioned Anglos about this faraway war, which seemed not to bear upon their lives one whit. El Paso had no plantations and therefore no slave economy, but many Anglo settlers came from Southern states. So, when the counting was done, just two had voted against secession.

O N MARCH 31, 1861, the Stars and Stripes fluttered down at Fort Bliss.

As part of Twiggs's disastrous surrender, Colonel Isaac V. D. Reeve marched his Union troops eight hundred miles east, to the Gulf of Mexico. The force headed to Fort Quitman, meeting up with troops there and continuing toward Galveston. Perhaps unsurprisingly, Magoffin, along with Simeon Hart, who had supplied troops with flour paid for by the US taxpayer, reaped the bounty: the departing troops left a year's worth of supplies, including food, in the hands of Magoffin and Hart, who'd designated themselves Confederate agents.

Most of those Union soldiers never reached the shores of Galveston. Instead, six companies of the Eighth Infantry were met in May by Confederate troops at Lucas Spring near San Antonio and were imprisoned there, despite the surrender agreement, which included safe passage. Magoffin, now a general in the Texas militia, organized a new unit, the Thirty-Third Brigade. He got busy supplying Confederate forces, including his sons Samuel and Joseph.[1] He also peddled an idea: from El Paso, the slaveholding Confederacy could invade northern Mexico, carving out a protectorate. It was a plan he'd once shared with former governor Sam Houston when both flew the American flag.

While the Civil War in the East raged between Northerners and Southerners, war in the Southwest was fought between descendants of Europeans, Anglo-Americans, and the Native people. By July, war in the Southwest was real. On the first day of the month, Confederate John Baylor and three hundred ragged ruffians of the Texas Mounted Rifles took over Fort Bliss, and on July 23, Mangas Coloradas attacked the last stagecoach out of El Paso for the duration of the war. His Apache killed all seven on board: Union sympathizers fleeing for California.[2] The Mescalero attacked all around Fort Davis to the east. Baylor then struck Union troops near Mesilla at the adobe Fort Selden, part of a string of forts up and down the Rio Grande in present-day New Mexico. Soldiers fought not only each other but the searing heat of summer and strangely freezing desert nights, along with the insects and snakes. Union troops burned their stores and withdrew upriver to Fort Stanton. Fleeing into the old Jornada del Muerto, they finally surrendered to Baylor's gray rebels.

Back in El Paso, Mills, the Unionist engineer and Magoffin's rival, had just returned from New Mexico, where he was observing Baylor's forces. While he was walking down the street on the Mexican side—which was neutral territory—six horsemen grabbed him, loaded him onto a horse, and raced north to cross the river. "Where do you intend to take me?" Mills demanded. At Fort Bliss, a major informed him tersely, "You are brought here a prisoner, sir." They locked Mills in a vermin-infested guardhouse and clamped a ball and chain on him. "The idea of kidnapping me did not originate with the Texan military," he later wrote, "but was instigated by citizen non-combatants—my own neighbors." So, which neighbor had Mills tossed in prison without charges?[3] Simeon Hart, of course.

With the Americans fighting among themselves now, everyone took quick advantage of the disorder. In Mesilla in early 1862,
three men were arrested and charged with being sympathetic to
the Union. A mob snatched them out of a military guardhouse and
lynched all three, though two survived; one was later clubbed to
death.[4] Mangas Coloradas led a bloody raid on the new gold mine at
Pinos Altos, above present-day Silver City. Baylor, the Confederate
commander, proclaimed himself military governor of the Arizona
Territory and shot and killed a newspaper editor in Mesilla who was
deemed pro-Union. Confederate general Henry Sibley then arrived
in El Paso with a large force and even grander designs: the takeover
of northern Mexico and seizure of California's gold fields and ports.

Much of 1861, as the historian W. H. Timmons put it, "was a
prolonged horror." And it was about to get worse.

FRESHLY PROMOTED TO brigadier general by none other than
the president of the Confederacy, Jefferson Davis, Henry Hopkins
Sibley was a distinguished soldier who had spent twenty-two
years in the West. Davis was suitably impressed with his plan: cross
thirteen hundred miles of forbidding desert, capture New Mexico,
present-day Arizona, the California gold fields, and the ports of San
Francisco and San Diego.

If this invasion succeeded, Davis and the Confederate leadership reasoned, it could change the war overnight. No longer a small
number of states strung along the East and Gulf Coasts, hemmed
in by the Union navy's increasingly effective blockade, the Confederacy would at once be transformed into a Pacific power. With the
shackles of the blockade smashed, the South would trade with the
world at will as gold poured into its coffers.[5]

Sibley was no homegrown Texas Ranger or state militia officer,
but when war called, as it increasingly did in the West, he had

answered. Louisiana-born to the influential physician and western explorer Samuel Hopkins Sibley, Henry was an 1838 graduate of West Point. He fought the Seminole in Florida and served in Mexico, battling bravely near Veracruz. After the Mexican-American War, Sibley fought the Comanche in Texas and the Diné in the New Mexico Territory. He pursued Mormons in the Utah Territory and quelled violence over slavery in Kansas. Yet his career in the US Army faded as his hair and beard grew gray and his drinking grew worse, and in the end he turned his back on the country he had once honorably served.

When the Civil War broke out, Sibley was at Fort Union, in the New Mexico Territory. He knew where his loyalties lay and immediately resigned his Union commission. He then headed across the continent to the Confederate president, bringing his plan to strike west.

In hindsight, many would see the invasion of New Mexico as Sibley's grandiose vision. But in reality, Davis had seized upon the idea of a big western offensive before Sibley set foot in Richmond. A West Point graduate himself, Davis apparently was influenced at the academy by the writings of Antoine-Henri Jomini, a Swiss officer under Napoleon who coined the phrase "the offensive-defensive": a curious combination of a generally defensive posture that didn't wait on the enemy to seize the initiative. Davis had an appreciation for the riches on the frontier: in the Senate, he had proposed that slave labor be imported for mining and agriculture in the West.

As president of the Confederacy, Davis initially said he had no interest in invading the West. But there were Confederate sympathizers in both Arizona and California, and they proved a handy excuse for doing so. Even the Union commander there reported at least twenty thousand sympathizers in California, and if the Confederacy "should ever get an organized force into this State, as a rallying point for all the secession element, it would inevitably inaugurate a civil war here immediately."

At his inauguration in Washington in March, President Abraham Lincoln seemed to anticipate the Confederacy's designs on the West, noting that the Constitution still applied to all states—and territories—that had not seceded. In April, Davis met with the Confederate secretary of war, Leroy Pope Walker, and the two discussed not just the importance of defending Texas, but how annexing New Mexico and Arizona would improve the situation.

Sibley presented his plan to the Southern president in July: after raising a force at San Antonio, he would march six hundred miles across the Texas Hill Country, the Edwards Plateau, and the Chihuahuan Desert to El Paso, settling in at Fort Bliss. Already a small rebel force, the Second Texas Mounted Rifles under Lieutenant Colonel John R. Baylor had dashed into El Paso, linked up with Arizona Confederates, and defeated a small Union force; Sibley proposed to vastly expand upon Baylor's initial success.

With a brigade of twenty-five hundred men, he would then move north up the Rio Grande into New Mexico before striking west. The detour would be necessary because supply lines to El Paso would have already been stretched and nearly exhausted; Sibley's entire strategy depended upon seizing supplies from his Union enemies to keep his force headed westward to California. Despite the huge risk of depending upon the enemy for supplies, Davis reasoned that it could work: it had taken only sixteen hundred soldiers to capture Santa Fe in 1846, after all.

Davis approved the expedition and gave Sibley command of the Confederate Army of New Mexico. But not everyone shared their optimism. The march up the Rio Grande had been fraught with danger for centuries; with burning desert on either side of the river and Apache lurking along its banks, the Spanish had named this track northward the Jornada del Muerto, or Journey of Death, for good reason.

Sibley had his work cut out for him. Governor Edward Clark was slow to provide troops. Texans worried about sending so many military units out west since they feared an invasion from the sea; they were hurriedly reinforcing shore batteries. Sibley went about scratching up troops for his brigade where he could, drilling them in the San Antonio sun.

IN 1863, SIBLEY retraced Oñate's route and crossed from Texas into New Mexico with twenty-five hundred men, leading his troops north along the Rio Grande and approaching the Union post at Fort Craig, 105 miles upriver from present-day Las Cruces. Taking Fort Craig was critical to Sibley's strategy; it was essential to capture Union supply routes before heading across the arid Southwest.

Seeing that Fort Craig was too heavily defended for a successful frontal assault, on February 13, Sibley deployed his forces in a line along the sandy west bank of the river, in the hope of luring the enemy from the stronghold. Three days passed, yet the Union colonel Edward Canby refused to take the bait. He distrusted his two thousand New Mexico volunteers, who were arrayed alongside a handful of Colorado volunteers and twelve hundred regulars. The colonel was reluctant to test them.

Confederate provisions had already started running low, and Sibley realized he could not simply outwait his Union foes. On February 18 he ordered his forces to ford the river, deploy on the east bank, and move six miles upriver toward Valverde, in a bid to cut off Canby from Union forces at Santa Fe.

A game of cat and mouse unfolded. Canby had correctly figured that the Confederates would take up the positions at Valverde, so as the rebels moved artillery to the high ground in order to bombard Fort Craig, the Union commander cut them off from the Rio Grande, their only source of water. Canby was a meticulous, by-the-books officer. General Ulysses S. Grant would later pay him the backhanded compliment of being "deliberate in all his work" and "an exceedingly modest soldier." His caution would prove both a blessing and a liability.

At 5:30 a.m. on the morning of February 21, a 180-man rebel scouting party conducted a reconnaissance down to the river. Retrieving water and spotting no enemy, they reported back that the area was free of Union forces. But as they withdrew toward the desert two hours later, they spotted them: Union cavalry in the woods downstream. Soon Union infantry, cavalry, and artillery arrived on the scene, and the air was pierced by the noise of a fierce duel that lasted through the afternoon.

Sibley spent those hours intoxicated, and a subordinate commander, Colonel Thomas Green, took control. With his soldiers thirsty and cut off from water, Green ordered a lancer charge into Union lines; an experienced Colorado militia company cut them down, killing or wounding twenty troopers and decimating the horses. At 4 p.m., with the outcome in his hands, the overly cautious Canby shied away from a frontal assault and ordered an attack on the center and left of the rebel lines.

The Confederate counterattack failed, but Green saw his opportunity and ordered three waves of 750 men total into a desperate attack. "Boys," Green shouted, "I want Colonel Canby's guns! When I yell, raise the rebel yell and follow me!" Desperate with thirst and needing to break through to the Rio Grande, screaming at the top of their lungs, the three waves of soldiers armed with pistols and shotguns fell upon the Union lines; the shock broke the back of the supporting forces protecting the artillery.

"Old Chas" Canby was the first to see the Confederate onslaught.

Wheeling on his horse, Canby tried to muster counteroffensives, riding up and down the river and rallying his commanders. But soon a semicircle of Texans, nearly half a mile long, was running through the lengthening shadows toward the Union battery. As the Texans closed, the battery, in the dense thicket, became impossible to defend.

Proving Canby's hunch, his New Mexico volunteers buckled and fled. Some Union troops followed, but the artillerymen stood and fought, blowing up their remaining ammunition before descending into the gore of hand-to-hand combat. The result was nearly three hundred Union troops dead or wounded; a single infantry company sustained a 71 percent casualty rate. Canby ordered a covering force to the north and withdrew to Fort Craig.

Green knew his Confederates had bled much that day—229 casualties, or a 10 percent casualty rate—and so decided not to pursue; he also agreed to a two-day truce, at the request of two Union officers under a white flag. The next day, Sibley and Green surveyed the situation and decided that attacking Fort Craig was now impossible. What might have been a Confederate rout turned into a Pyrrhic victory: Sibley won on the battlefield, but his dream of breaking through the Union lines and capturing vast stretches of the American Southwest was doomed.

The Confederates remained encamped on the battlefield, but there was no strategic victory. Canby and the Union survivors remained inside the walls of Fort Craig with their supplies. Sibley, meanwhile, was cut off from resupply from Texas. His hobbled forces resumed their march north, having not only failed to capture Union supplies but also endangered their own supply train, losing 160 mules and uncounted horses in the fighting. A stab at Santa Fe was their only hope before turning west toward California. To add to the sting, Canby sent the New Mexico militia to harass the Confederates as they pressed onward.

Sibley, according to one officer, was "heartily despised by every man in the brigade for his want of feeling, poor generalship, and cowardice." The bottle would remain his chief aide-de-camp as his troops plunged north, not west, into the bitter New Mexico winter instead of the warm California sunshine.

ON THE COLD New Mexico morning of March 28, 1863, Union colonel John P. Slough rode with his cavalry down the ruts of the old Santa Fe Trail. Like their commanding officer, his force of a thousand troops was not battle-tested, but the soldiers were well-rested, well-equipped, and well-fed, and the Colorado volunteers among them in particular were itching for a fight. Trailing the defending Union force was its wagon train, loaded with provisions and ammunition—indeed, wagon trains and supplies were what the fight here in northern New Mexico Territory was all about.

Coming up the trail, Confederate lieutenant colonel William R. Scurry led a nearly identical number of men through the predawn darkness: a weary, hungry, exhausted invasion force that would gamble everything here in the high desert. If they won, they could attack nearby Fort Union and gain needed supplies. But the Texans were ragged from battle farther south and unused to the bone-chilling, arid cold. Many of their officers were undisciplined, and Sibley, their commander, was drunk most of the time in Albuquerque.

More than a year before the titanic clash at Gettysburg—the high-water mark of the South's attempts to invade the Union in the East—the Confederate tide was now cresting in the West. In Tennessee, the bloody Battle of Shiloh, a Union victory, would unfold in just a few days. And here, where the high desert met the Sangre de Cristo Mountains and the high plains, the ambitious Southern strategy of invading the American Southwest and capturing California's gold, as well as its ports, would be put to the test.

No army since Hannibal's had passed the test Sibley had devised: surviving thousands of miles from home with little to no logistical train, with his troops fighting both the enemy and the elements. At 9:30 a.m. on March 28, the Union field commander, Slough, divided his force.

Slough quickly found himself in trouble: he encountered the enemy farther up the road than he expected, much closer to his base at Pigeon's Ranch than the Confederate encampment at Johnson's Ranch. Confusion reigned on both sides, but as the morning wore on, the Union commander pressed one clear advantage: his seven artillery pieces to the Texans' three. Seizing the initiative, ninety Colorado volunteers crouched and ran up the arroyo. Spotting them, the Texans fixed their bayonets, and a bloodbath ensued. The two sides fought at close range with revolvers, bowie knives, and shotguns. One Texan beat a Coloradan to death with his rifle.

Now, with the artillery advantage nullified by the proximity of the two sides, the ragged Texans were pressing the advantage, shoving the Union troops up the muddy arroyo. The Union forces finally broke ranks at Pigeon's Ranch, where they had begun, and Slough ordered a withdrawal to nearby Kozlowski's Ranch, an ideal place to make a stand. But while he was ceding ground, Slough was also building up a new advantage: through his steady withdrawals, the Union commander was frustrating and taxing the desperate Confederates, who needed to engage and win in order to move on Fort Union.

Meanwhile, the Union colonel Chivington was leading a flanking force that had missed the entire furious battle that day but had spotted the entire unprotected Confederate wagon train at Johnson's Ranch. There were thousands of animals and over eighty wagons, protected by a handful of artillerymen: the dwindling life-blood of the Texan invasion and the very belly of the entire army.

They quickly captured the Confederate artillery piece and scattered the handful of defenders. After setting fire to a few wagons containing clothing, Mexican blankets, food, ammunition, guns, camp equipment, and medicine, they placed powder kegs along all eighty of them and blew them to bits, one by one.

As word of the attack on what remained of their supplies spread among the Texans, they realized that regardless of the outcome against Slough, they were defeated. "Here we are," said one soldier, Bill Davidson, "1,000 miles from home, not a wagon, a dust of flour, not a pound of meat." Over 270 men lay dead, nearly evenly divided between blue and gray in the Battle of Glorieta Pass, but the Confederates' morale was crushed. They headed into undefended Santa Fe, scrounging for food and shelter. There, Sibley made a rare appearance and wrote a grandiose report to Richmond, claiming victory on the battlefield and asking for more troops. None came.

On April 17, 1862, Sibley finally ordered a full retreat: the surviving men would leave with only rifles, ammunition, and what each could carry on his back. One week's rations were packed onto the remaining mules; everything else was burned or abandoned, including the wounded, left to their own devices under a hospital flag.

The Texans headed southwest toward the Magdalena Mountains, crossing increasingly difficult terrain—freezing in the cold, dying of smallpox and pneumonia, and stalked by starvation. The reluctance of General Canby to shed more blood was all that stood between Sibley's tortured retreat and the outright destruction of what was left of his army. Harassed by the Apache, who even poisoned the water ahead by stuffing wells with dead animals, the survivors crossed blistering West Texas in the summer and reached San Antonio, where they had begun their quest, just as autumn approached. The *Austin State Gazette* called the entire invasion of the far West "a grand failure."

"I saw that gallant force march away, with drums beating and flags flying, and every man, from the general downwards, confident of victory," said one San Antonio resident, R. H. Williams. "[Then] I saw the first detachment of the remnant come straggling back on foot, broken, disorganized and in an altogether deplorable condition."

The return of Sibley's shattered brigade sent shivers down the spines of the people who lined the streets of San Antonio. The heady rush to secession and war now turned on what had meant destruction at Glorieta: the Union army, vastly better supplied, nearly countless in number, and equipped by mighty industry. Confederate ambition now revealed itself as mere audacity.

His reputation destroyed, Sibley was among the returning stragglers. Having lost 1,000 of the 3,200 men under his command equally to imprisonment and death, he was quickly stripped of his command and would never lead men again.[6] His only remaining battle was a losing one with the bottle—all because of that colossal, foolhardy invasion of that wild land, El Paso and the Southwest.

THE EUROPEANS, NAMELY the French, had seized upon the turmoil in America. Yet matters were no better in Mexico. Indeed, they were far worse. On November 29, 1861, an initial landing force of twenty-five hundred French troops arrived off the coast of Veracruz, Mexico. Nearly forty thousand followed.[7] Spanish troops had already entered the port city, engaging in heavy fighting. England's Royal Navy was in the harbor too. The Europeans had come to collect. Under Mexico's new president, Benito Juárez, the first Indigenous president in all of the Americas, the government stopped paying interest on debt incurred by previous governments.

Mexico was exhausted from a four-year civil war, the War of Reform, and the treasury was empty. After a while, the British and Spanish withdrew their forces and peacefully negotiated with Juárez. A full-blooded Zapotec, Juárez had taught himself to read, become a lawyer—and, as president, was and remains the most beloved leader in Mexican history.[8] The upper classes and the Catholic Church hated him for it.

The French had other ideas. Napoleon III, nephew of the famous dictator, had his eye on the silver mines of Mexico and knew how unpopular Juárez was with Mexican conservatives. On April 16, 1862, the French issued an open appeal for the Mexican public to support them. A pair of towns fell to the French as they headed west, retracing the steps of Cortés more than three centuries earlier. Several cities and towns declared their allegiance, including the overrun port of Veracruz. Bound for Mexico City, the French first headed for Puebla. Once there, a combined force of Mexicans under Porfirio Díaz—a future president himself—and Ignacio Zaragoza, a Texas-born army officer, held off the French, repulsing them finally on May 5, 1862.[9] That day would forever be known for Mexican bravery against overwhelming odds: Cinco de Mayo.[10]

But the invasion was hardly over. Zaragoza died just after the battle, stricken by typhoid. The French started landing massive reinforcements at Veracruz, some thirty thousand troops streaming inland. Convulsed by the Civil War, the United States was powerless to do anything about a European takeover at its border. Washington concluded that it might secretly arm the Mexicans but need not do anything openly that would offend the French, who were also receiving diplomatic overtures from the Confederacy.[11] The last thing the United States needed was a French attempt to undo the Union navy's blockade of Southern ports, where piles of Southern cotton were going nowhere; even worse was the notion that France might arm the South.

The French army and its foreign legion were finding, just like the Americans before them, that predictions of concluding a short and glorious war were mirages in the Mexican countryside. Brutal fighting dragged on for months until Puebla finally fell, on May 17, 1863. In Mexico City, President Juárez knew what would happen next and evacuated the government north to El Paso. The French took Mexico City on July 10 and proclaimed the Second Mexican Empire, really just a client state of France. Napoleon III gave the throne to an out-of-work Austrian Hapsburg prince, Ferdinand Maximilian Josef Maria von Hapsburg-Lothringen, who had a little naval training and was married to Napoleon's second cousin, Charlotte.[12] As a boy, he'd been charming, undisciplined, and talented at the arts. As a man, he had been passed over, by his own father, for the imperial throne in favor of his brother, Joseph. He and Charlotte were living in Trieste when he got the offer from Paris; aimless and pressured by Charlotte, who was the daughter of the Belgian king, Leopold I, he said yes. The imperial couple arrived in Mexico City in 1864.[13]

Meanwhile, the Mexicans fought like hell in massed, formal battle, and—again—as guerrillas. From El Paso, still in Mexico, Juárez personally directed the Mexican resistance against the French; the two sides fought an astonishing twelve hundred battles, from Veracruz to Acapulco and from Monterrey to Oaxaca.[14] The US Army began "losing" weapons shipments in El Paso; they were secretly being slipped to the Juárez government for use against the French.

Maximilian and Charlotte, known now as Maximiliano and Carlotta, lived lavishly at Chapultepec Castle, the old military academy, with a sweeping view of the Valley of Mexico. He ordered a grand new avenue cleared so he could see his entire capital without obstruction and acquired a country home near Cuernavaca.[15] On October 5, he issued the Black Decree, ordering military courts to condemn any armed Mexican to death. That meant any Mexican soldier captured in battle would be executed, and thousands lost their lives to French firing squads. The French turned a force north to capture Chihuahua—and the Mexican provisional capital of El Paso.

Chapter Ten

THE SEVENTH CIRCLE, 1863–80

YET ANOTHER ARMY converged on El Paso in 1862: the California Column of the US Army marched nine hundred miles east across the blazing deserts of their home state, present-day Arizona, and New Mexico during the peak of summer, arriving in August.

The force of twenty-five hundred men included infantry, cavalry, and artillery, and they were disciplined and capable. They crossed, wisely, in small groups, so as not to exhaust wells and waterholes. The army had stashed grain in mailboxes along the Butterfield stage line before the war. Troops and horses alike lived off that and whatever the land might yield. They fought two skirmishes along the way, but it wasn't just Confederate troops they would encounter.

The Apache leader Mangas Coloradas had combined his forces with those of his western counterpart, Cochise, who was also his son-in-law. Both men had suffered at the hands of the Americans, and that had changed their minds about war. Back in 1861, a rancher's son had gone missing. Cochise initially cooperated in the investigation, as his people were not in possession of the boy; he didn't know that another band, the Tonto Apache, had snatched him. Cochise went to meet with Lieutenant General George Bascom about the matter, bringing his wife, two children, his brother, and two nephews.[1] It was a trap: Bascom meant to capture Cochise, who slashed a hole in the tent, escaping alone through a hail of bullets. On February 5, Cochise sent a message asking for his family's release; Bascom refused. He wanted the boy. So Cochise went to war; his warriors attacked Mexican and American teamsters. They tortured and killed the nine Mexicans and took the Americans hostage, but there was still no deal, so Cochise's band attacked troops fetching water. In the end, the army released his wife and children—but hanged his brother and both nephews right there at Apache Pass.

As for Mangas, he had been taken captive by miners at Pinos Altos and tortured. His opinion of the Americans resembled that of his son-in-law. Together they forged an alliance to raise large forces of warriors, and they raised all hell, especially at Cooke's Valley below Cooke's Peak, a landmark for travelers and source of precious fresh water at its spring. The Apache made off with hundreds of head of cattle and sheep; they also tortured and killed Mexican herders, wiping out a hundred Americans and Mexicans in 1861.

Now the combined Apache force prepared stone breastworks for protection so they could fire on approaching Union troops. When an initial detachment, led by Captain Thomas L. Roberts, was two-thirds of the way through the pass on July 15, the Apache opened fire with deadly accuracy, some of them from the nearly point-blank range of barely thirty yards. Roberts's force of just over a hundred men was outnumbered by an Apache force of five hundred, so he quickly retreated to the mouth of the canyon and the open desert. Then Roberts advanced again—this time with the big guns up front. Two M1841 howitzers opened up on the Apache positions.[2]

Iron rained down as the guns fired nine-pound cannonballs from eight hundred yards. Under constant rifle fire, Roberts advanced the guns even closer, adjusting fire upward. Mangas was hit in the chest by the infantry's rifle fire. The Apache wouldn't budge until night fell, when they slipped away. They carried Mangas 150 miles to the Mexican town of Janos, found the doctor, and informed him that if he didn't save their chief, they would kill everyone in the town.

The next morning, the troopers found sixty-six Apache killed, while they had lost only two men. The soldiers also discovered nine dead civilians, killed by the Apache before the fight even started. The Battle of Apache Pass was the first time the US Army used artillery against Native Americans, and it had worked.

The main force left behind an infantry unit to build a fort and proceeded eastward. What lingered from the fight was not just the clever and deadly use of artillery by the California Column, but the instructions its commander carried with him. Like other Union commanders in the area, Colonel James H. Carleton was not only authorized but ordered to kill any Apache or Diné he found—on sight.[3]

The huge California Column entered American El Paso on August 20, 1862, and took up positions at the new Fort Bliss, while Carleton became military governor of New Mexico. The Civil War was effectively over in the Southwest by 1863, but there were scores to be settled between the locals, for sure. As for the US Army, it had other business: namely, genocide.

ON THE OTHER side of the Rio Grande, the Imperial Army seized Chihuahua but was turned back when it marched on El Paso. After settling into guerrilla warfare, ambushes, and nighttime attacks, the Republican forces under Juárez had to mix up their tactics against the French, who had pressed increasing numbers of Mexicans into their service. The number of French, Mexican, Belgian, and Austrian combatants fighting for the empire in Mexico soared to sixty-four thousand in 1865. The Imperial Army created a special counter-guerrilla unit.[4] Despite the skilled and brave fighting of the Republicans, Juárez controlled only a patch of the far north around El Paso, and his remaining army there numbered just three hundred. The future looked bleak.

But across the world, Napoleon III was increasingly worried about another European war in the offing, so he ordered French forces to withdraw from Mexico in three phases; Maximilian would be left with only Mexican conscripts and Austrian and Belgian troops. Maximilian's Black Decree had turned much of the civilian population against him and his empire. Mexican generals in America were pleading for help, and Juárez's chief emissary in Washington was arguing that the French would attempt to seize Texas and Louisiana. As the American Civil War drew to an end, the Mexicans recruited American soldiers to fight the French, offering generous pay and guarantees of free land; they even enlisted Ulysses S. Grant to help them organize an American expeditionary force and select a commander. After the assassination of President Lincoln in 1865, with the Civil War settled, President Andrew Johnson convened the cabinet, but his secretary of state, William H. Seward, sabotaged the idea of intervention. Officially, the United States remained neutral; nevertheless, guns flowed, particularly from California to El Paso, and they mysteriously disappeared even as they were shipped to Fort Bliss on the other side of the river. Of course, they wound up in the hands of Juárez's army.[5]

As the French withdrew, Juárez seized back the country bit by bit. Several thousand gringos crossed the Rio Grande and joined his army. Captains and lieutenants joined up. A private from the California Volunteers, F. J. Cassil, enlisted as did a surgeon, writing, "I have always had a lively interest in the fate of our sister republic ever since the Frenchman's foot ever polluted her soil."

On March 24, 1866, Mexican forces fought at Chihuahua under the command of a man who would become pivotal and powerful in the region: Luis Terrazas. He began the assault at 9 a.m., avoiding a cannonade out of concern for the cathedral. By 11 a.m., the Imperial forces surrendered. Some seven thousand men reinforced the city after an overland march from the Sea of Cortez; they were a mix of Americans and Mexicans—professional soldiers, adventurers, and miners from played-out gold and silver camps. Saltillo, Monterrey, and San Luis Potosi fell to the Republican forces. The tide was turning; over a hundred thousand men left the United States to fight the French. Colonel George Mason commanded an entirely American unit, the American Legion of Honor, stationed alongside Juárez in Mexican El Paso.

From Europe, Napoleon and Carlotta were urging Maximilian to get out of Mexico in 1866. He refused. Three armies of the Republic converged on the southern city of Querétaro on March 6, 1867; in the vanguard was the American Legion. Maximilian had concentrated most of his troops, nine thousand men, at Querétaro, but they faced over thirty-two thousand, and ten thousand reinforcements were en route. Juárez's forces laid siege. Their plan was simple: encircle the city, smash it with artillery, and starve the French out.[6] After all, Maximilian himself was inside. On May 14, 1867, after two grueling months of starvation and bombardment, the city fell; only half the Imperial force made it out alive, and Maximilian himself came out waving a white flag. Juárez's forces descended upon Mexico City, which fell immediately. Finally, with Maximilian and his generals imprisoned at Querétaro, Juárez proceeded to restore the Republic.

The war with France was over. Five years of conflict had involved soldiers from Mexico, France, the United States, Austria, Belgium, Poland, and Egypt. Confederates had crossed the border too, to fight for the empire. At least thirty-two thousand Mexican troops were dead, with more than eight thousand wounded, thirty-three thousand imprisoned, and eleven thousand executed. Some fourteen thousand Imperial troops had died;[7] to say the least, the Mexican venture was a costly distraction for Napoleon III.

But it was even more costly for Maximilian. Quite a few of the Americans decided to pay the former emperor a visit. The Mexican president had issued an important decree early in the war: a death warrant for Maximilian. In Paris, Carlotta pleaded with Napoleon to intervene. He refused, saying Maximilian had not done his job of pacifying and ruling Mexico. She went to Rome to beg the pope to intervene, but Piux IX too declined. Early in the morning of June 19, 1867, the Austrian archduke was led from his cell to the nearby Cerro de las Campanas, the Hill of Bells; he had already been condemned to death by a military tribunal under Juárez's decree. European governments pleaded for the Mexicans to spare him. Juárez refused.

An American officer commanded the backup firing squad. Maximilian spoke his final words in Spanish as the guns aimed squarely at him: "I forgive everyone and ask everyone to forgive me."

There would be no forgiveness that day; the Mexicans executed him there, on that barren hill, and carted his body to Mexico City to be put on display. The news didn't reach Paris until July 1, just as the Parisians and their emperor celebrated the opening of the Universal Exposition. The news shocked them, and it inspired Édouard Manet to create a series of haunting paintings depicting Maximilian's execution.

Carlotta, for her part, went mad. She lived out the rest of her days in an insane asylum.

THE WAR AGAINST France left an indelible imprint on the Mexican people. They had now defeated two great European powers—

Spain and France—leaving them with a great deal of patriotism, whatever the failings of their country's internal politics. Back in American El Paso, across the river from the former provisional capital of Mexican El Paso, the US Army began the task of stamping some order onto the wild country of the Mexican Cession. Not unlike the Union troops who occupied the South during Reconstruction, in this part of the country, the US Army was supposed to be the only law and order in town.

Troops poured into El Paso and the region around it; Fort Bliss moved farther east. The Fifth Infantry there was relieved by two companies of the 125th US Colored Troops: the so-called buffalo soldiers. Fort Bayard sprung up in the heart of Apache country. When the buffalo soldiers were moved to Santa Fe, two companies of the Thirty-Fifth Infantry arrived. Their job was to occupy American El Paso, which had become increasingly lawless and unruly. The fort was moved onto the property of Concordia, and more buffalo soldiers arrived.

The task across the region was twofold: put a foot on the neck of the local population and kill Native Americans. Troops organized and drilled militias of civilians, almost all of them with Mexican surnames, while the US Army fought the Mescalero Apache east of El Paso. Unlike the Mescalero in the heights of the nearby Sacramento Mountains, the Apache people from the Guadalupe Mountains attacked everything and everyone crossing West Texas to El Paso—including armed army supply wagons. Meanwhile, the army attacked a Jicarilla Apache and Ute settlement at Ojo Caliente, north of Santa Fe, killing six and driving over a hundred women and children out into the snow; they had to flee across the frigid river nearby. Horses were killed, and seventeen people froze to death.

Under orders from James Henry Carleton, the California Column commander and military governor, Kit Carson left Santa Fe with a force of volunteers and headed west.[8] In the dead of winter, on January 4, 1864, he launched a savage campaign against the Diné, also known as the Navajo. His men did not so much fight as conduct a scorched-earth campaign: burning out entire villages, killing livestock, and destroying crops, and in the process forcing eighty thousand Native Americans on the brink of starvation to march 340 miles to the Bosque Redondo, a forest of cottonwoods on the Pecos River at Fort Sumner.[9]

The Diné called it the Long Walk. Here is one account:

> It was said that those ancestors were on the Long Walk with their daughter, who was pregnant and about to give birth . . . the daughter got tired and weak and couldn't keep up with the others or go further because of her condition. So my ancestors asked the Army to hold up for a while and to let the woman give birth, but the soldiers wouldn't do it. They forced my people to move on, saying that they were getting behind the others. The soldier told the parents that they had to leave their daughter behind. "Your daughter is not going to survive, anyway; sooner or later she is going to die," they said in their own language. "Go ahead," the daughter said to her parents, "things might come out all right with me." But the poor thing was mistaken, my grandparents used to say. Not long after they had moved on, they heard a gunshot from where they had been a short time ago.[10]

Two hundred Diné people perished on the Long Walk; the survivors were herded into the Bosque on the Rio Grande. Ute scouts for the army snatched up Diné women and children to sell them into slavery to other tribes; the army did nothing. After all, Bosque Redondo was a concentration camp. Already the army had put hundreds of Mescalero Apache into the forest there. The Diné and the Mescalero had a lot of bad blood between them; the Mescalero raided Diné settlements all the time. There was little firewood or clean water; the river ran nearly dry in winter. The camp had originally been planned to hold five thousand people. Now there were twice that number. The corn was infested with worms, and the crop failed repeatedly.

For the army, Bosque Redondo was the first reservation west of Oklahoma. But even while spending $1.5 million a year on food, they couldn't keep the effectively imprisoned people fed. Smallpox broke out at the fort, and most of the Mescalero were infected. One out of four Diné people died at Bosque Redondo, some two thousand in all, buried in unmarked graves.

Finally the army gave up on removing the Diné and signed the Treaty of Bosque Redondo with Diné leaders. The treaty gave the Diné a reservation, today in northwestern New Mexico and northeastern Arizona, and obligated the United States to provide seeds, farming tools, and schools; in exchange, the Diné would stop raiding.

It was the end of a little-understood American tragedy, comparable to the Trail of Tears. The US Army had committed a crime against humanity. On June 18, 1863, the Diné began another long walk—back to their homeland of soaring mesas and grand valleys.

FROM EL PASO, the California Column fanned out, namely to kill the Apache, deploying as far east as Fort Quitman, up the Rio Grande Valley, and to posts deep in Chiricahua country.

In 1862, Mangas had second thoughts about all this warfare and sent an intermediary to inquire about a treaty. But Carleton, the military governor, had other plans. Having imprisoned the Diné and nearly wiped out the Jicarilla Apache, he turned his attention to the Chiricahua and, just beyond them, the Western Apache. The plan was to remove them all from their homelands—in other words, "utter extermination." In addition to his troops, he called for civilians to arm themselves and assist the army, enlisting two hundred O'odham and Maricopa scouts and even calling for armed Mexicans to cross the border.

"Every effort must be made to have a general rising of both citizens and soldiers, on both sides of the line, against the Apaches," he wrote as he issued general orders. Government policy was to eliminate the Apache. The men were to be killed on sight. Villages and food were to be burned and destroyed. The combined force of troops and volunteers would strike out in every direction: from the string of forts up the Rio Grande all along the border to the Gila River. The first target was the Mescalero, who lived in the high forests of the Sacramento Mountains. In October 1862, troops overran a camp at Dog Canyon, killing fourteen Apache, including two of their leaders, and wounding twenty more. But the Californians, joined by mostly Hispanic volunteers from New Mexico, took note of both their orders and Kit Carson's savagery. The Californians destroyed homes and fields of corn. As many as three hundred Mescalero people died in the winter of 1862–63. A Mescalero leader, Cadette, found and confronted Carleton up in Santa Fe, saying: "We are worn out; we have no more heart, we have no provisions, no means to live. Your troops are everywhere."

To the west in Arizona, miners hunted and killed the Apache. The war there was deeply racial: whites claimed to be victims as Yavapai and Tonto raids fell upon them. Indeed, a mindset of victimization set in, as whites came to characterize the Apache as vile and not really human. An Arizona rancher named King Woolsey lured a large group of O'odham, Maricopa, and Western Apache to a meeting at his camp, where he furnished tobacco, clothing, and pinole, which is a mixture of ground maize, beans, and seeds. Then, on January 24, 1864, Woolsey's men shot to death as many as thirty-three Native Americans.

Carleton had his war of extermination. He issued General Order No. 1, calling for the army to attack all of the Mimbres Chiricahua. On January 18, 1863, he sent a unit with Brigadier General Rodman West to do just that.

West's men arrived at Fort McLane near present-day Bayard, New Mexico, where some of them mixed with gold miners at nearby Pinos Altos and raised a white flag, inviting Mangas to come into camp and talk peace. When Mangas and a dozen escorts entered, armed troops suddenly burst out from hiding and pointed their weapons at the Apache, taking all thirteen captive. They then released twelve men and kept Mangas, hauling him fifteen miles to the fort. One soldier remarked: "Mangas was the most magnificent specimen of savage manhood that I have ever seen." The far shorter army commander, West, looked up at the old warrior, now in his seventies, and said he had murdered his "last white victim." The general also said that he and his family would be imprisoned but treated well.

It was a lie.[11] West walked away and told his sentries: "I want him dead."

Mangas went into a makeshift cell and covered himself with a blanket against the cold of night. Around midnight, the sentries started stabbing him with bayonets heated by the fire. They seemed to enjoy watching the old warrior flinch at the searing pain caused by the hot blades as they stabbed at his feet and legs.

Then they shot Mangas Coloradas to death. They pitched him into a shallow grave, and then dug him up.

So they could cut off his head.

Which they boiled.

West, who ordered the murder, was rewarded: first with a star as a brigadier general, and second by election to the position of US senator from Louisiana. He had ordered the illegal execution of a prisoner, considered a war crime today. Even in the 1860s, the conduct of the US Army in the Southwest might well have been judged a series of crimes; President Lincoln himself had general orders drawn up regarding wartime conduct, which became the predicate of the Geneva Conventions. But the army chose not to apply those orders to Native Americans.

Unpopular with the civilian population, Carleton, for his part, lost his brevet star, was reduced to lieutenant colonel in the regular army, and was sent to the Fourth Cavalry Regiment in San Antonio. He died there at the age of fifty-nine, in 1873. For his actions, particularly against women, children, and the elderly, he was a war criminal, but his biggest crime—indeed, his legacy—was that the wars he set in motion raged on and on. As the historian Janne Lahti put it: "The United States was chronically troubled by a fragile and unstable collective identity in need of constant securing and defining in the face of immigration, the vexed question of slavery and secessionism."[12]

THE AMERICAN POLICY of outright extermination of the Apache was determinate in forging a new American identity in the wake of the Civil War. The Apache largely refused the fate of life on a government reservation. Instead, the Apache fought back. Shocked and enraged, the Chiricahua, in particular, elevated a new man as their leader: Geronimo. Cochise struck American and Mexican settlements alike from his base in the rugged Dragoon Mountains, while Carson fought the Plains Apache in Texas. Mexican troops crossed the border to attack the Apache; an all-out war against the Yavapai broke out as civilian Americans and Mexicans, troops, and other Native Americans tried to wipe them out, massacring 150 men, women, and children on April 30, 1871. They then scalped all the dead and sold twenty-two children into slavery in Mexico.[13]

In 1872, now seventy years old, Cochise made peace in exchange for a tiny reservation in the Chiricahua Mountains, a rugged sky island of natural beauty gazing out over the vast desert.[14] The great chief died two years later, and his people buried him high in the rocks of the mountains, at a favorite campsite. Many then left to join the Mescalero in their sacred mountains, the Sacramento Range, which afforded more room. Geronimo, however, grimly hung on.

The longest American war did not take place in Afghanistan in the early twenty-first century.[15] It raged across Apacheria for nearly four decades.[16] While American history has chronicled—accurately and otherwise—the wars against the Plains peoples, most of the engagements of the Indian Wars were actually fought in the American Southwest. Yet despite having thousands of men, weapons, artillery, horses, and civilians in the field, the army killed only between six and nine hundred Apache over the course of decades. To be blunt, the Spanish and the Mexicans killed more Apache in less time than the Americans did, while brokering long, if tenuous, periods of peace. The American approach was blundering, excessive only in its cruelty.

The official US Army history of the Indian Wars concedes that

> The Apaches were among the Army's toughest opponents in the Indian wars. The zone of operations embraced the territories of Arizona and New Mexico, western Texas, and Mexico's northern provinces, and, despite the fact that hostile Apaches were relatively few in number and the theater was essentially a secondary one, they tied down sizable forces over a long period of time.[17]

What the army did accomplish was inflicting mass suffering on civilian noncombatants: women, children, and the elderly. For every warrior life taken, whole families suffered. The loss of any family member put lives at stake in the wild, but warriors also brought home food and other goods, and they hunted game. The entire population of all Native Americans in the United States in this period never hovered far above three hundred thousand, and the various bands of Apache likely never exceeded ten thousand after the American invasion of the Southwest. They did not merely endure the tragedy of loss, but they saw their odds of long-term survival fall.

Though Apache life was shattered, the Mescalero, Ojo Caliente, Chiricahua, and Western Apache survived as a people—if barely. The Mescalero and White Mountain reservations are beautiful, rich places, with red buttes, pine forests, and long valleys thick with grass, where their ponies still roam alongside wild mustangs. The Apache Wars were a horrible and shameful period of American history; indeed, the army's ability to get the Apache to turn on one another as scouts is a sad chapter. But the Apache people are a testament to human endurance: they escaped extinction.

THE US ARMY failed miserably in pacifying the Southwest by subduing Native Americans. Life in garrison for the troops was filled with manual labor, alcohol abuse, and disease from often filthy conditions. Regular soldiers had no physical training regimen, and the army performed poorly at best. After all, few tribes in the Southwest risked outright extermination over confinement to reservations and death camps like Bosque Redondo. A war that ground on for nearly forty years cannot be considered a victory—other than a Pyrrhic one. It's not winning, it's just trying not to lose.

If a secondary goal was to bring American law and order to bear on citizens, many of whom had been citizens of another nation, the army's occupation of the Southwest was an abject failure here too. Carleton, the military governor, was as ham-handed with the civilian population as he was with the Native Americans. Justice was rare, and when it did make an appearance, it was often arbitrary. Meanwhile, there was no order: the cycle of violence unleashed by enlisting civilians in the fight against the Apache, combined with refusing to bargain with them as the Mexicans and the Spanish had, destabilized the entire region for decades.

As a result, the people took the law—or rather, the violence— into their own hands. The practice of taking captives spread like wildfire. Americans, Mexicans, and Native Americans all captured one another and enslaved their captives. In fact, the biggest captive-slaver around was none other than the US Army. Carleton himself delivered a six-year-old Diné girl to the convent in El Paso; utterly traumatized, she was christened Maria and raised by an Italian nun. Geronimo's cousin, Nah-thle-ta, was captured by Mexicans and sold to a family in Santa Fe. The army would go in search of whites taken captive, but not Hispanic people in the same predicament. A woman seized by comancheros—gangs of Hispanics, Native people, and even gringos who traded and stole—was eventually deposited in El Paso, a tragic wreck of a human being. There was so much slavery going on in the Southwest that Congress had to specifically outlaw it.

America had seized the Southwest but couldn't control it. Instead, it helped spark a period of historic violence and misery. "A common thread that weaves the stories of all the captives together is race—one racial group attacking another. Many innocent people were simply trying to live their ordinary lives when another group decided it was justifiable to use violence to rob, beat, murder, kidnap, sometimes mutilate and enslave others and their loved ones," Noel Marie Fletcher wrote in *Captives of the Southwest.*

The last of the California Column mustered out in 1867, just as Civil War retributions among the gringos mounted. In their place came many others. As the army reshuffled and reorganized units, it fashioned four regiments of African American troops, many of them veterans of the Civil War: the Ninth and Tenth Cavalry and the Twenty-Fourth and Twenty-Fifth Infantry. The army sent these troopers to perform the toughest duties in the most violent places: as far down as the Lower Rio Grande Valley, and to Fort Bliss, in El Paso, and the network of little forts strung north, south, east, and west.

The Union army found out that Hugh Stephenson had supported the Confederacy financially by buying war bonds and seized his Texas property, including Concordia. He remained at La Mesa, but Mills, the Unionist, purchased the seized properties at the army auction and returned them both to the original gringo, it seems. Yet Stephenson took ill and died on the farm at La Mesa on October 11, 1870. Magoffin dashed to El Paso on the first stage-coach after the war and found his grand hacienda demolished by flooding. Moreover, he was not welcome in El Paso; he did not have a pardon, and now could get one only from the president of the United States. His petitions fell on deaf ears and, suffering from edema—perhaps the result of heart failure—he died in San Antonio in 1868.[18] Simeon Hart had once yelled at Mills at the outbreak of the Civil War: "Champagne for the secessionists and the noose for Unionists!" During the war, Hart seized the assets of Mills; now the tables were turned, and Hart died in 1874.[19]

In 1877, yet another war broke out: over salt. Much as James Magoffin had tried to corner the salt market in 1854, the Texan Charles Howard tried also to lay claim, this time with the massive salt deposits at the base of the Guadalupe Mountains to the east. *Salineros* of Mexican origin from San Elizario had always collected salt there, and the controversy quickly fell out along racial lines. Two of these Mexicans, José Mariá Juárez and Macedonia Gandara, went off to collect salt from the dry lake bed. A Virginian by birth, Howard hired a local lawyer, Albert Jennings Fountain, and sent the sheriff—who, with the collapse that year of the local government, was in his pocket—to arrest them. But the *salineros* had other ideas.

They grabbed Howard and held him hostage for three days in exchange for $12,000 and a guarantee of free salt. Howard, in turn, went back to El Paso and gunned down one of his local opponents. The largely Mexican American population flew into a rage. Twenty Texas Rangers arrived—and were promptly captured. It was the first and only time the Texas Rangers ever surrendered. The *salineros* executed three of them after a two-day siege, then dumped their bodies down a well. Part of San Elizario was destroyed; the town officials fled into Mexico, and the US Army sent its Black troops—buffalo soldiers of the Ninth Cavalry—to quell the fighting. In the end, twelve people were killed, fifty were wounded, and the fighting left $1 million in property damage as African American soldiers fought Mexican Americans.

The Americans had now infected the Southwest with a disease at least as bad as the smallpox the Europeans had brought: racism.

That hatred convulsed dangerously in all directions. Though the buffalo soldiers fought pitched battles out in the desert, flat-hatting across the creosote with rifles up, their ponies lathered and straining, the surge of new American whites to El Paso despised them. Indeed, the Blacks were often banned from El Paso, while the white officers and their genteel wives were entertained lavishly. In more remote frontier posts they often found greater acceptance among Mexican Americans and married into their families. Once their enlistment was up, more than a few stayed, settling in and around El Paso.

Yet with racial division, there was no law, only lawlessness and revenge. Anglo-American squatters stole millions of acres of land as state and territorial governments from Texas to California either dallied or simply ruled against Mexican Americans. While some of their ownership was documented, the promise by the United States in the Treaty of Guadalupe Hidalgo was broken. An untold number of Mexican Americans lost their lands because, having been thrown off them, they couldn't earn a living, so they couldn't pay their taxes. Outraged at the Camp Grant Massacre in Arizona, President Ulysses S. Grant demanded that the governor do something. He did, and when an all-white jury ended its work, all one hundred white defendants were found not guilty.[20]

The memories of the Salt War still glowed like the embers of a campfire.[21] No one was ever arrested nor brought to trial, despite a congressional investigation,[22] but San Elizario was stripped of its power as the county seat. Mexican Americans were not averse to taking matters into their own hands, either. Many years later, Howard's lawyer, Albert Jennings Fountain, crossed the desert basin from Lincoln County headed for Mesilla, near Tularosa, with his eight-year-old son, Henry. Two horsemen trailed in the distance. Then a third followed.

Fountain and his son were never seen again.

IN THE REMAINING years of the nineteenth century, the US Army changed strategies against the Apache: the formerly broad, unlimited conflict, pitching civilians against warriors, women, and children, became a shrewdly targeted, if still vicious, anti-insurgency war, often fought by Black cavalry and infantry. This was a lesson that would prove important, if still imperfect, to the army: negotiating while fighting. In territorial terms, the various Apache people were losing, being driven ever more tightly into reservations and off the lands they'd once roamed freely. The man chosen to finish the job was Brigadier General George S. Crook, skilled at both talking and fighting, diplomacy and war. He commanded all of Arizona but the Sixth Cavalry to the east in New Mexico.

With the death of Mangas, a new leader emerged among the Mimbreños and Warm Springs Apache: Victorio.[23] A square-faced, stern man born about a hundred miles north of El Paso, he had fought and raided with Mangas, as well as with Geronimo and Nana, two other rising leaders. To many students of Apache history, Victorio was as great a leader as Mangas Coloradas—or even greater.

In 1877, he accepted an offer from the United States to lay down his arms in exchange for a reservation in Ojo Caliente, New Mexico, the very heart of his people's home range. With three hundred people, he went to plots of land near Tularosa to await the opening of the reservation. Almost no sooner had they arrived, in August of that year, than they were ordered to march three hundred miles west to San Carlos: a reservation overcrowded with feuding bands of Apache. Its land was nearly impossible to farm, yielding half-ripe crops, and disease was rampant there. Nevertheless, the Apache made the march, their own reenactment of the Diné Long Walk. After three months at San Carlos, deep in misery and on the verge of starvation, Victorio and hundreds of people jumped the reservation.

For three years they plundered, raided, and pillaged all around El Paso, as far east as Fort Davis and occasionally into Mexico. No one could catch Victorio, and the job fell to the buffalo soldiers of the Ninth Cavalry, who employed new tactics. Instead of giving chase, they anticipated where the enemy might appear next, and there they waited in ambush. The all-Black Tenth Cavalry joined the fight; its white officers were a new breed, different from the blunderers of the California Column. The commander of the Ninth, Edward Hatch, was a brevet major general who'd risen from Civil War private to military governor of New Mexico. The man who led the Tenth, Benjamin Henry Grierson, had commanded an astonishing cavalry attack on Confederate troops in Mississippi and then fallen in love with the harsh beauty of West Texas.[24] He personally organized the Tenth, though many in the army looked down on a white officer who would lead Black troops.

By now, three thousand Chiricahua remained: an eastern band of Chihenne from the Rio Grande to the Mimbres River; the Bedon-kohe in the high Mogollon country; the Chokonen in Chihuahua and the Dragoon Mountains of Arizona; and the Nednhi in Sonora. To the east, the Mescalero people took in exiled Lipan Apache from Texas, numbering as many as twenty-five hundred altogether, and the Western Apache in Arizona numbered up to sixty-five hundred. But these people could be divided against the Chiricahua in return for favorable reservations and jobs as scouts: hunting their fellow Apache for the US Army.[25]

In July 1880, the two commands joined together out of Texas and New Mexico to hunt Victorio. The all-Black cavalry troopers ambushed him at the base of the Guadalupe Mountains, but after a three-hour fight, he and his Apache band escaped. They headed up into the Black Range, a densely forested, steep mountain range north of El Paso, but another unit there under a young officer cut the Apache off from the few sources of water. Victorio turned south and disappeared, it seems, into Mexico. At this point, the US Army violated its peace treaty with Mexico, entering the country in hot pursuit, without prior notice. At one point, five thousand men hunted Victorio and the runaway Apache: soldiers, Texas Rangers, and the Mexican army itself, led by none other than Colonel Joaquin Terrazas, who had driven the French out of Chihuahua fifteen years earlier.

Victorio's natural inclination was to climb up into the Sierra Madre; these mountains would provide the elevation and natural obstacles from which to mount a defense. But Victorio thought again; he would hide in plain sight, on the flat Janos Plain near a lonely landmark known as Tres Castillos—Three Castles—which was nothing more than a few piles of rock in the desert.

The Mexicans advanced as the Apache built rock walls and fought from caves all night long on October 14, 1880. Then, apparently they ran out of ammunition. The Mexicans finished off the last Apache warrior at 10 a.m. the next day. All told, some sixty-two warriors lay dead, along with sixteen women and children. Their survivors disappeared into prison and then were sold into de facto slavery in Mexico.

The victor, Terrazas, solidified his claim on Chihuahua. Already his family owned the old Ascárate spread and silver-mining operation at Corralitos. Like Ascárate, members of his family, directly or through marriage, owned millions of acres, possessed vast fortunes, and occupied key military and political positions—including the governorship—nearly constantly.

Asked if he was from Chihuahua, the son, Luis Terrazas, famously responded, "No. Chihuahua is mine."[26]

The Apache Wars did not end, as contemporary American lore would have it, when Geronimo and his thirty or so Chiricahua surrendered in 1886; for all his undoubted skill and ferocity, Geronimo represented a symbol of political defiance far more than a military threat to the United States. In military terms, the Apache Wars ended on October 15, 1880, on the flat Chihuahuan Desert south of El Paso. After all those years, the Apache way of life was over—forever.

Chapter Eleven

THE NINTH CIRCLE, 1881–1900

THE FIRST TRANSCONTINENTAL railroad was completed in the high deserts of Utah in 1869, with the driving of a single golden spike at Promontory Point. The second approached from two directions, advancing on El Paso from the east and California from the west; it promised to revolutionize everything from warfare to trade and, of course, transportation. Entire fortunes and cities were springing up like wildflowers after the rain along the rail lines, and more workers were constantly needed to extend them. People from Chile, China, and Mexico streamed into Texas. Dallas and Fort Worth swelled from sleepy river crossings and army posts to booming cities. The city of Abilene didn't even exist until March 1881, with the arrival of the Texas and Pacific Railroad; to the west, the Southern Pacific Railroad had come to Tucson the year before. Crews pounded rails into the deserts of New Mexico and West Texas, and both lines would converge in El Paso, connecting the Pacific and the Atlantic. The northern route through Utah would fade in importance because of the impassable winter snows of the Sierras; the southern route would gain in importance, snow-free year-round, an easier route to the deep-water ports on the Pacific.

But for El Paso and the Southwest to function as a society, economically and otherwise, the chaos of the Southwest had to abate. The United States purported to offer immigrants and citizens alike not just economic opportunity but justice for all: fairness under the law and its foundation, the Constitution. Yet the local government of American El Paso simply collapsed in the late 1870s, and the lawlessness of the countryside gave rise to vicious territorial struggles between giant ranching interests: the range wars. In the city, the hordes of killers, gunfighters, gamblers, prostitutes, and heroin dealers that followed the railroad were bent on shaking every dollar they could from temporary workers and locals alike.

Because many of these characters were not Native Americans or Mexicans, but white Americans from back east, these dangerous people were glamorized in the pulp novels of their day and well into the history books that followed. But in truth, they were far from glamorous. There isn't much that's funny about women consigned to prostitution, yet later historians seemed to nearly chuckle at their so-called graces. The widespread use of opium—heroin—is not exotic and enticing, and gamblers got paid handsomely to fleece Chinese rail workers. Assassins roamed, often wearing badges, themselves both gunfighters and enforcers. Some were reckless, ruthless young killers, like one William H. Bonney of New York, whose innocuous nickname, Billy the Kid, belied his true nature. The romanticizing of this period has hidden its cruelties.

America had suffered an identity crisis in the years after the Civil War. Black people were free from enslavement and were en masse looking for a way to join American society. The South was decimated, the North was desperate to embrace the Gilded Age, and the West was up for grabs. European immigrants flooded seaports from Boston to Charleston; there were no immigration controls or checkpoints. Many headed west to the Appalachians—and then beyond, to Texas and California. There they found no singular American culture to grasp. For many, simply being white put them ahead of Mexicans, Blacks, and Native people in the pecking order of seg-regation and violence. Though conflict was ubiquitous—El Paso was literally becoming "The Gunfighter Capital of the World"—the time was coming for a reckoning. Matters needed to be settled by law, and yes, even by force.

Up in the little mining town of Socorro, New Mexico, the *Chieftain* newspaper summed up the situation in El Paso succinctly: "Hell."

FOR THIRTY YEARS, the contagion of violence that broke out with the American conquest of its new Southwest had infected American El Paso.

In 1858, "Clown" Garner, a gold miner, swaggered about town, claiming he was going to have a big time by "killin' a Dutchman" that night. Later, he stumbled into Ben Dowell's saloon, downed a dozen brandies, and groused that he still could not get drunk. Quite suddenly, Thomas Massie, a professional gambler from Missouri, pulled a pistol on Samuel Schutz, a German Jewish immigrant, over the rent on a house, exclaiming, "Mr. Schutz, you told a damned lie!"[1]

Schutz let out a guttural cry and grabbed the barrel of the gun, struggling with Massie. Both men were strong. W. W. Mills, the Indiana Unionist, stepped up and demanded of the other men in the room, "Gentlemen, would you see the man murdered?"[2]

Yet no one moved a muscle. Unable to bear his pistol on Schutz, the gambler drew a knife and shoved it into his shoulder. Schutz stumbled out the door into the street, as Massie fired and missed; Massie fled, and Schutz lived. The next day, Dowell, the barkeep, told Mills, the newcomer: "My young friend, when you see anything of that kind going on in El Paso, don't interfere. It is not considered good manners here."[3]

That anecdote hung in the air for decades as a simple code for survival: look the other way. Over the years, the story gained currency in both local lore and history as a kind of tough man's street wisdom, when in fact, Mills was morally right. Standing idly by while a man is murdered—over rent he is owed—was reprehensible. That was not a lesson lost on Schutz's fellow immigrant, his young nephew Solomon, who had accompanied his uncles Joseph and Samuel from Westphalia before the Civil War.

Both of the older Schutz brothers had opposed secession and had to slip across the Rio Grande for a while, to avoid reprisals. Nevertheless, the Schutz men became successful merchants after the war and were instrumental in organizing Temple Mount Sinai, the first Jewish congregation in the El Paso region and one of the earliest in all of the American West. The Schutz brothers ran a store in an adobe building on San Francisco Street, and later Samuel built the city's first brick building. In 1880, Solomon took his turn at leadership and became postmaster.

The temple began to take shape not only because of the efforts of its future Jewish congregants, but with the help of Christian ones too: the Presbyterians and Methodists took up collections for their Jewish neighbors when the hat was passed for a temple building. They were part of the upper and middle classes of people who built homes in the heights, above the old Ponce ranch, corrals, and barracks, which were rapidly becoming storefronts down by the Rio Grande. Whatever their religion or denomination, this group of people took an interest in the restoration of law and order, which had collapsed in 1875 with the last municipal government. So in 1880, the youngest Schutz, Solomon, put himself up as a candidate for the city's restored office of mayor. He won.

Schutz was one of the first Jewish mayors elected in the United States;[4] only Portland, Oregon, could claim one elected earlier, in 1869.[5] El Paso also elected a Jewish alderman and installed its first

Jewish fire chief.[6] This group of Christians and Jews had a vested interest in stopping the lawlessness; El Paso was dangerous, dirty, and inhospitable to stable growth. They decisively put their support behind a simple ideal: the equality of all before the law, as it was embodied in the Constitution of the United States. They plowed political and financial capital not only into the restoration of government but also into public institutions, such as schools, museums, and libraries. The county building doubled as a Hebrew school; later, a Hebrew school opened its doors to Mexicans fleeing violence. Even the cemetery at the old Concordia Ranch of Hugh and Juana Stephenson was cleaned up.

Schutz set about collecting taxes and penalizing people who polluted the river water that filled El Paso's system of acequias: the canals and ditches that gave life to rose gardens, orchards, and fields alike. And he set his sights squarely on the gunfighters, whose unpredictable violence kept El Paso in a permanent state of chaos. He was not alone.

THE US ARMY had imposed a certain kind of peace in the Southwest, namely, by destroying the Apache way of life. But that peace did not extend to the violence of El Paso. Gunfighters, mostly white ones, frequently went beyond the reach of law, order, and even military force. Indeed, the army was no match for the most important event in El Paso's history in three hundred years: the arrival of the railroad and the lawlessness that followed in its wake.

In May 1881, the Southern Pacific Railroad arrived from California, laying tracks right through the parade ground of Fort Bliss. The arriving trains unloaded passengers and cargo alike inside the small, already cramped post hard up on the northern bank of the Rio Grande;[7] the army, meanwhile, gave up on the fort altogether and withdrew to a plateau northeast of the city. The army's move, coinciding with the abandonment of small frontier posts, marked the end of the wars against the Native peoples, most of whom settled into the confinement of reservations. It also marked the evolution of El Paso. Where once carts, wagons, and oxen left ruts and tracks headed north and south, now people and goods journeyed east and west too. Soon steel rails went toward New Mexico and Chihuahua. The old Camino Real, established three centuries earlier, now ran on coal, iron, and steel. Once a portal between continents, El Paso was now also a gateway across continents: an inland port, unequaled in reach by any other American city except New York and San Francisco.[8]

The trains brought wealth in the form of settlers, travelers, cargo, and commerce. The Anglo denizens of American El Paso wanted that wealth, as new banks and newspapers opened. Yet two cities lived side by side, sharing the same name. Mexican El Paso was the more established of the two and the more peaceful during this time. The year the railroad arrived there, the police locked up every American in town to prevent an outbreak of the violence that often spilled into the streets of American El Paso: gunfights, thievery, and jailbreaks, with a mob of gunmen roaming the streets firing randomly into buildings.[9]

On the American side, Mayor Schutz was constantly hiring—and losing—marshals. Some were incompetent, others were drunks, and still others were criminals themselves. His own marshal, George Campbell, resigned in exchange for the dropping of charges that he helped incite the riot of January 1881.[10] A deputy, Ed Copeland, was a saloon owner appointed to replace Campbell, but was stripped of the job the very next month for being unqualified. Texas Rangers were operating to the south but engaged in their own work-for-hire, raiding into Mexico to deliver a man for a mob hanging in exchange for $500. On April 11, thirty-six-year-old Dallas Stoudenmire, an imposing Alabaman, was appointed town marshal. Like many of the toughest men around, he was a Confederate veteran who was fast with a gun.[11]

Indeed, the ways of the old Confederacy had been steadily imported into American El Paso, and a large divide opened between people of Mexican origin north of the river and the white merchant class that steadily abandoned its riverbanks for a series of hills above. There, families such as the descendants of the Magoffins built towering Victorian homes from brick and wood; they were done with the old adobe. While many of them remained devoted to turning American El Paso into a hub of trade and commerce, they quite literally looked down on the burgeoning frontier city. Whereas public schools for Anglo and rich Mexican kids opened in 1883,[12] most boys and girls of Mexican origin would not walk through school doors until 1887. Black children would not get schools until 1891, and even then, schooling for both Mexican American and African American children would remain segregated and inferior to that in the schools of Anglos and upper-class Hispanics.[13]

For much of its three centuries, the El Paso region had been part of a multicultural society of Europeans, mestizos, and Native Americans whether it was in Mexico or New Mexico, both politically and culturally. (Indeed, there were frequent movements to break away from Texas and become part of New Mexico, or even to form a new state altogether.) But now the long arm of segregation had reached from Reconstruction-era Texas to the Rio Grande. The laws of Jim Crow twisted a society centuries in the making, dividing it by hue of skin and language.

THE RAILROAD EXPEDITED the import of racism into El Paso, and while this means of transport offered the prospect of riches, it also increased the city's lawlessness. Chinese workers, increasingly shunned in the run-up to the racist Chinese Exclusion Act of 1882, came nonetheless: from the south, after arriving at Mexican ports on the Pacific Ocean. Mexicans and Chileans came too. While these laborers earned a legal living through hard toil in the desert laying tracks, they often fell victim to predators: gunfighters, card players, opium dealers, barkeeps, and madames running prostitutes, whose single goal was to relieve the railroad workers—of any nationality—of their pay.

Schutz finally called the governor for help, pleading for Texas Rangers. Four different town marshals had been killed; a fifth, George Campbell, was spending most of his time drunk at Ben Dowell's notorious saloon, the site where those who could vote had done so to join both Texas and the Confederacy. Campbell fumed about his humiliation and muttered about revenge to a friend, John Hale, himself an enemy of the new marshal, Dallas Stoudenmire, an experienced gunfighter. Already, Schutz and the city council had forced Stoudenmire and Hale to enter a nonaggression pact, but it wasn't holding.

On April 14, 1881, two young Mexican vaqueros, Sanchez and Juarique, were found dead in the Bosque, the forest along the Rio Grande, at a location suspiciously near the ranch of one of the Hale brothers, all of whom were troublemakers and killers. The posse that found them was composed of seventy-five armed Mexican vaqueros looking for the two cowhands and nearly three dozen head of cattle. Johnny Hale, a rancher, was a known purveyor of stolen cattle. Schutz himself allowed the Mexican posse to cross the border, accompanied by a city constable fluent in Spanish. Two of Hale's hands were arrested for murder and hauled into a makeshift court in downtown El Paso, found guilty, and sentenced to death that very day.

Having been in court for the proceedings, Stoudenmire left and crossed the street for dinner. The constable went next door, to Dowell's saloon, to retrieve his guns and call it a day himself. It was then that the voluble Campbell began smack-talking the constable about his translations of the proceedings and his befriending Mexicans. Drunk and angry at the verdict, Hale grabbed one of Campbell's pistols and shot the constable, who slumped against the door, drawing his own pistol.

Stoudenmire flew out of the restaurant door, drawing his .44 revolvers and firing wildly; he hit and killed a bystander. Hale jumped behind an adobe pillar, but when he did, Stoudenmire shot him between the eyes. The constable shot Campbell in the wrist before passing out from blood loss. Stoudenmire fired at Campbell now, who clutched his belly and fell, yelling: "You big sonofabitch! You've murdered me!" Like that, four lay dead inside of five seconds.[14]

But it wasn't over. Schutz was running out of marshals, though he had no love for Stoudenmire, who lorded over American El Paso like a conquering prince. He spent city money that wasn't his, collected taxes, and even shot at the bell in the tower of Saint Clement's Episcopal Church. Schutz threatened to kill Stoudenmire in a duel, though he wouldn't have to. A friend of the Hale brothers hired yet another police officer to kill the Texas gunman turned lawman; the assassin failed, but the ensuing gunfight saw Stoudenmire down in the street, beaten to death.

With one of his own .44 revolvers.

Often depicted as an incidental figure in local history, Mayor Schutz was in fact a man who fought—and seems to have fought dirty—in the service of the America that had attracted him and his people, not only to immigrate to El Paso but to build a synagogue to their God there. He was instrumental in that effort even as he faced down the gunslingers, including those he hired to kill the other gunslingers. He lasted just a year in the job before decamping to Arizona—and converting to Catholicism. He quit politics to make pianos.

The accomplishments of Schutz have been overshadowed by the exploits of the era's acclaimed killers, none more so than Billy the Kid. Born in the slums of New York in November 1859 to an Irish immigrant mother, Cathryn McCarty, William trailed his mother west, first to a husband in Indianapolis, then to Santa Fe and Silver City. When William was staying at a boardinghouse, he and a friend, George Schafer, robbed a Chinese laundry. After being arrested, William shimmied up a chimney and escaped into Arizona. Arrested again in Arizona, he blundered by escaping back into New Mexico, where he was wanted and hunted. He compounded his troubles in a poker game, killing Francis "Windy" Cahill. He joined up with the cattleman John Tunstall, as much a gunman as he was a cowhand in the range wars with powerful, violent bosses, the equivalent of modern cartels. The Lincoln County War erupted when Tunstall was killed in 1878; the only prevailing force in the region, the US Army concentrated at Fort Bliss, did absolutely nothing as over sixty people were killed or wounded.

Nevertheless, Billy the Kid was just a bit too clever. He corresponded often with the territorial governor of New Mexico, Lew Wallace. Frequently, he pleaded for help, and just as frequently he offered to turn state's evidence, like any common snitch:

March 4 1881

Sir, I will keep the appointment I made but be sure and have men come that you can depend on I am not afraid to die like a man fighting but I would not like to be killed like a dog unarmed. I Expect you have forgotten what you promised me, this Month two years ago, but I have not and I think You had ought to have come and seen me as I requested you to. I have done everything that I promised you I would and You have done nothing that You promised me.[15]

Then he wrote: "I guess they mean to Send me up without giving me any Show but they will have a nice time doing it. I am not intirely [*sic*] without friends."[16]

There has been much speculation, but the historical record is fairly clear: Wallace used the Kid as a source of intelligence, particularly while Billy was in jail. When the governor departed office, he left Billy the Kid to die.[17]

In 1880, Pat Garrett, a gunfighter who moonlighted as a lawman, arrested Billy. The next year, he was to stand trial from an adobe jail in Mesilla, about forty miles north of El Paso and just off the plaza where Mexico had ceded territory to the United States. On April 28, 1881, Billy the Kid escaped jail—again. But this time he made the fatal mistake of killing two deputies. Garrett trailed the killer north, up the Rio Grande. Both neared the old adobe army post at Fort Sumner. Billy slipped onto a nearby ranch, and Garrett followed him. Garrett was not alone; his posse killed Billy's allies. But the fight wasn't yet over. On July 14, Garrett entered the remains of the old military post. Gun drawn, he questioned its occupant. Then Billy entered, saying, "Qué pasa?" Garrett turned and shot him twice in the chest. Billy the Kid was dead.[18]

GUNFIGHTING WAS A culture, and though the loss of one or two notorious gunfighters didn't bring that culture to an end, there were a few whose deaths marked a change. Billy the Kid was one, and John Wesley Hardin was another. A hero to some, Hardin had

shot dozens of people with hardly a second thought: he was a patho-
logical killer without parallel. Texas could not contain him. He
was the state's most notorious gunfighter, murdering people from
Central Texas to Florida. When finally jailed, Hardin was sentenced
to twenty-five years at the notorious state prison in Huntsville. Released in 1884, after serving seventeen of those years, he moved to
El Paso. Maybe he was drawn to its reputation for outlawry, but
he failed to see a deadly pattern: the locals in El Paso struck back
through their own assassins and then had little problem killing
them exactly the way they'd disposed of Stoudenmire.

On August 19, 1895, another El Paso lawman, J. D. Selman,
walked into a bar and shot Hardin in the back.[19] The last old gunfighter died without any glory whatsoever.

But the city didn't surrender to the gamblers, thieves, whores,
and killers. Many improvements were being made. Streetlights, fire
departments, and public schools went up in El Paso. Streetcars
ran on rails through the streets. The city council banned opium
dens. An opera house opened its doors, and major league baseball
drew crowds. When El Paso's Browns trounced Chicago 14–3, the
town went wild. A traveling performance of *Julius Caesar* arrived
in 1888; that same year, a concrete bridge replaced the old wooden
Santa Fe Street Bridge into Mexican El Paso. On the American side,
citizens donated money to move the army's Fort Bliss to a high
mesa[20] and organized a standing militia. The grand Myer Opera
House burned, but upon its repair, English, Mexican, and French
opera companies appeared in this showplace of the Southwest into
the twentieth century. A railroad running deep into Mexico connected points north into New Mexico; Oñate's Santa Fe Trail was
now made of iron as trains bustled east and west, north and south.
Women organized to form the Woman's Club, and in 1899, the
public library opened with four thousand books.[21] Neighboring

villages became towns and suburbs as a dusty, dangerous hamlet transformed into a bustling city of fifteen thousand on the north bank of the Rio Grande.[22]

On September 16, 1888, Mexican El Paso, El Paso del Norte, was renamed Ciudad Juárez for the beloved Zapotec president who had defeated the French and made the city the provisional capital of Mexico; citizens unveiled a powerfully crafted statue in his honor. As a result, American El Paso received sole ownership of the name that Oñate had bestowed three hundred years earlier: El Paso. The pass of the north.

AFTER A HALF CENTURY of violence and bloodshed, the twentieth century beckoned at this oasis in the desert: a crossroads between continents and an American city of laws, forged in Mexico. The new century would certainly bring war and difficulty but generally in the service of a higher American ideal: justice.

Part III

No mariner ever enters upon a more uncharted sea
than does the average human being born in the
20th century. Our ancestors know their way from
birth through eternity; we are puzzled about the
day after tomorrow.

—WALTER LIPPMANN

---------- **Chapter Twelve** ----------

REVOLUTION AND BETRAYAL, 1900–1920

A S THE TWENTIETH century dawned across the vast American Southwest, the increasingly Americanized cities sought to become more so—namely, more Anglo and white, both outwardly and inwardly. Historic adobe structures were demolished in favor of wooden and brick buildings in El Paso, which was by now a small American city, though not even in the top hundred.[1] But it boomed with copper, cattle, cotton, and trade. Churches and synagogues arose. In May 1900, the sheriff decreed that the streets were too busy for boys to play baseball in them. Horses and buggies careened along, usually avoiding pedestrians. An old ore smelter, with its workforce housed in shanties in the surrounding Smeltertown, was bought up by the American Smelting and Refining Company and folded into the fortunes of Henry Guggenheim's interests in New York.[2]

Mules pulled streetcars full of people up and down the streets and across the old Santa Fe bridge: into Mexican Juárez and back. The city was electrified in 1901, and on May 5 of that year, the ultimate personification of American power paid the city a visit: President William McKinley arrived by train on his way west. The crowd was tremendous, and the stop was more than mere coincidence; relations with Mexico had remained tenuous even as America had absorbed what was left of the Spanish Empire through war in 1898 just a few years earlier. But the government of Mexican president Porfirio Díaz could ill afford a hostile United States on its northern border, and McKinley, for his part, not only thanked the Mexican political officials and Díaz, but added that no one should worry about American militarism. Díaz, a hero in the war against France, had proclaimed himself president for life, and Washington had no problem with it, since he was as accommodating to American commercial interests as he was to the Guggenheims, who expanded their desert empire from the American Smelting and Refining Company to mines across the Southwest and deep into Mexico.

But McKinley aimed his departing remarks, the next day, at his audience in El Paso. This was now deeply Americanized territory, whatever its links to Mexico:

> I am glad to be in this cosmopolitan city. I am glad to know that assembled here within your gates are the men of all races, all nationalities and all creeds, but under one flag, the glorious Stars and Stripes. Acknowledging allegiance to no other Government but the United States of America, and giving willing sacrifice at any time, the country may call for the honor of our Nation and the glory of our republic. I am glad to know that this city believes in expansion. That it has been doing a great deal of itself in the last four years. That it has more than doubled its population in the last half of the present decade and given promise of still greater advancement and prosperity in the decade now at hand. You have here, my fellow citizens, the true national spirit, the spirit of enterprise, of development of progress, of building the structure of liberty and free Government on the broad and deep foundations of intelligence, virtue, morality, and religion.[3]

With that, the president waved farewell and boarded his private car, "Olympia," to resume his transcontinental journey.

THE US-MEXICO BORDER was perhaps one of history's greatest mistakes. In the haste and greed of the American occupation of Mexico City, the United States reached for the biggest land grab it could get, and a few years later, the Gadsden Purchase of 1854 only made it—and the mistake—larger.

When the border was mapped, its sheer artificiality became clear. Surveying expeditions had trouble locating it as they started out eastward from San Diego. Even when they drove border markers into the desert, blowing sands buried them or people simply stole them. Aside from the Colorado River and the mountains on the Arizona–New Mexico border, the desert was fairly featureless; only a general or mapmaker could love this notion of an international frontier. From El Paso onward, the boundary was set in the middle of the Rio Grande, which flooded and shifted channels constantly—alternately putting US territory in Mexico and Mexican territory in the United States.[4] As surveyors entered the rough country of the Big Bend, a land of soaring mountains and deep, rough-and-tumble canyons over the often-roaring river, much of the expedition had to inch along the Mexican canyon rims, where men and mules alike were lost.[5]

In reality, the Big Bend was the only constant geographic feature, and it was just a little more than a hundred miles of a nearly two-thousand-mile line on the map. People could cross anywhere; it wasn't illegal. The border controls that exist today were not even a thought in the early twentieth century. Besides, the border was not designed to keep Mexicans out of the United States—it was designed to let Americans into the West. Ultimately, this is how the Mexican population in the United States soared. American agriculture and industry alike wanted cheap labor.

In a sense, McKinley had been right about El Paso's diversity. The Mexican Cession, like El Paso itself, had been transformed into American territory by force, bloodshed, and finally the rule of law. But that law was deeply tainted. Another artificial border divided the community—segregation. The American shame of segregation has broadly been understood as a tale of the old Confederacy ultimately succeeding in separating and repressing African Americans who had been freed from chattel slavery. But with the flood tide of Anglo-Americans eclipsing Hispanics in the old Mexican Cession of the Southwest, segregation was a sinister fact of life for people of Mexican origin. Even if they were citizens, they were second-class citizens, at best, in their own land.

Within the boundaries of Texas, the era between 1910 and 1920 in Texas was known as La Matanza—The Slaughter. Just as Blacks were lynched from trees in the Deep South, thousands of Mexican Americans were hanged, dragged to death behind horses, and simply gunned down. In Rocksprings, Texas, a sandstone hamlet on the edge of the Texas Hill Country, Antonio Rodriguez, a twenty-year-old migrant worker, was accused of murdering a woman. A mob swelled and headed for the town jail, retrieving the prisoner. As the historian Monica Muñoz Martinez chillingly recorded: "They bound him to a barbed mesquite tree and encircled him with limbs of dry cedar. They saturated the heap with kerosene, set it on fire and burned Rodriguez alive. Despite the geographical isolation of Rocksprings, news of the murder and the impending lynching [had] spread like wildfire. Newspapers reported that thousands of local residents attended the lynching. The crowd that gathered to watch the spectacle of a live man burning to death went to great lengths to be there."

In Weslaco, down in the Rio Grande Valley, another man was jailed for fighting with an Anglo coworker. A mob hanged him.[6] An infamous photograph from the collection of Ralph Runyon at the

University of Texas in Austin depicts, in faded black and white, three Texas Rangers on the vast King Ranch in 1915. At first blush, they appear to be only dusty cowboys with lassos taut, posing for Runyon. But upon closer examination, the mangled remains of three men lie at the ends of those lassos: Jesús García, Mauricio García, and Amado Muñoz. Runyon scrawled this caption: "dead Mexican bandits killed at battle of norlo's [sic] ranch, Tex-Mex border."[7]

For decades after, Runyon's photograph could easily be purchased anywhere—on a postcard. The Texas Rangers were less a police force than they were, in many cases, state-paid mercenaries for hire, working for wealthy ranchers and killing at will, even shooting men in the back. When they weren't doing that, they were busy enforcing "Juan Crow," the Jim Crow laws of Texas. The Rangers alone were responsible for killing hundreds of Hispanics.[8]

A mob in Collin County, North Texas, accused Refugio Ramírez, his wife, and their teenage daughter, María Ines, of bewitching their neighbors[9]—then, cheering, burned all three to death. Ethnic Mexicans were often armed and fought back, and border outlaws like Juan Cortina and Joaquín Murieta inspired Mexican Americans and put fear into Anglos.[10]

The violence was common in Texas but spread too to New Mexico and California. It was often directed against Chinese and Chilean workers as well. Over the years, historians ignored this chilling brutality, leaving two scholars, William D. Carrigan and Clive Webb, to call the casualties "the forgotten dead."[11] What developed in the American psyche, as a result, was a common misconception: that ethnic and racial minorities were a tinderbox of mass racial violence against whites.

But the exact opposite was true, not just in the Southwest but across the nation: the white majority had the numbers and the will to bully, maim, and kill minorities, and this wasn't limited to people of other races. Throughout the Civil War, the Protestant

majority often used mob violence against Catholics in the East.
After the war, Italians became the target. From the late nineteenth
and into the twentieth century, white mobs turned on Blacks in the
South—killing at least a hundred in Slocum, Texas in 1910[12]—and
the Midwest, as well as against Hispanics and Asians in the Southwest and West.

In the farthest western corner of Texas, the Juan Crow era was
more subtle. Poverty was widespread in predominantly Mexican
American South El Paso and Chihuahuita, the little barrio by the
Rio Grande. As was the case in other cities in Texas, restaurants,
hotels, and transportation were segregated along racial lines. But
the cornerstone of the American apartheid era in the crossroads of
the Southwest was perhaps even more insidious: the schools. As
many as 40 percent of Paseños lived in dilapidated housing, often terribly unsanitary tenements with few bathrooms. City leaders
could thereby characterize Mexican American children as unclean
and placed them in separate schools, as was the case for Black children.[13] The Aoy School opened its doors to Hispanic children in
1897; the largest in the nation, it was terribly overcrowded. Three
subsequent elementary schools for two thousand children offered no
lunch, while schools for Anglo children served up the midday meal.

Though American citizens, children with Spanish surnames
went to separate and inferior schools, where speaking Spanish was
forbidden and subject to corporal punishment; African American
children were afforded a similarly second-class experience, and both
were subjected to the soft bigotry of low expectations.

Mexican Americans lived in the barrios where the river flooded,
while Anglo people lived in the hills above. The black-and-white
photos of the time reveal a stark existence for many: a brood of
serious-looking Black children arranged neatly in front of their
brick schoolhouse, a stern white schoolmaster off to the side; a
young Chinese man and a poor Mexican woman, a black shawl over

her head, crossing the Santa Fe bridge on foot—no streetcar for her; a brooding old cowboy with a boy, their buggy and skinny horse following behind them.[14]

The expanded American republic now stretched from Guam to Cuba, from Alaska to Texas, and to be considered American, those of the conquered cultures had to act American—that is, they had to act white.

For better and worse, America had finally put its stamp on the Southwest. The American Smelting and Refining Company smoke-stacks rose over El Paso, pumping out smoke that billowed with heavy metals: gold, silver, and copper. Electric streetcars replaced mule-drawn ones. The city imposed an obviously racist poll tax. A tin mine gouged into the east flank of the Mansos, now unroman-tically called the Franklin Mountains, the sparse mountain woods now cut down, the grasses stripped by the overgrazing of cattle, goats, and sheep. Suburbs sprang up, clinging to slopes and taking over farmlands. Indeed, many of the vineyards and cornfields were replaced by more valuable fields of cotton; the weathered, leathery brown hands of Mexican workers plucked the snowy fiber from its sharp bulbs. Mexican Americans, in particular, were supposed to be accorded the same opportunities as any other Americans, and by now, 75 percent of them had been born in the United States, not Mexico. Yet they were no longer the majority, and the Anglo majority made the rules. As a result, most Mexican Americans oc-cupied the lowest-paying occupations: 60 percent were farm work-ers or laborers.[15] Still, the wages were vastly superior to those in Mexico; increasingly, starving peasants in central Mexico migrated northward into the United States.

In 1909, another American president arrived. Revolutionary sentiment was rising in Mexico and Díaz, the dictator, was still Washington's preference. It was time to defrost relations between the two nations more directly, so President William Howard Taft visited El Paso to meet with Díaz; after all, the portly Taft and the *presidente* of now thirty years did have a border dispute simmering, as the Rio Grande changed course during the flood seasons, moving the international boundary. Parades of US and Mexican troops escorted their respective leaders to the meeting; children sang to the presidents in both English and Spanish; bunting hung from buildings.[16] This was the first time that the presidents of these two countries, among the first to fight for independence from Europe and pursue, imperfectly, republicanism, had come together.

Díaz agreed that the Americans could dam the Rio Grande upstream to water the valley farms. In 1916, 120 miles north of El Paso, a giant wall of concrete would rise in front of the roiling Rio Grande. It was among several feats of engineering of the period that dammed the great rivers of the Southwest. Its concrete walls were packed with native stone, as were the Hoover and Glen Canyon Dams. It was designed by the federal government's Bureau of Reclamation to tame the great river, end its seasonal flooding downriver to El Paso, and regularly provide water in the dry seasons to farmers and city dwellers alike.

As the dam rose at a narrow chokepoint—near where the explorer Juan de Oñate had departed from the river for the dreadful march across the desert to the east—bureaucrats named it Engle Dam, for a nearby railroad stop. The new dam wouldn't just harness the river; it would supply electricity too. Three thousand workers labored on it, housed nearby in a tent city. The Anglo workers and Mexican workers lived in segregated quarters.

As it closed, the dam was the tallest of its kind in America, and around the world it was second only to the Aswan Dam on the Nile in Egypt. It controlled the drainage of nearly thirty thousand square miles and irrigated nearly two hundred thousand acres. Slowly, the dam filled the canyon with over two million acre-feet of water. The upper camp for workers was inundated, along with much of the promontory that was a landmark for miles: Elephant Butte. That name stuck to the reservoir and the dam alike.

The remaining Rio Grande wasn't just tamed. It was broken.

After Díaz agreed to allow the construction of the massive dam, he went back to Mexico and nineteen months later was overthrown, plunging Mexico into revolution. Guggenheim's American Smelting and Refining Company bought the mine at Santa Rita, where Mangas Coloradas once fought. By 1910, fifty-three thousand people made El Paso home, as did another ten thousand in Mexico. El Paso was as populous as Fort Wayne, Charleston, or Harrisburg. By the standards of that time, the city had arrived.

However uneven and unfair, this was what passed for American progress in the new century of the American Empire.[17] Yet the people of Mexican origin, whether north of the Rio Grande or south of it, would not be ignored. It was a simple fact that the border drawn sixty years earlier between the United States and Mexico was the longest undefended—and indefensible—border in the world. The very idea that an imaginary line in the desert would somehow divide the fates of the two nations was an absolute folly. The Americanization of the Southwest, in a white nationalist sense, was even more absurd. National loyalty was one thing; the destruction of culture, as the Native Americans had suffered, was quite another. Americans and Mexicans were joined at the hip, despite who had the upper hand and in the tumultuous years ahead, their fates would be sealed—one way or another—together.

In 1910, there were far more Anglo-Americans in El Paso and the Southwest than there were Mexican Americans. The inequality that settled in was not merely El Paso finding itself within the boundaries of Texas, and by extension, the old Confederacy; it was also a matter of sheer numbers. The population had more than doubled since the turn of the century, reaching over fifty thousand, which placed it among the ten largest cities in the country.[18] Most of the newcomers were Anglos. Segregation in Texas and El Paso was unjust, certainly, but it also resulted from majority rule. Across the entire Southwest, from Texas to California, there were just two hundred thousand people of Mexican origin in a territory that now had seven million residents.[19]

Interestingly, in this era of widespread racism, the US Census Bureau counted Hispanics as white. Nevertheless, there was a great gulf between how Mexican Americans were counted and how they were treated.

All of that was about to get even worse with one of the deadliest conflicts the world at the time had ever known—the Mexican Revolution. It began in old Mexican El Paso, now Ciudad Juárez, with a rough-and-ready bandit and army deserter who often lived on the American side of the border. He was José Doroteo Arango Arámbula, who came to be known as Francesco "Pancho" Villa.

IN 1910, PRESIDENT Porfirio Díaz was reelected to another term in office. The illustrious hero against the French at the Battle of Puebla had served as president since 1877. But there was no magic to his continued popularity; the election was rigged and Díaz quickly jailed his rival candidate, Francisco Madero, who descended from a wealthy family in Nuevo León, the northeast corner of Mexico once pioneered by Portuguese Jews.

Díaz had done much. A mestizo, he had dismantled the last remnants of the old Spanish caste system. He celebrated the mestizo heritage of Mexico, building monuments and wide boulevards and modernizing the nation. He ordered thousands of miles of rail built, including to and through Ciudad Juárez to Mexico. Yet at the same time he concentrated wealth, leaving the criollos, those of Spanish descent, their haciendas and land. A handful of Mexican families had most of the nation's wealth in their vaults, bank accounts, and land holdings. The rest was siphoned away by foreign investors with the approval of the president.[20] Among them were Americans: William Randolph Hearst, the newspaper publisher, and the wheat king William Wallace Cargill.[21] Díaz needed their investments and, rightfully distrustful, he wanted to keep Washington happy, famously saying, "Poor Mexico. So far from God. And so close to the United States."

Díaz had also outlawed communal holdings of Indigenous communities, known as encomiendas, as well as agricultural holdings of the Catholic Church. Calls for land reform rang like a warning bell in 1906. Agricultural workers were increasingly saddled with debt, and when the economy slumped in 1910, their wages fell. Quite suddenly, the prospect of mass starvation in the land that had invented corn became quite real.

Escaping from prison in late 1910, Díaz's opponent, Madero, crossed into the United States; after arriving in San Antonio, he issued his Plan de San Luis Potosi, an open call for armed revolt against the Díaz regime. Copies were printed and secretly distributed across Mexico. The revolt was to start at 6 p.m. on November 20. At first, few heeded Madero's call—but one person did. Born in 1878 in the Mexican state of Durango, Pancho Villa could often be found on the streets of El Paso.

Madero passed through the city and reentered Mexico, taking up quarters in Ciudad Juárez, still known as El Paso del Norte, as Villa trailed along. There they quietly raised an army of twenty-five hundred men with Pascual Orozco, a self-made man who was already fighting in the surrounding state of Chihuahua. Orozco was a talented commander and a ruthless opponent, pinning notes to the jackets of dead federal troops: "Here are the wrappers. Send more tamales."

On April 7, 1911, they attacked.

THOUSANDS OF EL PASOANS gathered on the opposite bank of the Rio Grande to watch the fighting, which dragged on to the end of the month. Up on the bluffs of Sunset Heights, the wealthier classes arrived in buggies to see the spectacle below. Local saloons ferried them beer.

By May 8, 1911, the federal troops were running low on everything: men, bullets, but most of all water, and the weather was hot as summer approached. In Mexico City, a desperate Díaz tried to negotiate a ceasefire with Madero; Madero was interested in the president's offer, but Villa and Orozco ignored him and pressed their attack. On May 10, Díaz's troops finally surrendered, running up the white flag at noon. The surrender treaty was signed shortly after at the customs building.

The American journalist Tim Turner caught up with Madero later, at a ranch house. Turner wrote his account in *Bullets, Bottles, and Gardenias*:

> Hollow-eyed as he was he started in at once, sitting there on the edge of the bed. I remember that once he stood, and raised his hand in an oratorical gesture while he held in it a sock he had just removed. So, we talked as he undressed. Madero was talking away and I had nothing to write on. I looked around the room. There a long shelf was covered with brown wrapping paper the neat ranchman's wife had arranged, and this I took, and, laying it out on a table, started to catch up on Madero's words. I remember the paper had splotches of face powder and rouge on it. As he talked, it all seemed so easy.[22]

The Guadalupe Mountains, east of El Paso, were a stronghold
for Mescalero Apache raiders, who attacked stagecoaches
bound for California. *Courtesy of the Library of Congress*

Hueco Tanks has been home to people for millennia. *Left:* a depiction of
the intricate rock paintings left by inhabitants dating back thousands
of years. *Right:* a wealth of water collects in the limestone formation's
hollows, or *huecos*. *Courtesy of the Texas Parks and Wildlife Department*

Juan de Oñate, the explorer who named El Paso del Rio del Norte, the Crossing of the River of the North. His expedition predated the Pilgrims landing in Massachusetts by more than twenty years. *Courtesy of the University of Texas at El Paso Library Special Collections*

The northern reaches of New Spain, now known as Mexico. Northern New Spain included California and Colorado and even reached into present-day Wyoming. *Courtesy of the Bureau of Land Management*

The Jesuit Mission of Guadalupe was where the permanent settlement of El Paso del Norte, Chihuahua, Mexico, began. Native Americans came here for conversion and food. The mission endured floods, wars, and disease. *Courtesy of DeGolyer Library, Southern Methodist University*

The Catholic mission, erected at Ysleta Pueblo after the Great Pueblo Revolt of 1680, provided services, conversion, and food to Pueblo refugees and became the center of Pueblo life in El Paso. *Courtesy of the Library of Congress*

A scene in the Mexican-American War, 1846–48, depicting the battle for Chapultepec, in Mexico City. Thousands of Americans died from disease and wounds in the midst of unexpected resistance. At the castle, Mexican army cadets wrapped themselves in their national flag and leapt to their deaths rather than be taken prisoner by the Americans. *Courtesy of the Library of Congress*

The original Fort Bliss in 1850 after the war with Mexico, now the plaza in downtown El Paso. Fort Bliss was eventually moved to the high desert northeast of the growing American settlement. Here, the mountains of Chihuahua are in the background. *Courtesy of El Paso History Alliance*

The acequia system of irrigation, adopted from the Moors and brought by the Spaniards. *Courtesy of Texas Beyond History at the University of Texas at Austin*

The Rio Grande frequently flooded, as in this scene in 1916. The city, now named El Paso, endured such floods until the 1920s, even after the then largest dam in the country, Elephant Butte, was erected. *Courtesy of the C.L. Sonnichsen Special Collections, University of Texas at El Paso Library, Gertrude Fitzgerald Photographs, PH025*

Mangas Coloradas, the greatest chief of the Apache people. Born
in the eighteenth century, he alternately negotiated peace with the
Spanish, then the Mexicans, and finally the Americans, raiding
when treaties weren't honored, before being captured and murdered
by the US Army—and beheaded. *Courtesy of the Library of Congress*

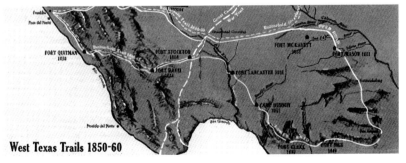

West Texas Trails 1850-60

The westward-bound trails after America took half of Mexico's
territory following the conclusion of the Mexican-American
War in 1848. *Courtesy of the National Park Service*

John Wesley Hardin, gunfighter turned lawyer in El Paso. He is buried in a cemetery in El Paso on the old Concordia Ranch. *Courtesy of the C.L. Sonnichsen Special Collections, University of Texas at El Paso Library*

Pancho Villa (*right*) at a revolutionary camp across
the Rio Grande from El Paso. *Courtesy of the C.L. Sonnichsen
Special Collections, University of Texas at El Paso Library*

Above and opposite: US soldiers descend on the El Paso
region during the Mexican Punitive Expedition,
which never caught Villa. *Courtesy of the Library of Congress*

Turned away from voting, Dr. Lawrence Nixon filed suit for discrimination prior to *Brown v. Board of Education.*
Courtesy of the University of Texas at El Paso Library Special Collections

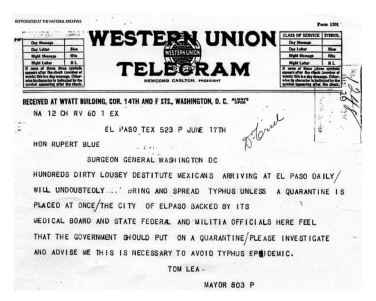

The mayor of El Paso, Tom Lea, used racist language in his call for the delousing of Mexican day workers. The dehumanizing practice resulted in two riots, as the workers were ordered to strip and be bathed in kerosene, gasoline, and ultimately Zyklon B gas, inspiring Hitler. *Courtesy of the El Paso Public Libraries*

The ASARCO copper smelter, the largest in the world, was acquired by the Guggenheim fortune. *Courtesy of the C.L. Sonnichsen Special Collections, University of Texas at El Paso Library, ASARCO collection*

Upriver, Elephant Butte Dam, the largest in America at the time, began stemming flooding in 1915 and was completed in 1916. *Courtesy of the Library of Congress*

MEXICAN IS U. S. ARMY HERO

Marcelino Serna, a Mexican immigrant and one of the most decorated US soldiers of World War I.
The Daily Morning Oasis

The dead of Texas's 36th Infantry Division, killed crossing the Rapido River in one of the largest Allied blunders of World War II, joined by the almost entirely Mexican American troops of El Paso's Company E. *Courtesy of the US Army*

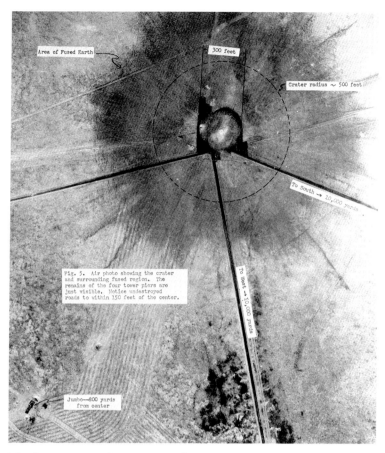

The first atomic explosion, north of El Paso, along the Jornada del Muerto
previously blazed by the Oñate expedition. *CNN; National Security Center*

*Courtesy of National
Aeronautics and Space
Administration (NASA)*

In the 1950s, El Paso was a hot spot for the famous and rich. Elizabeth Taylor married Conrad "Nicky" Hilton Jr. here in 1950; it was her first marriage, lasting just eight months. *Courtesy of MGM*

Raymond Telles (*left*), the first Mexican American mayor of a major US city, with President Lyndon B. Johnson. *Courtesy of the El Paso Public Libraries*

The Plaza Theatre in downtown El Paso in the 1950s.
Courtesy of the El Paso Public Libraries

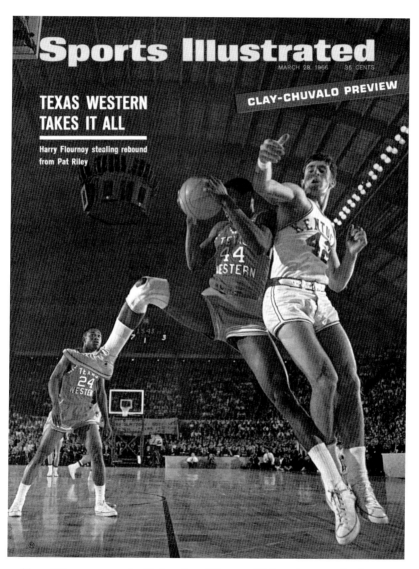

Texas Western, now the University of Texas at El Paso, became the first team with African American players beating an all-white team from Kentucky, the reigning champs, in the 1966 NCAA championship. © *SI Cover / Getty Images*

A view of contemporary El Paso's East Side, with the Franklin Mountains, rising to seven thousand feet above sea level, in the background. *Courtesy of the Library of Congress*

Downtown El Paso was connected to Mexico by streetcars for most of the twentieth century. Now service in El Paso has resumed. *Courtesy of the El Paso Public Libraries*

Much of it restored to its glory days of seventy years ago, downtown El Paso is home to a vibrant nightlife, replete with festivals year-round. *Ivan Pierre Aguirre*

Turner quoted their conversation and commented in his book, as if in poetic refrain to the wealthy revolutionary:

"All is favorable for us because we have the aid of the people."
It all seemed so noble.
"Our soldiers volunteer, they are fighting for ideals, for liberty and for their rights."
It all seemed so progressive.
"We are fighting for the Constitution, for the rights of suffrage and for general and free education."
It all seemed so fair and reasonable.
"I am friendly to the American people but against the trusts of any nation."
It all seemed so just.[23]

Finally, Turner wrote this: "A few years later it was all to seem so foolish."[24]

The news rocked the world.

Grizzled revolutionaries in big sombreros and bandoliers rode on horseback triumphantly through the rubble-strewn streets of Juárez, their lead rider holding the Mexican tricolor high.[25] They spared their prisoners' lives and asked for only one thing in exchange: Díaz, the old war hero turned dictator, had to resign his beloved presidency. He set sail and began his exile in, of all places, France—the nation he had fought as a young man. He would die just four years later.

When they learned that Madero had granted Díaz's trusted, vicious general, Juan Navarro, safe passage out of Juárez, Villa and Orozco flew into a rage and burst into a cabinet meeting. To pacify Orozco, Madero promoted him to brigadier general; he made Villa a colonel, instructing him to hunt down leftist opponents who thought Madero too moderate. Villa did so.[26] Yet nothing was quite as it seemed. Madero had spared the enemy general, certainly out of sincere humanism, but he also aimed to assert civilian control over his two new headstrong commanders, according to the Austrian historian Friedrich Katz. Despite his field promotion, the dark-haired, brooding Orozco was increasingly dissatisfied with what he was getting out of this war. Years later, Villa would accuse Orozco of being a double agent who was paid $50,000 to enlist Villa to kill Madero. Regardless, the stout, balding, and often smiling Villa seemed happy and loyal to Madero.

The revolution appeared to be practically over, its main goal achieved within a month. Yet like mirages in the Chihuahuan Desert, this too was an illusion. As entrants leapt into the fray on both sides, all bent on shaping Mexico to their will, benefit, or both, the revolution became a full-blown, multisided conflict, and it was escalating. Emiliano Zapata in the south was a revolutionary but came from a different walk of life and as a result had a different vision of Mexico than Villa, a northerner. Orozco was ordered to fight Zapata and refused. General Victoriano Huerta was an opportunist who faithfully served Díaz until he faithfully served Madero—then planned to betray him. Like many wars, it developed a momentum, a roaring life all its own, beyond any individual's control.

And as the conflict accelerated, it began to consume Mexico itself. Villa's troops seized the railroads and transported men, women, and horses by train to the front lines. Wives went with their peasant soldier husbands to battle. Women soldiers, known as soldaderas or Adelitas, joined or were pressed into service; taking up bandoliers and Winchester rifles, they went, skirts flying, into combat against machine guns. Women served as commanding officers, even in the federal army. Orozco's men kidnapped the women in Villa's army. Airplanes entered the fray, the first time they ever saw combat.[27] Madero ascended to the presidency, only to be toppled the next year by the traitorous Huerta.

The war's effects were no longer confined to Mexico. After all, the border established in the previous century was just an imaginary line across the desert and down the middle of a river. There was no natural defensive boundary for either Mexico or the United States, except the vastness of the desert itself. So even as Americans went south to join the revolution, desperate Mexicans went north to stay alive. In 1914, famine struck much of the country because of the war. In 1910, the year before the revolution, just twenty thousand Mexican migrants had arrived in the United States. That became fifty thousand refugees per year, then a hundred thousand.[28]

As Mexicans fled for their lives, their point of entry was that desert port, El Paso. As Ellis Island took in a peak of one million Poles, Russians, Italians, and Austro-Hungarians, all escaping hardship, in 1909 El Paso took in at least six hundred thousand Mexicans fleeing war. No passports, visas, or documents of any kind were required to make this passage. In fact, some Americans preferred Mexican immigrants to others, considering them more docile due to the strict religious and social hierarchies of their home culture, where many were subject to oppression; it was thought this background made them better laborers.[29] The complexion of El Paso and the whole American Southwest began to change. From El Paso, Mexicans headed to the orchards of Arizona and California and upriver to New Mexico to help build the big new dam at Elephant Butte, which would tame the Rio Grande's raging spring floods. They fanned out across the farm fields of El Paso and Las Cruces and worked the ranches of West Texas and eastern New Mexico.

At the same time, Villa's Army of the North successfully campaigned east and south, subduing all of Chihuahua and much of northern Mexico. Yet even during the war, he returned to his American home in El Paso. He had much business there: recruiting Americans, for one. His image, replete with mustache and sombrero, was plastered on posters all over town. In an Uncle Sam–like pose, he pointed a finger at the words "GRINGO, Pancho Villa wants you to join the Mexican Revolution."

He opened a recruiting office in downtown El Paso as out-of-work soldiers streamed to the border. Villa was, in fact, pro-American and secretly sought out officers in the US Army, very much wanting their help.

While most men could be found drinking and carousing after work, Villa was a devout teetotaler. His men liked their tequila and whiskey, but their commander, now a general, almost never drank hard alcohol. Yet he did indulge one curious addiction: ice cream. If anyone wanted to find the Mexican rebel, he could be located, cowboy hat off, tall boots shined, sitting in a coat and tie while politely sampling the creamy wares of the nearest confectionery.[30]

Villa's first campaigns in the Mexican north, in Chihuahua, Coahuila, and Sonora, had gone lightning-fast; he spent a great deal of time as a semi-retired gentleman general. But with President Madero's assassination in 1913, he saddled up and rode to war again. The fighting became harder as federal commanders now understood his tactics. He stumbled politically too, raiding the giant ranch and hacienda of British-born William Benton in 1915. Americans didn't mind Mexicans killing each other, but killing a fellow Anglo stirred public opinion against him.

Most of American history has portrayed Villa as an out-of-control outlaw turned general: cruel, ruthless, and a threat to the United States. Only some of that was true. Villa was quick to anger and could be vicious. He had run away from home as a boy after a ranch owner raped his sister, and the owner wound up dead. Villa raised himself as a boy and then a teenager, doing any work necessary, stealing food, and fleeing.

Yet as a revolutionary he believed in the cause, perhaps to a fault. Too much land was in the hands of hacendados like Benton and even worse, the Terrazas clan. Villa hated them with a wrathful, righteous vengeance, but he had another side too. He was generous but disciplined with his muchachos, who could veer out of control. Every penny he stole during the revolution he put back into his growing Army of the North, keeping little to nothing for himself. He worshipped the United States for its Constitution and principles, seeing its political order as a model for post-dictatorship Mexico and desperately seeking all kinds of American help. Contrary to nearly all American stories about Villa, he never, in fact, attacked the United States.

ATOP HIS HORSE, the short and stout Villa possessed a menacing look: large sombrero bent into the desert wind, bandoliers of big brass .30–30 bullets crisscrossing his chest, a trusty Winchester in the scabbard, a scowl etched onto his face beneath his big dark mustache.

In the ensuing depictions for American audiences, he represented every frightening thing about a Mexican: a violent and cruel bandit. Other Mexican figures before had been portrayed in the exact same way, making the border seem a frightful, faraway place and all Mexicans dangerous and untrustworthy.

In the twentieth century, there were really two Villas: the living revolutionary general and the archetypal myth. Villa never wore a uniform; he dressed as a plain old vaquero in the field and preferred khaki mufti with a vest and tie in the city. He was indeed responsible for atrocities, particularly early in the war; he shot a woman who screamed at him for killing her husband, and once had the wives of enemy soldiers executed. However, rumors have abounded that Villa was a womanizer, having many wives at any given time, and that is false. "During his lifetime, Villa had never bothered with conventional arrangements in his family life," the

Austrian-born Mexican anthropologist and historian wrote in Villa's biography. Yet while Villa was married four times, all bonds were legal—he never divorced, and one early wife died—even as he fought all through his thirties.

After much debate over the years, the Mexican Congress finally concluded in 1946 that he had just one widow and so awarded a government pension to her: his fourth wife, Soledad Sáenz Villa, who had married him in 1919.[31] During their marriage she often resided in Ciudad Juárez while he frequented El Paso. From her accounts and letters, he was a devoted husband and father. Eventually, she painted a portrait of him, eyes gleaming, with a dark handsomeness that most accounts overlooked. Her house was filled with landscapes and still lifes, yet the portrait of her husband stood out.

"This is my masterpiece," she quietly told the El Paso reporter Jessie Peterson in 1996. "The other paintings on the wall, . . . they are of little consequence."

"Handsome and strong," she continued, "this picture is the way I want people to remember him in their hearts."[32]

While Emiliano Zapata fought in the south for land reform, Villa believed in the cause and attacked the big haciendas of the ruling Terrazas family; he also fought in the name of public education for his people. Ignorance as much as a lack of land kept the Mexican people trapped; Villa himself had been functionally illiterate much of his life. Indeed, his wives Luz and Soledad—teachers by profession and nature—taught him when he returned from battle.

When the American leftist journalist John Reed met Villa and traveled with the Army of the North, he couldn't help but identify with the revolution. He noted that even in the heat of battle, where Villa was indeed ruthless, he was a happy, clever warrior. Before achieving fame with his book *Ten Days That Shook the World*, about the Russian Revolution in which he would perish, the young American penned *Insurgent Mexico*: "Villa found that he hadn't enough trains to carry all his soldiers, even when he had ambushed and captured a Federal troop train, sent south by General Castro, the Federal commander in Juarez. So he telegraphed that gentleman as follows, signing the name of the Colonel in command of the troop train: 'Engine broken down at Moctezuma. Send another engine and five cars.'"

The unsuspecting commander dutifully sent Villa another train, not knowing that on the other end of the telegraph was the enemy. Villa asked for orders and was told to return at once. He replied that he would and kept sending fake telegraphs. By the time the federal garrison learned that Villa was setting upon them, they had just an hour's notice to prepare—and fell easily.[33] In America he was a maligned bandido. But in Mexico he was known as the Centaur of the North.

The chief of staff of the US Army, General Hugh Scott, shared that opinion. In 1915, the fighting intensified. Famine gripped Mexico and the revolutionary leaders fell upon each other. With Madero, the revolutionary, dead and the hated General Victoriano Huerta ousted from the presidency, a wealthy landowner and rebel commander, Venustiano Carranza, seized the office. A student of the German kaiser Wilhelm II, he deepened Germany's already pronounced involvement in the revolution; there were German military advisers alongside federal troops, German machine guns, and at least a thousand German spies in the country, preoccupying Washington. German propagandists showed the Mexicans how to malign Villa in an attempt to undermine US support for him.[34] German and American naval forces frequented the port cities of Tampico and Veracruz, wrangling for de facto control of Mexico's vital oil supplies. Britain's Royal Navy, for instance, ran strictly on Mexican fuel.

Scott traveled to El Paso to meet Villa often, since much of the US Army was deployed along the Mexican border, even as World

War I was underway in Europe. Upon their first meeting, the two officers joined up in the middle of the old Santa Fe bridge and got into a car. As they conversed, Scott handed Villa a copy of the laws of war and told him that he had to stop executing prisoners.[35] Villa, who did not know of the Geneva Conventions, promptly did so. In 1915, the two men met on the front porch of a graceful house in the wealthy Sunset Heights area above downtown El Paso, listening to each other, faces etched with the expression of two trusted leaders passing wisdom and secrets in that perilous winter. It was Villa who informed Scott of Carranza's secret pact with the kaiser: he planned to be the next dictator of Mexico. Villa and Scott could be frank and argue, but it never diminished either's view of the other, nor their mutual desire that President Woodrow Wilson would allow American might in favor of the revolution and against dictatorship and Germany. Even El Paso crawled with German agents, according to the American physician R. H. Ellis, Villa's personal surgeon, who practically lived with Villa on the battlefield.

"We locked horns like two bull elk," Scott said, over a ceasefire proposal along the Arizona border. But the two shook hands and Villa agreed to what Scott wanted. "As every man in that room knew, Villa would carry out his promise once he made it."[36]

But in Washington, Wilson, the Georgia-born former Princeton professor who was now president of the United States, had other plans. While concerned about German involvement, Wilson was also a deep-seated racist; he looked down his pince-nez at brown-skinned Mexicans as much as at African Americans. Instead of siding with the revolutionaries, he sided with the dictator, Carranza. Wilson gave the order for US railroads to carry federal Mexican troops all along the border to attack Villa from the rear. Villa was dealt terrible blows and so was his army, even as Royal Navy codebreakers snatched German cables to and from Carranza. The Germans aimed to sow discord along both US borders to tie up

American and Canadian troops and keep them away from the war raging in France. Backing Carranza was a massive American blunder that would only be settled in France and at the cost of millions of lives.

Scott was shocked and ashamed. His own country had just betrayed its very principles, all to maintain a neutrality that would only end in a larger war and over a hundred thousand Americans dead. "General Scott stated that no man ever had as much right as Villa to turn against him, yet Villa maintained that Scott was the only honest man north of Mexico," Ellis, the doctor, recorded. Meanwhile, Carranza's forces not only attacked from American territory but staged atrocities and blamed them on Villa.

According to the eyewitness accounts of Ellis and other Americans who were with Villa, he did not even participate in the fateful raid on Columbus, New Mexico, on March 8 and 9, 1916—but out-of-uniform federal troops did. The savage attack raided an armory and burned much of the dusty little town in the New Mexico desert, killing eight people; at the time, it was only the second instance of a foreign power attacking the United States. Multiple Americans who were with Villa say the same as his doctor: the general was home in bed, deep inside Chihuahua, sick with a cold. The disguised federal troops, according to the author Frank M. King, recorded that they were led by a man the troops had never seen "made up to look like Pancho Villa."[37] After the attack, Carranza's troops—now in uniform but still in the United States—were captured by National Guard troops and confessed to the raid under General Manuel Obregon and a German agent, Luther Wertz.[38]

Walking right into the German trap, Wilson ordered American troops to invade Mexico to catch or kill Villa. For two months, his Punitive Expedition hunted down suspected Villistas and sent them back to Columbus to stand trial. Some were executed, yet many were acquitted. After two fruitless months, American troops withdrew to El Paso. The US Army then proceeded to triple-cross Villa: American troops and artillery made a night attack into Juárez on behalf of Carranza's troops.

"What does the world think about me; what is the consensus of opinion as to whether I'm dead or alive?" Villa, trying to mend after being shot in the leg, asked a visiting American as the tide of the war turned against him. Always, he wanted Americans to love him, to love the revolution, to love Mexico.[39]

On January 9, 1917, Berlin decided on unrestricted submarine warfare off the US and Mexican coasts. The war that Wilson could have fought earlier on behalf of democracy only swelled in scale, a now unavoidable storm. In Washington, he foolishly hoped for a peace deal and what he called, to Congress, "peace without victory."[40] Later that year, Royal Navy codebreakers made a unique find in a cable from Berlin to the embassy in Mexico City. The Germans wanted Carranza to enter the war on their side and against the United States—and Berlin would guarantee that the Mexican Cession, all of the Southwest, was returned.

We intend to begin unrestricted submarine warfare on the first of February. We shall endeavor in spite of this to keep the United States neutral. In the event of this not succeeding, we make Mexico a proposal of alliance on the following basis: make war together, generous financial support and an understanding on our part that Mexico is to reconquer the lost territory in Texas, New Mexico, and Arizona. The settlement in detail is left to you.

You will inform the president [of Mexico] of the above most secretly as soon as the outbreak of war with the United States is certain and add the suggestion that he should, on his own initiative, invite Japan to immediate adherence and at the same time mediate between Japan and ourselves.

Please call the president's attention to the fact that the unre-

stricted employment of our submarines now offers the prospect
of compelling England to make peace within a few months. Ac-
knowledge receipt.

—ZIMMERMANN[41]

The British passed the message to the US State Department,
which, in turn, gave it to Wilson. The March 1 *New York Times*
headline read:

GERMANY SEEKS ALLIANCE AGAINST US;

ASKS JAPAN AND MEXICO TO JOIN HER;

FULL TEXT OF HER PROPOSAL MADE PUBLIC.[42]

On March 20, after German U-boats sank three American
ships, Wilson met with his cabinet, and a majority demanded war.
Former president Theodore Roosevelt said: "If he does not go to
war I shall skin him alive."

On the night of April 2, Wilson asked Congress to declare war,
adding that the Zimmermann telegram was proof of Germany's
bid to "stir up enemies against us at our very doors." The United
States formally declared war on Germany on April 6, 1917. Three
years after the Mexican Revolution, on July 20, 1923, Villa would
be assassinated in Parral, Chihuahua, in a hail of machine-gun fire.
He was forty-five years old and left behind one young son, Antonio,
with the grieving Soledad.

THE YEAR 1918 was indeed fateful. That January, downriver from
El Paso, La Matanza came to call.

The village of Porvenir, Texas, was a small, dusty place, a collection of farmers, cowhands, and a school for children with names
like Bonilla, Flores, Gonzalez, Jáquez, Lares, Moralez, and Nieves.

In the darkness before dawn on the morning of January 24, 1918, Company B of the Texas Rangers arrived quietly on horseback. Along with four local ranch owners—Buck Pool, John Pool, Tom Snyder, and Raymond Fitzgerald—and a smattering of troops from the Eighth Cavalry, the Rangers ordered everyone out of bed. Men, women, and children stumbled out of their homes in the inky blackness. The ranchers were convinced that villagers were stealing cattle, so the Rangers then separated fifteen unarmed men and boys, marched them out of the village—and executed them. The surviving residents of Porvenir all fled to Mexico for their lives. The Rangers and ranchers tried to justify this barbaric act of mass murder, but Governor William Pettus Hobby in Austin wouldn't have it; he fired the Rangers, disbanded the company, and forced their commanding officer to resign.

Adjutant General James A. Harley, who commanded the Thirty-Sixth Division of the Texas National Guard, condemned the massacre, telling the resigning Ranger commander that "15 Mexicans were killed when they were under the custody of your men and after they had been arrested and unarmed. This was proven by all kinds of evidence, even by the confession of those who took part and by reports collected by this office and by Agents of the Government of the United States." He further stated that while the United States fought in World War I "to overthrow ruthless autocracy," the state of Texas would not "propose to tolerate it here at home."

History is personal; it happens to real people. The year 1918 was a momentous one for my family as well. In 1918, my maternal grandfather found himself orphaned by the Spanish flu in northern Mexico. An aunt took seven-year-old Antonio Delgado to the bridge into Laredo, Texas, and there left him alone with distant relatives who lived on a ranch. My paternal grandfather had been dropped at the St. Louis, Missouri, train station at the age of sixteen as his single mother pressed five dollars into his palm. He rode the rails out west as a hobo, a homeless man, until the United States entered the war. Then he left for the navy, embarked on a destroyer, and helped hunt German U-boats in the Atlantic as far as the Azores.

It was a brutal, punishing war, and by the time armistice was declared, on November 11, 1918, twenty million lay dead and twenty-one million had been wounded. Some two hundred thousand Mexican citizens, Spanish citizens, and Mexican Americans had gone to war in Europe for the United States.[43] It bought them no justice at home.

--------- **Chapter Thirteen** ----------

THE KLAN, 1921–39

I T CAN BE said that the struggle for civil rights in North America
had many different beginnings. Some would put it in the 1950s
or 1960s in the American South, as many textbooks claim.[1] Some
identify it as the landmark Supreme Court ruling in *Brown v. Board
of Education*, which struck down segregated schools in 1954. But
there is a case to be made that it began as a struggle for basic human
rights undertaken by women in El Paso during World War I.

On January 28, 1917, seventeen-year-old Carmelita Torres
leapt aboard the streetcar and crossed the Santa Fe bridge, just as
she had nearly every morning on her way to work as a maid in
El Paso. To her astonishment, as she disembarked on the American side of the bridge, US customs officers told her to strip. She
was to be physically inspected while completely nude. Then she
would have to take a shower and be doused with gasoline to disin-
fect her. Enraged, she enlisted thirty other women waiting to cross
to demonstrate against the US officers. By 8:30 a.m., two hundred
Mexican women blocked all traffic into El Paso. By noon, there
were several thousand. They marched on the crude disinfectant facilities. When customs officers tried to stop them, the officers were

met with hurled rocks and bottles, jeers, and profanity. When US Army troops arrived, the women screamed at them; one got hit in the face.

Streetcars couldn't cross. Traffic snarled. Women tore the cloth tops and horns of automobiles, smashed the vehicles' back windows, and commandeered streetcars. The rioting continued into the next day, aided now by men. Mexican troops from the dictatorship showed up on horseback and drew their swords. The women mocked, insulted, and even attacked them; their wrath was evidently more furious than hell. Rumors circulated among them that women who submitted to inspections and delousing were then being burned alive. It turned out too that soldiers had been taking pictures of women stripping and showering.[2]

The mayor of El Paso, Tom Lea, a Missouri lawyer, had been instrumental in initiating this dehumanizing practice. He had two powerful phobias: Mexicans and disease. He even wore silk underwear, as he'd heard that lice couldn't thrive on silk. Lea shut down four Spanish-language newspapers in El Paso and repeatedly ordered raids on the Mexican American population of Chihuahuita in search of typhus, after health inspectors had already concluded there was none; after five thousand raids, they finally found one case. Lea was also a member of the local Ku Klux Klan, which had spread across the South and now into Texas.

As the protests went on, the wealthy of El Paso became angry without their maids and gardeners. The chamber of commerce complained about workers unable to get to work. Finally, customs officials relented. No more stripping, showers, and inspections for people from Juárez. They would instead get a weekly pass and could provide certificates of health from their own doctors. Even though Congress passed harsh immigration restrictions within days, border businessmen lobbied for an exemption, and well into 1921 they

got it. Having referred to the workers as "all the dirty, lousy people coming into this country from Mexico," Lea grew incredibly
unpopular and served only a single term.[3]

As the historian David Romo has noted, Carmelita Torres
might have been as important a figure as Rosa Parks. Yet history
forgot her, and for this reason: though Lea may have fallen out of
favor, his views hadn't. Two things were alive and well in 1920s and
1930s America: the Klan and the Nazis.

BY THE 1920S, El Paso would be practically unrecognizable to
those familiar with it only a decade or so earlier. The oil boom
of East Texas oddly triggered an oil boom in El Paso in the early
1920s. But it soon became clear that there was no oil under the
desert, just water. The boom was a mirage that disappeared.[4]

Nevertheless, adobe buildings were demolished and replaced
with steel and brick. The grand cataracts that had forced the Spanish away from the river and into the desert were destroyed with
explosives. A new wealthy neighborhood went up between the old
Sunset Heights and the Franklin Mountains: elegant Kern Place,
with perfect vistas of downtown and far into Mexico. Henry Trost, a
young architect by way of Chicago, set up shop with two brothers and began to design hundreds of new buildings all over the
American Southwest. Trost refashioned much of El Paso with his
own hand, even designing the new Popular store of the Schwartz
family.[5] Mexican Americans were increasingly crowded into Chihuahuita down by the river and the Segundo Barrio just east of
Kansas Street.

Across the Southwest, Mexicans and Mexican Americans alike
challenged their presumed servility. The Mexican Revolution concluded in 1920 with the emergence of a centrist government and
effective one-party state; a following of laborers, workers, and the

military; a vast patronage; and a graft-ridden system, all cloaked in the language and symbols of revolution, which mimicked social democracy.[6] In the United States, nearly five hundred thousand people of Mexican birth now lived primarily in the Southwest, just as the Italian- and German-born populations had previously swelled on the East Coast.[7] Combined with the prewar Mexican American population, their total was nearly seven hundred thousand.

Many of the new arrivals were educated, and wealthy enough to get out of Mexico. Throughout the Southwest, these people were generally acceptable to Anglo elites; like those before them, these Anglos and Mexicans socialized, did business together, and married each other. Regardless of class, intermarriages sprouted like spring desert flowers. Chinese married Mexicans in Tucson; Mexican Americans married Blacks in Tucson and Las Cruces.[8] As a share of population, the non-Hispanic white population actually dipped in Texas;[9] the US census from 1920 did not differentiate between whites and Hispanics, classifying all as white. In 1921 in San Antonio, Latino workers organized the Orden Hijos de América, or Order of the Sons of America, to raise awareness of civil rights and to demand fair wages, education, and housing.[10] In the 1920s, twenty-nine states—and all of the Deep South—banned intermarriage between Blacks and whites, but even in Texas, marriage between Anglos and Hispanics was not only legal but increasingly common.[11] That same year, a new federal immigration law took effect, sharply restricting the number of immigrants from southern Europe and, at the urging of businesses in the Southwest, increasing immigration from, yes, Mexico.

All of which began to beg a new question: What—or rather, who—was white anyway? And what did it matter? Most of the cases that reached state supreme courts involved the marriage of a Black person to a Hispanic one, and in nearly all those cases, the picture that emerged was entirely muddled because a Hispanic person was officially white.[12] Or was this the case? Native Americans too were not officially considered, except by the census, to fall into any category other than white, though they hardly received preferential treatment.

John Lucas and Felicitas Leyva met after they both fled to El Paso. Lucas escaped one of the most deeply racist cities in the Lone Star State: Tyler, set deep in the Piney Woods of East Texas, a hot, humid place of towering trees, slow rivers, and fields full of chiggers, biting insects that mercilessly feed on human blood. Just after Lucas was born, Tyler experienced a wave of horrific lynchings. As an adult, he wisely got out, making his way to El Paso by 1917. Leyva crossed the Rio Grande, fleeing the Mexican Revolution with a four-year-old son. The two married in 1919—but not in El Paso. "El Pasoans wed in Las Cruces," read the tiny announcement in the January 29, 1920, issue of the *El Paso Herald*. He worked as a boilermaker, she as a maid.

"Las Cruces, New Mexico provided opportunities to Black El Pasoans that were denied by Texas law, including the right to marry a 'white' woman and get an education at the New Mexico College of Agriculture and Mechanic Arts," their granddaughter, Yolanda Chávez Leyva, a historian at the University of Texas at El Paso, wrote.[13] In the same year that Lucas arrived, another Black man from East Texas came to El Paso: Dr. Lawrence Aaron Nixon packed up his practice and fled his hometown of Marshall for the exact same reasons Lucas did.

But there was a backlash against these newcomers. The Anglo onslaught of settlers had peaked in population by the 1920s, just as the Mexican Revolution began to tip the scale with fresh immigrants through and to El Paso. The newest Anglos seemed unable to understand or accept living in what had been—until the Mexican-American War, the forty-niners, and the railroad—a racially and ethnically diverse region.[14]

Still, diversity flourished despite the racial tension. El Paso was accepting of nearly all comers, very much unlike most of Texas and the Deep South. Syrians and Lebanese Christians had trickled in during the nineteenth century, but after the shattering of the Ottoman Empire in World War I, they came in large numbers, worshipping as Roman Catholics even though most were Antiochian Orthodox, Greek Catholic, or Maronite. They competed with the Jewish merchant class before branching into manufacturing, medicine, and law.

This went on, with occasional resentments and skirmishes but overall acceptance, until the period after World War I, when a new force emerged in town: the Klan. Derived from the Greek word for band or circle, *kuklos*, the original Klan formed out of the ashes of the Civil War in Pulaski, Tennessee, in 1865. It was a wet nurse to racism and the shame of defeat. In its original incarnation, it was confined mostly to northeast Texas. When Congress banned the Ku Klux Klan as an illegal, secret conspiracy against the United States in 1871, the Klan in Texas quickly collapsed. But after World War I, a new Klan, modeled on the old one, appeared in the torchlight at a ceremony in Stone Mountain, Georgia. From there it spread like wildfire across the South and into Texas—this time, into El Paso itself. The Klan's strategy was shrewd, enlisting as many local politicians, bureaucrats, police sheriffs, business leaders, and lawyers as possible, thereby stockpiling power in secret. Of its hundred thousand members in Texas, many came from the elite and governing classes.[15] For the new Klan, it wasn't enough to strike fear into the hearts of African Americans and others. This time around it aimed to take power—something it had not been able to do during Reconstruction.[16]

No longer a secret enterprise engaged in violent crime, the new Klan was perfectly legal, out in the open, and protected by the First Amendment. It preached a gospel of white male supremacy,

Protestantism, and law and order, not as a competing ideology but as the definition of American nationalism. It staunchly opposed the emerging radicalisms of early twentieth-century America: agrarianism populism and socialism. From the Klan's Frontier Post No. 1, it selected its first target: the public school board. Even today, service on a school board can be a sly and effective stepping stone to power. If a movement can secure majorities on school boards, they can assemble majorities in cities, counties, and entire states, winning congressional districts and Senate seats. And if the states control the electoral process, as they did a hundred years ago, movements that control them can also gain control of the presidential electoral process by appointing members of the electoral college; after all, voters had only just gotten the power to elect their own senators with the Seventeenth Amendment in 1917.

In 1921, as El Pasoans were distracted by dreams of oil fortunes and by a feud that broke out between Catholics and Protestants, the Klan stunned the city: it captured the majority of seats on the local school board. Taking advantage of the strong feelings aroused by the feud between religious denominations, it had won by bashing Catholics, who, by the way, were the very first Christians in El Paso. The African American population in the city was too small to be a target; it had actually fallen by half, from just 3 percent, since 1910. Once on the board, the Klan became more interested in political performance art than meaningful work in education. It named, or renamed, schools for heroes of the Confederacy and the rebellion against Mexico; it banned books and engaged in anti-Catholic reprisals, firing school principals for attending non-Protestant churches. Running for office as members of the Democratic Party, which dominated Texas, the Klan set its next target: taking the county. One of its three candidates won. Next up: the city elections of 1923. If the Klan could win there, it would also control, most ominously, the police.

Richard M. Dudley was the Democratic candidate. A Kentuckian by birth and engineer by training, with experience in the Chihuahua railways and New York Harbor, he was also a banker by trade and had served in the state legislature. A square-faced, honest man, Dudley had been married to the same woman for almost thirty years, Fannie Moore of Tarrytown, New York, and the couple had no children.[17] P. E. Gardner was the Klan candidate, and as Dudley correctly made clear, there was but one issue facing the thirteen thousand voters who turned out on February 24, 1923: the Klan itself. In El Paso, a Catholic and increasingly Hispanic city, that was a lethal move, and Dudley defeated Gardner early in the evening with a two-thousand-vote lead. In fact, all of his Democrats defeated their Klan opponents for the city council. It was a crushing blow.

The *El Paso Times,* the dominant morning newspaper, was practically giddy the next day. The reporter Bob Chapman wrote: "El Paso is not a Ku Klux Klan town. This was the word sent out by El Pasoans yesterday to the country after an election which resulted in a decisive victory for the opponents of the hooded organization. R.M. Dudley won by 2,120 votes. He got 7,572 and P.E. Gardner got 5,452. There were 13,024 ballots cast according to unofficial but complete returns. The voting yesterday was for or against the klan. This was the only issue involved. The result showed El Paso was whole-heartedly against such a secret organization."[18]

It was the beginning of the end for the Klan in Texas; it was forced underground and eventually out of business in all but the farthest reaches of East Texas, after numbering 150,000 Klansmen at its peak. Women too were the key to the Klan's demise; the state was one of the first to ratify the Nineteenth Amendment, finally allowing women to vote, as it did in 1919.[19] Five years later, Texas held a race for governor. The Democrats already controlled the antebellum governor's mansion in Austin, just across the street from the sweeping lawns and pink granite of the capitol, with James "Pa" Ferguson, though the legislature impeached him for unduly interfering in the University of Texas at Austin. Although he was barred from state office, he could run for the US Senate, and did so in 1922: as an anti-Klan, anti-Prohibition, pro-populist, and pro-farmer candidate. He lost.[20]

In 1924, his wife, "Ma" Ferguson, stepped up. Many suspected she was just a stand-in for her husband, who sought to govern from the shadows. She ran on exactly the same platform, but came out more directly against the Klan. She also made it clear that "Pa" would, indeed, have a say in governing; by this she gained votes from his supporters. She squeaked into a runoff in the Democratic primary that spring and then crushed both her opponents. In the general election she faced off against a handsome, urbane law professor, George Charles Butte, who ran as a Republican but drew strong Klan support.[21] Ma Ferguson crushed him by nearly eighteen points.[22] As a political entity, the twentieth-century Klan was dead in Texas.

Ma Ferguson became the first woman elected governor in the history of the United States.

DESPITE THE KLAN'S drubbing at the ballot box, racism was very much alive and well in Texas and the Democratic Party.

In 1924, a tall, lean African American doctor from Marshall walked up to his polling station for the spring primary. Dr. Lawrence Nixon had built a successful life and practice in El Paso after fleeing East Texas. He paid his poll taxes of $1.75 for each election cycle and dutifully voted. He was also a member of the National Association for the Advancement of Colored People (NAACP) and had been for fourteen years. But in 1923, at the height of the Klan's influence in Texas, the state legislature had cravenly banned African Americans from voting in primaries, and the only one that mattered was the Democratic one. The national NAACP was seeking a challenger to the new law—and it chose Nixon in El Paso.

"We are looking for someone who is not afraid," the field secretary, William Pickens, said.[23] The quiet doctor agreed and arrived at the polling station, poll tax receipt in hand, on July 26, 1924.

Nixon later recalled: "The Judges were friends of mine. They inquired after my health, and when I presented my poll tax receipt, one of them said, 'Dr. Nixon, you know we can't let you vote.' 'I know you can't,' Dr. Nixon replied. 'But I've got to try.'"[24]

With the help of the NAACP, Nixon sued both election judges and sought damages from the state as well. When a federal judge in San Antonio dismissed the case, he appealed straight to the Supreme Court. In *Nixon v. Herndon,* the court ruled that "it seems to us so hard to imagine a more direct and obvious infringement of the Fourteenth [Amendment]."

The court further commented on the Fourteenth Amendment: ". . . while it applies to all, [it] was passed, as we know with a special intent to protect the blacks from discrimination against them . . . [and it] not only gave citizenship and the privileges of citizenship to persons of color, but it denied to any State the power to withhold from them the equal protection of the laws . . . What is this but declaring that the law in the States shall be the same for the black as for the white; that all persons, whether colored or white, shall stand."[25]

Undeterred, the Texas legislature quickly passed another law: granting power over primaries not to the state but to the two parties, namely the Democratic one, as Texas was still mostly a one-party state. The Democratic Executive Committee in Austin then adopted a new rule excluding African Americans from voting in primaries and, essentially, giving all power in state politics to white voters. Nixon sued again, citing the Thirteenth, Fourteenth, and

Fifteenth Amendments: abolishing slavery, establishing citizenship for Blacks, and stating that no rights shall be abridged to any citizen of the United States. For good measure, the Supreme Court ruling from his previous case was tacked on.[26] The new case, *Nixon v. Condon*, made its way through the federal court system.

The defendants tried to argue, rather cleverly, that the previous case did not apply because the state Democratic Party was not a part of the state government. But that was pure sophistry, and the court wasn't buying it: "The result for [Dr. Nixon] is no different from what it was when his cause was here before . . . delegates of the State's power have discharged their official functions in such a way as to discriminate invidiously between white citizens and black."[27]

Texas fought on to keep Blacks from voting; El Paso was paying a price for having joined Texas instead of New Mexico, a far more liberal and inclusive state. Nevertheless, the two Nixon lawsuits would eventually pave the way for the Supreme Court to finally issue an outright ban on segregating primary elections.

Not until 1944 did Nixon cast his first primary vote, after persistently demanding to do so for more than twenty years.

THE STRUGGLE WAS hardly over. Delousing made a return appearance as the 1930s approached. On January 19, 1929, the medical officer at the border delousing station, J. R. Hurley, tried a new approach. For the mere price of $25 he purchased a new agent with which to disinfect Mexicans: Zyklon B, a hydrocyanic gas that in higher doses could be more lethal than any poison gas used in World War I. It would, of course, go on to infamy in the next war, used by the Nazis in their grisly network of concentration camps.

The experiment on Mexicans in El Paso, was, in fact, closely watched by the Germans, who would insist on delousing residents of the Warsaw Ghetto in 1940 "at the point of a bayonet," as a

British epidemiologist put it. In the United States too, eugenics gained ground, a pseudoscience based upon race that masqueraded as a medically sound theory of hygiene. Anglos, Saxons, and Goths bathed properly and had good hygiene; everybody else didn't and had bad hygiene. These theories informed the immigration law passed by Congress in 1924. As the El Paso historian David Romo has put it: "The enforced baths and delousing stations were not about the elimination of sickness and disease. If so, they wouldn't have continued for decades after the typhus scare was over. Instead, the U.S. Customs sterilization plants were mostly about what sociologists call 'the medicalization of power'—about border agents armed with medical degrees taking over where the military had left off. The job of these petty bureaucrat doctors was to protect America from the dirty, the dumb, the destitute and the defective."[28]

Into this atmosphere of racist pseudoscience came economic catastrophe. On October 29, 1929, the New York Stock Exchange collapsed, the banks collapsed, and the world was plunged into the Great Depression. One of the first things the Hoover administration did was order the roundup of anyone with a "Mexican-sounding name." From California to Texas, agents swept up 1.8 million people and pushed them by train and bus and on foot into Mexico. At least half of them were American citizens; many had been born in the United States.[29] It was essentially the first family-separation policy in American history since the end of slavery. Of course, it would not be the last.

"Individuals who left at 5, 6 and 7 years old found themselves in Mexico dealing with the process of socialization, of learning the language, but they maintained an American identity," according to the historian Francisco Balderrama, who focused particularly on the harsh forcible deportations carried out by both local and federal authorities in Los Angeles, "and still had the dream to come back to 'my country.'"[30] Mexican Americans and Mexicans, young and old, packed their cars, boarded buses and trains, and headed south, just likes Okies from the Dust Bowl, who migrated westward in the same desperate fashion.[31]

Though El Paso had prospered in the 1920s, when it became known as the "Queen City of the Southwest," the city and its surrounding region were not spared the devastating effects of the Great Depression. Instead of working primarily as domestic servants, nannies, and cooks, women found their way into manufacturing. Yet the need for labor declined as the money simply dried up like an arroyo after the rain. At the same time, Anglos tried to displace Mexican American and Mexican workers in the field and on the factory floor. As far as wages went, it was a race to the bottom. A report from the state of Texas at the time found that in El Paso "long hours of drudgery and starvation pay are the rule rather than the exception."[32] Unions organized but couldn't stem the increasing poverty. Not while Mexican citizens would work for a dollar a day—or less.[33]

The Depression brought into sharp relief the conflicted relationship between Americans and Mexicans. On the one hand the former wanted—indeed, demanded—Mexican labor. There was general agreement that people of Mexican descent, whatever nation they lived in, were honest, hardworking people, whether they were doctors or gardeners. As one newspaper columnist, Anna Brand of the *El Paso Herald Post,* put it, "When you think of the streets that have been paved, the ditches that have been dug, the clothes that have been washed by faithful hard-working Mexican hands in this town, how can you imagine the town without them?"[34]

Nevertheless, there was still more than a tinge of ethnic loathing among white Americans toward any people who were not quite white enough—particularly when times got tough. But increasingly, people of Mexican descent were deciding they were not going to take it. Those who were citizens of the United States demanded all of the rights owed them based on that status. As the historian Yolanda Chávez Leyva wrote:

> The Great Depression was a decade of paradox for the Mexican community in El Paso. The Depression brought enormous changes; yet, change appeared minimal. Although Mexican women had been employed in the service and manufacturing sectors since the nineteenth century, the Depression created new expectations and a new sense of identity for some workers. These changes helped maintain old arguments about work and power, yet they also created new ways for women workers to participate in the debate. Increasingly, Mexican-American women and men challenged the racist characterizations of the "Mexican worker."[35]

IN GERMANY, PEOPLE took notice of what was happening in El Paso and all along the Mexican border, and grew interested in new ways to deal with an unpopular minority. A German scientist called for a similar use of Zyklon B, writing enthusiastically in 1937 and including photos of the El Paso gas chambers and diagrams of them. The 1939 issue of *Anzeiger für Schädlingskunde*, a pest-control journal, read: "WE ARE CLOSING THE BORDERS TO THE IMMIGRATION OF HARMFUL PESTS." An adjacent map hopefully suggested the location of delousing stations at border crossings, to be used on pedestrians or even trainloads of passengers, relying on "a steady stream of poison gas."

Adolf Hitler was watching too.

After he was thrown in prison in 1923 for staging the Beerhall Putsch in Munich, an attempted coup d'état against the Weimar government, Hitler had plenty of time on his hands, and he grew particularly fond of American racial policies. In his book *Mein Kampf,* he wrote: "Compared to old Europe, which had lost an infinite amount of its best blood through war and emigration, the American nation appears as a young and racially select people. The American union itself, motivated by the theories of its own racial researchers established specific criteria for immigration . . . making an immigrant's ability to set foot on American soil dependent on specific racial requirements on the one hand as well as a certain level of physical health of the individual himself."[36]

Mein Kampf became a bestseller when it was published in 1923, electrifying Germany. The historian Detlef Junker concluded that for Hitler, the United States was "*the* model of a state organized on principles of *Rasse* and *Raum {race* and *space}*"—race defined the population, and by extension, the nation.[37] There had always been fraternal German organizations, and during World War I, the United States had imprisoned, harassed, and discriminated against Germans. But Hitler replaced German international organizations in America with the German American Bund, an organization built of infiltrators, diplomats, and spies trying to tap into links to the racist state he was creating when he ascended to the chancellorship on January 30, 1933.[38]

Indeed, he quickly began patterning his new racial laws, which would kill twelve million people, half of them Jews, on those of one country alone: the United States.

---------- **Chapter Fourteen** ----------

A WORLD AT WAR, 1940–41

A S THE CLOUDS of war darkened over Europe and Asia, Fort
Bliss was still a sleepy cavalry post.

The renowned First Cavalry Division had been activated for
the first time at Fort Bliss, its mounted troopers parading on the
post and traveling a specially cut road over the Franklin Mountains to patrol the banks of the Rio Grande and go on maneuvers
in the desert with their associated artillery, signalmen, and supply train. Some of these exercises were huge: 280 officers, 4,000
men, 3,200 horses, and 1,500 mules spanned the gulches, hillocks,
and sagebrush plains. Tanks, artillery, airplanes, and ambulances
all joined in mock war against an entirely separate cavalry division
from Marfa on the dusty, hot landscape. Their distinctive oversized
unit arm patch—a yellow shield with a thick blue sash across it and
a blue horse-head profile in one upper corner—flashed in the sun
and dust.[1]

Yet the time of horse-mounted warfare was drawing to a close
by 1940. Germany had started the war with a huge cavalry, but
dive bombers, artillery, and tanks led the Blitzkrieg in Europe.
Horses, nearly all Western breeds or mixes, served in the initial

Japanese war in China but obviously could play virtually no role in long-range strikes across the Pacific or island-hopping.[2] The ten thousand men of the "First Cav" nevertheless prepared for war in Asia with their mounts, shipped by rail to the swamps of Louisiana and East Texas.[3] The Texas landscape could offer little in the way of preparation for most of the combat in World War II.

The neighboring New Mexico National Guard would ship out to Asia first. Tapped for a year's tour, eighteen hundred men of the 200th Coast Artillery Regiment—many of them Hispanic—mustered in Santa Fe late on January 6, 1941, where they were federalized and shipped south to Fort Bliss. The regiment came from a distinguished lineage: it was the longest continually serving militia in the United States. Originally Spanish, the unit was later commanded by the famed Indian fighter Kit Carson. In the Civil War, it defeated Sibley's brigade from Texas. Finally, in September 1880, these men were officially organized as the 111th Cavalry.

Horsemen for sixty years, the New Mexicans were converted to anti-aircraft defense in 1940, so they sharpened their gun skills in the desert ranges of Fort Bliss while training and drilling up to standards as federalized soldiers. Their three-inch "ack-ack" guns fired with a vertical range of over twenty thousand feet; the men practiced with these and their .50 caliber machine guns, including by night with searchlights. In September 1941 they traveled more than a thousand miles to San Francisco by means of a 250-vehicle truck convoy to be posted at Angel Island in the Bay. Though they had been chosen personally by General Douglas MacArthur, the men had no idea where they were going.

"We were a cross-section of New Mexico," one soldier, Luther Ragsdale, later said. "Professors, students, miners, lumberjacks, cowboys, rodeo performers, sheepherders, farmers, bus drivers. We had Navajos, Pueblos, Apaches, and Zunis. And everyone performed 120 percent."

Largely overlooked by history and popular culture, the people of the Southwest who served in the military—including large numbers of Native people, Hispanic Americans, and Mexican citizens—went into the world's greatest war for America. Despite having suffered discrimination and mass expulsions to Mexico, half a million men of Mexican origin served. Having once despised Mexican workers, the United States now flung open its doors to millions of them. An elite Mexican American unit from El Paso fought its way across North Africa and up the Italian peninsula with enormous bravery. The Mexican Air Force fought the Empire of Japan with precision and courage. The 111th followed suit.

Once aboard two troop ships, the USS *President Pierce* and the USS *President Coolidge,* the men of the 200th Coastal Artillery learned their destination: Manila. The mission there was to protect Clark Field. The United States had not yet entered the war, but the threat of being dragged into another global catastrophe was impossible to ignore. Aboard ship in the middle of the vast, blue Pacific, the men had no way of knowing what had already been decided in Japan. Faced with a crushing American oil embargo, the Japanese Cabinet had met on September 4, 1941, to consider plans from the Imperial General Headquarters and concluded that they were ready to go to war with the United States.

On September 24, Takeo Yoshikawa, the Japanese vice-consul in Honolulu, received an order from Tokyo. A former naval officer turned spy, he was to map Pearl Harbor into five zones, provide the number of battleships at anchor, and report back. He rented a second-story apartment with an impressive view of the harbor.

Out in the vast Pacific, except when huge ocean swells brought waves of nausea, the mood belowdecks on the American troop ships was good. Navy food was far better than GI food; the men had no set routine and rose from their racks when they wanted. The *Coolidge* even had a five-piece band, and the officers would sneak

down to their men's staterooms for hooch that the troops were buying from the swabbies.[4]

Still, there was a feeling of foreboding. Slipping under the
Golden Gate Bridge, Second Lieutenant Al Stuttman turned to Sergeant Winston Shillito, saying: "Some of us won't see that bridge
again."[5]

BORN IN 1915 in El Paso, Gabriel Navarrete had spent much of
his working life sweating in the hot repair shops of the huge railyard owned by the Southern Pacific Railroad just east of downtown.
To help him and his wife, Elvira Aguirre, make ends meet, he became a part-time soldier with the Texas National Guard, known for
its fighting in France in World War I and its unusual unit patch: a
flint arrowhead emblazoned with a big "T" for Texas. He enlisted
for a standard one-year contract on active duty.

Navarrete soon realized he had a knack for this soldiering business: he swiftly rose to the rank of sergeant at the training camp at
Camp Bowie in Brownwood, southwest of Abilene in the brushy
Texas Big Country.[6] To celebrate, he took a couple of friends, all in
uniform, into town, to a hamburger and milkshake joint. But the
sign on the window was clear: "No Mexicans or Dogs Allowed."

The woman inside ordered them around to the back door to
pick up their food from the kitchen. Angry, the men returned to
Camp Bowie, and Navarrete marched straight to his lieutenant's
office. "If this is the way American soldiers were going to be
treated," he demanded, "then I might as well join the Mexican
Army." Second Lieutenant John L. Chapin was not Hispanic, but
he was a son of El Paso, having grown up and attended Ysleta High
School alongside Hispanic boys, like the men he now commanded.
The officer tried to calm Navarrete, then went down the hall and
returned with a colonel.

Why exactly were the men not served?

"Because they are Mexicans and we don't serve Mexicans," Navarrete replied, parroting the business owner.

After a second attempt to be served, this time with the colonel in tow, also failed, the colonel declared the burger joint off-limits to *all* base personnel. That got the owner's attention; she rushed to the base to apologize. Tens of thousands of hungry men would not be allowed back unless the owner paid a $500 fine for refusing to serve the men of Company E, Second Battalion, 141st Regiment, Thirty-Sixth Division.

While much has been written in deserved adulation of the 442nd Infantry Regiment, composed entirely of Japanese Americans fighting in Europe, comparatively little has been said of another racially segregated group: the men of Company E, the all Mexican American and Mexican unit from El Paso. They were a tight-knit group, many sharing the same high school, the same slang. As the California author David Gutierrez describes them, "Company E was like a Bowie High School reunion. If you were from the Segundo barrio and someone asked you where you went to school, the reply was never Bowie High; it was always 'La Bowie.'"[7]

The company was filled with men who'd known each other, or at least of each other, all their lives. Some of their parents had crossed the Rio Grande. Some of them had had the boundary line cross them, as the new Western portion of America absorbed not just territory but its Mexican population. Some had been lifelong friends and even had the same first name, such as Los Dos Mannys: the Two Mannys. Two were encouraged to become officers; one of them was Navarrete. Both were rejected, likely because they were of Mexican origin. Some were from small Texas towns like Sonora and Del Rio. The occasional new guy had to contend with a company that had been together a long time, were some of the best crack shots in the US Army—and were mostly from the same barrio in El Paso, known as "El Chuco."[8]

Listening to the roster of one Spanish name after another as the men fell into formation, one veteran, Gabriel Salazar, later wrote, "Anyone would think we were a battalion from the Juarez garrison."

The men turned one of their own, Roque Segura, into a company cook so he could serve up the Mexican dishes they had grown up on. These were far better than the standard-issue "shit-on-a-shingle" (corned beef and gravy on toast) or "dog food" (corned beef hash) that were daily slopped onto most GI metal trays. Unfortunately for the men, one day a frustrated Segura untied his apron, tossed it aside, and walked out of the kitchen for good, yelling: "I came to learn how to be a soldier! Not a *pinche* cook!"[9]

It turned out that Segura was an even finer soldier than he was a chef. In fact, 100 percent of the men qualified as marksmen with their M-1 rifles, one of the first companies to do so; the company had won the regimental championship for eight straight years. On maneuvers in Louisiana, their division of Texans defeated the opposing Twenth-Seventh Infantry Division from New York. At Camp Bowie in November 1941, one man, Edmundo Moreno from El Paso, was such an excellent soldier, he was selected for elite commando Ranger training at Fort Sam Houston; he would return to train the rest.

Navarrete began to pack to go home to El Paso; his yearlong hitch in the National Guard was up, and he was eager to be with his wife and little boy again. His discharge date was just a few squares down the calendar: December 10, 1941.

AFTER TAKING ON a warship and spotter plane escort outside Hawaii, the New Mexicans endured a queasy ride through a howling typhoon. Finally, after they had spent two months at sea, the Philippine Islands came into view in November. With one troop ship ten full days behind the other, sailors unloaded their cargo of troops and equipment in bustling Manila Bay. Unbeknownst to them, navy codebreakers had intercepted a Japanese message to its Washington embassy: an all-encompassing agreement with Washington that would, among other things, end the oil embargo had to be completed by November 25. If not, the only other option was war.

The men of the 200th took up rotten quarters at Fort Stotsenberg, an old cavalry post next to Clark Field. Many of them, particularly the Native Americans and Hispanics, felt the uncomfortable stares from fellow soldiers nearby, who were not used to cowboys, professors, and shopkeepers whose names were not Smith or Jones. But the officers of the Twenty-Sixth Cavalry offered the ex-cavalrymen the use of their horses when off-duty, and the New Mexicans immediately dashed home letters for bridles, saddles, and more, with visions of tropical polo in their heads.

By December 4, a large Japanese convoy was sailing from Formosa—directly for the Philippines. The US Navy intercepted another message: "East winds, rain." The president concluded that this meant war, and General Douglas MacArthur ordered a full alert on Sunday, December 7, 1941; on the other side of the international date line, it was still December 6.

For most of the men in the Philippines, it was another languid Sunday in an exotic foreign land—once part of the same Spanish Empire from which they sprang and where the familiarities of Catholicism, the Spanish language, tortillas, and beans could be easily found. Some of the men watched a polo match; some sat and drank scotch in the afternoon; two went to the movies to watch a Dick Tracy film. One duty officer was so bored, he loaded his jeep with rum and distributed it to the men; the ensuing party lasted till just before reveille on Monday.

But there was not just one Japanese fleet on the move in the

Pacific, there were two, as army intelligence would confirm. The historian Dorothy Cave recounts it: "Toward morning, Cpl. Walter Johnson, at his station, listened to music on a homemade radio. Suddenly, an excited announcer broke in. Johnson gasped. He grabbed the phone. 'Tell the captain!'—his voice sounded like a stranger to itself. 'Tell him—they're bombing Pearl Harbor!'"[10]

---------- **Chapter Fifteen** ----------

WAR AND HOPE, 1941–50

THE ATTACK ON Hawaii took place at 2:20 a.m. Philippines time; the news reached Corporal Johnson shortly afterward and, eventually, General MacArthur's staff.[1] The Japanese approached the Philippines with the power of a typhoon, but far deadlier: over five hundred aircraft striking from Formosa, two hundred miles away; from bases in Indochina and Japan; and from carrier decks. Two entire army divisions, the Fourteenth and the Sixteenth, were afloat offshore, aboard ships of the navy's Third Fleet. The Japanese attacking force was massive, with three army divisions aboard. The Japanese pilots aboard their bombers could not believe their luck as they approached Clark Field: the entire Far East Air Force was wingtip to wingtip, just parked there in the midday light.

MacArthur had bungled the job.[2] While he had ordered the base on alert on Sunday, he received further orders at 5:30 a.m.: execute War Plan Rainbow 5, to strike any Japanese force within range. The air commander pleaded all through the early morning to launch his aircraft while MacArthur delayed, even as a destroyer came under Japanese attack off Luzon. Finally, at mid-morning, MacArthur authorized pursuit squadrons and bombers on patrol over the Philippines, still not on the attack. Then he changed his mind and ordered the bombers back to refuel, in order to bomb Formosa. The bomber pilots obliged. The response was simply chaos: many of the airborne fighters were circling Manila, not engaging over Clark Field while Japanese Zeros descended low to strafe aircraft, rupturing fuel tanks and setting aprons ablaze. The biographer William Manchester would later describe MacArthur, in his office, as "catatonic."

Manchester added, "By 1:37 P.M., when the last Japanese plane soared away, Clark was unrecognizable."[3]

THE JAPANESE ALSO struck a fighter base at Iba, where all but one P-40 aircraft was stationed. In the panic, MacArthur ordered the remaining airborne bombers to abandon the fight and head for safety in Australia. At 12:35, nearly fifty bombers unloaded over six hundred 130-pound bombs on Clark Field, at the effective safe altitude above the 200th Coast Artillery's 37 mm guns. The first Americans to open fire in the Philippines, the New Mexicans, banged away at the bombers and the low-level, strafing Zeros. As they hit, the Japanese bombs destroyed twelve of the seventeen B-17 bombers on the ground and damaged four more; only three escaped to Australia. The old P-40s that were aloft couldn't fly as high as the Japanese bombers, and half of them were destroyed on the ground or in the air. They were no match for Japanese Zeros over a hundred of which flew cover for the bombers. The New Mexicans downed five Japanese aircraft, and two of their own men died.[4]

The bombardment lasted just one hour and two minutes. Then, an eerie quiet settled over the remains of the base. "Except for sudden explosions, and wounded horses screaming in agony," Corporal Jack Aldrich recalled, "we were standing around in shock."[5] The Japanese lost but a handful of planes. The invasion began at the two islands of Mindanao and Luzon, south to north. The navy's Asiatic Fleet fought on but without sufficient air cover; within days, its surviving seaplanes withdrew to Dutch Indonesia, abandoning the Philippines and leaving behind a force of submarines that would prove, frankly, ineffectual.

The 200th, in the meantime, was split in two, and a new regiment was formed: the 515th, which was ordered to defend the skies over the capital, Manila, from follow-on attacks. By now, news of the attack had reached home by radio. As Glenn May, the historian, recounted it: "At home, New Mexicans listened tense-jawed. Proprietors turned up radios in stores and out on the sidewalks, where crowds gathered quietly. School children filed into auditoriums to listen. No one needed to be told it was a 'day of infamy,' but they wanted to hear it enunciated. Few families in the stricken state were without friends or family in the 200th."

On December 22, the main Japanese invasion force came ashore in the Philippines: over forty thousand men. Two American divisions were unable to repel them. The Twenty-Sixth Cavalry (which had offered its horses to the New Mexicans for sport) and Philippine scouts fared better, but sustained heavy casualties and fell back. On the day before Christmas, General MacArthur initiated War Plan Orange 3: with a few units blocking the Japanese, the primary American and Philippine force of eighty thousand men began to withdraw to the Bataan Peninsula. Four days later, MacArthur declared Manila an open city, so the Japanese might not destroy it. The New Mexicans abandoned Clark Field on Christmas Day and started hauling their guns, ammunition, and rations into the jungle. Private Evangelisto "Evans" Garcia said:

So many times, we were defending Manila. In December 1941, as we were defending the rear of the convoy leaving Manila, we could hear the Jap bombers coming. It was Christmas Eve, and

Christmas night. We had 37mm guns, so there was not a lot we could do against bombers. I ran to a Catholic church for cover with two other fellas.. There was a bridge close by that we had just crossed, and we could barely see the bombers coming. I said to myself "They're such poor bombers—if they try to hit the bridge, they'll hit the church." So I ran out of the church and got under the bridge, and the two other fellows followed. Here come the bombers. They hit one part of the bridge, but made a direct hit on the church. The fellows said "Evans, we're going where you go." I just sensed it that time.[6]

Over the next four months, the New Mexicans, now assisted by most of the 515th, scored nearly a hundred confirmed kills of attacking Japanese aircraft. They proved crucial in covering the retreat over Calumpit Bridge, spanning the deep Pampanga River, repeatedly pouring 50-caliber fire into Japanese troops trying to blow the bridges into Bataan and affording the retreating force of some forty thousand men an escape route.[7] But provisions were dwindling, and the infantry sustained heavy losses covering the rear. By March they were getting sick—malaria, dysentery, dengue fever, scurvy, beriberi—while suffering from dehydration and starvation.

"We ate elephant ears, and caught little fresh-water shrimp in the creeks—and you can get a lot of fish with a hand grenade," said Private John West. "We got to killing all the carabaos [water buffalo]. We ate wild hogs til we found out they were eating out of the slit trenches. And mangoes—I've seen guys in mango trees, with the Japs strafing and bombing—and they'd just stay up there gathering mangoes."

No reinforcements came. MacArthur didn't know that President Roosevelt had made a secret pact with British prime minister Winston Churchill: "Europe First." The increasingly besieged

Pacific—under invasion now in Dutch Indonesia, British Burma and Singapore, French Vietnam, and, of course, China and Korea—would have to wait. Japan's government even contemplated an assault on India. In late February, the War Department ordered MacArthur out of the Philippines.

AFTER A HARROWING sea voyage aboard four PT boats, MacArthur arrived at Del Monte Field on Mindanao for evacuation. Two B-17s touched down in the darkness under complete radio silence, and then, with the general's party aboard, they lifted off again, MacArthur in the radio operator's seat of one plane headed for Australia. The 200th was one of his favorite units.

On April 9, 1942, the 200th was ordered to destroy its heavy guns; the men smashed them with sledgehammers and pickaxes and then spiked barrels. With no reinforcements, the 200th and 515th were all that stood between the retreating Allied forces and the approaching Japanese Imperial Army. The other troops were in relative safety on the peninsula. Abandoning an airfield, the two remaining defense companies climbed a nearby ridge, armed with only their pistols, old Springfield rifles, and machine guns. At dawn, they fixed bayonets for close-quarter combat. The Japanese advanced out of the jungle with tanks churning behind them. Then came the word from Major General Edward King: all US and Philippine forces were to immediately surrender. As Jack Boyer, a soldier in the 200th, recalled: "Nothing in our training prepared us to be prisoners. But still, men did not lose their morale or spirit. We began to look for friends—to help each other, and to buddy up again. Though we were in shock, we still had that old feeling for each other."[8]

The Japanese began collecting captives: seventy-eight thousand men, eleven thousand of them Americans, including the 200th; they would gain ten thousand more in Corregidor. It was the largest surrender in American history. The 200th had been the last to fight, but the worst was yet to come: they were forced at gunpoint onto what would become known as the Bataan Death March, during which starving and sick captives were bayoneted, shot, or beheaded if they could not continue on the sixty-six-mile march from Maravilles, the deepest into the peninsula some had reached, to the railhead at San Fernando. Crowded, suffocating in the tropical heat, they were shipped to Camp O'Donnell. Along the way, the Japanese killed three thousand men.[9] Then the Americans were forced onward to Canatuban, where they would be imprisoned with the troops from Corregidor. Public executions and torture were common. The survivors ate dogs, cats, snakes, rats—anything. They labored for the Japanese, building runways and roads; some were shipped to Korea, Manchuria, and Japan.[10] They all became something they'd never imagined back at Fort Bliss or at home in New Mexico: slaves to a cruel and violent empire.

BACK IN EL PASO, President Franklin Roosevelt became the first American leader in history to work diligently at actually improving relations with Mexico. Roosevelt had been fortunate to have Mexico enter the war on the side of the Allies, though its forces were not yet in the field. In the spring of 1942, he met with the new Mexican president, Manuel Ávila Camacho; the two presidents connected at two other cities and finally at El Paso. People crowded the streets for a brief viewing of Roosevelt as he passed by in his convertible. Details of the talks were shrouded in secrecy; only lofty platitudes were shared in public speeches. As one reporter recorded:

Interrupting a lavish, seven-course dinner, the two continental leaders delivered radio addresses at Monterey without disclosing in any manner the real reason for their dramatic meeting. They spoke, instead, of differences between their two governments which already have been solved, of a joint solidarity in arms in a world at war, and of the values, now and for the future, of the good neighbor policy. They dealt strictly in generalities and words of friendship and Roosevelt promised that "the Government of the United States and my countrymen are ready to help" Mexico toward greater progress toward "the greatest possible— measure of security and opportunity." He referred to the issue now, apparently dead, created by Mexican expropriation of American-owned oil lands.

Roosevelt declared with studied emphasis: "We recognize a mutual interdependence of our joint resources. We know that Mexico's resources will be developed for the common good of humanity. We know that the day of the exploitation of the resources and the people of one country for the benefit of any group over another country is definitely over." A few minutes before, Ávila Camacho had said, in a conciliatory vein, that "neither your excellency nor I believe in negative memories."[11]

BUT BEHIND THE scenes, the two presidents were working on a trade: huge purchases of food and raw materials from Mexico and a simultaneous flinging open of the border gates to millions of Mexican workers as American men were drafted for war. After over a decade of throwing them out, Americans needed as many Mexicans as they could find for fields and factories alike. This effort came to be known as the Bracero Program: visa-less entry for workers. The

United States would close a huge labor gap while money flowed to Mexico; further, the United States would drop all claims related to the recent nationalization of the oil industry.

HALF A WORLD away, the boys from the barrio in El Paso found themselves in another desert: the sands of North Africa.

Aboard the troop ship *Brazil*, none had any idea where they were going; it was top secret. On April 13, the ship tied up along-side Pier 13 at Oran, Algeria, not far from where the slave Esteban had begun his journey to the American Southwest and nearly on the same latitude as their faraway hometown. The troops who went topside stared at a giant billboard on a nearby hillside, which help-fully said: "Welcome to North Africa 36th Division."[12] So much for the secrecy.

Already good soldiers, the men of Company E had been trans-formed into exceptional ones. The entire company underwent commando training under Great Britain's No. 1 Commando unit, whose own men had succeeded in daring raids against German-occupied Europe. All graduated with M1918 trench knives, which only commandos carried; the double-edged blade came with a spiked brass-knuckle handle, giving it a fierce look. Along the way, the men realized that they were accepted by their fellow troops and locals alike as simply Americans; the discrimination present in Brownwood was literally half a world away.[13]

By then, though, the Germans were abandoning North Africa and falling back to Europe, particularly Italy. The men passed time in camp and drew passes to visit the port and other Algerian cities as their division was folded into the Fifth Army. They embarked upon the USS *O'Hara* for Salerno. Once Sicily fell, Allied bombers unleashed a savage offensive on the Italian mainland. Anchored just offshore on September 8, the men ate heartily, and at 6:30 p.m., the voice of none other than General Dwight D. Eisenhower came over the radio, and his message was broadcast shipwide:

> This is General Dwight D. Eisenhower, Commander-in-Chief Allied Forces.
>
> As Allied Commander-in-Chief I have granted a military armistice, the terms of which have been approved by the Governments of the United Kingdom, the United States and the Union of Soviet Socialist Republics. I am thus acting in the interests of the United Nations.
>
> The Italian Government has bound itself to abide by these terms without reservations.
>
> The Armistice was signed by my representative and the representative of Marshal Badoglio and becomes effective this instant. Hostilities between the armed forces of the United Nations and those of Italy terminate at once.
>
> All Italians who now act to help eject the Germany aggressor from Italian soil will have the assistance and support of the United Nations.

All the Texans whooped, hollered, and broke into song. There was just one hitch: the German army was still in Italy. Italian troops were deserting en masse; German troops were capturing and disarming them.

Operation Avalanche, to expel the Germans, went into effect on September 9, 1943. Under the cover of darkness, the Texans hit Paestum Beach, the first American troops to set foot in Europe in the entire war.[14] The Germans opened fire; green tracers streaked by.[15]

The landing was awful; troops arrived on the beach with their clothes, gear, and weapons sopping wet. Naval artillery was too far offshore to be of any help. In the dark, men couldn't find officers or each other. But with the leadership of their sergeants, the men regrouped and opened fire with .30-caliber machine guns on the approaching Mark IV tanks.[16] One man, Ramon Guttierez, set up his Browning Automatic Weapon (BAR) on a stone wall and poured fire on the tanks; German machine guns returned fire from deep trenches.

Finally, the tanks withdrew. Then the men silenced the German machine gunners; one American even jumped into a trench and stuck his trench knife so deep into a German soldier, he almost couldn't get it loose. As dawn came, the Texans expanded their beachhead, protecting the right flank of the invasion force. The men of Company E proceeded to nearby hills to patrol for German forces. The Allied ships closed in, pounding the German artillery. When the Germans attacked the hills, the Texans went back into action. Guttierez opened up on a patrol, killing four Germans. A fifth rushed him and shot at him; Guttierez fell, and as the German neared, he grabbed the man's Mauser, pulling the German toward him—he unsheathed that trench knife again and drove it into the German's gut.

Death was everywhere. The town of Altavilla, where the men set up next, was destroyed. Gabriel Salazar, of El Paso, wrote: "I remember marching up the winding road toward Altavilla at night. We could smell the burning flesh of dead Germans who were trapped in their Tiger tanks. Their tanks had been destroyed by our anti-tank guns on the previous day. It was the sweet smell of death, rather like chocolate, sweet enough to turn your stomach. I hated the smell of chocolate for a long time after this experience."[17]

Salerno was a bloodbath for the Americans by the time the Germans withdrew on September 16, 1943. The 189,000 men of the Fifth Army who survived—over 5,000 were either killed in action or missing but assumed dead—paused only briefly to regroup. Despite the fierce fighting, which would win them the Distinguished Service Cross, the men of Company E had lost only two of their own. They picked up their gear and weapons and trudged inland and upward over the Italian peninsula.

Increasingly, the combat action messages that traveled up the chain of command were no longer awards recognizing heroism but rather sad telegrams that had to be delivered to families in El Paso. The Texans battled up the peninsula and fought for twenty-three straight days at San Pietro; after four attacks, they finally forced the Germans out. Then they went to Caserta and Naples for two weeks of sleeping, eating, and enjoying the Italian coast; they hadn't had a shower in two months, so they took the opportunity to clean up and rest. On January 1, 1944, they sat down to a piping hot turkey dinner with every trimming.[18]

Two weeks later, they pulled out from the Italian coast and headed inland to a short river, the Gari; on the opposite bank, two Panzer grenadier units opposed the Americans. On January 20, 1944, the Texans, including Company E, launched sixty rubber and wooden boats into the river under cover of darkness. Once on the other side, they were prepared to assault German positions around the town of San Angelo. Detecting their presence, the Germans opened fire with their artillery; men were killed by flying shrapnel and, loaded down with weapons, ammunition, and gear, drowned in the freezing river. Machine-gun fire made rags of the rubber boats, which promptly sank.

Only a few of the men of Company E made it to the other side to establish a beachhead near San Angelo. They then advanced on the Germans, who fought back with machine guns, mortars, tanks, and artillery. Men fell dead; the wounded were taken captive; the remaining combatants started running out of ammunition and were ordered to withdraw. John Chapin, the lieutenant in Company E who was now a captain, would posthumously win the Silver Star. The fighting had lasted just twenty minutes, and though 142 barrio boys went in, only 27 returned.[19] Sergeant Roque Segura was one who did not; he too was posthumously awarded the Silver Star for bravery.

A second attack took place two days later, before dawn. The Battle of the Rapido River was also a disaster, with over two thousand men killed, wounded, or hauled into German prison camps for the duration of the war. Outraged at the incompetence of his superiors, the company commander, Navarrete, having survived multiple crossings, put on his Class A uniform, grabbed his 45-caliber sidearm, and raced off in a Jeep to the battalion headquarters. There, he was directed to the division commander, Major General Fred Walker. A veteran of World War I, Walker confronted the young Hispanic from El Paso; he would not be involved in a duel with a junior officer.

Navarrete returned to the hospital to get care for his own battle wounds. He too got a Silver Star. It was his second.[20]

The commander of the Fifth Army, General Mark Clark, had had enough; he was junior to Walker and had been a student of his at the Army War College; he harbored suspicions about the fitness of his former professor.[21] Walker would be relieved of duty in 1944, despite his many successes, including the capture of Rome. Clark offered Walker a stateside post at the Infantry School at Fort Benning, Georgia.

WALKER HAD EFFECTIVELY been fired. The offer had clearly been approved by the top of the Allied command. The disaster at the Rapido River was a black mark on Clark's record; he began taking officers out of the Italian campaign to keep them from speaking as witnesses. After all, he had ultimately been in charge of the crossings and never objected to them. The Allied high command knew and punished him by denying him further glory: he was passed over to help lead the landings at Normandy.[22]

Nevertheless, the Germans' losses kept them from interfering with the simultaneous landings at Anzio. And for the Allies, that laid open the road to Rome, crucial to ending the war. Anglos and Hispanics had spilled and shed blood together; that would be an important, transformative moment in American history. With its two regiments combat-ineffective, the Texas Thirty-Sixth Division was nearly shattered, having lost seven thousand men since landing at Salerno.[23] Yet the survivors would go on to France and suffer more casualties. Inside Germany, the Thirty-Sixth Division, reduced to half the number that had left Italy, liberated the prisoners of Dachau and went on to defeat a Waffen SS force, oddly fighting side by side with Wehrmacht troops. In Austria, the Texans captured German field marshal Karl Rudolf Gerd von Rundstedt—the commander of all German forces on the Western Front—just in time for May 8, 1945, Victory in Europe Day. They captured the chief of the Luftwaffe, Field Marshal Hermann Goering.

The Thirty-Sixth went into the garrison in the beautiful Tyrolean countryside of Austria. It had suffered more losses than nearly any army division: nineteen thousand battle casualties, including reinforcements with thousands dead, since it came ashore. The division won twelve presidential citations; the men were awarded thousands of medals; fourteen, including Morris Crain of Company E, won the Medal of Honor.

When the war ended, Ramon Guttierez, the man with the trench knife, went home to Sonora, Texas, the only passenger on the bus. He stepped off, greeted the family in the crowd, and walked with his mother, Consuelo, to their church. The town packed the service and the fiesta that followed. But over subsequent nights, the nightmares, the howling and trembling, of posttraumatic stress arose. When daylight came, Guttierez never again talked about the war and brusquely changed the subject when it came up.

Another man from El Paso, Gabriel Salazar, later wrote of why he had begged a recruiter to allow him to join the army: "I think now the word 'belong' has more significance than one might imagine. Was I looking for manhood, feeling patriotism, seeking adventure or love? I know only that I wanted to belong to a group of young men whose lives were similar to mine. I knew I could never find such unpredictable experiences at home."[24]

BACK IN THE Philippines, General MacArthur, now the Allied commander for the Pacific, barked out his orders for the First Cavalry Division, landing in the archipelago without horses this time. The mounts had been left in El Paso. The division patches on their shoulders were no longer cavalry blue on yellow, but black on yellow: black was the color of armor.

"Go to Manila! Go around the Japs, bounce off the Japs, save your men, but get to Manila!" MacArthur demanded. "Free the internees at Santo Tomas! Take the Malacañang Palace and the legislative building!"[25]

Three mobile columns, tanks, artillery, and engineers with a medical unit dropped their heaviest supplies and charged toward Manila. Covering seventy miles in three days, the division reached Santo Tomas, where the Japanese held four thousand prisoners—mostly Americans, including the men of the New Mexico National Guard who had trained alongside the First Cav in El Paso. The First had reached Manila on February 3, 1945, opening the gates at Camp Powell near Santo Tomas and releasing the starving, sick prisoners.[26] Some New Mexicans were still held at another horrid camp, Canabutan; still others were at smaller camps.

MacArthur's haste and daring were driven by the successful Great Raid by army rangers, Filipino scouts, and guerrillas in January. The Great Raid had liberated over five hundred people. The First Cav freed two camps at Santo Tomas, releasing thousands of prisoners, including civilians, and grabbed hold of the legislature's building.[27] Some of the New Mexicans were still slaves in Japan. But one by one, they came stumbling out, very sick. Of the eighteen hundred men who arrived in the Philippines in 1941, only nine hundred managed to survive and surrender. Of them, just three hundred would survive their first year of freedom.

With the task of liberation behind them, the First Cav fought ferociously for Manila over twenty-eight days. As the Japanese defended their positions, they killed a hundred thousand civilians. When the First Cav triumphantly entered the city, it lay in ruins around them.[28]

IN THE FINAL days of May 1945, a squadron of P-47 Thunderbolt pilots roared down on a Japanese military convoy. Above them, American pilots harbored doubts about these greenhorns; they were new to the liberation of the Philippines and, to boot, they were Mexicans.

In his burly, fast fighter, Lieutenant Reynaldo Perez Gallardo swooped down on the convoy, pouring .50-caliber rounds into Japanese trucks in a low-level strafing pass. Then, as the vehicles burst into flames, Gallardo pulled his P-47 up into the Pacific sky, snapping into a victory roll, exposing himself to enemy fire. Over the radio an American voice crackled: "Look at that crazy Mexican!"

Crazy or not, this new bunch of fighter jocks—roughly thirty pilots of the three-hundred-strong 201st Fighter Squadron of the Mexican Expeditionary Air Force, nicknamed the Aztec Eagles—was now in the fight to free the Filipino people.

Other than Brazil, which sent troops to fight in Italy, Mexico was the only Latin American nation to actively fight the Axis, namely, the Japanese Empire. President Manuel Ávila Camacho of Mexico, an old soldier himself, had made the decision carefully.

Early on, sympathy for Nazi Germany had swirled among Mexican intellectuals. And Ávila Camacho was reluctant to side with the United States, his nation's perpetual enemy, with its frequent invasions and incursions. After all, General Douglas MacArthur himself had participated in the brief US seizure of the Port of Veracruz in 1914.

But on May 14, 1942, a Mexican oil tanker off the coast of Florida was intercepted by a German submarine, which torpedoed the vessel, spilling six thousand tons of oil and killing at least thirteen of the thirty-five crew members. A week later the Germans struck another tanker, killing at least seven Mexican sailors. During his visit to Mexico, President Franklin Delano Roosevelt had quietly urged Ávila Camacho to enter the war on the side of the Allies; in fact, Roosevelt wanted to avoid Woodrow Wilson's problem with Germans on the country's southern flank during the First World War. On May 28, 1942, Mexicans everywhere huddled to listen to the radio as the grave voice of Ávila Camacho declared war on the Axis powers. The second world war had arrived.

Mexico City was convinced that its deadliest enemy lay not in the heart of Europe but across the Pacific Ocean: Japan. The Mexican army had intercepted a Japanese plan to invade the United States via the Sea of Cortez on the Pacific coast. Troops would land in the state of Sonora, in northwestern Mexico, and drive north into the vulnerable American Southwest.

As a result, the Mexican government forced much of the country's large Japanese population to relocate to designated areas; some were detained in camps. Mexicans turned up at army bases across the country to volunteer, but Ávila Camacho was well ahead of them: he had already organized the 201st and sent it to the United States for training, even before he publicly announced the force.

The men, all volunteers, came from a cross-section of Mexico. Their commander, Colonel Antonio Cárdenas Rodríguez, was a combat veteran who had flown with the US Army Air Forces in North Africa; even so, some Americans did not feel that Rodríguez was pro-American enough, and they tried unsuccessfully to have him replaced. Now far from home, the Mexicans experienced something they had never known: discrimination because of their ethnicity. Indeed, many in the squadron suspected the Americans doubted their abilities as fighters.[29] Just like the men of Company E in Brownwood, Mexican pilots were refused service at local businesses.

On their way to war, the men of the 201st stopped first in San Antonio, where they were trained by the Women's Airforce Service Pilots. They were shipped to North Texas and then to Idaho to train on the plane that would take them to war: the Republic P-47 Thunderbolt. Designed as a fighter, the aircraft was also a flying tank—capable of close air support, dropping five-hundred-pound bombs and unloading its .50-caliber guns with ferocious generosity. Reinforced armor underneath made the plane able to take as much damage as it could dish out.

Gallardo, the lieutenant, was the scion of a powerful Mexican family who had transferred from the cavalry, and he loved pushing his great big fighter plane. When the squadron went to Greenville in North Texas, he dropped out of formation in his Thunderbolt and buzzed the town—flying right down the main street. On landing, he got busted to a desk job. "I was very sad," he said later. "But I knew that I would fly again one day, and I did." He was shortly reinstated, in time to conclude his training.

The American counteroffensive, meanwhile, began to pay dividends, though at a staggering human cost. The Battle of the Coral Sea hampered the Japanese navy; the Battle of Midway destroyed its prized aircraft carriers. US Army and Marine amphibious invasions—known as island-hopping—prevented an invasion of Australia and then slowly peeled back Japanese control of the islands extending southeast from the Philippines, even as thousands of lives were lost in grinding battles like the one at Guadalcanal.

Finally the prize was in sight: the Philippines and outlying islands like Guam and Tinian. From here, the Allies would be within range to bomb Japan's biggest islands—and even invade. MacArthur made his return, and the main American invasion force landed on the Philippine island of Luzon on January 9, 1945, engaging in pitched fighting with the Japanese.

Arriving in the Philippines aboard the USS *Fairisle* on April 30, 1945, the 201st was assigned to the US Fifth Air Force. The 201st went into action on its own near Vigan, where the Japanese were dug in, and the only way to get them out was to fly close against the mountain range, executing dangerous dive-bombing runs. The Mexicans got the job done, to the amazement of the Americans, who nicknamed the Mexicans the "white noses" for the paint on their cowlings. The pilots had to fly so close to the Japanese that one of the first aircraft took "two blows to the wings," according to Gustavo Vázquez-Lozano, the Mexican author who wrote a definitive work on the Mexican Air Force's participation in World War II.[30]

On June 1, 1945, the 201st attacked a Japanese ammunition depot. Because of three high cliffs and antiaircraft batteries, they would have to dive-bomb from high altitudes and then try to pull their heavy planes up and out. The Americans considered it suicide; the Mexicans had never dived-bombed in combat. Four pilots took off. Carlos Garduño Nuñez explained later: "Fausto was coming up behind me, right on my tail. First I dropped my bombs and I got out straight away, grazing the sea." Rising fast, he recalled, "my blackout happened, and when I got my vision back, my plane was ascending. I turned around to see if Fausto was behind me . . . but it was another plane."[31]

"They got Cachito!" the radio crackled. "Cachito" was the nickname of the squadron's youngest pilot, Second Lieutenant Fausto Vega Santander of Veracruz, who was only twenty-two. Various accounts describe him as having been hit by Japanese fire or losing control. His powerful P-47 lurched twice to the right and then spun into the Pacific at 350 miles per hour.

The 201st continued to attack Japanese positions day after day into June. As the rainy season set in, the 201st flew into combat to hit remaining Japanese infantry and anti-aircraft guns in Northern Luzon and the Marikina Valley east of Manila. The losses of the squadron's pilots mounted into July; MacArthur ordered his air forces to turn their attention northward to the Japanese territory known as Formosa, now Taiwan. The battle for the Philippines was largely over at a cost of thirteen thousand Allied lives—and over three hundred thousand Japanese. Now the fight would be taken directly to the enemy.

The remaining Mexicans flew dangerous, six-hour wave-top missions over nothing but open ocean to hit the Japanese in Formosa with half-ton bombs. "We saw more frequent airplanes from Japan on that 650-mile trip than ever before," Miguel Moreno Arreola said years later. "But they didn't want to have combat with us, because they knew our P-47s were better than their Mitsubishis. We could fly higher and faster."[32] So grueling were these missions that when they returned, pilots had to be pried out of the cockpit and helped off the tarmac.

From nearby Guam, the big American bombers roared off to fire-bomb Japan. Despite losses, no replacements came, and with fourteen aircraft wrecked, the 201st was becoming ineffective for combat after having logged two thousand hours of combat sorties, dropped 1,457 bombs on the Japanese, and put thirty thousand Japanese troops out of combat. So many of its pilots had been killed and its aircraft destroyed that the company was left in the Philippines when US fighters relocated to Okinawa. Then one night in

August the men gathered in a tent at Clark Field. They learned the United States had dropped atomic bombs on two Japanese cities, and the enemy was finally offering to surrender; the test of "The Gadget" at Trinity Site, north of El Paso, had been successful in July.[33]

The First Cavalry Division boarded ships for the occupation of Japan. First, they went about liberating American prisoners of war. One was Ramon Villa Sr., a Texan in New Mexico's 200th Coast Artillery. He had lost seventy pounds in captivity. Asked years later for his advice to anyone in such a harrowing and desperate situation, he answered simply: "I would say, don't give up."[34]

The most extensive war ever fought was over; the men returned home to parades and flowers. "I can vividly remember our welcome home to Mexico," Captain Luis Pratt told an interviewer in 2003. "As we traveled through the towns toward Mexico City, we were greeted by cheering crowds and confetti and marching bands."[35]

The men went home to El Paso, Mexico City, West Texas, and New Mexico. Historians would later overlook or forget them; a recent popular volume on the Bataan Death March makes almost no mention of them. As Professor Maggie Rivas Rivera at the University of Texas at Austin and her colleagues have recorded, Hispanics in general seemed to occupy a nebulous and even arbitrary space within the spectrum of American racism.

When twenty-five-year-old Trinidad Botello, from the small central Texas community of San Saba, was discharged from the US Army in the fall of 1945, a clerk recorded his particulars: brown eyes, black hair, five feet, five inches tall, 145 pounds, US citizen. Under "Race," where only three choices were offered—"White," "Negro," and "Other (specify)"—the clerk typed "Mexican." The following year, his younger brother, Crisantos D. Botello, was likewise discharged from the army. His particulars were almost identical: brown eyes, black hair, five feet, five inches tall, 140 pounds, US citizen. But under "Race," this clerk typed "White."

In fact, five Botello brothers served in World War II. Besides Trinidad and Crisantos there was John, who was inducted in summer 1943 and discharged in November 1945; Simon, sworn in during November 1942 and discharged in summer 1946; and Gregorio, who joined the navy and was discharged in 1945. Simon was categorized as "White," John as "Mexican," and Gregorio as "White." So, three of the five brothers were considered white and two Mexican. The Botello brothers' discharge papers illustrate the capriciousness of Hispanic racial categorization in that period. The racial assignments of Mexican American and other Hispanics were inconsistent throughout World War II—and to this day continue to bedevil demographers, makers of public policy, historians, and even family members.

In an interview in 2000, a veteran from West Texas recalled being prodded by a drill instructor to state whether he was Spanish or Mexican. Aniceto "Cheto" Nuñez recalled, "I told him, 'I was Mexican, but when the war started I became a white man.'" The instructor persisted. Mexican? "No, I was not born in Mexico," replied Nuñez. "I was born in Fort Stockton, but they called me Mexican. And when the war started, I became a white man."[36]

After sixty million dead, twenty-five million more wounded, and all the pain, fear, and sacrifice on home fronts around the globe, the future was looking brighter in the American Southwest. Returning Hispanic soldiers felt at one with their fellow service members and their mutual country. Mexico won a seat on the United Nations Security Council. The aftermath of war, as had been displayed following World War I, is almost always change: political, economic, and social. Change was coming to El Paso, the Southwest, and America itself: the final quest for equality.[37]

Part IV

War is always a matter of doing evil in the hope that good may come of it.

—SIR BASIL LIDDELL HART,
BRITISH ARMY CAPTAIN, JOURNALIST,
AND MILITARY THEORIST

Chapter Sixteen

CIVIL RIGHTS, 1951–59

I N THE LATE autumn of 1950, the tallest smokestack in the world rose from the old Guggenheim copper smelter, bounded to the east by the remnants of the rocky hills Oñate's expedition once circumvented and to the west by the languid Rio Grande. It was a triumph of capital, blast furnaces, and hardscrabble human will over the ore veins of the Southwest. At the base of the smokestack, raging fires of more than 1,500 degrees Fahrenheit melted down copper and separated it from other minerals. Workers lived in on-site shantytowns that laced nearby arroyos, such as La Calavera Canyon. The American Smelting and Refining Company (ASARCO) had bought the land, charged the workers $2 rent per year, and then, to avoid attracting squatters, surveyed the lots and deeded the property to workers and their heirs.[1]

From the smokestack belched arsenic. A local doctor proposed to the city that he monitor the emissions for health effects, but his plan was quietly scuttled. The stack was the most visible symbol of ASARCO's hemispheric empire, which stretched across the American West and southward to Mexico and soon to Peru as well.

All around, El Paso was marked by mid-century modernism. A full century after its founding, Fort Bliss was transformed from

a cavalry post to the center of nearly all army training and experi-
mentation in air-defense missiles and rocketry. The airfield at the
post was carved out and modernized into Biggs Air Force Base,
home to the silvery streamlined, swept-wing B-47 nuclear-armed
bomber, which flew higher and faster than any other heavy strategic bomber. Instead of adobe forts, gleaming US Air Force bases
sprouted up the Rio Grande and out onto the eastern prairie of
New Mexico.

Scientists captured from the German SS after World War II and
their families were quickly moved to Fort Bliss; an errant V-2 missile had even struck the outskirts of Juárez.[2] The new generation
of American missiles of war and space explorations were actually
the work of men who had worked for the Nazis and not that long
before had unleashed a reign of terror upon Great Britain's cities.
Their blond-haired, fair-skinned children went to the Anglo public
schools from which the Hispanic and African American children
of Texas were barred.[3] El Paso County grew to nearly two hundred
thousand people, a jump of nearly 50 percent from before the war.
The city was now bigger than Albany, Eerie, Tampa, and Sacramento.[4] The population of Ciudad Juárez, meanwhile, soared by
150 percent. It thrived at night and on weekends, with soldiers
and airmen frequenting its bars, nightclubs, and restaurants—as
well as strip shows and prostitutes.[5] Hollywood's most glamorous
stars were about to discover the original El Paso and the newer one
alike. Baseball, namely, the El Paso Texans of the Mexican League
and later the Texas League, seized the hearts of El Pasoans.

The memory of combat was never far away, of course—the rail
to Los Angeles was named the Bataan Memorial Trainway for the
sacrifice of Southwestern soldiers in the Philippines—but the end
of the war had changed nearly everything. Not only was the post-
war economic boom lasting well into the ensuing decade, but expectations of equality and opportunity were rising.

Discharged from the US Army in 1945, after a vicious winter fighting at the Battle of the Bulge, Corporal Juan Martinez returned to his hometown of El Paso where he too had gone to La Bowie, Bowie High School. He married María Talamantes on June 1, 1947. The couple would have five children: Martha Morrison, Carmen Reid, Irma Felix, David, and Victor. In Europe, his officers had encouraged him to pursue an education; with the financial aid of the GI Bill, extended to almost all thirty million American veterans, he enrolled at the Texas College of Mines and Metallurgy.

"[You could] probably get through college," Martinez recalled his officers saying. "You may not even finish it, but give it a try."[6]

The Bracero Program of temporary labor from Mexico had been a smashing success—delivering four million workers to American farm owners. As a result, Mexico was now the source of more immigrants, even on a temporary basis, than any other nation in the world.[7] The snowy-looking cotton crops that lined the banks of the Rio Grande beckoned to be picked, and in October 1949, Mexican workers lined up on the south bank of the Rio Grande while growers waited with empty trucks on the other side. Mexico wouldn't let them cross the bridges because of a *bracero* wage dispute with the United States, so border patrol officers waved them into the river, whereupon they were promptly arrested—and immediately paroled to the waiting farmers.[8]

King Cotton would have his workers, the law be damned.

It was a sign of things to come in the ensuing two decades: a cry for fairness by Mexicans and a demand for uncompromised equality for Mexican Americans, as well as African Americans. No longer a faraway hinterland, the booming borderlands—from Laredo and Del Rio to El Paso, Tucson, and Tijuana—were now an increasingly significant part of the national economy and the fight for justice. American presidents would begin to use the border to serve their own political interests as well as national security during the Cold War. There were American citizens in the borderlands who wanted their fair share of the national project. If it was not given, then power would simply have to be taken.

THE LATE 1940S had shown such signs of promise.

Two presidents visited El Paso during this period: the sitting president, Harry S. Truman, and a future president, General of the Army Dwight D. Eisenhower, fresh from commanding the Allied forces in Europe. Still in uniform and on an inspection of Fort Bliss, Eisenhower arrived first on February 25, 1946—touring the anti-aircraft school, the airfield, and the army hospital with local reporters and photographers. His place of lodging was an open secret, and it wasn't the Bachelor Officers Quarters, typically made available to VIPs on the post. Instead, he bunked at the Hilton, the one built by Conrad Hilton, who still lived there. Thousands thronged the hotel, hoping to catch a glimpse of one of the most famous generals in history, even though he'd already announced he would make no public statement.

Taciturn would be a diplomatic way of describing Eisenhower's demeanor during his visit. Always a chain smoker, he and his entourage dined privately in the hotel restaurant. One aide complained that the Mexican food was too spicy for his taste. Eisenhower, by contrast, dug heartily into a huge meal. As the *El Paso Times* then reported: "At the Hilton Hotel Sunday night, the chief of staff disposed of a full plate of enchiladas, tacos, fried beans, tamales, etc., in short order. Then he attacked a large plate of avocado salad and tortillas in earnest. He said it was his first experience with avocado salad but quickly pronounced it his favorite dish."[9]

It was only the second time Eisenhower had eaten Mexican food, he said. Born in Denison, Texas, but raised in Kansas, he had never had Mexican or Black friends or teachers. His whole career was shaped by a segregated army, except largely for the Mexican American troops. His favorite place to relax with a round or two of golf was the Augusta National Golf Club in Atlanta, a perfect example of the intersecting divides of race and class. Though not an overt racist—like Woodrow Wilson, for example—Eisenhower was uncomfortable with issues of race and ethnicity. He preferred to avoid the topic, just as he skirted the grateful people who rang his hotel.[10] He considered the Mexican border a national security concern that ranked just behind the Soviet Union in importance.

The aftermath of the war revealed a tightly woven city—El Paso–Juárez—with merely a shallow river dividing it. With more work and wartime income, half of the civilians in El Paso now had health insurance; members of the military and their families had free health care. Penicillin and wastewater facilities improved general health significantly. Workers were increasingly unionized, including those at ASARCO, earning far more stoking those furnaces than non-union workers did. The student body at the College of Mines and Metallurgy was nearly 15 percent Hispanic, compared to just 1 percent at the state's flagship campus, the University of Texas at Austin. Women worked as secretaries, nurses, bus drivers, taxi drivers, and newspaper reporters, but with men returning from abroad, those opportunities began to dwindle. Juárez became more than a destination for drunken weekend leave as its industrialization increased. The race riots that plagued Los Angeles and Detroit never materialized in El Paso, though political power was held tight by a small group of rich white men—for a while.[11]

More than two years later, on the morning of Saturday, September 25, 1948, the *Baltimore Sun* endorsed New York governor Thomas E. Dewey for the presidency: "Mr. Truman has been a weak and uncertain Chief Executive whereas Governor Dewey, on his record, is an able and decisive man."[12]

Almost exactly at the same time, and 1,999 miles away, the staff at Union Depot in El Paso abruptly closed the bar and restaurant.[13] Alighting from his train, at 9 a.m. sharp, President Harry Truman appeared at the podium before the flashbulbs of photographers and the eager ears and eyes of reporters and the public alike.

Claiming credit for rising incomes, the huge reclamation projects of the Southwest that put thousands to work, and electrification, Truman blasted Republicans as elitist, incompetent, and in the hip pocket of the electrical utility industry in particular, which wanted first dibs on the power from federal dams like Elephant Butte. He said of Democrats: "This is the party that believes that all the people, not just a few, should benefit from low-cost public power. The record concludes that this is what the Democrats stand for. It is a record of action."[14]

Since Roosevelt, Texas had become divided, with white conservative Democrats on one side and progressives, Hispanics, African Americans, members of the working class, and even small farmers on the other. These were the words they, and the crowd in El Paso, were waiting for: a party of "all the people, not just a few."

Truman was a product of Missouri, which had been divided over race since at least the Civil War. He told racist jokes and used racial slurs. The prevailing wind among politicians at that time was not to show support, or even empathy, for nonwhites. But in a 1947 exchange of letters with his sister, Mary Jane Truman, he hinted at a change, admitting he was to give a speech to the National Association for the Advancement of Colored People (NAACP). Truman lamented that Walter Francis White, a skilled lawyer and brave investigator of lynchings, who had been close to Eleanor Roosevelt though rebuffed by her husband, could rise to lead the NAACP and still be considered a second-class citizen. This attitude was more akin to the one he presented in El Paso the following year.[15]

In 1949, El Paso, a seemingly unlikely place for civil rights milestones, reached another: the beginning of the end of segregated college sports. The New Year's Day Sun Bowl at the College of Mines would pit the local team, the Miners, against the Lafayette College Jaguars of Easton, Pennsylvania—but because of the Jim Crow rules of the University of Texas system, no African American player could set foot on the field. This would prevent the halfback standout, David Anthony Showell of Lafayette, from playing. Protesting students shut down the campus and dashed off a telegram to President Truman. The *New York Times* reported the controversy; Sun Bowl officials and everyday El Pasoans alike were humiliated and felt stirred up against the university.[16] The same kind of stand-off took place over an integrated California team, Loyola Marymount, in 1950, and finally the college in El Paso was officially granted an exception to the requirement that games be segregated. In 1951, the integrated University of the Pacific and Texas Tech University played at the Sun Bowl; the next year, the university at El Paso integrated all sports, permanently.

At the national level, President Truman, who upended Dewey and served another four years, went on to desegregate the entire US military by executive order, form an employment commission to enforce fair hiring practices, and create the Civil Rights Committee.

Succeeding Truman in 1952, the chain-smoking hero of Europe, Eisenhower, had different plans.

IT WAS THE veterans, namely Mexican American ones, who came to demand complete equality. They had more than earned what was due them.

Of all places, Texas was where they organized. The League of United Latin American Citizens (LULAC) had sprung up in the late 1920s in Corpus Christi, and the G.I. Forum arose in San Antonio in 1948, at the hand of Héctor P. García, a physician and World War II army surgeon who resumed civilian practice by attending to the health of the city's impoverished barrios.[17] The league became increasingly active in California too, trying to keep Mexican Americans working even as deportation threatened them and drawing a sharp distinction between American citizens and imported Mexican labor—a distinction that Cesar Chavez, the leader of farm workers, would later sharpen.

The G.I. Forum focused on fighting discrimination, and veterans were its vanguard. Its first public campaign arose when the remains of a Mexican American private killed in action, Felix Longoria, were returned to his family in Three Rivers, Texas, three years after the end of the war. The local funeral parlor flatly refused to bury him because he was Mexican American. Immediately, this became known as the "the Longoria Incident" and got the attention of a publicity-conscious junior senator who knew Mexican Americans in Texas; he'd grown up with them and taught them. This was none other than future president and then Texas Democratic senator Lyndon Johnson, who immediately arranged for the slain private to be buried at Arlington National Cemetery. When Longoria's remains were interred, Johnson was graveside, along with a personal representative of President Truman.[18] The Longoria Incident proved to be a lesson that Johnson, a longtime segregationist, would not soon forget.

With another war underway on the Korean Peninsula, there was no more pricey chit to full American citizenship and upward mobility for the least privileged than serving in the military, and the rising number of Hispanic men—who constituted half the population of El Paso—generally understood that. Once more, a hundred thousand Hispanics and Mexican citizens shipped out to the Far East, where fifteen Hispanic soldiers and marines won the Medal of Honor for valor under horrendous fire.

In 1953, as Eisenhower entered office, his top foreign challenge was dealing with the Soviet Union and its hydrogen-bomb arsenal. To him, domestic issues, such as the lunch counter sit-ins by African Americans across the South and, as he'd foreseen, the Mexican workers coming into the country, both legally and not, were a headache. In addition to the flows of Mexican laborers, there was rapacious demand from American farm operators—so much so that outright bribery ran deep, even as wages remained stubbornly low and living conditions in the field appalling. What's more, just as in 1949, Immigration and Naturalization Service (INS) officers arrested undocumented Mexicans, then promptly released them to the state of Texas, which in turn sent them out as farm workers. All in all, it was a good racket for farm owners and operators. Eisenhower appointed the former chairman of the Republican National Committee, Herbert Brownell, as attorney general, then installed under him a cast of former armed forces officers bent on militarizing the approach to the Mexican border. Eisenhower watched as the number of Mexicans detained rose to over eight hundred thousand.

Cotton producers profited mightily, far and wide. In 1952, George Stith, a cotton-field manager in Arkansas, told Congress: "As soon as the Mexicans were brought in the wages started falling. Wages were cut to $3.25 and $3 per 100 pounds. In many cases local farm workers could not get jobs at all . . . I think there were about 25,000 Mexican nationals hired in 1949. In 1950 there was a small crop of cotton but more Mexicans were brought in to pick cotton and it was all picked out before the end of October. The cotton plantation owners kept the Mexicans at work and would not employ Negro and white pickers."[19]

Early the next year, Brownell produced the plan: mass expulsion of undocumented Mexicans, families, and even Mexican American citizens from the United States. This was intended to open farm work to Americans home from war. Mexicans, according to this view, were no longer needed. The plan was to be implemented by the retired general Joseph Swing, a friend and classmate of Eisenhower's at West Point.[20] The commander of the Eleventh Airborne in the Pacific during the war, Swing was, with his troops, the first to enter and occupy Japan. Congress grew nervous because Brownell's plan called for more than deportations; it also meted out penalties and fines to owners of businesses and farms. But the man who designed and led the greatest invasion in history, Operation Overlord, approved the new plan: Operation Wetback.

In mid-1954, a combined force of agents, state police, local police, and military personnel fanned out across South Texas, arresting farm workers from cotton, citrus, and vegetable fields alike. They apprehended nearly five thousand on the first day and then another thousand daily. Many of those rounded up were treated and transported inhumanely through El Paso to the Mexican interior. Others were crammed aboard ships at steamy Port Isabel, bound for Veracruz. At least six drowned by jumping overboard, and a mutiny broke out aboard one vessel. Organized labor showed no sympathy, and neither did the G.I. Forum, which even published a book called *What Price Wetbacks?*[21]

In Los Angeles, the results were heartbreaking. People merely suspected of being undocumented were rousted out of neighborhoods and forced into a makeshift camp at Elysian Park. The *Los Angeles Times* lavished the word "wetback" upon its stories published in June as the roundups went on: "Wetbacks' Detention Camp Slated," read one. "Wetbacks Herded at Nogales Camp," read another; the article that followed made note that over eleven hundred people were sweltering in the Southern California heat.[22] American-born children were ripped away from their Mexican parents or taken with them to a country they'd never known. Entire families were torn apart; some American citizens were caught up in the mayhem; many people of Mexican origin voluntarily left for Mexico, including citizens who gave up on the idea of the American dream.

Many never knew why they were swept out like garbage, used and then discarded, first in the 1930s and now in the 1950s. "They never talked about it," said the oral historian Elena Herrada. "There was a lot of shame associated with it . . . They didn't know why they got deported. They didn't know what they did to bring that on. The only thing they knew was that they were Mexicans—and this only happened to Mexicans."[23]

The federal government claimed to have deported 1.1 million people—the largest mass deportation in American history and one of the largest in the history of humankind. Most estimates have steadily cut down that claim, noting that at least as many people left America of their own accord as were deported. Their legal status, the desire to reunite with family members who had been deported, or simple disillusionment in their nation, the United States, motivated their departure. The result of deportation in America was the same, either way: suspicion of and hostility toward many Mexican Americans increased throughout the country.

In 1954 a pair of landmark rulings forced Eisenhower to pick a side in the civil rights struggle: *Topeka v. Board of Education* and *Brown v. Board of Education* ruled that all children had the right to public education and then struck down segregation altogether. In El Paso, a dozen African American students immediately enrolled at the College of Mines, the first in Texas's all-white public universities to accept Black students. Southern states would fight the court for years. But on June 22, 1955, the El Paso School Board abolished segregation in all schools—the first in Texas to do so. "I feel that this is an historic event," Dr. Vernon Collins, the president of the local NAACP, said that night. "I suppose that the signing of the Declaration of Independence took place at a meeting much like this, where routine business was carried out along with the historic."[24]

BACK IN EL SEGUNDO BARRIO of El Paso, one young army veteran, Raymond Telles, was getting relentlessly nagged by his father. Life in El Segundo could be hard. The Anglo politicians never got the streets paved, the rains turned into floods, and the barrio never got connected to the city sewage and water system. The young veteran's father, Ramón Telles, was himself a tough man, working as a meat packer and taxi driver and training into middle age as an amateur boxer. His three boys were instructed to never hang out with gang members, to get good grades, to defend themselves if attacked, and to go to church. They received a strict Catholic upbringing at home and at school: ties, uniforms, and all. Ray, the oldest, once found his father's cigarettes and went out behind the house for a smoke. Immediately, he sensed that his mother had noticed him. Scared, he gulped down the smoke, which made him sick, and stuck the burning cigarette into his shirt pocket. But his mother hadn't actually seen him; doing the laundry later, she found the burnt shirt pocket. She gave Ray an ass-whipping, and when Ramón got home, he gave Ray an ass-whipping too.

By the mid-1950s, the younger Telles was an accomplished married man. He'd served in the Texas Thirty-Sixth Infantry like other boys from El Paso, but he'd never made it to Italy, which probably spared his life. He was a skilled company clerk; he'd gone to business college before the war and then worked. He was rapidly promoted to sergeant and then selected for Officer Candidate School for the US Air Force in Miami, where he trained alongside none other than the actor Clark Gable. Later promoted to captain, Telles was posted to Mexico City as the air force attaché, where he conducted two top-secret missions—one was to illegally provide the Mexican air force with planes, despite opposition from Congress.

Telles also reported on the infiltration of the Mexican military by the Soviets and served as an aide to Eisenhower during his visit to the Mexican capital after the war. During the 1950s, the CIA station there, inside the American embassy, swelled to the largest CIA post overseas with the exception of the one in Moscow. Summoned during the Korean War, Telles served as executive officer of the Sixty-Seventh Tactical Reconnaissance Group, retiring as a full colonel. Leaving the service for home in El Paso, to be with his wife, Delfina, and the rest of his family, he took a desk job at the white Spanish revival federal prison upriver, which was known as La Tuna, the Spanish term for red prickly-pear fruit: sweet to the tongue, but bearing tiny spines.

Still, his father hounded him: he wanted Ray to run for political office. In his taxi job, Ramón had gotten to know Anglo politicians. When election season rolled around, they predictably wanted him to deliver the vote of El Segundo Barrio. Frequently, the answer was unsatisfactory, and the votes went undelivered. Yet if a boy from the barrio could win real political power, that would change. At first Raymond pushed the idea away. But he was always prepared to do his duty, and eventually he understood that running for office wouldn't be something he was doing for himself. It would be for *others*: his children, wife, parents, brothers, and El Segundo itself. Here it was, almost the 1950s: television stations were flickering to life, and yet *they* still had sewage rotting in the streets. He knew the people of the barrio deserved better.

"The best thing that happened to the Mexican-American was being taken by the army," his brother Richard Telles told the biographer Mario T. García. "They started to learn about equal rights. If I'm gonna die for my country, then I want a piece of cake."[25]

No person of Mexican heritage had occupied a position of political power since the refounding of Texas in 1883. Not a single one. But as an office worker turned veteran, Raymond Telles could appeal to soldiers at Fort Bliss—Mexican American veterans, including his old comrades from the Thirty-Sixth—and with his executive skills and credentials, he could defuse Anglo objections based solely on ethnicity. So he agreed to run in 1948, becoming, naturally, the county clerk.

After years of spotless service in that position, at the behest of Mexican American leaders and with the editorial help of a progressive—Ed Pooley, the editor of the afternoon *El Paso Post*—Telles ran for mayor in 1957. While the city had forcibly annexed all of Ysleta, where Pueblo people lived, beginning in 1680, the whole area was now overwhelmingly Hispanic, and a whole new bloc of Mexican American voters came into the El Paso fold, where they were easily picked up by Telles. The news shot around the country: Telles had become the first Hispanic mayor of a major American city. He did so fully three decades before Henry Cisneros would become mayor of San Antonio and nearly fifty years before Antonio Villaraigosa would assume the same job in Los Angeles.

In October, a serious-looking Telles, with his short dark hair, held up his right hand as the US district judge R. E. Thomason read the oath of office. He then somberly turned to the crowd, the largest ever to attend a mayoral swearing-in, and said: "[It is] with pride and extreme humility we assume these grave responsibilities. We cannot do the job alone and I ask all the people of El Paso to help us meet the problems before us. The people of El Paso have spoken and we are grateful for the vote of confidence given us. We hold no malice toward any individual or group. With the help of God and the co-operation and help of the people, we will have a successful administration."[26]

As for the sewage problems and the dirt roads of El Segundo, pipes were laid, sewage was drained, and roads were paved. But Telles advocated for improvements beyond his own neighborhood. A new city-county building went up, as did a hospital. Separately, the air force replaced all its bombers at Biggs Air Force base with brand-new B-52 Stratofortresses. In the jet age, the original Southern transcontinental railroad through Nogales, Arizona, and on to California was abandoned. Horse racing came to nearby Sunland Park, New Mexico. Riding an economic boom and continuing to work meticulously, Telles cruised to reelection in 1959.[27]

"No Mexican-American community had done what the Chicanos of El Paso managed to do in 1957, that is, mount a massive grassroots campaign and elect one of their own as mayor of a major Southwestern city. The political influence that Mexican-Americans enjoy today is in large measure the legacy of this milestone," said García, the biographer and professor at the University of California at Santa Barbara. "When Henry Cisneros was elected mayor of San Antonio in 1981, the national media trumped it up as this momentous breakthrough, the first time that a Mexican American had been elected mayor of a major Southwestern community. Well, that kind of treatment doesn't hold up in light of Telles' victory in 1957. Furthermore, in Telles' time, there were still tremendous obstacles to Mexican-Americans becoming elected. Telles was truly a pioneering Mexican-American politician."

Upon completing his second term in office, Telles got to know another up-and-coming veteran turned politician: John F. Kennedy.

RAYMOND TELLES, ALONG with a powerful US senator from nearby New Mexico, Dennis Chavez, took an immediate shine to the charismatic senator from New York. For his part, John F. Kennedy had no real knowledge of Hispanic Americans and no experience with gaining their support in a political campaign.

But Chavez did. The first Hispanic Democrat in the Senate, he never strayed from his New Deal roots; he tangled with the red-baiting Republican senator from Wisconsin, Joe McCarthy, and turned into a Cold War hawk, fighting cuts to military spending. Chavez's state benefited from ever-expanding nuclear weapons laboratories, air bases, and test ranges.[1] And he saw in Kennedy an approach to national security and the Soviet Union that neatly dovetailed with his own.

Beyond the politics of the presidential season, Kennedy and Telles spoke two or three times privately. Kennedy confided his genuine concern for the country, equality, and looming famines, wars, and instability around the world. Acknowledging these issues, Telles offered his help: "[Kennedy] wanted to bring peace to the world and wanted to bring our young people to have a better understanding of their country. He wanted to help the poor, the underprivileged. He wanted to help people regardless of their color, religion, race, or political affiliation."[2]

Even before Kennedy launched his presidential bid in 1960, Chavez commenced a drive to recruit Hispanic voters: "Viva Kennedy." Though centered on Mexican American voters in the Southwest, it reached across the country to Michigan, Florida, and New York, pulling in Latinos of nearly every nationality. Los Angeles City councilman Ed Roybal convinced Kennedy of the value of the effort, as Viva Kennedy clubs formed in neighborhoods from coast to coast. On September 11, 1960, barnstorming the country in a presidential bid against the outgoing vice president, Richard Nixon, Kennedy came to El Paso to give a speech at the Cortez Hotel. This luxury establishment had been built on the site of the old saloon, where elections were held and grievances were settled out front, via gunfight.

"Texas twice, in 1952 and 1956, has jumped off the Democratic bandwagon," Kennedy teased, referring to Eisenhower's two wins there. "We're down to see if it's going to be a habit." Naturally, the crowd applauded and laughed. Referring to his running mate, the Texas senator Lyndon Johnson, as "old Lyndon," he talked of El Paso as the gateway it had always been, then called on Texas to lead the states in making him president.[3]

With the help of Telles and many others, Kennedy did win Texas and the White House. After the inauguration, in February 1961, Telles was home ready to mount a third bid for mayor, when the call came—the president wanted to dispatch Telles to Costa Rica as ambassador. Telles rejected it out of hand. For most anyone, it would have been considered an honor, but Telles sensed that serving in San José would derail his electoral ambitions. A sleepy backwater of a diplomatic posting, Costa Rica was not a major player on the world stage, and he was only forty-five, at the prime of his political career. He had been planning to return to El Paso, win another term as mayor, and then run for the congressional seat.[4] But at a meeting in Washington, Chavez, Kennedy, and Johnson all told Telles to take the ambassador job. Privately, Telles sensed he was getting screwed by his good friends: "they did a little bit of arm twisting, you know." It could be that people like Johnson and other Texans didn't want him energizing the liberal wing of the Democratic Party in the Lone Star State, which was constantly locked in battle with the conservative wing. In the end Telles accepted, if warily.

The post was not without some merit. Telles had contacts with Latin American militaries there from his army air force days. Costa Rica was beautiful and largely free of the revolutionary forces of revolution and the Cuban and Soviet interference that caused problems elsewhere. His mission was to help form an economic alliance led by the United States.

Kennedy had campaigned on equality and changing the nation's immigration laws, saying, "We must remove the distinctions between native-born and naturalized citizens to assure full protection of our laws to all, . . . the protections provided by due process, right of appeal, and statutes of limitation can be extended to noncitizens without hampering the security of our nation."

As part of his Cold War, Kennedy wanted to reach out to people in what was then called the Third World, to win their hearts and minds. Immigration law was part of his arsenal against Soviet influence. In 1962, Kennedy signed the Migration and Refugee Assistance Act, which was created to help foreign nationals from the Western Hemisphere fleeing persecution in their home countries—especially Cubans fleeing Fidel Castro. On signing the act, Kennedy said, "The American people will be assured that this government's leadership will be maintained in the great humanitarian endeavor of helping the world's stateless and homeless people."[5]

But Telles was out of the action.

Whenever Kennedy toured the Southwest, he did invite Telles to fly up from Costa Rica to accompany him. Telles helped negotiate a tricky boundary dispute with Mexico, and Kennedy asked him to join him on a fall campaign trip to Dallas. Telles later wrote:

> I did travel with him, and the last time was in July of 1963. And the interesting part about it, before he went to Dallas, he had asked me to come and join him there. But unfortunately, at that moment, there were certain official matters that came up in Costa Rica that had to be taken care of, and I didn't believe that it was the thing to do, for me to leave at that point. So I called the White House and advised one of his aides to please tell the President the situation, that I would like to suggest that I remain there, but if he said, "Come," well, I'd go. So they did. I got word back from the President. He said, "Well, if in your judgment, you think you better stay there, go ahead." So I did.
>
> And then I got a letter from him on that Friday when he was killed. I received it the same day. He had written it before he left Washington. He was telling me, of course, that he was sorry that I couldn't meet him in Dallas, but he wanted me to be sure and see him the next time I was in Washington. He wanted to talk to me. Well, you can imagine how I felt, getting the letter the day that he died.

He held the letter in his hands, knowing that Kennedy was dead in Dallas, the victim of an assassination. The day was, of course, November 12, 1963.

THE KENNEDY AGENDA survived the slain president; for decades, his image hung in many Hispanic households. Nevertheless, the thirty-sixth president of the United States, Lyndon Johnson, took

the oath of office aboard Air Force One, en route back to Andrews
Air Force Base, and soon vowed to cement his predecessor's legacy,
albeit in his own way. For reasons not entirely explained, he left his
old friend Telles in Costa Rica—for his entire presidency.

As a progressive, Johnson was a curious figure. After all, he
had little progressivism to show in his track record. He had offered
a consistent no vote on all but the most inconsequential pieces of
civil rights legislation. A Texan, Cold Warrior, and wheeler-dealer
who steered friends into federal projects and was lavishly repaid in
turn, Johnson, it seemed, was more of a representative of the liberal
wing of the Republican Party. And yet his presidency's first order of
business was one of Kennedy's last: a new civil rights law to outlaw
discrimination on the basis of race, sex, color, religion, or national
origin.[6] Johnson seized on it like a longhorn tangling with a mountain lion. On July 2, 1964, the former committed defender of Jim
Crow signed the bill into law.

In Washington, Johnson cemented another of his predecessor's
dreams: overhauling the nation's immigration laws, which essentially remain the same today. Kennedy had believed that the system
of immigration quotas by country, favoring white Europeans, presented a problem in the midst of the Cold War. The Soviet Union—
along with its proxy, Cuba—supported violent revolutionary wars
in Latin America, Africa, and Asia, and attempted to win the hearts
and minds of those who lived there. The United States, Kennedy
and Johnson reasoned, could not possibly build goodwill in these
places by keeping their people out of this country. A new immigration act would group them by region. Latin America would
be allowed a certain number of immigrants. Asians—long barred
from the United States—and Africans would have increased access.
Those with relatives in the United States who were already American citizens would receive preference.

Johnson turned to Kennedy's brother, Ted, to steer the bill

through Congress. In a telephone conversation on March 8, 1965, the two men talked about strengthening their working relationship and dispelling rumors about a strain between supporters of Johnson and Kennedy. The public, however, was nearly evenly divided as to whether the changes to immigration law were desirable.

On a bluebird fall day, October 3, 1965, Johnson flew to New York and sat down at a makeshift desk in front of the Statue of Liberty, with Lower Manhattan looming in the foreground. He said: "Over my shoulders here you can see Ellis Island, whose vacant corridors echo today the joyous sound of long ago voices. And today we can all believe that the lamp of this grand old lady is brighter today—and the golden door that she guards gleams more brilliantly in the light of an increased liberty for the people from all the countries of the globe."[7]

The new law was passed, a major break with the previous xenophobic and racist laws that had discriminated against Asians, Jews, and southern Europeans as well as Africans, Mexicans, and other Latin Americans. The law, however, would also prove problematic and require Congress to make significant adjustments in the coming years—especially as the Cold War ended. Then, the need for national security changed.

THE COUNTRY WAS making strides toward justice and equality, and musicians often led the way. Instead of white singers producing a sort of African American music, as Elvis Presley had done, Ray Charles, Gladys Knight, Diana Ross, Marvin Gaye, Aretha Franklin, and many more crowded the charts and jammed the airwaves to a ready generation of baby boomers, the sons and daughters of the veterans of recent wars. In 1959, the country-western singer and songwriter Marty Robbins recorded his hit "El Paso," produced by the legendary Don Law, who made the only known recordings of the blues giant Robert Johnson. The Spanish-style guitar work and Robbins's voice—*Out in the west Texas town of El Paso, I fell in love with a Mexican girl*—told the story of a cowboy who falls in love with Faleena; a gunfight with a rival ensues at Rosa's Cantina, and afterward, the cowboy must flee, chased by vigilantes to his death. It was a western movie tucked into a perfect song, and though over four minutes long, it reached number one on both the country and pop charts and won a Grammy. So successful was this song that Robbins returned listeners to El Paso in 1966, to follow up on the story of the beloved Faleena, who in the end commits suicide after the loss of her cowboy love. These hugely popular songs featured a controversial theme: the mixing of ethnicities.

In El Paso, a young high school basketball coach showed up for work at Texas Western College. Born in Enid, Oklahoma, in 1930, Don Haskins had bounced from one small-town high school in Texas to another until that moment: he had been offered a salary, dormitory housing for him and his little family, and a Division I job coaching the Miners. With hardly a scholarship to dole out, he began prowling the big cities of the Midwest and the East, looking for talented players who wanted a way out of the inner city. He did something previously unknown in the largely segregated National Collegiate Athletic Association: he both recruited and played Black athletes. It was not against the rules; it simply wasn't done. And playing more than one Black player at a time against an all-white team was *never* done.

Soon nicknamed "the Bear" for his imposing, cinder-block appearance—he was built like a brick shithouse—Haskins took heat from within the university for recruiting African Americans. "I don't see Black and white, I see players," he snorted back at critics, the university president, and reporters alike. His first Miners team notched an 18–6 record. His second team posted a 19–7 mark during the 1962–63 season and made it to the first NCAA national tournament in the school's history. But nothing would ever compare to the 1966 season. The Miners hit the road that autumn with seven Black and five white players: Bobby Joe Hill, David Lattin, Orsten Artis, Nevil Shed, Harry Flournoy, Willie Worsley, Willie Cager, Louis Baudoin, Jerry Armstrong, David Palacio, Dick Myers, and Togo Railey. The players found genuine acceptance in El Paso, eating heaps of Mexican food and breaking out of the dormitory to drink in Juárez—but despite Supreme Court rulings and the new civil rights law, they encountered plenty of hatred on the road, especially in the rest of Texas. They were consistently one of the top five defensive teams in the country. While more than a few of his players could dunk like crazy, Haskins not only taught but enforced a dull yet deadly set of defensive principles. He focused on the collective nature of defense over the individual showmanship of scoring, however much his players resisted it. "I can't emphasize too much that good defense is team defense," he said in a training film. "Long hours of drilling make your reactions automatic when the chips are on the line."[8]

The Miners nearly ran the table that fall, winter, and into the next spring. Before they knew it, they were headed to Wichita and the beginning of another national tournament. They made it to the national championship game, where they would play Kentucky, the greatest basketball program in the nation, inside Cole Field House at the University of Maryland in College Park.

Led by Adolph Rupp, the Kentucky Wildcats had won the Southeastern Conference for years, made annual appearances at the NCAA tournament, and advanced to the finals four times. Rupp was known as the "Baron of the Bluegrass," for both his stately ways and commanding record. He had survived a point-shaving scandal, bribes to players, and the first "death penalty" in NCAA history, when the Wildcats were barred from playing during the 1952–1953 season.

The ball tipped off at 10 p.m. Eastern in front of over fourteen thousand people, packed like sardines inside Cole Field House. Much of the country hunched over radios and at Texas Western, students sat in their cars and listened. Rupp started five white players; Haskins started five Black ones. "I really didn't think about starting five Black guys. I just wanted to put my five best guys on the court," Haskins said. "I just wanted to win that game."[9]

The Miners roared out of the box, taking the lead with ten minutes to go in the first half and not letting go of it, ever. In the second half, the Wildcats cut the Miners' lead to one until the Miners widened the gap. Kentucky closed within one again with eight minutes to go, and then the score rose: 50–40 in favor of Texas Western. When the lead stretched to eleven, with just over three minutes to play, Haskins rested his starters with white players.

On the Kentucky side of the boards, the phone rang increasingly, interrupting Rupp in the game of his life. On the other end of the line, the president of the university, John Oswald, was frantic. "Kentucky coach Adolph Rupp privately complained of incessant calls from his university president," the historian Taylor Branch wrote. "'That son of a bitch wants me to get some n——s in here,' he said. 'What am I gonna do?'" After all, he hadn't a single Black player on the bench. He had tried to recruit Black players himself but couldn't find those willing, and he was pressured by his president to back off after asking if the university could leave the thoroughly segregated Southeastern Conference.

The unstoppable force had met the immovable object—and it moved; the Miners triumphed 72–65. As they received their giant trophy, and the national championship, bedlam erupted in El Paso. Anglo students in button-downs and short hair ran around in the dark, yelling and holding their index fingers in the air: they too were number one. Black and Hispanic students drove around campus, honking and flashing headlights. As the *El Paso Times* put it, "The entire downtown area and Texas Western College campus was in a hectic uproar. Thousands of horn-blowing cars and exuberant fans swept through the San Jacinto Plaza area. People screamed 'We're number one!' At the Plaza, the din of auto horns was so loud, it was impossible to talk. One pickup truck was seen driving around with three drummers in the back playing snare drums."[10]

The cops let everybody blow off their steam. The next night an impromptu dance at the college attracted four or five thousand people: students, soldiers, and everyday residents. While the band played and thousands danced, others got into mischief—starting illegal bonfires, shooting off fireworks, and busting open fire hydrants. When the cops showed up, they got booed and showered with empty bottles. "You are number one in the nation," Lieutenant Bo Trast said over a police loudspeaker. "Let it remain that way. Don't spoil the record."[11]

The crowd dispersed, many heading to the dance and the rest just trailing off. A few more bottles rained down. But it had taken just a dozen police officers to disperse the crowd, with no one arrested, no one hurt, and no violence within the crowd. It was just a case of college kids in El Paso, a hard-partying town.[12]

But the game transformed what was left of segregation in sports, well over a decade after that transformation had begun in El Paso. College sports, especially the racist Southeastern Conference, could not go on without African American players; segregationist teams knew that by not recruiting the best of any color, they would be on a losing path—forever.

"The workmanlike 72–65 victory by Texas Western turned a pitiful mismatch into churning reappraisal," the historian Taylor Branch wrote. It was "the game that changed American sports."[13]

THOUGH MIRED IN Vietnam and hastily building the New Society, President Johnson returned to El Paso time and time again.

At long last, the Chamizal dispute over the changing course of the Rio Grande was settled in 1964. Mexico received back about a square mile of territory that it had claimed since the end of the two countries' conflict in 1848. Five thousand residents—including Mexican American veterans—were finally provided a fair-market payment for their homes and moved to other parts of the city, in the process losing their historical neighborhood to what was left: just a small, manicured national park with an obelisk commemorating the settlement. The mighty Rio Grande was temporarily dammed upstream so that construction crews could re-create the channel of 1848: pouring a concrete channel that would permanently chain the mighty river to that course.

Johnson ceremoniously shook hands with Mexican president Adolfo López Mateos as the deal was inked and the concrete dried. The Mexican newspaper *Exélsior* called the Chamizal settlement "the greatest victory of Mexican diplomacy." López Mateos had also been on the receiving end of much American praise and help ever since the Kennedy administration.[14]

The Bracero Program was abolished in 1965. The future lay in American capital leveraging cheap Mexican labor—in Mexico. The farm unions, led by Cesar Chavez, had won most of their fights for higher wages and better living conditions, especially in California. The two presidents approved the beginning of a new free trade system, creating so-called "twin plants," or maquiladoras.

Quickly, American corporations rushed to the border. They could set up a front office in the United States, a manufacturing plant in Mexico employing cheap labor—and pay no import tax when the finished goods crossed the bridges into the United States. These companies lured hundreds of thousands of Mexican workers and a healthy smattering of American executives and their families, including mine. Maquiladoras sprouted all along the border: from

Tijuana to Nogales to Juárez, Laredo, and along the Mexican state of Coahuila. Like El Paso, all these towns became not just Mexican manufacturing hubs but also American inland ports. Instead of ships, trucks and trains hauled the cargo away.

Behind the scenes, Mexico increasingly supported the United States in the Cold War. Not only did the CIA station in Mexico City grow—especially after Kennedy's assassin, Lee Harvey Oswald, a former marine who had lived in Russia, checked in and debriefed in Mexico City—but a string of Mexican presidents, including López Mateos, became handsomely paid informants for the agency.[15] López Mateos was handled by the courteous station chief, Winston Scott. His successor, Gustavo Díaz Ordaz Bolaños, was also on the agency's payroll, but shrewdly misled Scott about his intentions toward rising student protests in 1968. The Mexican government's crackdown on students in Mexico City, called the Tlateloco massacre, killed hundreds. The United States was blindsided. The asset skillfully became the handler.[16] Nevertheless, the Cold War partnership endured and free trade, even globalized trade, was coming as part of the forging of alliances.

On December 13, 1968, Johnson and Díaz Ordaz met again on the Santa Fe bridge in El Paso, over the Rio Grande. El Paso was a stopover: the American president was on his way to South Vietnam one last time, to see the troops in the war that had cost him another term. The two men enjoyed a warm, even brotherly relationship. They were not dissimilar in character, after all: persistent, slippery, intent, and quite capable of inflicting violence.[17] At 11:53 a.m. that day, Johnson attended a luncheon with his Mexican counterpart and said:

Long after our words of today are gone and forgotten, something more important is going to endure—channels between men, bridges between cultures, border commissions which link the human values that Mexico and America hold dear. These, my friends, will never pass away if we are true to our heritage.

Together, we have shown that borders between nations are not just lines across which men shake their fists in anger. They are also lines across which men may clasp hands in common purpose and friendship. And throughout our periods of respective service, no head of state, no leader of any nation has worked closer, cooperated better, or extended the hand of friendship more than the most distinguished President of Mexico, and we are all grateful for it.

In the years to come, Mr. President, the American people are going to demonstrate to you and your people that we are worthy of your trust and your confidence and we are going to return the hand of friendship that you have extended all the time to us. Gracias, amigos.[18]

The Mexican president responded with a toast: "You have crossed the border several times to visit our country, always on business and with official commitments. We now very cordially repeat the invitation that you visit us for pleasure. You will not be received with the ceremony that the high office you have held requires, but with the same cordial hospitality by the Mexicans in general and by my wife and myself, your friends."[19]

The ever-loyal former mayor of El Paso, Telles, was not in attendance. Johnson had left the former rising star in Costa Rica throughout his presidency, returning him to the United States as chairman of the International Boundary and Water Commission— which would oversee the new old boundary—only as he was on his way out the door, in early 1969. Telles would later serve President Richard Nixon as chairman of the Equal Opportunity Employment Commission. Then he faded from public life, moving to California to be near his daughter, Cynthia. He uttered scarcely a critical word about his exile and the extinguishing of his career—and never a critical word about the late president, Kennedy. He died in Sherman Oaks on March 8, 2013, one of the most important political figures in twentieth-century America whom almost no one had heard of.[20]

AFTER THEIR LUNCHEON in El Paso, the two presidents went to the Santa Fe bridge to send the signal to blow up the temporary dam upriver and let the water into the channel. They dutifully pressed two huge red plastic buttons as the expectant crowd waited for the water, now tamed by steel and concrete, to rush under the bridge.[21] But only a trickle reached them. To relieve the awkward embarrassment of two heads of state, the engineers had to fake it: they released water from the main river back into the river channel, faking it. This time, the water dutifully obliged, rushing into its new cement conduit.[22]

The border was now a major economic opportunity. The populations along it swelled—in Juárez, beyond the city's capacity. The economies boomed. The future never looked brighter.

Chapter Eighteen

HELL PASO, 1971–89

ON JULY 5, 1971, the temperature in El Paso soared to 100 degrees Fahrenheit.[1] I know because I was there, dressed in shorts, standing in a front yard made entirely of cinnamon-colored sand, barren of any kind of plant life, in front of my family's new white-brick three-bedroom ranch-style house.

I had turned seven earlier that year, and when school ended, my father and mother packed the car with me, my sister, the two dogs, and our belongings and drove 604 increasingly dry, desolate desert miles from Laredo, Texas, to El Paso. I remember looking out the car window in shock: the hot, humid brush country of Laredo was no walk in the park, but El Paso was the bleakest edge of the earth. We arrived in June and rented an executive apartment paid for by my father's employer—where he was promptly bitten by either a venomous spider or a scorpion and rushed to the emergency room, where I thought he would die. It was a harsh welcome.

When he recovered, we plunked down in our empty new house across the street from a seemingly endless cotton field. The Allied Van Lines truck soon pulled up and the house quickly filled with our belongings. In August, as is customary in the Southwest, I would start at a new school up the street, with no familiar friends, sights, or sounds from Laredo. From the front yard I could see nearly endless sand dunes to the west; from an equally sandy back-yard, the barren Franklin Mountains to the east. Front and back, back and front: no matter how many times I rubbed my eyes, I was lost in some kind of desert.

History is personal. My mother and father had joined the stam-pede not so much to settle the Southwest, but to urbanize it. My father had already moved his mother to Scottsdale to start her new life after my grandfather, the World War I sailor, died in 1957.[2] By 1971, metropolitan El Paso was home to 340,000 people; the population within the city limits was on par with Miami, St. Paul, Omaha, Honolulu, and Long Beach.[3] Fueled by the need for work-ers for American companies, Juárez—a ten-minute stroll away—was home to another 400,000. The combined urban area, joined at the hip, was home to nearly as many people as Washington, DC, or Cleveland, though the latter was closer in nature: El Paso–Juárez, to borrow from the poetry of Carl Sandburg, was a "stormy, husky, brawling, City of the Big Shoulders."

Smokestacks belched, from the ASARCO tower, now the tall-est in the world, and others. Hundreds of thousands went to work in the American factories in Juárez; others packed the bridges as they went to work and shop. Thousands of American executives, with permits to work in Mexico, left their families in their new households each day, driving their big American cars past buses, crowds, cops, and electric trolley cars. My father, James, would pull up in his champagne-colored Ford LTD and tip the old man in an official-looking uniform who guarded the company parking lot to look after the car as he crossed the street in a short-sleeved shirt and tie, briefcase packed with legal pads, pens, a pipe, and a slide rule, and disappeared inside the bunkerlike building of A. C. Nielsen.

El Paso was not alone in the new Southwestern boom: from Dallas to Los Angeles, the farmlands were carved into subdivisions.

Houston was the fastest-growing city in America, surpassing one million residents. And nobody could match the growth of Southern California.[4] Yet what was at work wasn't just the quantitative swelling and dense urbanization of the Southwest; it was qualitative as well. Until 1970, the US Census Bureau lumped Hispanics in with Anglos as white, with Spanish-surnamed people counted in the Southwest and Puerto Ricans counted in the East. In 1970, it relabeled all Hispanics as people of Spanish origin—whatever that meant. That year there were nearly nine million Hispanics in the United States; 20 percent reported being foreign-born.[5] The vast majority lived in the Southwest, where, at the conclusion of the Mexican-American War, there had been just fifty thousand.[6]

But there was more subtlety to this picture. First, even as the Chicano movement rose and shook over a century of discrimination especially in California—while faltering, by comparison in Texas, much of the Mexican American population created a new model of assimilation. No longer the melting pot that Jews and southern Europeans encountered in the East, the Southwest for Mexican Americans married participation in the life of the nation—voting and soldiering, with another war raging in Southeast Asia—with a fierce defense of language and culture. After all, though they had fought and won de jure equality, Mexican Americans were not de facto equal. In 1970, Hispanics made up 4.3 percent of the American population—and more than 70 percent of the people living below the poverty rate.[7]

Yet there was still another complicating factor: intermarriage. While this was generally legal between Hispanics and Anglos in the Southwest, that right was denied to couples consisting of a Black and a white partner. Then the Supreme Court struck down state laws that banned intermarriage in *Loving v. Virginia* in 1964. In 1967, 3 percent of marriages involved people of differing races and ethnicities. By the early 1970s, that rate had doubled—and then it skyrocketed.[8] The most common pairing was a Hispanic spouse with an Anglo one.[9] Their children, and their children's children, would inherit two languages and two cultures along with their American citizenship.

As these couples and families embraced the duties of citizenship, voting, and soldiering (including service in Korea and Vietnam) while retaining a fierce love of Mexican culture, they brought something new to America, and on a large scale, which would have ripple effects for decades to come. Mexican Americans, of whatever background, populated not just dense cities but the fastest-growing parts of America; they weren't necessarily rooted, like Dominicans, Puerto Ricans, and Cubans, to urban barrios in New York or Miami.

Yet these are all statistics and maps, in the end. It's best to tell what it really was: a love story.

MY FATHER, JAMES, grew up a poor Catholic kid in rural Arkansas, as had his father. After leaving the navy, his father, Robert, became an oil wildcatter (a prospector), then a strawberry farmer (just as sugar was being rationed during World War I), and finally a sheep rancher.

My mother, Josefina, grew up in a lapsed Catholic working-class family in Monterrey, the steel-mill capital of Mexico. Her father, Antonio, had been orphaned by his Spanish mother and Mexican father during the Spanish flu pandemic that swept the globe. Dropped off with relatives in Laredo, Texas, he returned to Mexico after just a year and put himself to work. Having not grown up in a church, he became an atheist and a member of a small and secretive sect: the Rosicrucians, who drew their beliefs from hermeticism, Jewish mysticism, and Christian gnosticism.[10]

James finished high school, graduating in the class of 1954

from St. Paul's in Pocahontas, Arkansas, near the Mississippi River delta. My father enlisted in the US Army. Smart, with an easy smile, he made his way to the Signal Corps—where the intelligent trainees went, as they go into cyberwar today—at Fort Gordon, Georgia, then departed from San Francisco on a troop ship bound for Okinawa, as the occupation of Japan lifted. He immediately fell ill with a nearly fatal case of malaria. Recovering, he stayed on and marveled at Japan, then went to Germany, to an old SS base called Panzer Kaserne in the deep woods of Böblingen, Bavaria. Assigned to the 160th Signal Group in 1955, he helped provide communications for the entire Seventh Army, which was spread out in Europe over a hundred installations.[11]

By night, he hunched over his radio in the back of a truck, on maneuvers with the First Army, as Warsaw Pact tanks and troops mirrored the GIs on the other side of the border. In his off-time, he traveled to France and Spain, watched a Redstone missile launch, and went to mass. He got a German shepherd—and a blonde German girlfriend. Dispatched to the noncommissioned officer school in nearby Stuttgart, he returned to Panzer Kaserne with the three stripes of a buck sergeant. Just twenty years old in 1956, he was, by all accounts and his own home movies, a happy young man with a big canine grin.

In Monterrey, Mexico, Josefina as a young woman had joined the large and growing Mexican working class. Just a year younger than James, she had grown up with two brothers and an equal number of sisters. Josefina considered herself thoroughly modern: she drank Coke and loved the movies, and when her high school education ended at age sixteen, she studied English and attended business school. Always artistic—she loved making up stories about neighborhood pets as a child—she got a job hand-painting glass at a nearby factory.

Shuffling home in the starry, snowy night after midnight mass on Christmas Eve, 1955, James entered his barracks and was told the duty officer wanted to see him. Reporting in, he was handed a stack of travel orders and informed, sadly, that his father had passed away in Arkansas. Given a bereavement pass, he was to board a plane home immediately. Nearly thirty hours later, he landed and went to the hospital. The family buried Robert in the Catholic church graveyard in Arkansas, and then, one by one, nearly all drifted away. My grandmother, Sue, had never worked outside the house before; she enrolled in college to become a schoolteacher. She took her youngest, Vickie, to Arizona.

Once affairs were settled, James still had time on his leave and wanted to smile again, so he hopped the bus for a fourteen-hour ride to a place he'd never been: Mexico, specifically Monterrey, the nearest big city. He arrived speaking nary a word of Spanish. Bored one afternoon, he went to the movies and spotted, just ahead of him in line, a beautiful, petite Mexican woman giggling with her friends. He tapped the shoulder of the guy in front of him—who turned out to be a soldier himself, in the Mexican army—and asked if he knew English. The other soldier said yes and was immediately enlisted to translate. As the movie line shuffled forward, my father asked my mother if she would go out with him for a Coke the next day. She said yes.

When the next day came, James arrived at the appointed place and time and waited . . . and waited . . . and waited. Josefina stood him up. With his leave coming to an end, James crisscrossed the streets every day, hoping to find her, an act now viewed, less favorably, as stalking. On his last afternoon before having to leave Monterrey, he spotted her crossing the street. They had that Coke, finally. And then they dated long-distance by letter for much of the next five years.

After he left the army in 1960, James moved to Mexico City, where Josefina lived with her parents; they embraced him. He loved

Cecilia's cooking and taught Antonio to play poker. Supported by the GI Bill, he enrolled at Mexico City College, and attempts were made to recruit him as a CIA asset, a job he absolutely refused. Then, on December 23, 1961, Josefina and James were married in a Catholic ceremony. Afterward, they set off by train northward to start their hopeful new life together in America.

IN THE 1970S, El Paso had the feel of a boomtown. Powerful and well-financed developers bulldozed whole mesas along the base of the Franklin Mountains to make way for suburbs. Texas Tech University medical school, based in Lubbock, built a teaching hospital in El Paso. In 1973, Texas Western College became the University of Texas at El Paso and, aided by the new immigration laws, built the fastest track and field teams in the United States, seizing the NCAA indoor title in 1974. This was followed by a second the following year and a third in 1976, under coach Ted Banks.

Don Haskins had played African American players at Texas Western, and Banks went further: he recruited scholarship athletes from the Netherlands, Kenya, and South Africa. Some of these athletes complained of their incomplete educations, about being mired in "softball electives" and even graft. Coach Banks denied it all. But, predictably, there was a backlash against legal immigrants who received scholarships. As one *New York Times* headline would read:

TEXAS—EL PASO'S USE OF FOREIGNERS

RAISES QUESTIONS.[12]

Coach Banks left. Regardless, the Miners won their fourth indoor track championship in 1978. Mexican Americans were excelling in many fields. The El Paso native Lee Trevino was a star professional golfer. Tucson-born Linda Ronstadt was the biggest woman in rock and roll.

Closer to home, families like mine were common: I had friends throughout my school years who were part Mexican and part American. Photos show lovely Mexican wives of ex-GIs at company parties, including at the Juarez Country Club, drinking and mingling with Mexican-born executives and their wives, with all of us kids playing on the deep-green golf course.

As a child I heard only one slur against Mexicans. This happened in middle school, when my mother arrived in her Volkswagen to pick me up. Milling around with other boys, I heard someone say: "Hey, your maid's here!" Fists flew, and scrapes and bruises resulted. I got into the car and my mother asked, "What happened?" I replied sternly, "Nothing." I wound up fighting, like most little boys of the time, with just about anyone: Anglos, Mexican Americans, cowboys, and in Juárez, anyone who picked a fight with anyone's little brother. But I was also friends with everybody—the Mexican American kids in A Building of Coronado High School and the white nerds in the library, before and after school. My little sister, Janet, was funny, pretty, olive-skinned to dark brown, intelligent and popular; only once did she have to rumble with a chola girl. Ours was nearly a privileged existence: we were firmly established in the expanding American middle class.

By the time I was in high school, my friends were Mexican American, popular Anglo kids, unpopular Anglo nerds, shitkickers in the Future Farmers of America, stoners, Jews, Colombians, Argentinians, and more; there were, admittedly, just two African American kids in the student body of over two thousand. Most African Americans lived east of the mountains. I quit playing football and started smoking weed and drinking beer, venturing across the Santa Fe bridge to Juárez for some serious partying. My first cocktail: a tequila sunrise. My first blackout: tequila. My worst blackout

occurred while working a summer job on a ranch in Colorado: tequila, and I passed out in the frigid trout waters of Goose Creek behind a bunkhouse. But even as the region grew in population—to
nearly a half million in El Paso alone by 1980—and wealth, two
deadly problems arose: The first was inequality, and poverty could
be terminal. The second was the rise of the cocaine cartels.

For more than a century, ever-taller smokestacks rose in El Paso
for one simple reason: clean air laws in the United States were getting tighter, but those restrictions counted less here. Nearly all the
plumes of smoke, which contained dangerous heavy metals, such as
arsenic and lead, fell on Mexico, specifically, the outskirts of Juárez,
just across the narrow river. There, shantytowns clung to desert
hillsides, and newcomers to the border could build cheaply.

"They could basically pollute as much as they wanted, because
it was going into another country that had no ability to stop us," El
Paso's mayor, John Cook, said later.[13] In the 1970s, the Centers for
Disease Control stepped in where the city and the state of Texas had
turned their backs. Epidemiologists found that more than half of
the children in Smeltertown had lead levels four times the acceptable limit. A follow-up study brought worse news.

"We found in these children who seemed to be healthy that
they had reduced IQ, slowing of their reflexes, [and] impairment of
their motor coordination," said Dr. Philip Landrigan, the epidemiologist who led the research nearly forty years ago. "This was one of
the very first demonstrations that lead could cause toxicity on the
human brain in children who appeared to have no symptoms." In
the shadow of the smokestack and the statue of Christ, high on the
old Sierra de los Muleros—now Mount Cristo Rey—workers who
had been grateful for their jobs for generations now found that their
children were permanently sick, simply from living in the company
town.

The city sued the mining giant. The liberal *Herald-Post* lashed out, calling Smeltertown "a grimy feudal kingdom spread beneath the company castle." The city tried to evacuate the people, but it was the only home many had ever known, and they resisted. Children were bused to schools six and seven miles away, including the one I attended, Zach White School. In 1975, another study found unsafe lead levels in children up to age nineteen within a radius of one mile. Finally, the residents were forced to move to new public housing. Their old homes were razed.[14] One kid, Andy Ortega, became my classmate and friend.

El Paso had allowed this poisonous shame to take place in plain sight. A local doctor had wanted to conduct a study on the health of the population of Smeltertown, but city politicians brushed him off. Other safety issues were allowed to slide too. Workers wearing respirators ran heavy machinery in Vulcan temperatures, and some were crushed to death.[15] Still, no one wanted to mess with a company making nearly $2 billion in revenue per year.[16] (As it turned out, ASARCO would ultimately be fined nearly that amount.) The discovery of so much poisonous lead caused the federal government to eventually ban lead in all gasoline across the country. The situation in El Paso was a national disgrace, revealing the divide between those who "got theirs"—including my family and neighbors—and those put to work in the furnaces of millionaires, whose children became permanently impaired, right under our collective nose.

THERE WAS A lot of weed in El Paso. My friends raised it under lamps hidden in closets. A judge's son sold it. And quite regularly, the Drug Enforcement Agency (DEA) announced busts of tens of thousands of pounds of it. There was so much weed in El Paso, I don't remember ever having to buy it. One night, with my friends Eric and Martin, we were out of papers, so I grabbed a checkbook carbon and rolled the biggest blunt I'd ever seen. We laughed as smoke filled the Volkswagen. Then we drove to Village Inn on Mesa and ordered the biggest breakfast on the menu: eggs, bacon, pancakes, toast, hash browns, everything. Then we ordered it twice more. The waitress gave us a frown every time. It was 2 a.m.

The weed trafficking was so lucrative and Mexico so close that a successful family, the Chagras, descended from Lebanese immigrants, decided to get in on it. One of them, Lee Chagra, a lawyer, lived right down the street from us, on Frontera Road, in a white mansion behind iron gates. We went to church with his family at Saint Matthew's on Riverbend. Their youngest girl, my sister's age, seemed quiet and was pretty, with big, beautiful eyes. Her brother, Lee Jr., about my age, was known as a big-spending partier.

Across the river, Mexican drug gangs that had long trafficked in weed and black tar heroin in Sinaloa and Juárez would do business with Americans: pilots, truck drivers, crooked cops. But two of the Chagra brothers, Lee and Jimmy, had bigger ideas. They would become the middlemen, and one of them, Jimmy, was a clever lawyer to boot.

They were not unopposed. At Fort Bliss, the federal government set up the El Paso Intelligence Center, a giant spying operation into Mexico and across the Southwest in 1974. DEA agents weren't the only ones listening to wiretaps and monitoring radar at the center; there were FBI agents, CIA analysts, army troops, and airmen—even members of the coast guard, the navy, and the border patrol, not to mention different contractors. They all eventually extended their electronic spyglass to look into Colombia, and then the entire Western Hemisphere, feeding tactical, operational, and strategic intelligence to federal, state, local, tribal, and global law enforcement.[17] They gathered so much information that plenty went to the cutting room floor.[18]

Increasingly, the DEA was publicly sounding the alarm that El

Paso was the hub of all drug trafficking in the Southwest; whether that was true, or was propaganda aimed at securing more funding, remains unclear. Two things were crystal clear, though: cocaine came from Colombia through Mexico to the United States, and guns— including automatic weapons—came from the United States, then mostly passed through Texas, and were ultimately sold in Mexico. Drug addiction and violence went hand in hand.

The Texas senator John Tower persuaded John Wood to leave civil law and become the federal district judge in El Paso. Wood was hard on drug traffickers, usually setting bond at $250,000 and meting out the maximum imprisonment possible upon conviction.[19] He reveled in his nickname, Maximum John.[20] But in this tense situation, the temperature kept rising.

Jimmy Chagra was the audacious one of the brothers. Brazenly, he rented a DC-3 to get one of his crew back; when it crashed in Colombia, the man was injured. Sensing more opportunity in Florida, Jimmy lit out in 1977. There, he set up a dummy corporation to siphon money out of Mexican accounts. He'd never slipped up, but now things changed. The DEA hadn't been able to pin a deal on him directly, even by putting his fingerprints on it beforehand, but now they could. And Jimmy, the lawyer, had helped him set up the dummy company.

Joe Chagra, another brother who had joined Lee's law practice, was sick of it. Both of his brothers spent money like wild men on boats, booze, and broads—in the parlance of the time—not to mention on gambling and, of course, drugs. The Mexican cartels, especially in Sinaloa, had partnered up with the Colombians to move more cocaine into the country; Lee snorted it daily, and the DEA nearly got him in Tennessee. His marriage teetered, and he went to Las Vegas to relieve the strain.

"You must have dropped close to half a million back there. You sonuvabitch, how are you gonna pay off those markers?" his traveling buddy asked, as the hotel graciously provided a limousine to the airport.

"I don't know," Lee replied.[21]

Back in El Paso, Lee's gambling losses made it increasingly impossible to cover the deficits at the law firm. Joe shouldered them more and more.

"Every morning when I drive down to the office, I get sick at my stomach," Joe told Patty, his sister, according to the great crime writer Gary Cartwright of *Texas Monthly*. "I never know if we have fifty thousand dollars in our account or fifty cents."[22]

Nevertheless, as Christmas 1978 approached, Lee was in a good mood after a big court win in Tucson. When he was cheerful he handed out $1,000 here, $10,000 there, and even $50,000, the total came close to half a million. With his cowboy boots propped on his desk, he celebrated big time. As clients, acquaintances, friends, and family streamed in, Lee sat behind his desk, the *patron*, suitably enough, with five ounces of cocaine at his side.

But he was alone in his office as the Sun Bowl came on TV and the door buzzer rang. Lee peered into the closed-circuit television to see who it was. He didn't recognize the first man, who was closest to the camera; he said they were seeking representation for a fellow soldier at Fort Bliss. He opened the door—and they shot him to death. It was, in the end, a stupid robbery attempt. The two men had been tipped off by a Chagra acquaintance connected to the gangster Joe Bonano, who had told them that Lee was handing out money for Christmas.[23]

When Jimmy stood before Judge Wood on drug-trafficking charges the next year, Lee was not there to represent him. And so, from prison, before his trial, he gave the order for a hitman to assassinate Wood. Jimmy doled out $250,000 to a man named Charles Harrelson of Midland, Texas, who on May 29, 1979, put a bullet in the back of Wood's head with a high-powered rifle. Harrelson, the father of the actor Woody Harrelson, then just a teenager, coldly smiled as his double life sentence—plus five years—was read out.[24]

Jimmy now faced two trials. He actually beat the rap on the Wood assassination, the first such murder of a federal judge in a century. But he took the pinch for obstruction of justice and then another thirty-year sentence for drug trafficking too. Lee Jr., with whom I attended high school, also went down for drug trafficking.[25]

Unknown to nearly everyone, Jimmy had cut a deal with the feds and outlived both his brothers. He took a thirty-year sentence for drug trafficking—after confessing to the assassination of Judge Wood and trying to kill the local US attorney. He was sent to the United States Penitentiary in Atlanta in exchange for the release of his wife, Elizabeth, who had been convicted alongside him on the drug charge. His health failing, he left Atlanta in 2003 for the witness protection program. He never lost his flair, though. He got married a third time in Las Vegas under an assumed name, left behind seven children, and turned up dead of cancer in a trailer park in Mesa, Arizona, on July 25, 2008.

MY HIGH SCHOOL counselor looked at my file, looked at me, and said, "You know, I think I can get you in the army."

He meant an enlistment. Well, I'd already gotten accepted to a picky, elite college on a small scholarship, so except for holiday visits home, I really didn't look back after 1982. I spent summers driving trucks across North Texas, in summer school, and training to be an army officer in Kentucky. After I'd finally gotten to see a little more of the world, El Paso, with its factories, trucks, and rail-yards, was no longer my cup of tea.

Working port cities—I think of Baltimore or New Orleans before both were gentrified into shopping malls by the Rouse

Company—can be pretty ugly. It's just the nature of the beast: a view of endless shipping containers, railways, cranes, refineries, fuel depots, and trucks picking up and dropping off. A contemporary of mine from El Paso who is now a Texas state senator, Mary Gonzalez, remembered a nickname for our hometown: "Hell Paso."

During a winter visit home in the 1980s, I went to watch a punk band at a dilapidated hotel on Mesa Avenue. Some good punk came out of El Paso, like Mars Volta and my buddy Ron Marks's Texas Instruments. But the motel was a dimly lit shithole. I noticed garbage in the hallways as I left. It was a metaphor for my hometown, ugly and cheap. The novelty of the boomtown had worn off under the grinding gears of global capitalism.

"I gotta get out," I told myself. So I did.

Chapter Nineteen

DRUGS AND MONEY, 1997–2011

I N THE SPRING of 1997, a four-ship flight of olive-drab helicop-
ters thundered into the western Sierra Madre of Mexico, flying
low and fast, the thudding sounds of the chopper blades bouncing
off the canyon walls.

In front rode two Mexican generals; in the back a photographer
and me. The pilot of the lead Bell Jet Ranger showed off his skill
fresh from his training, courtesy of the US Army at Fort Rucker,
Alabama. He wasn't just flat-hatting for the generals; the low approach would conceal the Jet Ranger and its three trailing UH-1
Super Hueys until the last minute.

Suddenly popping straight up, the entire four-ship formation
settled onto a narrow ridge. The troops behind us fanned out under the blades to secure the perimeter. The field below was full
of beautiful red poppy flowers, ripe for the heroin trade of Sinaloa.
This time there would be no firefight, as occasionally there was when
poppy farmers decided to defend the fields. A few soldiers stood
perimeter with their Colt M16A1s while the rest slung arms and
grabbed machetes, lopping the tall shoots, head and ball, the blos-
som, and bundled them up. Down the Sierra Madre to Michoacan
and Guerrero, troops flew in and followed suit.

As the helo engines whined down to a stop, my photographer colleague got to work and I sidled up to the two generals, the senior one clearly not knowing that I understood and spoke fluent Spanish. "Look," the squat, bald officer told his taller subordinate, "don't bother me with this shit again." The taller one-star responded that he was just following orders. The soldiers diligently started whacking down a single plot easily worth tens of millions of dollars; they stacked the poppies as high as they could reach, doused the pile in gasoline, and set it afire. Gray smoke wafted away across the mountains.

All this—the arms, equipment, camouflage uniforms, Kevlar, and upgraded engines—was the handiwork of the US government, via the Clinton administration. For the first time since World War II, the United States was overtly, if quietly, lending the Mexican armed forces a multi-billion-dollar hand.

This fight was against the Mexican cartels, who had gotten so powerful that they had killed off many of their Colombian overlords in the cocaine trade and taken over, adding their own homegrown heroin and weed. These eradication missions seemed like overkill to me, until I stopped to consider that a single such mission back in 1984 had chopped down $8 billion worth of crop in Chihuahua, next door to El Paso. As payback the DEA agent Kiki Camarena had been tortured and killed the next year, compliments of the Sinaloa cartel of Rafael Caro Quintero himself. The Mexican cartels had simply gotten too powerful—controlling entire cities—so the CIA and the Green Berets took a hand.

My photographer headed home the next morning. I checked out of my hotel in Acapulco—owned by the Mexican military—for another one down the beach, where I could write. It was the first time the Mexican army had opened the kimono, so to speak, about US military aid, still a sensitive topic. By now, I had spent a lot of time writing about Mexico: the new free trade agreement known as the North American Free Trade Agreement (NAFTA), Chiapas, and now, the new and improved "war on drugs."

Things had gotten sticky. Whenever I checked into my hotel near the American embassy in Mexico City, the line clicked with surefire wiretaps. Repeated devaluations of the peso by the government, reckless federal spending, and the swelling of government ranks by financing its oil supplies had wiped out most people's savings, my mother's included. I offered to bring my aunt's kids to the United States for college, but she declined. President Carlos Salinas stole everything but the silver on his way out the door—into exile in Ireland.

Composing a lengthy first draft of the final piece of the series in my hotel, I found it hard to know what to say. Clearly, this maneuver with the poppies had been a dog-and-pony show for the news outlets; our photos and articles would get picked up by the Associated Press, and American readers would see the tough and effective new face of the war on drugs. But the real story was the cartels—how they posed a threat to power, order, and money. NAFTA had turned Mexico and Canada into much, much more than a trading bloc worth more than $6 trillion at the time, and the agreement had been negotiated in nearly as much secrecy as American military aid. As a reporter covering NAFTA in Mexico City and Washington, I had to develop all manner of sources inside both governments as well as outside—because the negotiations were classified as "top secret" under two presidents, George H. W. Bush and Bill Clinton. No detail would be officially revealed until it was a fait accompli; only up or down votes in both houses of Congress would determine the outcome. The stakes were high.

The money involved in NAFTA made the money involved in Mexican drugs—in the tens of millions in profits per year at the time—look like chump change. With billions of investment dollars flowing into Mexico, intended to turn big profits on Wall

Street and keep more Mexicans at home, instead of immigrating to the United States, the United States couldn't risk letting the cartels destabilize things. But, as usual, nothing went according to plan: rural Mexico emptied out as big American and Mexican corporations took over farmland as part of NAFTA, and Mexico became, initially at least, even more impoverished and chaotic.

Two days after turning in my article, I grabbed the phone to call my editor about what I'd just seen on the news: the grumpy general from my helo flight, Jesús Hector Gutiérrez Rebollo, was under arrest in Mexico City, charged with drug trafficking. The old, bull-necked general had a reputation for being as honest as he was gruff, yet he had turned, just two months after his appointment as the nation's top drug enforcer—and was now on the payroll of a new kingpin, Amado Carrillo Fuentes, leader of the up-and-coming Juárez cartel across from El Paso. I confessed to my editor that I was embarrassed; he had been right under my nose. Then again, everyone was embarrassed: the Mexicans and their new president, Ernesto Zedillo; the Clinton administration and its drug czar, the retired army general Barry McCaffrey; the CIA and the Pentagon—everybody but the DEA, which had sniffed out the connection by means of a Mexican military informant. Gutiérrez was fired, jailed, and eventually sentenced to nearly forty years in prison, where he would die. Money, drugs, violence, and competing bids for power—Mexico teetered on the brink of becoming another Colombia.[1]

Stories from the drug world involved such shocking violence, they seemed unbelievable. Carrillo, the leader of the Juárez cartel, died while having plastic surgery to make his face unrecognizable. Carrillo's men then proceeded to torture the surgeons, kill them, and place them into a steel barrel, which they then filled with concrete.

But NAFTA was where the *real* money was. The agreement

was not just a trade treaty, nor did it simply establish a common market without tariffs. Through NAFTA, Wall Street would finance the industrial development of Mexico to benefit the biggest corporations in the world, so they could increase their profits by means of paying lower wages. Here they would manufacture all kinds of consumer goods, from televisions to cars, and avoid taxes when shipments crossed international boundaries. The Cold War was over; NAFTA became a testbed to see whether these flows of capital could be replicated on a global scale, thereby extending a web of American soft power, particularly to what would become the biggest factory floor in the world: China.

WITH HIS ECONOMY reeling under a crushing $100 million in debt, Mexican president Carlos Salinas de Gortari, a slight, balding technocrat, had asked President George H. W. Bush for a formal trade agreement in 1990. Soon, the Canadian prime minister, Brian Mulroney, was involved too. The biggest hurdle to the historic deal was the Mexican cartels.

In Washington, the Bush administration assumed, incorrectly, that Mexican drug trafficking would fall with the Colombian cartels; instead, the Mexicans moved in and took over. As a result, Congress was in an uproar about Mexico. Salinas placated the Americans by quickly arresting Miguel Felix Gallardo, leader of the Guadalajara cartel. Salinas got a big reception for this achievement in Washington. But Salinas was likely just playing favorites; a new cartel was springing up in his home state, Nuevo León, in the Mexican northeast.

"People desperately wanted drugs not to become a complicating factor for NAFTA," said John P. Walters, a senior official for international drug policy in the original Bush White House. "There was a degree of illicit activity that was just accepted."[2] If violence erupted in Mexico, it would easily scare away American investment.

Bush is best remembered, perhaps, for being on watch as the Soviet Union collapsed and subsequently declaring the "New World Order," a unipolar world led by the United States. But behind the scenes, the issue of economics held enormous importance. When Detroit demanded that Bush curb the imports of Japanese cars, he rebuffed the automakers; he was far more concerned with propping up the economy of Japan, an important ally. He actively shepherded American industries to relocate in the former eastern bloc, and as the former ambassador to China, he was always keenly interested in bringing that nation into an American-led world.

"If democracy is to be consolidated, the gulfs that separate the few who are very rich from the many who are very poor, that divide civilian from military institutions, that split citizens of European heritage from indigenous peoples, these gulfs must be bridged," Bush said shortly after signing NAFTA. "Economic reform must ensure upward mobility and new opportunities for a better life for all citizens of the Americas."[3]

The US economy had dropped into a brief recession that didn't feel global. Bush lost his bid for reelection—but he got the negotiations over the line. He signed the North American Free Trade Agreement in December 1992, on his way out of office, and would build a friendship with his successor, Bill Clinton, in part because of the treaty. It would be up to Clinton to wrangle approval from Congress.

Until the treaty went to Congress, its text was locked as tight as a safe—unless, that is, one was a lobbyist for the industries that would be affected, and their Wall Street bankers. Up in Ottawa, papers on the status of negotiations for the cabinet were heavily redacted and nevertheless marked "FOR EYES ONLY."[4] Indeed, when legal disputes arose under the treaty, the resulting tribunals would be entirely closed to the public, whether Canadian, American, or Mexican. Even the judgments were kept secret; only a few of the secret tribunal documents were ever leaked.[5] These amounted to billions of dollars' worth of judgments involving corporations, national governments, and even public health. The system was wide open to abuse; in one case, a Louisiana funeral company challenged a Mississippi jury verdict against it by claiming it was protected by the free trade treaty.[6] In another, a Canadian corporation, Metalclad, tried to fight a $900 million judgment against it under Mexican law for harming the environment and making people sick.[7]

Nevertheless, Clinton picked up the treaty and immediately ran with it, surrounded by Wall Street advisers, getting Congress to approve it without changes, and giving it a final signing on December 3, 1993. "NAFTA means jobs, American jobs, and good-paying American jobs," he said, echoing Bush, in "an era in which commerce is global."[8]

It would not be the first time President Clinton would tell a lie. NAFTA was marketed and sold one way but worked in exactly the opposite way. During Clinton's second term, Mexican exports rose to six hundred times their level at the beginning of the decade.[9] The surge of American investment increased Mexican productivity, boosted profits, and made Wall Street stocks and portfolios soar. The treaty helped the Mexican economy rebound, for sure, but there was another big winner: Wall Street, which could cease worrying about Mexico defaulting on its huge debt, as Argentina had. Said Lawrence Krohn, a senior economist at the Union Bank of Switzerland, "Default would have meant chaos."[10]

Not everyone emerged a winner. While NAFTA cost taxpayers basically nothing, it did cost some seven hundred thousand American workers their jobs. Manufacturers shed American workers primarily in California, Texas, Michigan, and across the industrial Midwest.[11] They liked the lower wages available in the interior of

Mexico; putting up factories along the border was nearly as cheap too, and an infrastructure was already in place. The surging trade was an initial boon to inland ports along the Mexican boundary line, from Tijuana to Laredo.[12]

Indeed, a Laredo banker, Dennis E. Nixon, rose during this time to national political power as a kingmaker. No other individual in the private sector had been more insistent about the trade treaty across presidential administrations. Along with Wall Street, his little Laredo bank swelled to become one of the largest in the nation; it was eighty-third in assets and the largest minority-owned bank in the United States.

But in reality, the wealth that lasted was pocketed by investors like Nixon and his Wall Street colleagues. After the initial investment in more border factories, the wages in the interior became increasingly attractive, and binational cities such as El Paso–Juárez and Laredo–Nuevo Laredo became transshipment points whose construction was, usually, publicly financed.

Rail lines, bridges, interstate highways, and cargo-only airports had to be built, expanded, and repaired with taxpayer money. Governments competed to make passage faster and more efficient for companies. The first intermodal port—interconnecting trucks, rail, and cargo aircraft—was rapidly built at Santa Teresa, New Mexico, just across the state line from El Paso's western suburbs. Taxpayers stretched the runway there to nearly ten thousand feet: longer than the one at Edwards Air Force Base, California, and long enough to easily land not only a 747, but even a space shuttle.[13] The federal government poured $5 million into a short stretch of road to connect trucks from Sunland Park to a crowded Interstate 10.[14]

But as it came and went, trade left little on the table for El Paso. Already a poor city by American standards, El Paso lost twenty-six thousand jobs in the first dozen years of NAFTA.[15] Wages fell. After surviving a sex scandal and impeachment in the Republican House of Representatives, Clinton set his sights beyond North America. China was hot on Mexico's heels as a trading partner, with Beijing ranking third in the late 1990s. Clinton increasingly turned a blind eye to human rights abuses in Tibet and the network of political prisons, the *laogai*, named for the old Soviet gulags. China joined the World Trade Organization as a full-fledged member on December 11, 2001. At last, there would be a factory floor even cheaper than Mexico's.

Chinese wages hovered at about 57 cents per hour.[16] Mexican wages were about $2.70 per hour.[17] The day after the deal was inked, the stock market recouped all eighty-four points of losses from the previous week.[18]

"In the broadest possible picture, NAFTA probably provided a very minor increase in real incomes in the [United States]," said the University of Virginia's John McLaren, who co-authored a 2016 study documenting NAFTA's effect on US wages. "But for an important minority of blue-collar people who already had lower wages, it was a big negative . . . El Paso was one of the most affected."[19] El Paso, with its low-wage manufacturing economy, would see wages fall further as manufacturers slipped across the border to enjoy even lower wages.

At the same time, no matter who was the president in Mexico City, the American-supplied war on drugs at best splintered the drug cartels, which would simply reconsolidate. In 1997, an assassin, or *sicario*, roamed the streets of Juárez; he killed six people in a restaurant, the biggest mass murder by organized crime in Mexico at the time. The bounty was astounding: $5 million for a single hit. As he explained to his biographers at the time, when his wife asked what he would do if someone came to kidnap their children, he gruffly snapped: *"No me preguntas eso."* "Don't ask me that." He gained fame in the wildly fictionalized movie *Sicario* and lived by a simple creed: *"Un ojo por un ojo."*

An eye for an eye.[20]

The law in Juárez was survival of the fittest.

EVEN AS AMERICAN demand for cocaine surged, remarkably, the national security apparatus worked: the agents, spies, soldiers, and contractors blunted the cartels right at the border. That didn't mean that drugs didn't get through, however; most did. But the widespread violence that fell on Tijuana, Juárez, and Nuevo Laredo never fell on their American sister cities at nearly the same scale; most of the cartels were confined right at the Rio Grande.

If the border was callously used for profit—black-market and white-shoe alike—at least one new president could be counted on to better understand and perhaps improve it: George W. Bush.

Yes, W.

The former governor of Texas and forty-third president of the United States was the only Bush born in Texas. Educated in the Ivy League, he pulled a stint in the Texas Air National Guard and started his oil venture, Arbusto—Spanish for "bush"—in Midland-Odessa. After joining in the ownership of the Texas Rangers, he defeated Ann Richards for the governorship on November 8, 1994, snapping Democratic rule in Texas, which stretched back to the Civil War. He had struck up a relationship with the new Mexican president as well: a fellow cowboy-boot-wearing border-state governor from Sonora, Vincente Fox. A fellow conservative, Fox had defeated the ruling party for the first time in a free and fair election.

NAFTA had helped some inside Mexico but displaced others—especially farm workers, as international companies took over the fields. The growing Mexican diaspora prompted Bush to campaign on reestablishing a formal Mexican worker program with a path to eventual US citizenship. As governor, Bush had fared well with Hispanic voters, and his team set their sights on that bloc in 2000. Reforming immigration was to be central to Bush's office.

In January 2001, Bush announced his first trip as president: straight to Mexico. He would cement a "special relationship" with the country, just as Franklin Roosevelt had with Great Britain.[21] The two leaders met in Monterrey and recited a litany of issues, including immigration laws, drugs, and tinkering with NAFTA. Then they adjourned to their respective capitals. Fox traveled to Washington for a full-fledged summit on September 4, 2001.[22] But by then, Bush was getting vague about changes to the immigration laws and system. Republicans, especially those in the Senate, opposed him, though big business sided with him. A streak of nativism among voters had nearly cost his father the nomination back in 1992, and now it was building again—opposition to guest workers, amnesty, and Mexican immigrants in general was growing virulent.

And then, exactly one week later, came 9/11.

Of course nothing was the same in the aftermath, for the entire nation. Mexico slid from the windshield of the American agenda and out the rearview. The intelligence community reeled at the failure, and the nation plunged into war. As he sought reelection in 2004, Bush did something that was, for him, surprising: he shifted toward his own party by sounding the alarm about immigrants, winning congressional approval to send six thousand active-duty troops to the US-Mexico border.[23] It bought time to train an equal number of border patrol agents—or, in the post-9/11 world, US Customs and Border Protection. But it was also a stunt to galvanize the Republican right.

Stoking fears that the Mexican border might pose another 9/11 seemed to come straight out of nowhere—actually, it came from Karl Rove, the president's chief political adviser. He had earlier gotten

Bush to tack toward Hispanic voters, most of whom were Mexican American citizens and generally sympathetic to immigrants because they knew or were related to them, given the size of the Mexican diaspora in the United States, then over eleven million.[24] Congress also ordered seven hundred miles of border fencing, costing over $1 billion.[25] Just as they had become involved in Afghanistan and Iraq, the giant military contractors, led by Lockheed Martin, Raytheon, and Northrop Grumman, stepped up with bids for government business, this time to militarize the Mexican border.[26]

"We are launching the most technologically advanced border security initiative in American history," Bush said, as he dispatched none other than Rove to Congress to sell security and his immigration plan.[27]

All of it did little, except to squeeze Mexican undocumented immigrants from one sector that was too hard to cross to others that were easier. It did nothing to stem the number of foreigners entering on visas at American airports and then simply staying here. They increasingly came from China and from African nations.

Nevertheless, the politics were perfect. Bush's immigration plan sank from sight, but Americans approved of the optics of troops on the border—again. By a 2-to-1 margin, those polled said they favored Bush's plan to deploy troops, yet voters were still evenly split on a path to citizenship. Bush had made the pivot seamlessly.[28]

Overlooked in Washington, however, was a crime wave in Ciudad Juárez. Women were drawn to work in the factories of the border, a ticket out of claustrophobic lives as wives and mothers in a desolate corner of rural Mexico. Working in the factories of foreign companies meant decent pay, their own spending money, and a social life in a sprawling city of over 1.2 million people. Foreign companies liked hiring women too. Managers found them punctual, dependable, motivated, quick to learn—and without the discipline problems that often accompanied men, of any nationality, in their late teens and early twenties.

In October 2001, Claudia Gonzalez arrived exactly four minutes late to work to find the gates to her place of employment locked. The next month, her remains and those of seven other women were discovered in a shallow grave. All eight had been raped, mutilated, and strangled to death. From the mid-1990s through 2015, five hundred young women turned up this way. About a hundred others disappeared, presumably into that ancient, terrible human practice: sex trafficking. The police were slow to investigate nearly all cases; higher courts, even international ones, had to force them to search fields and houses.[29]

Might the local police have been in on it? Taking bribes from rackets and then protecting them was standard operating procedure, after all. Why make an exception now to such barbarity? "They've sent a message that there isn't the capacity to investigate crimes nor to punish the guilty," the lawyer David Pena said of the investigators and prosecutors. "We believe they were covering up for the real guilty parties. The actual guilty ones remain free."[30] When the police arrested two men—exactly two—for committing all five hundred murders of teenage girls and young women, the grieving mothers were outraged.

The United States did not have the stomach to intervene. Weighed down by defeat in Iraq and Afghanistan, and facing a collapsing economy and financial system, Bush finished his second term having failed on the border with Mexico, as others had. He had taken a complex set of realities and reduced them to Republican Party politics. He blamed Congress.

He had squandered nearly all of his political capital in his response to 9/11 and the subsequent wars; there was nothing left to substantively improve the relationship with Mexico, and border

cities like El Paso. American presidents always did as they liked
with the Southwest: they ignored it, panicked over it, or played
great power politics with it, but even Wilson had never played it
for strictly domestic political gain.

ON THE BLUSTERY Chicago night of November 8, 2008, a trim,
hopeful man looked out into the crowd, into flashing cameras, cell
phones, and stage lights. Barack Obama had campaigned, in part,
by promising change to those at the border, especially Latinos. He
had even taken the old chant of Cesar Chavez's farm workers: "*Sí, se
puede!*" "Yes, we can!"

Then President-elect Obama spoke to an enthralled majority,
who could see themselves in his words:

> If there is anyone out there who still doubts that America is
> a place where all things are possible; who still wonders if the
> dream of our founders is alive in our time; who still questions the
> power of our democracy, tonight is your answer.
>
> It's the answer told by lines that stretched around schools
> and churches in numbers this nation has never seen; by people
> who waited three hours and four hours, many for the very first
> time in their lives, because they believed that this time must be
> different; that their voice could be that difference.
>
> It's the answer spoken by young and old, rich and poor,
> Democrat and Republican, black, white, Latino, Asian, Native
> American, gay, straight, disabled and not disabled—Americans
> who sent a message to the world that we have never been a col-
> lection of red states and blue states; we are, and always will be,
> the United States of America.
>
> It's the answer that led those who have been told for so long
> by so many to be cynical, and fearful, and doubtful of what we

can achieve to put their hands on the arc of history and bend it once more toward the hope of a better day.

It's been a long time coming, but tonight, because of what we did on this day, in this election, at this defining moment, change has come to America.[31]

After the first eight years of the twenty-first century, Americans were exhausted by war, financial collapse, two recessions, the threats of terrorism, job losses, college loans, and the sinking feeling that their version of the American dream had slipped away, replaced with chaos. Here, at last, was a moment of respite; the glimmer of, yes, hope, that the country might be able to dig itself out.

Just forty-seven when he assumed office, the forty-fourth president of the United States was among the youngest in American history. And he inherited a mess: the wars in the Middle East and Afghanistan, a shattered economy, a giant federal deficit fueled by the largesse of military spending and tax cuts, and a hostile Republican Congress. Like Bush when he first campaigned, he had tapped into Mexican American anxiety about how their families were treated in trying to come to this country. If they came without papers, there was still no path to citizenship, no matter how long they lived and worked here—and paid taxes and contributed to the Social Security they would never collect. But whether Obama knew it or not, a large shift was underway: Mexicans were no longer coming to the United States in the numbers of the previous century's diaspora. Indeed, the year he was elected, they stopped coming; more went back to Mexico than came to the United States. Wages in Mexico had fallen, and as wages in China surpassed them and rose to nearly $4 per hour, Mexico seemed like a good place for global capital to resettle again, for a while.

Other immigrants started to arrive in their place, namely, from Central America. Whether Obama knew it or not, Mexicans and

Mexican Americans in this country did not identify with these new-comers. They had little more than a vaguely common language be-tween them, and often not even that. Many Central Americans came from much harsher conditions than those of Mexico, displaced as the Mexican cartels were increasingly driven into Guatemala, Honduras, and El Salvador. And many of the new immigrants didn't speak Span-ish. They spoke Q'eqchi' and Tzeltal, Mayan languages descended from the greatest of classical civilizations, which began in the Amer-icas five thousand years ago, before the pharaohs ruled the Egyptians.

Though he was a leader seeking change and promising greater justice at the US-Mexico border—now home to twelve million people—Obama turned away from it. Drugs and security were, pre-dictably, the top agenda items in his talks with the Mexican pres-ident, Enrique Peña Nieto.[32] The Mexican cartels were expanding into still more heroin and increasingly cheap artificial fentanyl to feed the American appetite; these were urgent concerns.[33] A milita-rized offensive that had begun under Peña Nieto's predecessor was proving disastrous; some seven thousand people died in Mexico in 2009 as a result of the drug war, while over a thousand Mexicans were kidnapped.[34] The offensive cut the heads off drug cartels, and like hydras, they produced even more. Now, instead of organized cartels, organized crime spread throughout the country—wreaking violence, havoc, and murder, and stealing everything not nailed down.

Meanwhile, Americans were buying less heroin and more fentanyl; the artificial opioid was the future, with a kilo worth $1.8 million on the street. Some two million Americans had an opioid disorder and tens of thousands died yearly from overdoses.[35] Unlike cocaine and real heroin, fentanyl was nearly all profit—which, in turn, bought more politicians and police back in Mexico. Though the national government in Mexico City was cleaner than ever, the states and cities were rife with corruption: local politicians, clerks, and cops got side gigs with criminal enterprises.

With less than a year left before reelection, the border was a headache the Obama administration just did not want. Nevertheless, on May 10, 2011, the president arrived in El Paso, bearing the rising spring heat. White shirtsleeves rolled up, Obama made opening remarks strikingly similar to those of another young president: Kennedy. He was funny and disarming.

But it was a rote speech, aimed at a national Latino audience that was changing before his eyes. Obama underscored his dedication to sweeping new immigration laws; like Bush, he teetered between stances of justice and toughness, noting that he was busy building fencing, dispatching drones, and bulking up the customs and border protection. Obama recited the required figures about the increased seizures of drugs and the declining apprehensions of border jumpers. A Reuters headline summed it up: "Obama's Immigration Speech Is No Game Changer."[36]

"Actions definitely speak louder than words, and this was no different from speeches we have heard in the past," said Pablo Alvarado, director of the National Day Laborer Organizing Network. "The conversation at the dinner table is 'what has he done for Latinos?' The answer is 'nothing.'"[37]

Well, that wasn't exactly true. Obama did deport nearly four hundred thousand immigrants that year—something that wasn't in his speech, but it did help him cement a second term. To the Republican right, Latino citizens in general began to seem like a threat to power; they tried to govern for a whiter and older base. As evidenced by the election results, that America was in decline. Obama failed to disrupt this Republican narrative about the border, and his immigration bill, like Bush's, would go nowhere in a Republican Congress. But he would, after reelection, go on to set a new record. Obama deported more immigrants than any president in American history: 1.5 million people.[38]

Part V

We, the people of this continent, are not fearful of foreigners, because most of us were once foreigners.

—POPE FRANCIS, ADDRESSING
THE US CONGRESS

Chapter Twenty

STRANGERS IN THE LAND OF EGYPT, 2018

O N JUNE 28, 2018, I drove up to the only American concentration camp I'd ever seen. It was the first of its kind since World War II. Locked inside, behind the chain-link fence topped with concertina wire, were children.

A sprawling tent city opened in the quiet farm town of Tornillo, just downriver of El Paso. The pecan orchards and cotton fields brought bucolic memories of my early life upriver. But this place, hemmed in between the Rio Grande and I-10, had a nefarious purpose: like several others along the United States–Mexico border, the Tornillo facility was intended to hold children apprehended for entering this country illegally.

Other facilities, like the converted Walmart in Brownsville, were the equivalent of short-term holding cells, where parents and children were separated and then processed out to other facilities. In contrast, the Tornillo facility, already home in 2018 to perhaps dozens of teenage boys, would hold hundreds of minors, possibly for months at a time. No reporters were allowed inside. Whatever the federal government chose to call it, this was an internment camp: a concentration camp for kids.

West Texas became a new front in the Trump administration's

war on undocumented immigrants. And this war, like all, took prisoners. Some nine hundred adult immigrants were locked up in the El Paso County jail. Children were held at facilities run by a private outfit, Southwest Key Programs. The government was planning to incarcerate still more people on military bases in El Paso, Abilene, and San Angelo.

Like a lot of wars, this one was long on secrecy. When I approached the facility, I was brusquely told to leave. The local customs and border protection spokesman claimed to know nothing about the camp just steps outside his station's back door. The Health and Human Services Department returned no phone calls. Representative Beto O'Rourke, a Democrat from El Paso who led a march here, was told he would need to wait two weeks for an appointment; his colleague, Joe Kennedy III of Massachusetts, was simply turned away.

However, Representative Will Hurd, a Republican whose district included Tornillo, and State Representative Mary Gonzalez, a Democrat who also represented Tornillo, did get into the camp late at night. In an interview, Gonzalez described inmates as sixteen- and seventeen-year-old boys, assigned to sleep twenty to a tent. A big tent, closest to the gate, served as a mess hall. All were air-conditioned. The place was livable, Gonzalez said—but "also dehumanizing."

In a handful of photos released by the Department of Homeland Security, the metal, military-style bunks were stacked one on top of the other; the tent ceiling seemed close enough to touch from the top bunk. The mess hall was brightly lit and furnished with folding chairs and plastic folding tables. The photos showed a dozen smaller tents on concrete, with a yard of gravel and portable toilets outside, where temperatures would soar into the hundreds. There were one or two command posts—one trucked in from the Texas state government—as well as an ambulance and medical van, along with caseworkers, therapists, and nurse practitioners, according to Representative Gonzalez. A soccer goal stood on a dirt field.

Further information was vague and contradictory. Some reports said that only unaccompanied minors were being held at the camp, but O'Rourke said he was told that about 20 percent of the boys at Tornillo had been separated from their parents. The facility was officially supposed to hold a few hundred boys, but Hurd said he was told on the tour that it might be expanded to hold four thousand.

There was something strange about a secret facility surrounded by dozens of journalists and camera crews. It was the most famous camp in America at that moment. "So why," Representative Gonzalez asked after her tour, "are they trying to keep it a secret?"

The simple explanation was shame. This was not something liberal democracies are supposed to do. The last time the US government separated children from parents on this scale was in the late nineteenth century, when Native American boys and girls were forced into boarding schools so they could be taught to act white. Before that, only the institution of slavery stripped away children wholesale. Both were the original sins of the American story, and yet here we were again.

The Trump administration seized two thousand children from two thousand parents in six weeks, according to its own statistics, using a law that was already on the books when Trump came into office. With that 1996 law, the Clinton administration began locking up undocumented immigrants, and the Bush administration accelerated the process. The Obama administration held entire families briefly in cells called *hieleras*—or iceboxes, because they were so cold—before their immigration hearing. But until 2018, no one held children captive *apart from* their families.

These places were reminiscent of the American internment camps of World War II. Coincidentally, one of the most notorious was called Crystal City, located 110 miles southwest of San Antonio. It held over three thousand people of Japanese, German, and Italian descent during World War II, including native-born American citizens. But even that camp was more humane: schooling was provided for children, who were kept with families, said Carl Takei, an attorney with the American Civil Liberties Union whose own grandparents had been split by that war: his grandmother in a camp and his grandfather fighting for the US Army in Europe.

The government called Tornillo and other similar sites "detention facilities," a term implying that the occupants were, first and foremost, lawbreakers. But "internment facilities" seems more accurate. This term has been used to denote places of confinement, without trial, for prisoners of war, citizens of other nations, and political prisoners. With its troops, walls, and arrests, the Trump administration was effectively waging war on a comparatively peaceful stretch of its own country—creating a crisis where no crisis actually existed.

The term "detention facilities" also implied that some measure of due process was in effect, but this was really not the case. The teenagers might have seen an immigration judge, but in an administrative, nonjudicial proceeding. If history was any guide, they probably wouldn't even get an immigration lawyer. The government said it could hold them for nearly two months. If it was true, then the camp in Tornillo would grow to be ten times its current size. It was unclear when, or how, any of these boys would find their families again.

And yet, there was something else hanging in the hot summer air, a whiff of the Rio Grande and the place where the Oñate expedition had rested on the banks hundreds of years earlier. This saga was no longer about immigrants: undocumented, illegal, or seeking asylum and freedom from persecution in their home country, totally legal in the United States and a basic, universal human right. To the Trump administration, immigrants, whatever their actual country of origin, were just more people of Mexican descent crowding into the United States. And that was unacceptable. The president had, after all, launched his campaign with these words:

> When do we beat Mexico at the border? They're laughing at us, at our stupidity. And now they are beating us economically. They are not our friend, believe me. But they're killing us economically. The U.S. has become a dumping ground for everybody else's problems . . . When Mexico sends its people, they're not sending their best. They're not sending you. They're not sending you. They're sending people that have lots of problems, and they're bringing those problems with us. They're bringing drugs. They're bringing crime. They're rapists. And some, I assume, are good people.[1]

It wasn't just Mexicans who were a problem—in fact, net immigration from Mexico had ceased eight years earlier. Mexican Americans were a problem too. In other cities, in other speeches, it was the Chinese and even the Japanese whom Trump railed against, though Japan was among our great allies of the late twentieth century. One of his first acts as president was excusing white nationalists in Charlottesville—one of whom killed a woman with his car—for chanting these words: "The Jews will not replace us!" The new president said forthrightly, "There were very fine people on both sides."

Black and Hispanic Americans would increasingly be denied the vote; women would, because of Trump's appointments to the Supreme Court, be denied the pursuit of life and liberty. Jews and others would be killed in hate crimes. Here in Tornillo, in a centuries-old bundle of war and peace and love and death, that was all being foretold. The beginning of the end of American democracy was here in Tornillo, with its apt Spanish name: "The Screw."

BY MIDDAY ON a Saturday in November 2018, the desert sun was high, and the little protest felt like an act of futility and powerlessness. About two hundred people, Jews and Christians, clustered near an eight-foot stone gate at the Tornillo facility, singing and praying for hundreds of Central American children held by the federal government. Two cop cars and chain-link fences topped with concertina wire kept them a good 150 yards out of the children's sight and well beyond their hearing. Every twenty minutes, buses with tinted windows arrived, ferrying still more children. The group sang "Olam Chesed Yibaneh," "We Will Build This World from Love," as a folk guitar strummed. Signs with statements like "Let My People Go," with a drawing of Moses, were taped to the fence. One driver, his federal uniform and badge clearly visible, brazenly leaned on the horn of a bus marked "Homeland Security."

A towering, curly-headed young Reform rabbi, Joshua Whinston, his head covered by a yarmulke and his big shoulders draped by a prayer shawl, told the knot of people to follow him. If the police turned them back, they should return to the gate that served as a designated protest zone. "We didn't come here to get arrested," he cautioned. There were Jews, Episcopalians, Catholic Sisters of Mercy, and even schoolgirls from the Catholic Loretto Academy, who left for second period back at school in El Paso with tears streaming down their faces. Dutifully, the group shambled toward the police, who had seen this drill here so many times, they could ladle the tension with a spoon. Sure enough, the group turned and shuffled back.

These protesters had emerged from the fearful sorrow of the October 2018 Pittsburgh massacre that killed eleven Jewish people in their own synagogue; this hate crime was burned into the national conscience. They had traveled from Illinois, Michigan, Ohio, and other points to El Paso, here to help refugees from Honduras, Guatemala, and El Salvador, putting themselves at risk. After all, the suspected Pittsburgh gunman had railed against Jews and immigrants in online posts before the massacre.[2] Deadly violence against Jewish, Hispanic, Black, and Asian people was on the rise in Donald Trump's America; hate crimes were reaching their highest level in a decade. Most were based on race or ethnicity, followed by religion and sexual identity, ultimately comprising nearly eight thousand assaults, including murder.[3]

Nevertheless, the young rabbi, Whinston, was stirred enough by the moment to lead his people into this faraway desert. Yes, the government made their journey nearly fruitless. But here, faith confronted power in a place that was now ground zero in the firestorm over the changing complexion of America. The desert backdrop of their pilgrimage was richly instructive, filled with the footsteps of immigrants, including Jews, and the first actual site of that uniquely immigrant celebration, the reason for making this journey now: Thanksgiving.

Whinston's voyage to the border began in an unlikely place, thirty-seven years earlier, in sunny Southern California. He was the prototypical upper-middle-class Jewish kid from the West Coast: involved with Jewish youth-group music in high school or waiting in suburban San Diego for the annual experience of Jewish summer camp. After college at the University of California at Santa Barbara and a stint at Hebrew Union College–Jewish Institute of Religion in Los Angeles, he wound up in leafy Ann Arbor, Michigan, with his wife, Sarah, three small children—ages three, six, and eight at the time—and a Reform congregation at Temple Beth Emeth.

Of course, now he was a grown man with a whole flock of responsibilities. He could recite chapter and verse of scripture. Whinston enjoyed a stiff Maker's Mark after work. Yet he carried himself with the earnestness of an oversized teenager. He had a warm smile and seemed privately unsure at times, and his beefy cheeks turned pink when he got overheated, which in 2018, he definitely was. It began in the summer, when he drove a Guatemalan refugee, Yeni Gonzalez, from Ann Arbor to Pittsburgh, to be reunited with her three small children who had been at the Tornillo internment camp.

America was jailing children separately from their parents, and nearly eighteen hundred miles removed, in Ann Arbor, Michigan, Whinston's congregants at Temple Beth Emeth asked what they could do. The question nagged at him. Being Jewish had taught him "that it is more important to welcome the stranger than honor the presence of God," Whinston said. The admonition, which came from the biblical exile of the Jews, was from Exodus 22:21: "Thou shalt neither vex a stranger, nor oppress him: for ye were strangers in the land of Egypt." His own favorite Talmudic teaching was the story of Abraham in Genesis 18:1–8, when God appeared to Abraham at his tent on the plains of Mamre and Abraham fed a trio of strangers in the shade of a nearby tree. And, of course, Jews have been immigrants—often unwanted—for much of their history. They fled the Spanish Inquisition in the seventeenth century and European oppression in the nineteenth. "I've been saying this stuff since I was a kid," said Whinston. "How do I say all those things and now not do something?"

Drones flew over the camp as it expanded in the summer of 2018, photographing teenage boys marching in single file. Elsewhere, pictures were smuggled out of Texas Immigration and Customs Enforcement facilities from the air-conditioned *hieleras,* showing children shivering under Mylar blankets on concrete floors. An audio file also leaked, recording one little girl sobbing to be released while another begged to call her aunt, using a phone number she had memorized.[4] The American public was outraged, and despite congressional inaction, the courts issued an injunction against the practice known as family separation, though it never really ended.

Back in Ann Arbor, it occurred to Whinston to make a pilgrimage, into the desert and the very heart of the Trump centerpiece. But he had no idea, exactly, how to do it. In September 2018, he had called a person who definitely would know: Miriam Terlinchamp, the fast-talking, rabble-rousing blonde rabbi of Temple Sholom in Cincinnati, who had already done a little time in jail along the way. On the other end of the line, Terlinchamp recognized the flash of righteousness in Whinston's voice. "That was the way I felt when Maribel was deported," she said.[5]

In 2017, Maribel Trujillo Diaz was snatched off the streets of Cincinnati by US Immigration and Customs Enforcement (ICE) agents; she had entered the United States illegally fifteen years earlier and was in the process of seeking asylum from drug cartels when she was apprehended to be deported to Mexico, returning to her family after seventeen months there.[6] Terlinchamp got busy with the logistics of organizing not just her congregation, but also other temples and churches, to free the Mexican immigrant, who was bouncing from jail to jail. Both the Democratic senator Sherrod Brown and the Republican senator Rob Portman appealed to the government to let Trujillo Diaz plead her case. She feared being killed if she was expelled to Mexico and had in fact learned that her family was also targeted for execution. In September, a federal judge freed Diaz and ordered a new asylum hearing. Terlinchamp had found that turning faith into acts beyond the bimah, the temple's pulpit, requires relentless pushing and pressing, "leaving some of us out there on the field." She was in.

The journey would be 1,728 miles to the most controversial, maligned, and mischaracterized place in America: the US-Mexico border, stretching 1,933 miles from the cold Pacific Ocean to the warm, shallow Gulf of Mexico. By 2018, about 2.3 million people lived in the El Paso region in Texas, Mexico, and New Mexico, none of them separated by more than a short drive or a brisk walk; it was a combined metropolitan area with the population of Pittsburgh, but it might as well have been the moon. In El Paso, the bars, nightclubs, and, yes, whorehouses present in my youth had been bulldozed, but by the time the Mexican drug war rolled around in the early 2000s, with bodies turning up by the hundreds in the Chihuahuan Desert, Americans were already staying away in droves. The nearest big city—still in Texas—was six hundred miles away. The rugged Franklin Mountains bisected the city with its pile of rocks and creosote. Nearly bald dunes lined the river. Winters were bone-snapping cold, spring was a three-month dust storm, and summer's heat was an experience just this side of hell.

In a stroke of evil genius, this was, in fact, chosen as the perfect place to hide an entire class of reviled people, namely, the asylum seekers. After the Tornillo tent camp went up, the military made ready to incarcerate entire families of immigrants[7] at Fort Bliss. Home to the First Armored Division, the post was so big that not a single trooper could be seen from the perimeter road. Thousands of immigrants effectively disappeared into one million acres of desert.

The very remoteness of the border made it easy to malign. President Trump had called Mexicans "rapists" and the Central American caravans an "invasion," depicting a region so much in crisis, it required a wall and a force of up to fifteen thousand troops whose greatest risk, so far, was dying of boredom within sight of a Whataburger in South Texas. And Trump was no longer alone in overdramatizing the troubles of the area. Mississippi's then interim Republican senator, Cindy Hyde-Smith, claimed, "I have been in the Rio Grande River with a bulletproof vest and machine guns all around."

Frankly, though, it was all bullshit. My eighty-five-year-old mother lived about half a mile from the river. I went there in shorts days before Hyde-Smith made her statement and watched a father, daughter, and their dog from the levee; the biggest threat was a shiver at sunset. After all, the border is remote, but not lonely. Some ten million people live along it, from San Diego–Tijuana to Brownsville–Matamoros. And in 2018, American border cities had the lowest rates of violent crime in the country, even though the drug war had raged right across the boundary for years. While Baltimore led American cities in violent crime, according to FBI statistics, El Paso didn't even crack the top forty. Instead of zombie immigrant hordes streaming across the international boundary, some two million people crossed the US-Mexico border every single day—legally. Even the word *border* was a misnomer, suggesting a place that separates lands. In Spanish, the word was *frontera*, as in "frontier": a place where lands meet.

My hometown was still a rough-around-the-edges kind of place, certainly. Redbox movie rentals passed for culture until they were destroyed by Netflix. This was a blue-collar, tattooed town, where trucks and trains rumbled north and south all day and night, against a skyline that was more refinery and railyard than skyscraper and green space. English was welcome but Spanish was spoken. Some of the best food in town was at the H&H Car Wash. When the day was done, you might wash it away with a craft brew at the Black Orchid, but a tall-boy Tecate from a can in the front seat of your truck was a whole lot likelier. El Paso had among the highest illiteracy rates in America, the crummiest health care, and the most epic poverty.

Intermarriage between Latinos and Anglos here was so common as to be unremarkable; it was least common in Mississippi. Sitting in a Walmart parking lot on a Friday in 2018, I noticed all kinds of people streaming by. There were license plates from Texas, New Mexico, and Chihuahua and a trio of young Mennonite Anglo women, with no makeup and long skirts, perched on a pickup tailgate after a long-distance shopping trip. They descended from people who actually migrated the other way, from the United States into Mexico. The closer Americans were to the border, the less they feared it. The farther a Republican lived from it, according to a Pew Research Center study,[8] the more they clamored for a border wall. The genius of Donald Trump was that he seized on this, making everyone here essentially disappear—and the alternate universe he conjured at his rallies scared the shit out of Americans.

By the time they arrived in El Paso in November, it was clear that Rabbi Whinston's little band of the faithful was more than a little nervous, their emotions still raw from the aftermath of the slayings in Pittsburgh. In Texas, on the eighth floor of the Embassy Suites, by the roar of Interstate 10, they gathered to go over their plan: visit migrants stuck on the international pedestrian bridge, protest in Tornillo, and volunteer by performing mundane chores such as washing the clothes of the migrants whom the government was suddenly dumping on the streets of El Paso. Yet there was new cause for alarm. The local Reform synagogue had been besieged with threatening calls all day because of their arrival; one caller who'd read news stories online about their journey to the border spewed anti-Semitic filth for ten straight minutes. There were lots of questions from the group about safety, passports, and basic constitutional rights. What would they do if border agents arrested them?

Whinston rode an emotional roller coaster. On one hand, he had the adrenaline spike that activism can spark, and it coursed through his blood like good heroin. But he was also frightened. Pittsburgh had scared him. After the shootings, he talked himself out of his fear, but now that he was here, as threats were being phoned in to the local synagogue, it wasn't working, and he was visibly deflated.

Terlinchamp, meanwhile, was all business. She pushed a congregant with a hotel-supply company to donate three thousand brand-new towels, only to hear from people in El Paso that there was no room to store that many. Then she learned from the large Catholic charity Annunciation House that three thousand was precisely the number needed for all the Central Americans being shipped in and released on the streets after their "credible fear" interviews—wherein asylum seekers must establish that they have a credible fear of returning home in order to be considered for asylum—and these people all needed showers. "The Jewish God is a God of abundance," she said, her eyes flashing; she almost looked giddy. Then her mood stiffened, and she pulled closer. "And if the face of 'Never Again' can't step into this space," she said, referring to herself, "then tell me this. Who in the fuck is it going to be?"

As dawn arrived, with the low-slung sun of autumn, I thought Whinston and his little band probably didn't need to be worried about violence; El Paso had little history of modern hate crimes. They needed to worry that the government was winning by keeping the migrants out of reach and even out of sight.

THE VERY NEXT morning, my car radio crackled with a report that a militia was coming to patrol the border.

In reality, it was just a ragtag handful of old men with pistols, from states as far away as Alabama. They showed up in Columbus, New Mexico, a windblown little desert outpost eighty miles west of El Paso, on the US-Mexico border. One was a seventy-one-year-old retired cop from Michigan, no less—Whinston's home state. The mayor of Columbus made it clear that these outsider geezers were not welcome. "A lot of people who never come here, they have a misunderstanding," Mayor Esequiel Salas told the *Albuquerque Journal*.

In 2018, the migrants whom Whinston and his band had come to witness to, march for, and help were conspicuous in one frustrating way: by their absence. The crowds of Hondurans, Salvadorans, and Guatemalan refugees who had been gathering on the international pedestrian bridge, hoping to apply for asylum, had simply vanished. Claiming that an advancing cold front posed too great a humanitarian danger, the Mexican government had cleared out the women and children; as the visiting Jews, Episcopalians, Catholics, and Disciples of Christ traipsed to the bridge, there was no one left.

Moving on to the internment camp at Tornillo, they could not see the child prisoners from the designated protest area. It was possible that the buses coming through with still more kids would carry word of the protesters' presence to those behind the razor wire. The few arrivals who could be glimpsed in silhouette waved back, but that was all. After unsuccessfully trying to march to the gate, Whinston's group milled around outside the stone wall. A few people then scattered along a dirt road into an alfalfa field that paralleled the perimeter. Sure enough, before too long, the farmer called the county sheriff and black-and-whites to warn off the trespassers.

The bureaucrats, federal agents, and cops were winning: they made the very object of concern, outrage, and even faith just vanish. On Facebook, a few photos circulated of Central Americans removed from the bridge by the Mexican authorities; eerily, each man in the picture stared back, posing with a number written in black marker on his forearm. Justin Hamel snapped a shot of a few teenage boys inside, waving. But that was it. That was all. Almost nothing was really known about the conditions inside the camp—except that it kept growing. In June, when the internment camp had opened, it held up to four hundred in reportedly austere but serviceable conditions, with twenty kids—mostly boys—in ten bunks to a tent and temporary medical facilities. By the time of the protest in November, though, nearly eighteen hundred kids, ages thirteen to seventeen, were there, one in five of whom were girls, according to the Health and Human Services Department. The camp was set to swell to thirty-eight hundred—to the tune of hundreds of millions of dollars.

The industry of holding immigrant children had suddenly ballooned into a billion-dollar business. In Austin, the state government insisted that none of its resources were being used there, but I'd seen a big trailer marked with a state seal and the words "Emergency Management Division" go in; later, a white van with the same markings went by. "They lied to us when we were there," said Bruce Lesley, the president of First Focus, an advocacy group for children and families in Washington, DC, and an El Paso native. "They told us it was going to be strictly temporary." The group was also threatened, he said, not to criticize the camp; doing so would risk losing access altogether. Nevertheless, there was no formal schooling for these young people. There was a telephone that kids could use to report abuse, but they had to be supervised by staff while doing so, according to the group's site-visit report. Mental health care was available only in a crisis, despite the fact that these internees had experienced thousands of miles of travel, followed by privation, separation, and the specters of physical and sexual abuse.

The people Whinston's protest group had come to help were invisible—yet religious faith itself is an exercise in embracing the unseen. As about two hundred Americans gathered, from points near and far, they would go home with something tangible, inspired by their experience, as Whinston himself had been. They would speak to others about what they did and saw, and those others might take an interest. "Look, I may not change what the president does," said a Baptist in the crowd. "But he's not going to change me."

As the light fell from the sky, the people whom all this was about finally emerged into a converted dining hall at the Catholic seminary, where they would sleep on cots: a woman, a couple of toddlers, and a handful of ponytailed girls; then a man, a boy, and more. In the lengthening shadows, the visiting Midwesterners, some wearing University of Michigan ball caps or yarmulkes, hustled big plastic bags stuffed with the towels Terlinchamp had procured into the adobe-colored buildings on the broad but humble campus, with a tile mural of the Virgin Mary, owned by the Catholic church. One woman struck up a game of duck-duck-goose with the kids, translating it as *pato-pato-ganso*. The little girls smiled and chased her, laughing. Then it was time for dinner.

About eighty people, mostly women and children from Guatemala, Honduras, and El Salvador, formed a line past the olive-drab cots in the harshly lit main hall. Unlike those still in federal custody, they had prevailed at their "credible fear" interviews and were released—pending asylum hearings in immigration court, which are typically scheduled months, even years, into the future. Most of the women wore ankle bracelets. Though many people were housed here, the hall was neat as a pin, with cleaning supplies tacked at the front. The line shuffled down a narrow hallway and passed a pantry overflowing with bread, cereal, and canned goods. Whinston and his group piled roast chicken, cherry tomatoes, and potato salad onto paper plates for the strangers as the warm air filled with the aroma of food and the patter of Spanish.

One of the few men in the room, Juan Francisco Artiaga, still bundled in a big down jacket, lifted forkfuls of rice to his mouth. Dangling from his neck was an inexpensive plastic rosary, just given to him by Father Tom Smith, a steely-haired Franciscan in the back of the room. Artiaga was here with his son, Ronnie, age thirteen. The thirty-seven-year-old laborer had first arrived hundreds of miles away in Presidio and had been bused here. Every one of these Americans, he says, had apologized to him for the way their country had treated him and his boy. "But you have nothing to apologize for," he said, breaking into a broad-toothed grin. "The president is doing what he thinks he has to do to protect the nation. And the people have been good and generous with us. Look at all this," he said, waving at the smiling faces and mounds of food in a clean, safe place. His boy's growth is stunted, clearly, from too little food and too much field labor; he was skinny to the point of emaciation and had endured captivity, jail, and standing before a judge to plead his case.

Artiaga came to America to work, perhaps as a construction laborer, and could not return home for fear of being killed. The war on drugs had forced many Mexican cartels and gangs into Central America, endangering those who lived there. "The judge said to me, 'Thank you for your honesty,'" he recounted.[9] "He even released me without an ankle monitor." His next stop was New Jersey, where he would check in with the government, pending a final judgment on his asylum application. "I have nothing at all in my heart but gratitude, for God and for how we have been treated here," he said, his eyes welling up briefly. "And I will never be able to repay God for this."

This simple meal was actually a feast, not unlike the one shared by Oñate's expedition and the native Suma and Manso peoples centuries ago, in that liminal space that would become El Paso. A brief respite in a lengthy struggle. Whinston towered over these latest pilgrims, serving them heaps of vanilla cake thick with frosting. He couldn't speak a lick of Spanish and they couldn't speak any English; some didn't even speak much Spanish, in fact, as Nahuatl or Pipil is still the preferred tongue for some Guatemalans. But Whinston was beaming, this big American giant, passing out plates, as those cheeks of his turned rosy red. I asked him why he was smiling. "I wanted them to see a white person smiling back at them," he answered. "I wanted to connect."

The celebration was winding to a close. The Central Americans thanked and shook hands with every American they saw, as they shuffled out through the dining room door. Whinston's team wiped down tables with bleach and bundled up leftovers.

The Trump administration announced plans to hold future asylum seekers indefinitely.

Chapter Twenty-One

"EVERYTHING DOWN HERE STICKS, STINGS, OR BITES," 2019

THE BRUSH COUNTRY along the Rio Grande on the Texas-Mexico border, hundreds of miles south of El Paso, grows thick: a jagged, tangled landscape of thorny trees, prickly pear, and grass so tall, it could hide a horse. Eight-foot rattlesnakes blend in among rocks and feral hogs wallow beneath mesquite thickets.

By the spring of 2019, one of the great quests of Donald Trump's presidency was building what he called "a big, beautiful wall" along the Mexican border. But if Trump was to ever get the funding for his long-promised wall, he would have to plot a course through Texas. In reality, there would be no wall stretching the whole eight hundred miles from Laredo nearly to El Paso, no "concrete structure from sea to sea," as the president once pledged. Taking this land would constitute an assault on private property and require a veritable army of lawyers, who would be no match for the state's powerful border barons.

More than 250 years ago, José de Escandón, a Spanish army officer, established the first colonial settlements along the Rio Grande in South Texas. Later, the Spanish crown divided the land into *porciones*, or "plots." Down in the Lower Rio Grande Valley the plots were small, radiating from the river. These fertile slivers could sustain more livestock, crops, and people than the more arid land upriver, which was removed from the warm gulf moisture. Over generations, the plots were subdivided by heirs into tinier and tinier holdings.

Starting in 2006, when Congress passed the Secure Fence Act under George W. Bush, the US government used eminent domain to seize these plots and put up barriers as high as eighteen feet; more than 345 condemnation suits by the federal government resulted in a strip of land 128 miles long, according to a 2017 investigation by ProPublica and the *Texas Tribune*. Yet years later, dozens of cases were still tied up in court, and settlements were wildly unequal: a retired schoolteacher got $21,500 for two acres, a lawyer and banker who hired one of the state's biggest law firms got nearly $5 million for six.

The cost was staggering. The most recent takeover of thirty-three miles in the valley set taxpayers back $641 million—or $19.4 million per mile—for a hodgepodge of fences, vehicle barriers, and some bollard fencing, with lots of gaps. And no one could really say, definitively, whether this project was worthwhile. No federal agency has systematically audited what all the barriers cost and what, if any, effect they have had.

"First, this suggests that this is all theater. There is no operational decision-making about what will actually work, because there's not really a security crisis," said Denise Gilman, a law professor at the University of Texas at Austin, at the time. "Instead, these federal agencies rush, saying, 'We've just got to get the wall up,' when what we need is real, targeted law enforcement."

As messy as land seizure was in the valley, it would have been even messier upriver, toward El Paso. The original Spanish *porciones* grew larger as the soil grew more arid, and that disparity remained visible in 2019; on the drive to Laredo, tiny plots gave way to expansive ranches controlled by richer landowners who had more power to oppose eminent domain. I knew this place. Though I was no cowboy, until recently I lived on a working cow-calf operation, and I've known a few ranchers. Over the years, some have allowed me to hunt and fish on their land and treated me like family.

Although many big ranchers and landowners backed Trump, they were conservative in the most traditional sense. They actually believed in small government, free enterprise, free trade, and private property—and nobody was going to put a wall through their brush. These men and women were a pretty private bunch too. You wouldn't find their names in the newspaper, screaming bloody murder.

But they knew how to make their presence felt. In 2015, a couple of dozen border barons from the Laredo region summoned local politicians, cops, and representatives from customs and border protection. It was a private, even secret event: no cameras, no press. According to Steve LaMantia, who led the group, the landowners warned the feds not to build a wall through their land. To underscore their point, they held another meeting. And just in case it wasn't crystal clear, they planned another one.

"The general sentiment—to a person—is that everybody is in favor of additional border security," said LaMantia. But seizing land through eminent domain? "That is diametrically opposed by everybody, from Zapata to Del Rio."

LaMantia was reserved about his family's holdings. He would admit to just a cattle ranch and natural-gas wells that front about five miles of the Rio Grande. But the land had been in his family's hands for generations, while the clan made its fortune in beer. Its company, privately held L&F Distributors, controlled the entire Anheuser-Busch operation from the Lower Rio Grande Valley to El Paso. It was a big, big business.

"Everything down here sticks, stings, or bites," he said, jokingly, about the mesquite-studded landscape. But he wasn't talking about just the flora and the fauna. These landowners were few, but they were powerful. Campaign contributions could dry up. Local sheriffs could get the message to stop cooperating quite so much with border protection agents.

"There are people there who have the resources that can fight this," said Democratic representative Henry Cuellar, whose district hugs the river from Mission to Laredo.

Dennis Nixon was one such person. The president of the International Bank of Commerce in Laredo, he was a potent force in Texas and national politics. He fought for NAFTA in the 1990s, but he backed Trump, who vowed repeatedly to dismantle the trade agreement, over Hillary Clinton in 2016 because the Obama administration, in his view, was rough on banks like his. (His community bank has assets of $12.2 billion.) Now he opposed a border wall.

The border barons had the people of their state behind them: Texans consistently opposed the wall in polls. But they were never represented by their US senators. Fearing Trump, Republican senator John Cornyn turned from staunch opponent of eminent domain to total squish, saying that some fencing was needed—without saying how much, or where. Senator Ted Cruz backed $25 billion for Trump's wall in December 2018 and suggested, preposterously, that Joaquín "El Chapo" Guzmán, the jailed Mexican drug kingpin, could pay for it.

Despite Republican subservience to Trump, Democrats in Congress would manage to stand fast against Trump's wall. Every single member of Congress from the border, from Brownsville to San Diego, opposed it, including the sole Republican, Will Hurd of Texas. If Trump declared a national emergency, Congress could act to terminate it. And if Congress couldn't get its act together, the last line of defense for the border barons was federal court.

Texas had just successfully opposed a federal taking of farmland along the Red River border with Oklahoma. Although the
courts had upheld eminent domain under the Secure Fence Act, a
national security declaration was another matter. The border barons
had standing in court to challenge a declaration—they would be
directly affected—and they would have reason on their side. After
all, apprehensions of undocumented immigrants were now down
from 1.6 million in 2000 to 300,000. There was no disorder in
the streets. Crime in every border city was way down, among the
lowest in the nation.

And here was the kicker: the borderlands between Laredo and
El Paso saw the smallest number of undocumented immigrants
anywhere along nearly two thousand miles of border, according to
customs and border protection's figures at the time. Yet "the president can declare whatever he wants," said Gilman. "They could just
challenge the premise that this is a national-security crisis."

If the border barons lost in court, that still wouldn't mean victory for Trump. They could simply have chewed up the wall by
chewing up the clock on Trump's time as president. They could
have demanded an injunction, blocking the government from
taking the land before arriving at a settlement. And their lawyers
could wrap the government up in years of haggling over dollars.

Here was the final, insurmountable barrier to Trump's wall:
money. The government had already paid nearly $1 million an acre
for that six-acre plot in the Rio Grande Valley, potentially setting a
precedent. If the Trump administration seized seven hundred miles
of private land, one mile wide, along the border—640 acres per
square mile—the tab could come to $448 billion. That's nearly
twenty times the cost of the wall itself. "The federal government is
much more cautious in taking land from wealthy landowners," said
Gilman. "Agencies just say, 'Let's build a wall elsewhere.'"

At that point, "elsewhere" might have meant Big Bend National Park. It was federal land, after all. Environmentalists would point out that the park's Chisos Mountains are home to golden-fronted woodpeckers, mule deer, and black bears; many of these creatures would be blocked from crossing back and forth to Mexico if Trump got his wall. Trump, though, had never shown interest in environmental concerns.

The land beyond the park, en route from Presidio to El Paso, was owned by still more land barons, only of a different sort. Most didn't come by their land through royal land grants; some didn't even have a long family history there. But these owners were usually rich, influential big-city dwellers: lots of bankers, lawyers, and doctors with lots of clout in Congress. They didn't want Trump's wall either, and they could easily bankroll legal challenges.

"The closer people get to the border, the less enchanted they are with the wall," said David Yeats, the CEO of the Texas Wildlife Association, a San Antonio–based association of ten thousand large landowners who own about one-quarter of Texas. "And we are a private-property state. Border security is critical, but there's a big difference between a wall and security." Like everybody else I spoke to, Yeats pointed to the same solution the polls and Democrats identified: more border security, including agents, patrols, drones, and sensors.

In Texas, Trump might have wound up getting just a few sections of his wall, concentrated in cities, where the structure—concrete or steel slats, or some alternative—would have been redundant, with the tangle of barriers already there. But nobody thought a thirty-foot wall would do anything more than invite thirty-two-foot ladders—as, ultimately, it did.

Trump, like most other people in Washington, didn't know what he was getting into down in El Paso. He didn't know his history, and certainly not his Texas history. Someone should have told him that the most popular symbol of resistance here is the Gonzales battle flag. Hastily painted on cloth in 1835 by Texan rebels, it was hoisted at the outset of revolution against Mexico. The rebels dared the Mexican army to seize back an artillery piece with these words: "Come and take it."

So, yes, everything down here stuck, stung, or bit. The border wasn't just a line on the map to a New Yorker who'd never even seen it. It was a real flesh-and-blood place.[1]

THE BORDER WALL, of course, was never just a steel barrier to keep out immigrants. It was part of a campaign to demonize an entire part of America, by demanding that it conform with the emerging ideology of white nationalism, the attempt to seize power by a people who were becoming a minority in a polyglot America. The US-Mexico border was not only where American history began, but where it began denying a largely white story that moved east to west, marginalizing or destroying everyone else in its path. While it was ethically galling to see a provincial and spoiled billionaire, who knew nothing but New York, denigrate the region where most Americans live, it was also coldly, calculatingly shrewd.

What had developed in American political opinion was fear among some whites about losing their place at the top of the country's pecking order as their numbers dwindled because of decreasing birth rates. By 2050, whites would no longer constitute a majority.[2] (The last time whites became a minority in a major nation was the end of the apartheid in South Africa in 1990.) At the same time, their fears of immigrants in general and the borderlands with Mexico specifically increased proportionate to their distance from the border. These two curves of fear could be exploited and turned into a useful emotion: anger.

President Obama was half Black and half white, yet he was considered America's first Black president. I was teaching college at the time and noticed my Hispanic students beginning to refer to themselves as not white, though in the terms used for the census, they were white. I too began to suppose I was no longer white. Slavery's one-drop rule was back, it seemed: a single drop of anything else meant you weren't white at all.

Up at Yale University, the psychologist Jennifer Richeson conducted a series of experiments. White nationalism was on the rise in much of the democratic world, from Hungary to Austria, France to Great Britain, as well as in North America. She asked white participants to read the news about becoming a minority in their own country, then indicate which racial and ethnic groups they would rather be with in social situations, such as work. The participants indicated they would prefer to be with members of their own race, ranking whites the highest, Asians second-highest, Blacks third—and Hispanics dead last. Other studies in the United States and Canada replicated the results independently.

It might not have been animus that motivated people to respond that way. It might simply have been fear of the unknown, of being a minority. Other studies found that white families moving to the suburbs were carefully picking explicitly white suburbs, not diverse ones where Hispanics, Asians, and Black people lived. The psychologist Jonathan Haidt said: "As multiculturalism is emphasized more and more, there emerges a reaction against it on the right, which is attractive to the authoritarian mind and also appeals to other conservatives. And this, I think, is what has happened. This is what Trump is about—not entirely, of course, but certainly this is a big factor."[3]

While Trump could whip up support by demonizing the border to people in the Midwest, for example, people in the border states knew better. Fully 56 percent of people surveyed in California, Arizona, New Mexico, and Texas disapproved—or strongly disapproved—of Trump's handling of the region; only a little more than one-third approved. And 60 percent disapproved of his administration's single real policy: incarceration of men, women, and children.[4]

ON A HOWLING February night, I found myself at the El Paso County Coliseum. In my youth, it was a cow palace that did double-duty for rodeos and Aerosmith concerts. Several million dollars later, it was a brightly lit arena with no stench of manure.

Tonight, however, it was the site of the battle of the border, an epic desert showdown between two gifted politicians, each marshaling around ten thousand people: one blessed with the truth, the other peddling lies. Yet to Donald Trump's mystifying credit, the lie survived to fight another day. We tell some tall tales here in Texas, but no Texan was a match for this president.

As day broke in my hometown on February 11, 2019, it looked like Trump's lies about the border had finally run out. Amid his showdown with Democrats over the proposed border wall—which had already led to an unpopular thirty-five-day government shutdown—Trump was coming to El Paso to make his case once again: "Build the wall." The people of El Paso, with the local hero and presidential Hamlet Beto O'Rourke as their public face, had a response: "We're safe not because of walls, but in spite of walls. We're safe not in spite of immigrants, but because of immigrants."

Ahead of the president's visit, normally taciturn local politicians turned on Trump for falsely claiming in recent weeks that El Paso, the second-largest border city in America, had been swamped by an immigrant crime wave until a fence went up. The English-language daily, the *El Paso Times*, proclaimed: "Local leaders ready to tell El Paso's story." The Spanish-language daily, *El Diario,* heralded the city as "El Paso, National Battleground." The officially nonpartisan yet Republican mayor, Dee Margo, laid into Trump on

Twitter: "El Paso was *never* one of the *most* dangerous cities in the U.S."

As Air Force One approached, winds whipped up to fifty miles per hour while people streamed toward the County Coliseum. There, Trump held what amounted to his kickoff rally for the 2020 election. Yet this was not Trump country. After all, he'd branded the entire border, where tens of millions of Americans live, a violent wasteland. Business leaders groused that the president had been bad for business, endangering $70 billion in local trade with Mexico while scaring away businesses with tales of immigrant mayhem. The County Commissioners Court was on the record opposing the wall cutting through downtown. El Paso voted nearly 3–1 against him in 2016.

For a moment, it seemed the president would finally get his comeuppance here—a definitive and undeniable repudiation of his monstrous and unpopular pet project. On the merits, Trump should have lost the battle hands down. The crime rate in El Paso peaked in 1993. Then it fell steadily for years, finally settling at about 370 violent crimes per 100,000 people: lower than the usual city El Paso's size, such as Boston, or the national average.

Organized by some fifty local groups, the March for Truth gathered outside, with at least as many people as there were inside at Trump's rally, if not more. The marchers wound their way to a field directly across from the Coliseum. Some skewered him: "Not today, Satan," read one sign. But most people, like Cathy Benavidez, a retired social worker, came to defend their hometown's reputation. "I'm just embarrassed by what Trump has said because it's not true," Ms. Benavidez said. Her hand-lettered sign said, in glitter, "Stop the wall, stop the lies, El Paso has always been safe."

Not far from Trump's rally, Beto O'Rourke appeared in shirt-sleeves, despite the plummeting temperatures. With his usual upbeat attitude, he spoke to thousands of people at an opposing rally;

he would soon make a furtive run for president. In a brief interview over the rising voice of a mariachi singer, he said: "This is El Paso, so I want to take every opportunity to support the cause, the culture, and the community." O'Rourke helped bring out ten thousand supporters, according to local organizers; maybe as many as fifteen thousand. Trump brought sixty-seven hundred to the old rodeo arena, according to the fire department, with a few thousand more stamping their feet in front of the parking lot Jumbotron. The truth—or at least the facts—had made steady progress in El Paso.

But that didn't stop the lies. Trump claimed that thirty-five thousand people came to see him, while just two hundred went to see O'Rourke. There is nothing Trump won't lie about. He even encouraged followers to chant "Finish That Wall," though there's been no construction on any kind of wall since he became president—only fences, which had been on order since 2006. I tried to count the lies told during his speech but had to stop after ten.

But the truth was plodding forward, putting its boots on one at a time, while a lie raced halfway around the world. Trump's tales of kidnappings and mayhem were far racier than the truth. Sure, El Paso had problems; the international bridges carried tens of millions of people, cars, trucks, and railcars each year, and they were not getting inspected. But that was boring. El Paso did have a crisis, too much poverty and too little education, but that was complex. In contrast, Trump's lies were simple, heart-pounding, mesmerizing—and that's what made them powerful.

The president's biggest cheerleader, Lindsey Graham, was absolutely right when he said "the wall has become a metaphor." Henri Rafael, a Trump fan I met at the rally, was right too: "It's not about the wall anymore." His friend in a pink MAGA hat, Monica DeMoss, chimed in: "These people need to go out and work."

The wall was about whatever grievances people nursed: welfare, immigrants, race, class, socialism, you name it. But word came that evening that congressional negotiators would give Trump about $1 billion for more steel barriers, which he could call a wall. He could declare victory, even though it would be anything but. He would get his monument: a metaphor that effectively divided the nation, even if a real wall never divided the border in El Paso.

I left the event a little early, to beat the inevitable traffic nightmare, and drove downtown. I hadn't eaten and needed a drink. For one of the first times ever, I felt like I was experiencing a form of vertigo. In Trump's world, everything that was down was up and what was up was down, and the lies were so outlandish, they disoriented me. Frankly, inside the Coliseum I felt unsafe as a credentialed member of the news media; I could see people in the crowd staring, even scowling at me. I headed to the empty bar downstairs at the Doubletree and ordered a cheeseburger and a martini. The bartender had the television set to the local news, which was broadcasting portions of the events I'd just attended.

"So, what do you think?" the bartender said, nodding his head toward the screen.

I weighed my response and took a slug of the martini: "I think that guy, Trump, is going to get somebody killed."[5]

-------- **Chapter Twenty-Two** --------

THE DAY HATE CAME TO EL PASO, 2019

AND HE DID just that.

The year before Trump took office in the White House, Hispanics comprised 11 percent of the victims of hate crimes, according to the Federal Bureau of Investigation. Yet in just the first two weeks after the 2016 election, there were thirty-four attacks on Latinos in the biggest cities alone: a 176 percent increase over the previous daily average, according to data compiled and analyzed by the Center for the Study of Hate and Extremism at California State University.[1]

"Post-election, I could tell that there was a change," reflected Pricila Garcia, age twenty, the daughter of Mexican immigrants living in Cleburne, Texas. Her mother was called a "stupid Mexican" in the grocery store, and she started having panic attacks as she crossed into the predominately Anglo side of town. "People became a little more brave with their words, especially when it came to hateful things that they said."[2]

In Eugene, Oregon—a liberal college town—hate crimes nearly doubled, from forty-seven to eighty-eight. Three were violent attacks on Latinos. In another, Brandon Scott Berry, age twenty-seven, approached a landscaping crew and began yelling, "I'm going to cut your head off and nobody will care because I'm white and you're not!" He shoved Edu Martinez over and over again, pushed his cell phone into the face of another worker, and then called the police— who promptly arrested Berry on charges of intimidation and menacing. In a trial that lasted one day, Berry was quickly acquitted.[3]

Trump did not invent white nationalism. It was already on the rise as the nation changed colors, hues, and gender identities before everyone's eyes. "By 2010, there were Latino families in Arizona that were being told to go back to their country, to go back to Mexico—these are people that have lived in Arizona for generations," said Democratic representative Ruben Gallegos, who himself received multiple death threats. In Los Angeles, a transgender woman from Guatemala was stabbed to death and her house set on fire, leaving her corpse unrecognizable.[4]

In Miami, three men showed up at the house of a Guatemalan worker with the words: "We're Guat hunting." The men were armed with a rock, a metal rod, and an ax handle. David Harris, age twenty-two, Austin Taggart, also age twenty-two, and his brother, Jesse Harris, age twenty-one, proceeded to crush the skull of Onésimo Marcelino López-Ramos, killing him. He was just eighteen years old.[5]

Trump didn't invent anti-Hispanic hatred, but he weaponized it more effectively than any American politician in history. It would have deadly consequences in El Paso.

SATURDAY, AUGUST 3, 2019, promised to be a hot one. The weather forecasters predicted another miserable high of 104 degrees Fahrenheit. It was also getting near the back-to-school season. I had been in Los Angeles and rode the Sunset Limited train to El Paso overnight. For some reason, I had been unable to sleep as we crossed the desert in the dark. Grumpy and tired when I reached my mother's home—the one I had grown up in—I made for the spare bedroom to lie down and sleep: curtains drawn against the sun, air conditioning turned up against the heat.

Clear on the other side of the city, people headed out to stock up on school supplies. For the El Paso Fusion, a youth girls' soccer team, this was a fundraising day; they sold fresh-squeezed juice and chicharrones—pork rinds—in front of a Walmart superstore near the airport. "Hey," coach Benny McGuire said to his sleepy daughter, Madison. "It's go-time. Let's raise some money for your team."[6] By 9 a.m., the girls, many in pigtails, and their parents were there, talking to strangers and selling cold juice on a hot day. The temperature had already reached 100 degrees.

They could not know it, but a certain man had pulled into the lot in a dark sedan, having driven at least ten, perhaps eleven or twelve hours—some six hundred miles, all the way from Allen, a northern suburb of Dallas. He was tall, awkward, pale to the point of translucence, and just twenty-one years old. Patrick Crusius was a loner and a loser. Unknown in high school, he sporadically attended community college. Kicked out of his home by his mother, he roomed with his grandmother. His mother had already had to call the police on her son, alarmed that he owned an AK-47-style assault rifle—which was perfectly legal in Texas.[7] The police asked if he'd threatened anyone or himself. She said no. The police did nothing.

His parents had split up; Bryan Crusius was a therapist and Lori Crusius a hospice nurse. What had most bothered Crusius, sitting in his car, was how his lily-white suburb back home had changed. The white non-Hispanic population had gone from 80 percent to half that. Hispanic and Muslim families, increasingly priced out of Dallas, went north. Alone online, Crusius had spent his time on 8chan, a far-right message board. But there were other influences around him. A flier in the county warned "Muslims, Indians, Blacks, and Jews" to leave Texas and "go back to where [they] came from" or face "torture starting now." I had seen the same at the university in Texas where I taught—on the day after the 2016 election. At the community college Crusius attended, Collin College, fliers appeared, warning against immigrants and interracial dating.

Originally interested in becoming a software engineer, Crusius wrote earlier that summer: "I'm not really motivated to do anything more than what's necessary to get by. Working in general sucks, but I guess a career in software development suits me well."[8]

He had also read "The Great Replacement" by the French author Renaud Camus, translated from his 2010 book, *Abécédaire de l'in-nocence:* a racist lament, claiming that native French people would be replaced by immigrants from North Africa and other parts of the Arab world. Many of his ideas were rooted in Nazi-occupied France, and he argued that this period was no different— that the new occupants of France, who came without weapons, needed to be resisted just as violently.[9] Crucially, Camus's work had become important to a long line of mass killers, most recently twenty-eight-year-old Brenton Tarrant, who in March had killed forty-nine people worshipping in a New Zealand mosque.

Inside his car, Crusius reached for his phone and uploaded a file to 8chan. Titled "An Inconvenient Truth," his contribution to literature was more than two thousand words long. It began with this simple sentence: "In short, I agree with the Christchurch shooter."

INSIDE THE WALMART, all kinds of people were busy shopping.

In their mid-twenties, Gilbert and Jordan Anchondo—he Hispanic, she Anglo—were doing back-to-school shopping for their little family. He was burly and handsome, with a thick shock of black hair; he'd been in a little trouble before and they'd had a rocky time. But finally, they married and had two children; the two of them were devout Jehovah's Witnesses. That evening, they were to have a small house party and birthday celebration for their little girl—all wrapped into one. Gilbert, like his brother Tito, was a fan of President Trump.[10]

Arturo Benavides, age sixty, wandered the aisles nearby, ready to pay up and leave. He was a broad-smiling, gray-haired retired bus driver who had also served in the US Army. Elsa Marquez, age fifty-seven, a mother of two, had driven over from Juárez. At eighty-six years of age, Angie Englisbee came shopping here every Sunday. Javier Amir Rodriguez had just turned fifteen and was about to start his sophomore year of high school.

People lined up at the bank by the front door. Alexander Gerhard Hoffman, sixty-seven, was a German citizen who had settled in Juárez. Just outside, Juan Velazquez, seventy-seven, and his younger wife, Nicholasa, parked the car; the two walked toward the sliding glass doors, passing the little girls selling juice and chicharrones. The time was exactly 10:15 a.m.

Crusius posted his manifesto to 8chan:

"This attack is a response to the Hispanic invasion of Texas," it read, before eerily and coolly describing the killer's preferences of weapons and ammunition, politics and economics, and racist philosophy. His idea was devastatingly simple: killing Hispanics would stop immigrants from coming and drive citizens to leave. "I am simply defending my country," he said, "from cultural and ethnic replacement brought on by invasion."[11]

The rest was the uneducated rambling of a man-child: he blamed corporations and the Republican Party for Hispanics becoming, inevitably, the majority of the Texas they had first settled. He feared they would turn the state blue, after it had been solidly red for more than two decades.

So Crusius got out of his car and strode to the store, opening gunfire as he went. Benny McGuire screamed at the little girls: "RUN!" They flew across the parking lot, pigtails streaming in the hot summer wind.

At 10:30, Crusius killed a woman who had parked in a handicapped space. Then he fired on the girls' coaches and parents, catching one, Memo Garcia, in the stomach and hitting both Guillermo Garcia and his wife, Jessica Coca Garcia, who took three bullets in the leg.[12] Crusius turned and struck Nicholasa Vasquez in the face, knocking her to the ground. Then he shot her husband dead. Walking through the sliding glass doors, Crusius killed Benavides, the retired bus driver, who was checking out. He turned to his right and opened fire on everybody standing at the bank. Blood covered the floors. Gloria Irma Marquez, the grandmother, was killed.[13]

Inside, trapped and terrified people ran in every direction. A worker hustled some out through the back. An artist, Guillermo Glen, with the help of another shopper, loaded a wounded woman into a shopping cart to evacuate her as shots continued to ring out, the Romanian-made AK-47 firing with a distinctively loud report every time.[14] At 10:39, someone dialed 911. Crusius strode down the aisles one by one, shooting forty-four people, killing half of them so far. Ten shots fired from an AK-47, not in rapid succession but in cunning staccato. First a shot. Then a long pause. Then one after another after another. And then there was the shout in Spanish: "Ay, no!"

Then he found the young Anchondo family.

Andre jumped in front of the killer and was immediately riddled with bullets. Jordan gripped the baby in her arms and turned away.

Crusius shot her to death.[15]

ON AUGUST 7, 2019, Trump boarded Air Force One. First it touched down in Dayton, the site of the most recent American massacre. Then it took off again for the three-hour flight to El Paso. Four days had passed. Two more people had died in the hospital, bringing the total to twenty-two. Exactly seven were citizens of Mexico.[16]

If consoling the nation in a time of need was a vital and yet simple task of the American presidency, Trump failed miserably. The forty-fifth occupant of the White House littered his consolation tour with not only petty insults but, just to rub salt into the wound, doses of renewed racism too. Most striking, however, was how alone and outnumbered the president was: rejected, ostracized, and told to go home.

The people—brown, Black, white, and every hue in between— who streamed to the massive makeshift memorial put up behind the Walmart defiantly defended El Paso's diversity. For perhaps the first time in Trump's angry, racist, and cruel presidency, the tables were turned against him. He was on the receiving end of popular righteous indignation, a response to his white nationalist politics and governance.

Trump issued the usual condolences but never backed off. He doubled down like a wild gambler in a casino. Leaving the White House on Wednesday morning, he had already said, "I think my rhetoric brings people together," adding that he was "concerned about the rise of any group of hate. I don't like it, whether it's white supremacy, whether it's any other kind of supremacy."

As if some *other* kind of violent political ideology has been responsible for killing people—Blacks and whites, Jews and Latinos, from Charlottesville, Virginia, to Pittsburgh, Dayton, and El Paso. Leaving Dayton, Trump insulted the mayor and a senator from the safety of Air Force One and, of course, Twitter.

Trump even jabbed a racist poke at El Paso, ridiculing the former Democratic representative Beto O'Rourke's Spanish first name, though he is of Anglo descent: "Beto (phony name to indicate Hispanic heritage) O'Rourke, who is embarrassed by my last visit to the Great State of Texas, where I trounced him, and is now even more embarrassed polling at 1% in the Democratic Primary, should respect the victims & law enforcement—& be quiet!"

While it was bad manners for a nation in mourning, it was more than that: a fresh dose of the kind of racism that had, just days ago, proven deadly. In an era in which minorities are becoming majorities, as in Texas, and intermarrying with Anglos, who was Trump to infer someone's race and ethnicity based on a name? At the makeshift memorial to the twenty-two killed for the hue of their skin while shopping at a Walmart, I spoke with a young soldier from the First Armored Division at nearby Fort Bliss. Big and burly in his camouflage uniform, Private First Class Richard Riley, age twenty, stood with arms crossed, staring silently at the piles of flowers, plastic hearts, and white crosses, one for every victim. Behind his dark glasses, his eyes welled up. "I just can't believe it," he said. "I'm Hispanic too. And I can't believe that these people were killed because they were."

El Paso was not a volatile, rioting city where the president could expect trouble. But along the president's route from the airport to a hospital, people lined the roads, largely expressing rejection. "What's more important," asked one man's sign, "lives or reelection?" American and Mexican flags sprouted together in the August heat. Signs with quotes bearing his name taunted him with his own sayings: "We cannot allow these people to invade our country." A "Not Welcome" sign covered the stage at a park, making clear the people's opinion of the president. The front page of the *El Paso Times* was entirely blacked out, with only this headline: "Mr. President, We Are Hurting."

How people actually lived here stood in stark contrast to Mr. Trump's white nationalism, which consistently separated Americans into old-fashioned and outdated racist categories. Six in ten Americans had family on the other side of the trickling Rio Grande, according to a study by the El Paso Community Foundation, while six in ten Mexicans just across the border had family on the American side. Like the Anchondos, 30 percent of Latinos married outside their ethnicity, usually to an Anglo. Nationwide, one in six marriages wasn't simply intercultural but interracial, according to the Pew Research Center.

Racial violence in America is almost never a two-way street. Instead, it has been visited upon the minorities by the majority: whites. What were historically called "race riots" were actually one-sided assaults led by white people: Anglo-on-Latino in Texas, white-on-Chinese farther west, white-on-Black in Oklahoma and the Deep South. And so it continued here in my hometown.

As if to symbolize just how out of touch Trumpism was here and in much of America, a woman wearing a bright-red MAGA hat, who approached the makeshift memorial at the Walmart, was quickly surrounded by over thirty people chanting: "Take it off! Take it off!" She refused, yelling back that the president should be accepted here—but her voice was drowned out. Later, young people appeared, dressed in black, chanting: "White violence, White House."

Another president might have sensed the feeling in the air in El Paso and changed course, played the unifier. Instead, Mr. Trump displayed just how small he is, no matter how big his mouth or powerful his office. He never once appeared in public or before the media.

But he did do this. At 6:01 p.m., after little more than two hours in El Paso, he safely boarded Air Force One again, and it was wheels up into the sky. Melania, his wife, had come along, and she tweeted a picture of the president standing in a hospital room. He was grinning widely, with his usual thumbs-up. Standing next to him was Melania, coldly smiling too and holding a baby in her arms. It was Paul, the Anchodos' baby: the other orphan of the slain couple. Neither of the Trumps looked at the infant, who gazed to the side, a helpless political prop for those complicit in the cause that took his parents.[17]

Three years later, in 2022, I went to the memorial of the victims down in Ascarate Park, named for the Mexican family whose daughter was the first known Mexican woman to marry an American man here in El Paso: Juana Ascárate, who wed Hugh Stephenson in 1828.

The memorial is a circular plaza, a somber place. On each stone tablet around me were the names of the dead, now twenty-three in all: after nine months in the hospital, the wounded Guillermo "Memo" Garcia had finally succumbed. He was one of the girls' soccer coaches. But the nation had moved on. Trump's controversies, more violence, a pandemic, a riot at the Capitol, and a new president's tenuous hold had swept my hometown out of the forefront of the country's mind. The Walmart had reopened its 220,000 square feet, though out front was a modest memorial of glass and light: La Candelara. I told an editor I wanted to do a story on the anniversary of the massacre, but the idea was rejected.

And that's what descended on El Paso: the grief, the shock, the shattered lives—and the feeling of being rejected by our nation. President Biden didn't visit on the first or second anniversaries. While we mourned the twenty-three dead, who left behind hundreds of grieving family, friends, and acquaintances, the survivors had to grapple with not only physical wounds and trauma, but also the deep psychological wounds that made merely surviving difficult. I've seen this time and again, in similar situations. Most of us experience a more distant form of survivor's grief. Why were we spared? The randomness of death's shadow rattles us to our core.

The very notion of equality seems to be vanishing from American society and certainly in Texas. After the massacre, Governor Greg Abbott was found sending fundraising emails about halting the Hispanic "invasion." Of course, most immigrants who pass through El Paso aren't Mexicans at all: they're from West Africa, Haiti, Cuba, and South and Central America. Today the Texas Republican Party wants the United States to declare that the immigrants begging for asylum are generally ineligible—that they are also an "invasion."

The killer, Crusius, is still in jail, the longest a mass shooter has languished without trial (I long ago dispensed with calling his crimes "alleged"; after all, he confessed to the police). Texas's prosecution of the killer was first botched by a local district attorney and, since then, has not resulted in even a trial under a prosecutor appointed by Republican governor Greg Abbott in Austin, who—like the shooter—has described undocumented migration as an "invasion." The federal government charged Crusius with a slew of hate crimes yet dropped any death penalty in exchange for a confession and life in prison.

The Biden years that have followed have done little to nothing to ease domestic tensions or the numbers of migrants coming from all over the world, other than to undo the most despicably cruel of Trump's policies. America cannot, after all, singlehandedly control economic collapse and chaos in other hemispheres, let alone around the world. Believing otherwise is just empty hubris. And the Republican Congress has blocked the simplest and most effective measures, such as paying for more immigration judges to speed up approvals—and deportations—for people seeking asylum. As usual, Washington politicians would rather have the issue than solve the problem.

TODAY OÑATE, THE sixteenth-century explorer, is a mere statue at El Paso's airport. The descendants of El Griego, the Greek soldier, helped Santa Fe and El Paso, and one, Danny Griego, became a music writer in Austin and then Nashville. The descendants of native people thrive in El Paso's Lower Valley.

Of course El Paso has its troubles: a stubborn brain drain of young people, a new immigration reality in which today's arrivals don't settle here so much as head for the bigger coastal cities to find family, friends, and entire enclaves of fellow countrymen.

Over the time I spent writing this book, I have come to understand that El Paso has been more than a model multiethnic society. It was one of the first battlegrounds for American democracy, justice, and equality. The place where I grew up is remarkable for its multicultural society inherited from the Spaniards, Mexicans, and Native people, for its tragic figures, like Benito Juárez and Pancho Villa, and for its brave souls, like the housekeepers who rioted against Zyklon B and Dr. Nixon who challenged Jim Crow. El Paso's cultural exports include the Academy Award–winning actor, F. Murray Abraham, and air brush artist Gaspar Enríquez, depicting Chicano life in what is now the nation's twenty-third largest city, also known as El Chucho. Today, El Paso barely trails Washington, DC, in population and is more populous than Detroit, Boston, and Las Vegas. El Paso continues to change American culture, most recently with the global hip-hop superstar Khalid, an African American US Army brat who once grew up around Fort Bliss and has since been given a key to the city. El Paso is a powerful yet overlooked engine of change, in pursuit of an ever more perfect democracy. I will note for the record that I did try to interview El Paso's luminaries in business, philanthropy, and politics for this book. From billionaires to politicians, not a single one of them nor their assistants ever returned my calls.

You always take a hometown for granted, and I have been stunned to learn the things I have while researching this book. I got to witness the earliest humans of the Americas, the cruelty of the Apache Wars, the trickery of the United States in pursuit of territorial gain, and all the strides forward made here, like desegregating college football. These things took place, and most of America didn't notice. Including me.

The sweeping desert and rugged mountains of this big country are heart-stoppingly beautiful. I have been mesmerized by the Davis Mountains to the east and the Organ Peaks National Monument of southern New Mexico. I also believe that the rugged Franklin Mountains should have their Spanish name restored to Sierra de los Mansos, honoring the Spanish heritage of the city and the Native Americans here first, possibly descended from original or at least early inhabitants. I have come to think that El Paso and Texas to the Pecos River should secede from the state and join New Mexico. Texas today is steadily stripping American citizens—women, Hispanics, African Americans, trans people, and everyone who is not a straight white male—of the rights guaranteed by the Constitution. I believe El Paso, the onetime seat of the government of New Mexico, would be safer there, and a boon to that state's economy. El Paso would provide a big anchor in global trade; New Mexico could invest in its largest new city, tapping its massive sovereign wealth fund, to bolster a return while temporarily delaying a huge increase in its tax base. Austin is steadily stripping away voting, human, and women's rights, which Santa Fe is unlikely to ever do. El Paso has nothing in common with the conservative suburbs of the Texas Triangle. And forget the tourist marketing slogans of Fort Worth and Abilene; the West begins in El Paso. And in short, El Paso needs Texas like most of us need a hole in the head. It's just a better fit than Texas, a state currently and tragically teetering on the brink of fascism when it should be rightfully leading the way into the American future.

I was gone from this place for a long time. But as I look out the window, the air is fresh from monsoon rain and the falling sunlight is soft. I love El Paso. And now I know the truth.

This isn't just where America began. If we're lucky, it can show America how to begin again.

---------- Acknowledgments ----------

THERE ARE MORE than a few people I would like to thank for the opportunity to write this book about the American Southwest. And if I leave anyone out, please forgive me.

First, I'd like to express my gratitude to Peter Hubbard, the publisher of this work, who was encouraging and enthusiastic about the project and also trusted me at important turning points in what is a long and complex story. My dear friend Holly Regan helped both early and later as the research took shape on the page as words; we've known each other for ten years now, and I'm proud to call Holly a colleague. I met a new friend as well, Susan Barnum, who was managing the Southwest and Border Collection of the El Paso Libraries. Susan helped me locate obscure journals found nowhere else, and she pointed the way for much of the early section of this book. She even took time to have a peek as the work unfolded. The finest and most dedicated journalist in the region, Bob Moore, now CEO of El Paso Matters, kindly shared his wisdom and perspectives. Claudia Ramirez at the library helpfully found many of the historic images in the finished work. At Mariner Books, Katie Adams put much-needed finishing touches on the work, encouraging me to do so as well. The Mariner team artfully crafted this final version, and so I express my undying gratitude to the bold Jessica Vestuto, who kept us going, as well as her colleagues Lisa Glover, Susanna Brougham, Kim Lewis, Emily Snyder, and the brave Janine Hernández-Díaz.

My dear friend Dr. Luis Urrea of El Paso took time to read chapters as they came along and provided diplomatic critiques—but mostly ceaseless encouragement. James Hyde of Austin also took time to look at an early draft and provide good direction, as did my dear mother, Josefina. And I definitely am grateful to all the people mentioned here who provided expert wisdom concerning archaeology, geology, and natural history, and the historians who have trodden this path before. Leon Metz has chronicled El Paso's deadly gunfighter days and provided an excellent chronology; David Romo's works offer a distinctly Latino view, particularly around the time of the Mexican Revolution, a formative time for that nation and ours as well.

I certainly want to thank bestselling author Janice Windle and her daughter, Virginia, for entertaining the roughest original idea for this work and giving their encouragement. Finally, I wish to thank my friend and agent Jane von Mehren. Betraying her skills as a previous book editor, she persistently but kindly pushed me to do a better job in shaping the proposal, and without it, there would have been no book. I'm very fortunate to know her.

Notes

PROLOGUE

1. John Upton Terrell, *Estevanico the Black* (Los Angeles: Westernlore Press, 1968), 12.
2. Oviedo y Valdez, Gonzalo Fernandez, and Harbert Davenport, "The Expedition of Pánfilo de Narváez," *Southwestern Historical Quarterly* 28, no. 1 (1924): 56–74, http://www.jstor.org/stable/30234907.
3. Terrell, *Estevanico the Black*.

1. 1598

1. "Cape Henry Memorial Cross," National Park Service, accessed June 28, 2022, https://www.nps.gov/came/cape-henry-memorial-cross.htm.
2. Stan Hoig, *Came Men on Horses: The Conquistador Expeditions of Francisco Vázquez de Coronado and Don Juan de Oñate* (Boulder: University Press of Colorado, 2013), 159.
3. Miguel Encinas, *Two Lives for Oñate* (Albuquerque: University of New Mexico Press, 1997).
4. The Tiwa language was part of the Tiwa-Kioa-Tanoan root language.
5. W. H. Timmons, "Rodriguez-Sanchez Expedition," Handbook of Texas Online, updated January 26, 2019, https://www.tshaonline.org/handbook/entries/rodriguez-sanchez-expedition.
6. Texas State Historical Association, "Rodriguez-Sanchez Expedition," n.d., https://www.tshaonline.org/handbook/entries/rodriguez-sanchez-expedition.
7. W. H. Timmons, "El Paso Documentary I: The Significance of the Oñate

Expedition in El Paso History," *Password: Journal of the El Paso County Historical Society* 25, no. 1 (Spring 1980): 1.

8. Eugene O. Porter, "The Spanish Occupation of West Texas and New Mexico," *Password: Journal of the El Paso County Historical Society* 10, no. 3 (1965): 79.

9. Hoig, *Came Men on Horses,* 159.

10. Bob Miles, "Early Roads," *Password* 31, no. 1 (1986): 76.

11. Porter, "The Spanish Occupation," 85.

12. Timmons, "El Paso Documentary I," 159.

13. Timmons, "El Paso Documentary I," 159.

14. Porter, "The Spanish Occupation," 89.

15. Patrick Beckett and Terry L. Crockett, *The Manso Indians* (Las Cruces, NM: COAS Publishing and Research, 1992).

16. Beckett and Crockett, *The Manso Indians,* 137.

17. Official diary of the expedition, as kept by Juan Pérez de Donís, in Marc Simmons, *The Last Conquistador: Juan de Oñate and the Settling of the Far Southwest* (Norman: University of Oklahoma Press, 1991), 161.

18. Timmons, "El Paso Documentary I," 160–61.

2. ANCESTORS, 38,000 BCE–1550 CE

1. Miles, "Early Roads," 76.

2. Rex E. Gerald, "A Youth's Introduction to the Indians of the El Paso del Norte Area," *The Artifact* 22, no. 1 (1984): 41.

3. Simmons, *The Last Conquistador,* 103.

4. "Oñate Expedition First Colonists," Sociedad de la Entrada, 2006, http://www.entrada1598.com/mdia/onatenames.pdf.

5. "Heraklion," Wikimedia Foundation, last modified July 16, 2022, 18:40, https://en.wikipedia.org/wiki/Heraklion.https://en.wikipedia.org/w/index.php?title=Heraklion&oldid=1202084881.

6. "Tlaxcala (Nahua state)," Wikimedia Foundation, last modified July 12, 10:32, https://en.wikipedia.org/wiki/Tlaxcala_(Nahua_state).

7. José Antonio Esquibel, "Parientes: Founders of the Villa de Santa Fe #5, The Griego-Bernal Family," *La Herencia* 16, no. 4 (Fall 2008): 43–45, accessed November 1, 2021, https://www.ancestry.com/sharing/15911857?h=b3acc3, https://www.hgrc-nm.org/herencia.html.

8. Rodofo Acuna-Soto, David W. Stahle, Matthew D. Therrell, Richard D. Griffin, and Malcolm K. Cleaveland, "When Half of the Population Died: The Epidemic of Hemorrhagic Fevers of 1576 in Mexico," *FEMS Microbi-*

ology Letters 240, no. 1 (November 2004): 1–5, https://doi.org/10.1016/j. femsle.2004.09.011.

9. Miles, "Early Roads," 77.

10. A full-sized wagon at the time carried four thousand pounds, or two tons, of cargo. Juan de Oñate Expedition, 1598, Geni, https://www.geni.com /projects/Juan-de-O%C3%B1ate-Expedition-1598/5321.

11. *Changing Pass: People, Land, and Memory*, Permanent Exhibition Gallery, El Paso Museum of History, El Paso, Texas.

12. *Changing Pass*, El Paso Museum of History.

13. Miles, "Early Roads," 76.

14. Miles, "Early Roads," 76.

15. Miles, "Early Roads," 76.

16. Simmons, *The Last Conquistador*, 108.

17. Simmons, *The Last Conquistador*, 108.

18. Simmons, *The Last Conquistador*, 117–18.

19. Joe Sando, *Pueblo Nations: Eight Centuries of Pueblo Indian History* (Santa Fe, NM: Clear Light Publishers, 1992).

20. Sando, *Pueblo Nations*, 132.

21. Hoig, *Came Men on Horses*, 175.

22. Hoig, *Came Men on Horses*, 176–77.

23. Simmons, *The Last Conquistador*.

24. Simmons, *The Last Conquistador*.

25. Hoig, *Came Men on Horses*, 196.

26. Carmel McCoubrey, "Richard MacNeish, Agricultural Archaeologist, Dies at 82," *New York Times*, January 30, 2001, https://www.nytimes.com/2001 /01/30/us/richard-macneish-agricultural-archaeologist-dies-at-82.html.

27. Martha M. Hammersen, "The Prehistoric Mogollon Culture and Its Regional Aspects in the El Paso Area," *The Artifact* 10 (January 1972): 1–15.

28. Rex E. Gerald, "The Indians of the El Paso del Norte Area," monograph (El Paso: The El Paso Archaeological Society, 1984).

29. Hammersen, "The Prehistoric Mogollon Culture," 6.

30. Gerald, "A Youth's Introduction," 4.

31. Kate Sutherland, *Rock Paintings at Hueco Tanks State Historic Site* (Austin: Texas Parks and Wildlife, 2006).

32. Sutherland, *Rock Paintings*, 10.

33. Gerard, "A Youth's Introduction," 3.

34. Author interview with Dr. David Carmichael, University of Texas at El Paso, June 15, 2022.

35. Author interview with Carmichael, June 15, 2022.
36. Gerald, "The Indians of the El Paso del Norte Area."
37. Hammersen, "The Prehistoric Mogollon Culture," 6.
38. Gerald, "A Youth's Introduction," 4.
39. UNESCO, "Archaeological Zone of Paquimé, Casas Grandes," World Heritage Convention, accessed November 22, 2021, https://whc.unesco.org/en/list/560/.
40. Todd L. VanPool and Christine S. VanPool, "Visiting the Horned Serpent's Home: A Relational Analysis of Paquimé as a Pilgrimage Site in the North American Southwest," *Journal of Social Archaeology* (October 2018), https://journals.sagepub.com/doi/abs/10.1177/1469605318762819.
41. Jay W. Sharp, "The Mysteries of Paquimé: Collapsed in the Mid-Fifteenth Century," *DesertUSA*, accessed November 25, 2021, https://www.desertusa.com/desert-people/paquime.html.
42. Michael E. Whalen, "Wealth, Status, Ritual, and Marine Shell at Casas Grandes, Chihuahua, Mexico," *American Antiquity* 78, no. 4 (October 2013), https://www.jstor.org/stable/43184965.
43. Karl Taube, "The Symbolism of Turquoise in Ancient Mesoamerica," *Academia* (November 2012), https://www.academia.edu/4069017/The_Symbolism_of_Turquoise_in_Ancient_Mesoamerica.
44. Author interview with Tim Roberts, Cultural Resources Coordinator–Region 1, Texas Parks and Wildlife Department, May 1, 2021: "The Mesoamerican influence at Hueco Tanks can hardly be overstated."
45. Sutherland, *Rock Paintings*, 13.
46. Hammersen, "The Prehistoric Mogollon Culture," 23.
47. National Park Service, "Prehistoric Background," National Historic Landmark Nomination, Form 10–934 (Rev 12–2015) OMB Control, 16.
48. Hammersen, "The Prehistoric Mogollon Culture," 23.
49. Author interview with Tim Roberts, Big Bend Center, Texas Parks and Wildlife, Fort Davis, Texas, June 1, 2022.
50. Hammersen, "The Prehistoric Mogollon Culture," 11.
51. Hammersen, "The Prehistoric Mogollon Culture," 11.
52. Bentley, Mark T., "On the trail of Naja," *Password: Journal of the El Paso County Historical Society* 37, no. 4, Winter 1992, 74.
53. Bentley, "On the Trail of Naja," 57.
54. Deborah Lawrence and Jon Lawrence, *Contesting the Borderlands: Interviews on the Early Southwest* (Norman: University of Oklahoma Press, 2016), 8.
55. Sando, *Pueblo Nations,* 28–30.
56. Sando, *Pueblo Nations*, 28–30.

57. Sando, *Pueblo Nations*, 27.

58. Michael E. Smith, "The Aztlan Migrations of the Nahuatl Chronicles: Myth or History?" *Ethnohistory* 31, no. 3 (Summer 1984), https://doi.org /10.2307/482619.

3. THE GREAT REVOLT, 1680–1700

1. Hoig, *Came Men on Horses*, 197.

2. John L. Kessell, *Spain in the Southwest: A Narrative History of Colonial New Mexico, Arizona, Texas, and California* (Norman: University of Oklahoma Press, 2002), 82, https://www.google.com/books/edition/Spain_in_the _Southwest/m_GtnPfC-98C?hl.

3. Ann M. Palkovich, "Historic Population of the Eastern Pueblos: 1540– 1910," *Journal of Anthropological Research* 41, no. 4 (Winter 1985): 401–26, https://www.jstor.org/stable/3630572.

4. Don Juan de Oñate to the Viceroy, the Count of Monterey, March 2, 1599, in Herbert Bolton, ed., *Spanish Exploration in the Southwest, 1542–1706* (New York: Charles Scribner's Sons, 1908), https://wps.prenhall.com/wps /media/objects/170/174877/03_settl.HTM.

5. Porter, "The Spanish Occupation," 85.

6. Hoig, *Came Men on Horses*, 258.

7. Hoig, *Came Men on Horses*, 252.

8. Hoig, *Came Men on Horses*, 252.

9. "14th Century," Wikimedia Foundation, last updated June 24, 2022, 14:23, https://en.wikipedia.org/wiki/14th_century.

10. Robin Farwell Gavin, *Traditional Arts of Spanish New Mexico* (Santa Fe: Museum of New Mexico Press, 1994), 4.

11. Gavin, *Traditional Arts,* 184–85.

12. Gavin, *Traditional Arts,* 191–94.

13. "Salinas Pueblo Missions National Monument: Montainair, New Mexico," National Park Service, accessed January 10, 2022, https://www.nps.gov /nr/travel/american_latino_heritage/Salinas_Pueblo_Missions_National _Monument.html.

14. Sando, *Pueblo Nations*, 57.

15. "San Gabriel de Yunque-Ouinge: San Juan Pueblo, New Mexico," National Park Service, accessed January 22, 2022, https://www.nps.gov/nr /travel/american_latino_heritage/san_gabriel_de_yunque_ouinge.html.

16. Hoig, *Came Men on Horses*, 6.

17. "Popé," Encyclopædia Britannica, last modified January 1, 2022, https:// www.britannica.com/biography/Pope-Tewa-Pueblo-leader.

18. "NM Climate Division 8," CLIMAS: Climate Assessment for the Southwest, University of Arizona, accessed January 22, 2022, https://climas.arizona.edu/nm-climate-division-8-climate-reconstruction.

19. Charles Wilson Hackett, "The Revolt of the Pueblo Indians of New Mexico in 1680," *Quarterly of the Texas State Historical Association* 15, no. 2 (October 1911): 105, https://www.jstor.org/stable/30243029.

20. W. H. Timmons, "Otermin, Antonio de," Handbook of Texas Online, updated May 1, 1995, https://www.tshaonline.org/handbook/entries/otermin-antonio-de.

21. Margaret Wood, "1680—The Pueblo Revolt," *In Custodia Legis: Law Librarians of Congress* (blog), Library of Congress, October 31, 2013, https://blogs.loc.gov/law/2013/10/1680-the-pueblo-revolt/.

22. Hackett, "The Revolt of the Pueblo," 105.

23. "The Pueblo Revolt of 1680," New Mexico Nomad, accessed January 26, 2022, https://newmexiconomad.com/the-pueblo-revolt-of-1680/.

24. Hackett, "The Revolt of the Pueblo," 109.

25. Hackett, "The Revolt of the Pueblo," 111.

26. Hackett, "The Revolt of the Pueblo," 115.

27. Hackett, "The Revolt of the Pueblo," 127.

28. Hackett, "The Revolt of the Pueblo," 93–147.

29. "El Paso Missions," Texas Beyond History, accessed February 5, 2022, https://www.texasbeyondhistory.net/paso/history.html#exodus.

30. "El Paso Missions," Texas Beyond History.

31. Leon C. Metz, *El Paso Chronicles* (Mangan Books, 1993), 11.

32. "French and Indian War," Encyclopædia Britannica, last modified May 6, 2021, https://www.britannica.com/event/French-and-Indian-War.

33. Beckett and Crockett, *The Manso Indians*, 3.

34. Metz, *El Paso Chronicles*, 11.

35. W. H. Timmons, "El Paso, TX," Handbook of Texas Online, updated December 15, 2021, https://www.tshaonline.org/handbook/entries/el-paso-tx.

36. Metz, *El Paso Chronicles*, 11–12.

37. Phillip W. Evans, "Roanoke Voyages," NCPedia, 2006, https://www.ncpedia.org/roanoke-voyages.

38. Texas State Historical Association, "El Paso, TX," n.d., https://www.tshaonline.org/handbook/entries/el-paso-tx.

39. Thomas H. Naylor, "The Extinct Suma of Chihuahua: Their Origin, Cultural Identification, and Disappearance," *The Artifact* 7, no. 4, 1.

40. Beckett and Crockett, *The Manso Indians*, 16.

41. Beckett and Crockett, *The Manso Indians*, 48.

42. Miles, "Early Roads."

43. Beckett and Crockett, *The Manso Indians*, 48.

44. Charles Wilson Hackett, "The Retreat of the Spaniards from New Mexico in 1680, and the Beginnings of El Paso, II," *Southwestern Historical Quarterly* 16, no. 3 (January 1913): 259–76, https://www.jstor.org/stable/30234558.

45. Metz, *El Paso Chronicles*, 11.

46. Metz, *El Paso Chronicles*, 11.

4. MUSTANGS, 1700–1720

1. Jamye Gilbreath, "Explore Ruidoso's Wild Side: The Wild Horses of Lincoln County," *Focus NM*, July 26, 2018, https://www.focusnm.com /regional/explore-ruidosos-wild-side-the-wild-horses-of-lincoln-county/.

2. "Spanish Mustang," Wikimedia Foundation, last modified December 20, 2020, 19:43, https://en.wikipedia.org/wiki/Spanish_Mustang.

3. "Barb horse," Wikimedia Foundation, last modified July 27, 2022, 19:30, https://en.wikipedia.org/wiki/Barb_horse.

4. Marie-Luce Hubert and Jean-Louis Klein, *Mustangs: Wild Horses of the West* (Buffalo, NY: Firefly Books, 2007), 10–11.

5. S. C. Gwynne, *Empire of the Summer Moon: Quanah Parker and the Rise and Fall of the Comanches, the Most Powerful Indian Tribe in American History* (New York: Scribner, 2010), 28–35.

6. Hubert and Klein, *Mustangs*, 13.

7. Gwynne, *Empire of the Summer Moon*, 28–35.

8. Hubert and Klein, *Mustangs*, 13.

9. Hubert and Klein, *Mustangs*, 13.

10. Hubert and Klein, *Mustangs*, 13.

11. Sinclair Ross, "The Outlaw," in *Thundering Hooves: A Collection of Horse Stories*, ed. Christine Pullein-Thompson (New York: Kingfisher, 1996), 128.

12. "Population Trends in Boston, 1640–1990," Boston History and Architecture, accessed February 28, 2022, http://www.iboston.org/mcp .php?pid=popFig; Tim Lambert, "A History of New York City," *Local Histories* (blog), March 14, 2021, https://localhistories.org/a-history-of-new -york-city.

13. "The History of the Vaquero," *American Cowboy*, accessed March 15, 2022, https://www.americancowboy.com/ranch-life-archive/history-vaquero.

14. Arnold Blumberg, "The *Jinetes*," *Medieval Warfare* 3, no. 1 (2013): 18–21, https://www.jstor.org/stable/48579016.

15. "Burgundy Cross Flag 1506–1785 (Spain)," CRW Flags, modified July 28, 2015, https://www.crwflags.com/fotw/flags/es_brgdy.html.

16. This section is adapted from Richard Parker, "As Texas Dries Out, Life Falters and Fades," *New York Times*, August 13, 2011, https://www.nytimes.com/2011/08/14/opinion/sunday/as-texas-dries-out-life-falters-and-fades.html.

17. Jamie Young, *Diocese of El Paso: Centennial History* (Strasbourg, FR: Éditions du Signe, 2013), 14.

18. "El Paso Missions," Texas Beyond History, accessed April 1, 2022, https://www.texasbeyondhistory.net/paso/history.html.

19. "El Paso Missions," Texas Beyond History.

20. Paul R. Sheppard, Andrew C. Comrie, Gregory D. Packin, Kurt Angersbach, and Malcolm K. Hughes, "The Climate of the US Southwest," *Climate Research* 21 (July 2002): 219–38, https://www.int-res.com/articles/cr2002/21/c021p219.pdf.

21. W. H. Timmons, *El Paso: A Borderlands History* (El Paso: Texas Western Press, 1990), 27.

22. Timmons, *Borderlands History*, 27.

23. Timmons, *Borderlands History*, 29.

24. Timmons, *Borderlands History*, 28.

25. Young, *Diocese of El Paso*, 14.

26. Young, *Diocese of El Paso*, 31–32.

27. John D. Inclan, ed., "The Descendants of Don Juan Perez de Onate and Dona Osana Martinez de Gonzalez," Somos Primos, updated May 27, 2007, https://www.somosprimos.com/inclan/onate.htm.

28. "Family Tree of Cristóbal de Narriaondo Pérez de Oñate," Family Search, accessed April 25, 2022, https://www.familysearch.org/tree/pedigree/landscape/LCTP-PFJ.

29. Sando, *Pueblo Nations*, 69.

30. Jennifer Agee Jones, "To Make Them Like Us: European-Indian Intermarriage in Seventeenth-Century North America" (master's thesis, College of William & Mary, 1994), https://dx.doi.org/doi:10.21220/s2-140a-vn25.

31. George D. Torch, "Isleta Pueblo on the Camino Real," *Carta: El Camino Real de Tierra Adentro Association* 6, no. 2 (Spring 2010): 8.

32. "The Jefferson Monticello: Mexico," Thomas Jefferson Foundation, accessed April 26, 2022, https://www.monticello.org/site/research-and-collections/mexico.

5. THE AMERICANS, 1800–1820

1. Elliott Coues, *The Expeditions of Zebulon Montgomery Pike: To Headwaters of the Mississippi River Through Louisiana Territory, and in New Spain, During*

the Years 1805–6–7 (Salt Lake City: Project Gutenberg, 2013), 2:374–380, https://www.gutenberg.org/cache/epub/43775/pg43775-images.html.

2. Herbert E. Bolton, "Papers of Zebulon M. Pike, 1806–1807," *American Historical Review* 13, no. 4 (July 1908): 815, https://doi.org/10.2307/1834266.

3. Coues, *Expeditions of Zebulon,* 1:ix.

4. "The Man Who Double-Crossed the Founders," National Public Radio, April 28, 2010, https://www.npr.org/2010/04/28/126363998/the-man -who-double-crossed-the-founders.

5. Bolton, "Papers of Zebulon," 806.

6. Coues, *Expeditions of Zebulon*, 2:773.

7. Elizabeth A. H. John, "Walker, Juan Pedro (1781–ca. 1828)," Handbook of Texas Online, updated February 16, 2019, https://www.tshaonline.org /handbook/entries/walker-juan-pedro.

8. "Lowcountry Digital History Initiative: The Spanish and New World Slavery," African Laborers for a New Empire: Iberia, Slavery, and the Atlantic World, accessed April 29, 2022, https://ldhi.library.cofc.edu /exhibits/show/african_laborers_for_a_new_emp/the_spanish_and_new _world_slav.

9. Richard Gunderman, "How Smallpox Devastated the Aztec—and Helped Spain Conquer an American Civilization 500 Years Ago," *PBS News Hour*, February 23, 2019, https://www.pbs.org/newshour/science/how -smallpox-devastated-the-aztecs-and-helped-spain-conquer-an-american -civilization-500-years-ago.

10. Rabbi Stephen Leon, *The Third Commandment and the Return of the Anusim* (Santa Fe, NM: Gaon Books, 2017).

11. In the early 2000s, a young American scholar argued that the rediscovery of Jewry in the Southwest and Mexico, led by Stanley Hordes, New Mexico's state historian, was a case of mistaken identity, largely misidentifying fringe Christian churches that claimed a strong Hebrew heritage. *The Atlantic* published one such acerbic article. Later, *The Atlantic* admitted its "takedown" was mistaken, as DNA testing increasingly revealed Sephardic Jewish genes throughout Latin America and the Southwest. Sarah Zhang, "The Genetic Legacy of the Spanish Inquisition," *The Atlantic*, December 21, 2018, https://www.theatlantic.com/science/archive/2018/12 /dna-reveals-the-hidden-jewish-ancestry-of-latin-americans/578509/.

12. Leon, *Return of the Anusim*.

13. Herminia Ballí de Chavana, "Joaquín de Hinojosa Land Grant," Handbook of Texas Online, updated August 3, 2020, https://www.tshaonline .org/handbook/entries/joaquin-de-hinojosa-land-grant.

14. A. C. Spencer and Sidney Paige, *Geology of the Santa Rita Mining Area, New Mexico* (Washington, DC: US Department of the Interior, 1935), 6, https://pubs.usgs.gov/bul/0859/report.pdf.

15. Metz, *El Paso Chronicles*, 37.

16. C. L. Sonnichsen, *Pass of the North: Four Centuries on the Rio Grande* (El Paso: Texas Western Press, 1968), 100–103.

17. Sonnichsen, *Pass of the North*, 101.

18. Martin Donell Kohout, "Stephenson, Hugh (1798–1870)," Handbook of Texas Online, October 1, 1995, https://www.tshaonline.org/handbook/entries/stephenson-hugh.

19. W. H. Timmons, "Hart, Simeon (1816–1874)," Handbook of Texas Online, updated January 1, 1995, https://www.tshaonline.org/handbook/entries/hart-simeon.

6. CONCORDIA, 1821–46

1. Teresa H. Alatorre, "1997: Women Part of Area's History," *El Paso Times*, January 19, 2011, https://www.elpasotimes.com/story/news/history/blogs/tales-from-the-morgue/2011/01/19/1997-women-part-of-areas-history/31520789/.

2. "Dona Juana Maria Ascarate Family Tree," Ancestry, accessed May 3, 2022, https://www.ancestry.com/genealogy/records/dona-juana-maria-ascarate-24-6n25z7.

3. "Obituary: Alfredo C. Flores," Dignity Memorial, accessed May 3, 2022, https://www.dignitymemorial.com/obituaries/el-paso-tx/alfredo-flores-10300461.

4. James Magoffin Dwyer Jr., "Hugh Stephenson," *New Mexico Historical Review* 29, no. 1 (January 1954), https://digitalrepository.unm.edu/cgi/viewcontent.cgi?article=1836&context=nmhr.

5. Sonnichsen, *Pass of the North*, 106.

6. C. E. Campbell, *Mines, Cattle, and Rebellion: The 275-Year History of the Corralitos Ranch and Its Impact on American and Mexican Relations* (Sunset Beach, CA: Green Street Publications, 2014), 23–24.

7. Kohout, "Stephenson, Hugh."

8. Campbell, *Mines, Cattle, and Rebellion*, 25.

9. Martin Donell Kohout, "Ponce de León, Juan María (unknown–1852)," Handbook of Texas Online, updated August 4, 2020, https://www.tshaonline.org/handbook/entries/ponce-de-leon-juan-maria.

10. Metz, *El Paso Chronicles*, 22–23.

11. "Juana Maria Ascarate Stephenson," Find a Grave, accessed May 11, 2022, https://www.findagrave.com/memorial/62786064/juana-maria-stephenson.

12. Sonnichsen, *Pass of the North*, 106.

13. Alatorre, "1997: Women Part of Area's History."

14. His name also may have been Manuel, according to the historian W. H. Timmons. https://www.tshaonline.org/handbook/entries/sonnichsen -charles-leland.

15. W. H. Timmons, *James Wiley Magoffin: Don Santiago—El Paso Pioneer* (El Paso: Texas Western Press, 1999), 28–29.

16. Martin Donell Kohout, "Magoffin, James Wiley (1799–1868)," Handbook of Texas Online, updated November 30, 2019, https://www.tsha online.org/handbook/entries/magoffin-james-wiley.

17. "List of Conflicts in Mexico," Wikimedia Foundation, updated March 20, 2022, 16:52, https://en.wikipedia.org/wiki/List_of_conflicts_in_Mexico.

18. Wilfred H. Callcott, "Santa Anna, Antonio Lopez de (1794–1876)," Handbook of Texas History Online, updated May 9, 2022, https://www .tshaonline.org/handbook/entries/santa-anna-antonio-lopez-de.

19. James Haley, *Apaches: A History and Culture Portrait* (Norman: University of Oklahoma Press, 1997).

20. Marc Simmons, "Trail Dust: Mangas Coloradas Was a Powerful Apache Chief," *Santa Fe New Mexican*, July 11, 2014, https://www.santafenew mexican.com/news/local_news/trail-dust-mangas-coloradas-was-a -powerful-apache-chief/article_c610ef08-d34c-581c-9338-0d116a387c83 .html.

21. Rex W. Strickland, "The Birth and Death of a Legend: The Johnson 'Massacre' of 1837," *Arizona and the West* 18, no. 3 (Autumn 1976): 257–86, http://www.jstor.org/stable/40168505.

22. "James Kirker, the King of New Mexico," American Studies at the University of Virginia, updated September 1, 2009, http://xroads.virginia .edu/~Hyper/HNS/Scalpin/children.html.

23. Timmons, *James Wiley Magoffin*, 28.

24. "Under the Rebel Flag: Life in Texas During the Civil War," Texas State Library and Archives Commission, last updated May 5, 2021, https:// www.tsl.texas.gov/exhibits/civilwar/index.html; Kenneth Howell, *The Seventh Star of the Confederacy: Texas During the Civil War* (Denton: University of North Texas Press, 2011); "1861: Opening Act," Texas State Library and Archives Commission, last updated February 19, 2016, https:// www.tsl.texas.gov/exhibits/civilwar/1861.html; National Historical GIS,

"1860 Census," University of Minnesota, accessed August 15, 2022, https://data2.nhgis.org/main; Ralph A. Wooster, "Notes on Texas' Largest Slaveholders, 1860," *Southwestern Historical Quarterly* 65, no. 1 (July 1961): 72–79, https://www.jstor.org/stable/30236192; Sam Houston, "The Proslavery Argument Against Secession," speech, Austin, Texas, September 22, 1860, http://www.civilwarcauses.org/houston.htm; James L. Haley, *Sam Houston* (Norman: University of Oklahoma Press, 2002); Guy Carleton Lee and Francis Newton Thorpe, *The History of North America: The Civil War from a Southern Standpoint* (Philadelphia: G. Barrie and Sons, 1903); Ralph A. Wooster, *Civil War Texas: A History and a Guide* (Austin: Texas State Historical Association, 1999); Ralph A. Wooster, *Lone Star Blue and Gray: Essays on Texas in the Civil War* (Austin: Texas State Historical Association, 1995); Walter L. Buenger, "Secession Convention," Handbook of Texas Online, last updated July 1, 1995, https://www.tshaonline.org/handbook/entries/secession-convention.

25.   Mirabeau B. Lamar to James Webb, February 23, 1842, Mirabeau B. Lamar Papers #2126, Texas State Library and Archives Commission, https://www.tsl.texas.gov/treasures/giants/lamar/lamar-webb-1.html.

26.   H. Bailey Carroll, "Texan Santa Fe Expedition," Handbook of Texas Online, updated June 13, 2020, https://www.tshaonline.org/handbook/entries/texan-santa-fe-expedition.

27.   Metz, *El Paso Chronicles,* 233–34.

28.   Ira G. Clark, "Six Who Came to El Paso, Pioneers of the 1840's," *Hispanic American Historical Review* 44, no. 4 (November 1964): 641, https://read.dukeupress.edu/hahr/article/44/4/641/159183/Six-Who-Came-to-El-Paso-Pioneers-of-the-1840-s.

29.   Timmons, *James Wiley Magoffin,* 44.

30.   Robert W. Merry, *A Country of Vast Designs: James K. Polk, the Mexican War, and the Conquest of the American Continent* (New York: Simon & Schuster, 2009).

31.   "American Experience: The California Gold Rush," PBS, accessed May 13, 2022, https://www.pbs.org/wgbh/americanexperience/features/goldrush-california/.

32.   "American Experience: The California Gold Rush," PBS.

33.   US Senate, "The Senate Votes for War Against Mexico," May 12, 1846, https://www.senate.gov/artandhistory/history/minute/Senate_Votes_for_War_against_Mexico.htm.

34.   Sean Wilentz, "Into the West," *New York Times,* November 20, 2009, https://www.nytimes.com/2009/11/22/books/review/Wilentz-t.html.

35. Adam Zeidan, "Stephen Watts Kearny," Encyclopædia Britannica, last updated October 27, 2021, https://www.britannica.com/biography/Stephen-Watts-Kearny.

7. MARS RETURNS, 1846–48

1. "Mexican War Campaigns," US Army Center of Military History, accessed May 15, 2022, https://history.army.mil/html/reference/army_flag/mw.html.

2. "Mexican War Campaigns," US Army Center of Military History.

3. Timmons, *James Wiley Magoffin*, 35–37.

4. "Manuel Armijo," A Continent Divided: The U.S.–Mexico War, accessed May 16, 2022, https://library.uta.edu/usmexicowar/item?bio_id=57.

5. Susan Shelby Magoffin, *Down the Santa Fe Trail and into Mexico*, ed. Stella M. Drumm (Lincoln: University of Nebraska Press, 1982).

6. Magoffin, *Down the Santa Fe Trail*.

7. "The Training Ground: The Impact of the Mexican-American War on the Regular Army," American Battlefield Trust, accessed May 24, 2022, https://www.battlefields.org/learn/articles/training-ground.

8. Sonnichsen, *Pass of the North*, 111.

9. Sterling Price, "From New Mexico," *Wilmington Journal*, April 30, 1847, https://www.newspapers.com/clip/41291870/1847-col-prices-account-of-the-taos/.

10. Sonnichsen, *Pass of the North*, 112.

11. Sonnichsen, *Pass of the North*, 113.

12. Sonnichsen, *Pass of the North*, 114.

13. Antonio Ponce de León, "Battle of Brazito Report," 1846, AC 180-P, Fray Angélico Chávez History Library, Santa Fe, New Mexico, https://nmarchives-dev.unm.edu/repositories/10/resources/175.

14. Sonnichsen, *Pass of the North*, 117.

15. Sonnichsen, *Pass of the North*, 117.

16. Metz, *El Paso Chronicles*, 37.

17. Ponce de León, "Battle of Brazito Report."

18. "Mexican War Campaigns," US Army Center for Military History, January 15, 2022. https://history.army.mil/html/reference/army_flag/mw.html.

19. Megan M. Bishop, "Vitamin D Sub-Set Analysis from the Flash Study—a Longitudinal College Student Cohort" (master's thesis, California Polytechnic State University, 2012), fig. 2, https://www.researchgate.net/figure/37-th-Parallel-Latitude-of-the-United-States-Except-during-the-summer-months-the-skin_fig1_304219637.

20. "The Treaty of Guadalupe Hidalgo," National Archives, updated June 9, 2022, https://www.archives.gov/education/lessons/guadalupe-hidalgo.

21. Frank Del Olmo, "Line Drawn in 1848 Shaped Who We Are," *Los Angeles Times*, March 1, 1998, https://www.latimes.com/archives/la-xpm-1998 -mar-01-op-24253-story.html.

22. "US-Mexico Border," Find Latitude and Longitude.com, accessed May 26, 2022, https://www.findlatitudeandlongitude.com/l/us-mexico +border/5750314/.

23. Micheal Clodfelter, *Warfare and Armed Conflicts: A Statistical Encyclopedia of Casualty and Other Figures, 1492–2015*, 4th ed. (Jefferson, NC: McFarland & Company, 2017).

24. By comparison, the casualty rate was 2.5 percent in World War I and World War II, 0.1 percent in Korea and Vietnam, and 21 percent for the Civil War. Of the casualties in the Mexican-American War, 11,562 died of illness, disease, and accidents. Ronald C. White, *American Ulysses: A Life of Ulysses S. Grant* (New York: Random House Publishing Group, 2017), 96.

8. INFERNO, 1849–60

1. "Hugh Stephenson," Find a Grave, accessed May 25, 2022, https://www .findagrave.com/memorial/149793149/hugh-stephenson.

2. "Hot Properties—Eight of History's Most Fought Over Places," Military History Now, September 15, 2014, https://militaryhistorynow .com/2014/09/15/hot-properties-seven-of-historys-most-contested-places/.

3. Richard L. Nostrand, "Mexican Americans Circa 1850," *Annals of the Association of American Geographers* 65, no. 3 (September, 1975): 388, http:// www.jstor.org/stable/2561888.

4. "Texas Almanac: Population History of Counties from 1850–2010," *Texas Almanac*, 2010, https://www.texasalmanac.com/drupal-backup/images /topics/ctypophistweb2010.pdf.

5. Nostrand, "Mexican Americans," 390.

6. Nostrand, "Mexican Americans," 381.

7. Nostrand, "Mexican Americans," 378–90.

8. Haley, *Apaches*, 186–88.

9. Haley, *Apaches*, 186–88.

10. Metz, *El Paso Chronicles*, 34.

11. Metz, *El Paso Chronicles*, 37.

12. Metz, *El Paso Chronicles*, 37.

13. Sonnichsen, *Pass of the North*, 131.

14. Sonnichsen, *Pass of the North*, 132.

15. Sonnichsen, *Pass of the North*, 137–38.

16. Arthur H. Leibson, "Schutz, Solomon C. (unknown–unknown)," Handbook of Texas Online, updated February 19, 2019, https://www.tshaonline.org /handbook/entries/schutz-solomon-c.

17. This section is adapted from Richard Parker, "Four Words for Syrian Refugees—Howdy. Welcome to Texas," *Dallas Morning News,* December 8, 2015, https://www.dallasnews.com/opinion/commentary/2015/12/08 /richard-parker-four-words-for-syrian-refugees-howdy-welcome-to-texas/.

18. Janne Lahti, *Wars for Empire: Apaches, the United States, and the Southwest Borderlands* (Norman: University of Oklahoma Press, 2017), 29.

19. Lahti, *Wars for Empire*, 30.

20. Frederick Webb Hodge, ed., *Handbook of American Indians North of Mexico: Part 1* (Washington, DC: Smithsonian Institution Bureau of American Ethnology, 1907), https://www.google.com/books/edition/Bulletin _Smithsonian_Institution_Bureau/lARNdKvvqewC.

21. Lahti, *Wars for Empire*, 55–56.

22. Lahti, *Wars for Empire*, 40–41.

23. Lahti, *Wars for Empire*, 60.

24. Timmons, *Borderlands History*, 54.

25. Lahti, *Wars for Empire*, 123.

26. Dee Brown, *The Gentle Tamers: Women of the Old Wild West* (Lincoln: University of Nebraska Press, 2012).

27. Leon C. Metz, "Mills, William Wallace (1836–1913)," Handbook of Texas Online, updated December 1, 1995, https://www.tshaonline.org/handbook /entries/mills-william-wallace.

28. Metz, "Mills, William Wallace."

29. This section is adapted from Richard Parker, "Sam Houston, We Have a Problem," *New York Times,* January 31, 2011, https://opinionator.blogs .nytimes.com/2011/01/31/sam-houston-we-have-a-problem/.

30. "Under the Rebel Flag," Texas State Library and Archives Commission; Howell, *The Seventh Star;* "1861: The Fighting Begins," Texas State Library and Archives Commission; University of Minnesota, 1860 Census; Texas State Library and Archives Commission, November 24, 1860; Wooster, "Notes on Texas' Largest Slaveholders"; Houston, "Address on Succession"; Haley, *Sam Houston;* Randolph B. Campbell, *An Empire for Slavery: The Peculiar Institution in Texas, 1821–1865* (Baton Rouge: LSU Press, 1991); Lee and Thorpe, *The History of North America;* Wooster, *Civil War Texas;* Wooster, *Lone Star Blue and Gray;* Buenger, "Secession Convention."

31. Jerry Thompson, "Mexican Texas in the Civil War," Handbook of Texas Online, updated June 17, 2016, https://www.tshaonline.org/handbook /entries/mexican-texans-in-the-civil-war.

9. THE FIFTH CIRCLE, 1861–62

1. Cameron Saffell, "The Magoffins in the Civil War," Texas Historical Commission, March 2011, https://www.thc.texas.gov/historic-sites/magoffin -home/history/magoffins-civil-war.

2. Metz, *El Paso Chronicles*, 92.

3. W. W. Mills, *Forty Years at El Paso, 1858–1898* (El Paso, TX: Carl Hertzog, 1962), 37–54.

4. Metz, *El Paso Chronicles*, 50.

5. Beverly Becker, "Letters from the Front and Other Writings," The Civil War in New Mexico, archives, August 25, 2011; Joseph G. Dawson III, "Texas, Jefferson Davis, and Confederate National Strategy," in *The Fate of Texas: The Civil War and the Lone Star State*, ed. Charles D. Grear (Fayetteville: University of Arkansas Press, 2008), https://muse.jhu.edu /book/12895; Martin Hardwick Hall, "The Formation of Sibley's Brigade and the March to New Mexico," *Southwestern Historical Quarterly* 61, no. 3 (January 1958): 383–405; Jerry Thompson, "Sibley's Brigade," Handbook of Texas Online, updated March 29, 2018, https://www.tshaonline.org /handbook/entries/sibleys-brigade; Jerry Thompson, "Sibley, Henry Hopkins (1816–1886)," Handbook of Texas Online, updated August 1, 2019.

6. Don E. Alberts, "Sibley Campaign," Handbook of Texas Online, February 1, 1996, https://www.tshaonline.org/handbook/entries/sibley-campaign.

7. "Second French Intervention in Mexico," Military Wiki, updated March 23, 2020, 10:45, https://military-history.fandom.com/wiki/Second _French_intervention_in_Mexico.

8. Walter V. Scholes, "Benito Juárez," Encyclopædia Britannica, updated July 14, 2021, https://www.britannica.com/biography/Benito-Juarez.

9. "Zaragoza, Ignacio Seguín," Handbook of Texas Online, updated August 5, 2020, https://www.tshaonline.org/handbook/entries/zaragoza -ignacio-seguin.

10. "Zaragoza, Ignacio Seguín," Handbook of Texas Online.

11. US Department of State, "French Intervention in Mexico and the American Civil War, 1862–1867," Office of the Historian, accessed May 28, 2022, https://history.state.gov/milestones/1861-1865/french-intervention.

12. Richard O'Connor, *The Cactus Throne: The Tragedy of Maximilian and Carlotta* (New York: G. P. Putnam's Sons, 1971).

13. "The Mexican Campaign, 1862–1867," Napoleon.org, accessed May 26, 2022, https://www.napoleon.org/en/history-of-the-two-empires/timelines /the-mexican-campaign-1862-1867/.

14. Hubert Howe Bancroft, *The Works of Hubert Howe Bancroft*, vol. XIV, in *History of Mexico, vol. VI: 1861–1887* (San Francisco: The History Company Publishers, 1888), https://archive.org/details/historyofmexico14 bancrich/page/n7/mode/2up.

15. Alan Palmer, *Twilight of the Habsburgs: The Life and Times of Emperor Francis Joseph* (New York: Atlantic Monthly Press, 1994).

10. THE SEVENTH CIRCLE, 1863–80

1. Robert M. Utley, "The Bascom Affair: A Reconstruction." *Arizona and the West* 3, no. 1 (Spring 1961): 59–68, http://www.jstor.org/stable/40167363.

2. Mark T. Fiege, *The Mountain Howitzer at Big Hole National Battlefield: A Technical and Historical Report* (Wisdom, MT: Big Hole National Battlefield, 1984), http://npshistory.com/publications/biho/mountain-howitzer .pdf.

3. George H. Pettis, *The California Column: Its Campaigns and Services in New Mexico, Arizona and Texas, During the Civil War, with Sketches of Brigadier General James H. Carleton, Its Commander, and Other Officers and Soldiers* (Santa Fe: New Mexican Printing Co., 1908).

4. Robert Ryal Miller, "Arms Across the Border: United States Aid to Juárez During the French Intervention in Mexico," *Transactions of the American Philosophical Society* 63, no. 6 (1973): 1–68, https://doi.org /10.2307/1006291.

5. Miller, "Arms Across the Border."

6. "Mexico," *New York Times*, April 7, 1867, https://www.nytimes.com /1867/04/07/archives/mexico-progress-of-the-siege-of-queretarothe -starvingout-process-in.html.

7. "Second French Intervention in Mexico," DBpedia, accessed June 1, 2022, https://dbpedia.org/page/Second_French_intervention_in_Mexico.

8. History.com, "Kit Carson Begins His Campaign Against Native Americans," *This Day in History* (blog), November 13, 2009, https://www .history.com/this-day-in-history/kit-carsons-campaign-against-the -indians.

9. Smithsonian Institution, "The Long Walk," National Museum of the American Indian, accessed June 2, 2022, https://americanindian.si.edu /nk360/navajo/long-walk/long-walk.cshtml.

10. Smithsonian Institution, "The Long Walk."

11. Jay Sharp, "The Night They Shot Mangas Coloradas: Chiricahua Apache Chief," DesertUSA, accessed June 3, 2022, https://www.desertusa.com /ind1/Colradas.html#ixzz7GUeLXlkn.

12. Lahti, *Wars for Empire*, 20.

13. Chip Colwell-Chanthaphonh, "Western Apache Oral Histories and Traditions of the Camp Grant Massacre," *American Indian Quarterly* 27, nos. 3 & 4 (Summer/Fall 2003): 639–66, https://muse.jhu.edu/article /174606.

14. "History Timeline of the Apache Wars," Preceden, accessed June 5, 2022, https://www.preceden.com/timelines/285060-history-timeline-of-the -apache-wars.

15. Dan L. Thrapp, *The Conquest of Apacheria* (Norman: University of Oklahoma Press, 1967).

16. Hunter Bassler, "America's Longest War Was Partially Fought in Arizona," NBC 12 News, KPNX-TV, December 9, 2021, https://www.12news.com /article/news/history/apache-wars-arizona-longest-united-states-military -conflict/75-73bb071d-4f47-43c0-8a98-303414fa45fe; Edward R. Sweeney, *Making Peace with Cochise: The 1872 Journal of Captain Joseph Alton Sladen* (Norman: University of Oklahoma Press, 2008).

17. US Army, *American Military History* (Washington, DC: Center of Military History, 1989), https://history.army.mil/books/AMH/amh-14.htm.

18. "James Wiley Magoffin," Texas Historical Commission, accessed June 13, 2022, https://www.thc.texas.gov/historic-sites/magoffin-home/history /james-wiley-magoffin.

19. Timmons, "Hart, Simeon (1816–1874)."

20. Karl Jacoby, "The Trial," Shadows at Dawn, 2008, https://www.brown .edu/Research/Aravaipa/trial.html.

21. C. L. Sonnichsen, *The El Paso Salt War* (El Paso: Texas Western Press, 1971).

22. Texas State Historical Association, "Salt War Turns Bloody," *Texas Day by Day*, accessed June 10, 2022, https://www.tshaonline.org/texas-day-by -day/entry/769.

23. Joseph A. Stout Jr., "Victorio (ca. 1825–1880)," Handbook of Texas Online, updated February 9, 2019, https://www.tshaonline.org/handbook /entries/victorio.

24. Bruce J. Dinges, "Grierson, Benjamin Henry (1826–1911)," Handbook of Texas Online, updated October 27, 2020, https://www.tshaonline.org /handbook/entries/grierson-benjamin-henry.

25. Lahti, *Wars for Empire*, 27–29.

26. Campbell, *Mines, Cattle, and Rebellion,* 25.

11. THE NINTH CIRCLE, 1881–1900

1. Mills, *Forty Years*, 17–18.

2. Mills, *Forty Years*, 17–18.

3. Mills, *Forty Years*, 17–18.

4. Arthur H. Leibson, "Schutz, Solomon C. (unknown–unknown)," Handbook of Texas Online, updated February 19, 2019, https://www.tshaonline.org/handbook/entries/schutz-solomon-c.

5. "Jewish Political Milestones in the United States," Jewish Virtual Library, accessed May 30, 2022, https://www.jewishvirtuallibrary.org/jewish-political-milestones-in-the-united-states.

6. Martin Zielonka, "From 1880's to 1928," Temple Mount Sinai, archived April 6, 2017, http://www.templemountsinai.com/Who-We-Are/History/Early-History-1880's--1928.

7. Leon Metz, *Desert Army: Fort Bliss on the Texas Border* (El Paso, TX: Mangan Books, 1988), 63.

8. "Tower 47—El Paso," Texas Railroad History, updated January 25, 2021, http://txrrhistory.com/towers/047/047.htm.

9. Metz, *El Paso Chronicles*, 71.

10. Metz, *El Paso Chronicles*, 71.

11. "Dallas Stoudenmire," Find a Grave, accessed June 5, 2022, https://www.findagrave.com/memorial/8332262/dallas-stoudenmire.

12. "About Us," El Paso Independent School District, accessed June 5, 2022, https://www.episd.org/domain/224.

13. *Alvarado v. El Paso Independent School District*, 426 F.Supp.575 (W.D. Tex. 1976), https://casetext.com/case/alvarado-v-el-paso-independent-sch-dist.

14. *Gunfights of the Old West*, directed by Jackson Polk (Capstone Productions Inc., 2004), videodisc, 30 min.

15. Franklin County Historical Society, "Excerpts from Letters Written by Billy the Kid to Lew Wallace," Billy the Kid and Lew Wallace, accessed June 14, 2022, http://www.franklincountyhistoricalsociety.com/Lew_Wallace/billy_the_kid/billy_the_kid.html.

16. Franklin County Historical Society, "Excerpts."

17. Jon Tuska, *Billy the Kid: His Life and Legend* (Westport, CT: Greenwood, 1994).

18. Leon C. Metz, *John Wesley Hardin: Dark Angel of Texas* (Norman: University of Oklahoma Press, 1998).

19. Trish Long, "The Age of Gunfights in El Paso," *El Paso Times*, August 29, 2015, https://www.elpasotimes.com/story/mobile/2015/08/29/age-gunfights -el-paso/71939366/.

20. Metz, *Desert Army*.

21. Metz, *Desert Army*, 115–38.

22. Timmons, "El Paso, TX."

12. REVOLUTION AND BETRAYAL, 1900–1920

1. Timmons, "El Paso, TX."

2. Metz, *Desert Army*, 136–77.

3. Trish Long, "Past Presidential Visits: William McKinley in 1901," *El Paso Times*, February 6, 2019, https://www.elpasotimes.com/story /archives/2019/02/06/el-aso-past-presidential-visits-william-mckinley -1901/2797181002/.

4. Leon C. Metz, *Border: The U.S.-Mexico Line* (Fort Worth: Texas Christian University Press, 2008).

5. Duff C. Green and Ronnie C. Tyler, "Exploring the Rio Grande: Lt. Duff C. Green's Report of 1852," *Arizona and the West* 10, no. 1 (Spring 1968): 43–60, http://www.jstor.org/stable/40167292.

6. Evan Rothera, "Rothera on Carrigan and Webb, 'Forgotten Dead: Mob Violence Against Mexicans in the United States, 1848–1928,'" Humanities and Social Sciences Online, July 2014, https://networks.h-net.org /node/20317/reviews/35705/rothera-carrigan-and-webb-forgotten-dead -mob-violence-against-mexicans.

7. "Texas Rangers," Bullock Museum, accessed June 30, 2022, https://www .thestoryoftexas.com/discover/campfire-stories/texas-ranger.

8. Lily Meyer, "The Texas Rangers: Good Guys No More," *Los Angeles Review of Books*, October 31, 2018, https://lareviewofbooks.org/article/the-texas -rangers-good-guys-no-more/.

9. William D. Carrigan and Clive Webb, "'*Muerto por Unos Desconocidos*' ('Killed by Persons Unknown'): Mob Violence Against Blacks and Mexicans," in *Beyond Black & White: Race, Ethnicity, and Gender in the U.S. South and Southwest*, ed. Laura F. Edwards, William D. Carrigan, Clive Webb, Stephanie Cole, Sarah Deutsch, and Neil Foley (College Station: Texas A&M University Press, 2004), 43, https://www.google.com/books /edition/Beyond_Black_and_White/uIENhDJSh5sC.

10. William D. Carrigan and Clive Webb, "The Lynching of Persons of Mex-

ican Origin or Descent in the United States, 1848 to 1928," *Journal of Social History* 37, no. 2 (Winter 2003): 411–38, http://www.jstor.org /stable/3790404.

11. Rothera, "Rothera on Carrigan and Webb."

12. David Martin Davies, "Should Texas Remember or Forget the Slocum Massacre?," *Texas Matters*, Texas Public Radio, January 16, 2015, https:// www.tpr.org/show/texas-matters/2015-01-16/should-texas-remember-or -forget-the-slocum-massacre.

13. Jonna Perillo, *Educating the Enemy: Teaching Nazis and Mexicans in the Cold War Borderlands* (Chicago: University of Chicago Press, 2022), 33.

14. Photo Exhibition, El Paso History Alliance, January 28, 2022, https:// www.facebook.com/search/photos/?q=el%20paso%20history%20 alliance%201900&sde=Abop57lPcXhacwMNVrmUjycDI4OP0OGa -DBXae710NjFNfhmfFSxqWID9udXatUqjI4YOe_2FFiAuKZSDSW17 tIbcGVrNUEBYE7uSNfesSqEpriEGVDZFcTPXHGQr-ktvOzZY5IzI7e fUOk9FWYQ3DEv.

15. Brian Gratton and Emily Klancher Merchant, "An Immigrant's Tale: The Mexican American Southwest, 1850 to 1950," *Social Science History* 39, no. 4 (Winter 2015): 528.

16. Trish Long, "City Swept Up in Taft-Diaz Meeting, First for a U.S. and a Mexican President," *El Paso Times*, September 15, 2021, https://www.el pasotimes.com/story/news/2021/09/15/city-swept-up-taft-diaz-meeting -el-paso-times-tales-from-the-morgue-trish-long/8332826002/.

17. "Top 100 Biggest US Cities in the Year 1910," Biggest US Cities, accessed June 17, 2022, https://www.biggestuscities.com/1910.

18. "City Population History from 1850–2000," Texas Almanac, accessed June 18, 2022, https://www.texasalmanac.com/drupal-backup/images /CityPopHist%20web.pdf.

19. Library of Congress, "A Growing Community," Immigration and Re-location in U.S. History, accessed June 20, 2022, https://www.loc.gov /classroom-materials/immigration/mexican/a-growing-community/.

20. Mark Wasserman, "Foreign Investment in Mexico, 1876–1910: A Case Study of the Role of Regional Elites," *The Americas* 36, no. 1 (July 1979): 3–21, https://doi.org/10.2307/981135.

21. Wasserman, "Foreign Investment."

22. Timothy G. Turner, *Bullets, Bottles, and Gardenias* (Dallas: South-West Press, 1935).

23. Turner, *Bullets, Bottles*.

24. Turner, *Bullets, Bottles*.

25. Bain News Service, *Revolutionists Entering Juarez*, 1911, glass negative, Library of Congress, https://www.loc.gov/pictures/item/2014690215/.

26. Bain News Service, *Revolutionists Entering Juarez*.

27. Tony Burton, "Did You Know? The World's First Aerial Bombing: The Battle of Topolobampo, Mexico," MexConnect, March 14, 2008, https://www.mexconnect.com/articles/1171-did-you-know-the-world-s-first -aerial-bombing-the-battle-of-topolobampo-mexico/.

28. Alexander Greene, "Mexican Immigration to the United States and Its Effect on Mexican Culture and the Family Structure," LatinxKC, accessed July 10, 2022, https://info.umkc.edu/latinxkc/essays/spring-2017 /mexican-immigration-family/.

29. Jason Steinhauer, "The History of Mexican Immigration to the U.S. in the Early 20th Century," *Insights: Scholarly Work at the John W. Kluge Center* (blog), March 11, 2015, https://blogs.loc.gov/kluge/2015/03/the-history -of-mexican-immigration-to-the-u-s-in-the-early-20th-century/.

30. "Pancho Villa Loved Ice Cream," January 28, 2022, El Paso Museum of History, https://www.digie.org/en/media/4771https://www.facebook.com /TracesofTexas/posts/pancho-villa-far-left-with-mustache-and-boots -eating-ice-cream-at-a-confectioner/1849630448402409/.

31. Associated Press, "Pancho Villa's Wife, 100," *New York Times*, July 12, 1996, https://www.nytimes.com/1996/07/12/world/pancho-villa-s-wife -100.html.

32. "Juana Torres," Frost, Gilchrist, and Related Families, last modified August 8, 2022, https://frostandgilchrist.com/getperson.php?personID =119198&tree=frostinaz01.

33. Ricardo Vaz and César Mosquera, "John Reed, Revolutionary Journalist," *Utopix*, October 17, 2020, https://utopix.cc/content/john-reed -revolutionary-journalist/.

34. R. H. Ellis, *Pancho Villa: Intimate Recollections by People Who Knew Him*, ed. Jessie Peterson and Thelma Cox Knoles (New York: Hastings House Publishers, 1977), 130–31.

35. Cornell Law School, "Geneva Conventions and Their Additional Protocols," Legal Information Institute, accessed July 11, 2022, https://www .law.cornell.edu/wex/geneva_conventions_and_their_additional_ protocols.

36. Ellis, *Pancho Villa*, 142.

37. Ellis, *Pancho Villa*, 148.

38. Jay Bellamy, "The Zimmerman Telegram: And Other Events Leading to America's Entry into World War I," *Prologue Magazine* 48, no. 4 (Win-

ter 2016), https://www.archives.gov/publications/prologue/2016/winter
/zimmermann-telegram.

39. Eileen Welsome, *The General and the Jaguar: Pershing's Hunt for Pancho Villa: A True Story of Revolution and Revenge* (Lincoln, NE: Bison Books, 2007).

40. Bellamy, "Zimmerman Telegram."

41. "Plot Uncovered!" *New York Times*, March 1, 1917, 1.

42. Bellamy, "Zimmerman Telegram."

43. Military Newspapers of Virginia, "Heritage Spotlight: Hispanic Men, Women Have Played an Integral Role in America's History," *Military News*, September 19, 2014, https://www.militarynews.com/peninsula-warrior /news/heritage_spotlight/heritage-spotlight-hispanic-men-women-have -played-an-integral-role-in-america-s-history/article_94178927-c1f2 -58e8-9b02-656081f48eba.html.

13. THE KLAN, 1921–39

1. "Timeline of the American Civil Right Movement," Encyclopædia Britannica, accessed July 13, 2022, https://www.britannica.com/list/timeline-of -the-american-civil-rights-movement.

2. David Dorado Romo, *Ringside Seat to a Revolution: An Underground Cultural History of El Paso and Juarez, 1893–1923* (El Paso, TX: Cinco Puntos Press), 219–28.

3. Alexander Cockburn, "Zyklon B on the US Border: A Grim History Lesson of What Happened in the 1920s When Fears of Alien Infection Inflamed American Eugenicists," *The Nation*, June 21, 2007, https://www .thenation.com/article/archive/zyklon-b-us-border/.

4. Owen White, *Out of the Desert: The Historical Romance of El Paso* (El Paso, TX: The McGath Company, 1924), 303.

5. Lloyd C. Engelbrecht and June F. Engelbrecht, "The Popular Dry Goods Company: El Paso, Texas," Henry C. Trost Historical Organization, 1990, https://www.henrytrost.org/buildings/popular-dry-goods-company/.

6. "Institutional Revolutionary Party," Encyclopædia Britannica, updated September 28, 2021, https://www.britannica.com/topic/Institutional -Revolutionary-Party.

7. US Census, "Country of Birth of the Foreign-Born Population," in *Fourteenth Census of the United States Taken in the Year 1920* (Washington, DC, 1922), 2, https://www2.census.gov/library/publications/decennial/1920 /volume-2/41084484v2ch08.pdf.

8. Sal Acosta, "Racial Fluidity in the Borderlands: Intermarriages Between Blacks and Mexicans in Southern Arizona, 1860–1930," *Journal of the*

Southwest 56, no. 4 (Winter 2014): 555–81, https://www.jstor.org/stable/24394958.

9. "Minorities Are the New Majority in Texas," The Texas Politics Project, accessed July 18, 2022, https://texaspolitics.utexas.edu/archive/html/cult/features/0501_02/slide2.html.

10. "Latino Civil Rights Timeline, 1903 to 2006," Learning for Justice, accessed July 19, 2022, https://www.learningforjustice.org/classroom-resources/lessons/latino-civil-rights-timeline-1903-to-2006.

11. Charles F. Robinson II, "Legislated Love in the Lone Star State: Texas and Miscegenation," *Southwestern Historical Quarterly* 108, no. 1 (July 2004): 65–87, http://www.jstor.org/stable/30239495.

12. Martha Menchaca, "The Anti-Miscegenation History of the American Southwest, 1837 to 1970: Transforming Racial Ideology into Law," *Cultural Dynamics* 20, no. 3 (November 2008): 279–318, https://doi.org/10.1177/0921374008096312.

13. Yolanda Chávez Leyva, "Bridging the Story: The Life and Times of John Lucas," *Fierce Fronteriza* (blog), March 14, 2018, https://www.fiercefronteriza.com/fierce-fronteriza-blog/bridging-the-story-the-life-and-times-of-john-lucas.

14. Don E. Carleton, "Reviewed Work: *War, Revolution and the Ku Klux Klan: A Study of Intolerance in a Border City* by Shawn Lay," *Southwestern Historical Quarterly* 90, no. 2 (October 1986): 202–4, http://www.jstor.org/stable/30237020.

15. Christopher Long, "Ku Klux Klan," Handbook of Texas Online, updated May 28, 2021, https://www.tshaonline.org/handbook/entries/ku-klux-klan.

16. Katherine Kuehler Walters, "The 1920s Texas Ku Klux Klan Revisited: White Supremacy and Structural Power in a Rural County," (PhD diss., Texas A&M University, 2018), https://oaktrust.library.tamu.edu/bitstream/handle/1969.1/173554/WALTERS-DISSERTATION-2018.pdf?sequence=1&isAllowed=y.

17. Arthur H. Leibson, "Dudley, Richard M. (1862–1925)," Handbook of Texas Online, updated December 1, 1994, https://www.tshaonline.org/handbook/entries/dudley-richard-m.

18. Trish Long, "Dudley Beats K.K.K. By 2,120," *El Paso Times*, February 25, 1923, https://www.elpasotimes.com/story/news/history/blogs/tales-from-the-morgue/2008/10/30/dudley-beats-kk/31515009/.

19. League of Women Voters of Texas, "The Woman Suffrage Movement in Texas," Texas Woman's University, updated November 3, 2021, https://

twu.edu/institute-womens-leadership/the-woman-suffrage-movement
/the-woman-suffrage-movement-in-texas/.

20. Fred M. Shelley, "Ferguson, James and Miriam (1871–1944; 1875–1961)," *Encyclopedia of the Great Plains*, ed. David J. Wishart (Lincoln: University of Nebraska, 2011), http://plainshumanities.unl.edu/encyclopedia/doc /egp.pg.025.

21. Ernest R. May, "Butte, George Charles (1877–1940)," Handbook of Texas Online, updated April 19, 2016, https://www.tshaonline.org/handbook /entries/butte-george-charles.

22. "Election of Texas Governors, 1900–1948," Texas Almanac, accessed July 20, 2022, https://www.texasalmanac.com/articles/election-of-texas -governors-1900-1948.

23. Trish Long, "El Paso Doctor Sued to Change Laws That Took Vote from Blacks," *El Paso Times*, August 11, 2009, https://www.elpasotimes.com /story/news/history/blogs/tales-from-the-morgue/2009/08/11/el-paso -doctor-sued-to-change-laws-that-took-vote-from-blacks/31514949/.

24. Michelle D. Esparza, "The Story of Dr. Lawrence A. Nixon, a Black Doctor in El Paso, Who Successfully Challenged Two Discriminatory Texas Statues in the U.S. Supreme Court," *El Paso Bar Journal* (Fall 2020): 5–6, https:// elpasobar.com/WorkPanda/Archivo/Us__Files/Documents/Journal /EPBJfall2020.pdf.

25. Esparza, "The Story of Dr. Lawrence A. Nixon."

26. *Nixon v. Condon*, 34 F.2d 464 (W.D. Tex. 1929), https://law.justia.com /cases/federal/district-courts/F2/34/464/1481906/.

27. *Nixon v. Condon*.

28. Romo, *Ringside Seat*, 243.

29. Abraham Hoffman, *Unwanted Mexican Americans in the Great Depression: Repatriation Pressures, 1929–1939* (Tucson: University of Arizona Press, 1974), i–vi.

30. Alex Wagner, "America's Forgotten History of Illegal Deportations," *The Atlantic*, March 6, 2017, https://www.theatlantic.com/politics/archive/2017 /03/americas-brutal-forgotten-history-of-illegal-deportations/517971/.

31. Francisco E. Balderrama and Raymond Rodríguez, *Decade of Betrayal*, rev. ed. (Albuquerque: University of New Mexico Press, 2006).

32. Yolanda Chávez Leyva, "'Faithful Hard-Working Mexican Hands': Mexicana Workers During the Great Depression," *Perspectives in Mexican American Studies* 5 (1995): 71, https://repository.arizona.edu/handle /10150/624819.

33. Leyva, "Faithful Hard-Working," 71.

34. Leyva, "Faithful Hard-Working," 63.

35. Leyva, "Faithful Hard-Working," 78.

36. Romo, *Ringside Seat*, 240.

37. Stephen Rohde, "The United States—A Model for the Nazis," *Los Angeles Review of Books*, September 3, 2017, https://lareviewofbooks.org/article/the-united-states-a-model-for-the-nazis/.

38. Sander A. Diamond, "The Years of Waiting: National Socialism in the United States, 1922–1933," *American Jewish Historical Quarterly* 59, no. 3 (March 1970): 256–71, https://www.jstor.org/stable/23877858.

14. A WORLD AT WAR, 1940–41

1. Si Dunn, *The First Cavalry Division: A Historical Overview, 1921–1983* (Dallas, TX: Taylor Publishing Company, 1984).

2. Aaron Skabelund, "Memories of Japanese Military Horses of World War II" (paper presented at the British Association of Japanese Studies Conference, Hokkaido University, Sapporo, HOK, May 2011), https://www.soas.ac.uk/history/conferences/war-horses-conference-2014/file94822.pdf.

3. Cavalry Outpost Publications and William H. Boudreau, "The Early Years, 1921–1941," 1st Cavalry Division, updated January 4, 2013, https://www.first-team.us/tableaux/chapt_01.

4. "The 200th Coast Artillery Regiment and the Bataan Death March," White Sands Missile Range Museum, accessed February 22, 2022, https://wsmrmuseum.com/2022/02/22/the-200th-coast-artillery-regiment-and-the-bataan-death-march/2/.

5. "200th Coast Artillery," White Sands Missile Range Museum.

6. Lorene Bishop, "History of Camp Bowie," City of Brownwood, accessed July 7, 2022, https://www.brownwoodtexas.gov/323/History-of-Camp-Bowie.

7. Dave Gutierrez, *Patriots from the Barrio: The Story of Company E, 141st Infantry, the Only All Mexican American Army Unit in World War II* (Yardley, PA: Westholme Publishing, 2019), 28–29.

8. Gutierrez, *Patriots from the Barrio*, 30–39.

9. Gutierrez, *Patriots from the Barrio*, 40.

10. Dorothy Cave, *Beyond Courage: One Regiment Against Japan, 1941–1945,* rev. ed. (Santa Fe, NM: Sunset Press, 2006).

15. WAR AND HOPE, 1941–50

1. John T. Correll, "Disaster in the Philippines," *Air Force Magazine*, November 1, 2019, https://www.airforcemag.com/article/disaster-in-the-philippines/.

2. Pacific War Historical Society, "The Japanese Attack Finds General MacArthur Unprepared," The Pacific War, updated November 23, 2009, https://www.pacificwar.org.au/Philippines/Japanattacks.html.

3. William Manchester, *American Caesar: Douglas MacArthur, 1880–1964* (Boston: Little, Brown, 2008), 230–31.

4. "A Brief History of the 200th and 515th Coast Artillery," Bataan Corregidor Memorial Foundation of New Mexico, accessed July 10, 2022, https://www.angelfire.com/nm/bcmfofnm/history/briefhistory.html.

5. "200th Coast Artillery," White Sands Missile Range Museum.

6. "Philippines Campaign (1941–1942)," Wikimedia Foundation, updated July 13, 2022, 21:19, https://en.wikipedia.org/wiki/Philippines_campaign_(1941%E2%80%931942); "200th Coast Artillery," White Sands Missile Range Museum.

7. "Brief History of the 200th," Bataan Corregidor Memorial Foundation.

8. "200th Coast Artillery," White Sands Missile Range Museum.

9. Michael Ray, ed., "The March and Imprisonment at Camp O'Donnell," Encyclopædia Britannica, accessed July 25, 2022, https://www.britannica.com/event/Bataan-Death-March/The-march-and-imprisonment-at-Camp-ODonnell.

10. "200th Coast Artillery," White Sands Missile Range Museum.

11. John J. Dwyer, "The End of U.S. Intervention in Mexico: Franklin Roosevelt and the Expropriation of American-Owned Agricultural Property," *Presidential Studies Quarterly* 28, no. 3 (1998): 495–509, http://www.jstor.org/stable/27551897.

12. Dwyer, "The End of U.S. Intervention."

13. Gutierrez, *From the Barrio*, 56–60.

14. John C. L. Scribner, "36th Infantry Division: The 'Texas' Division," Texas Military Forces Museum, accessed July 26, 2022, https://www.texasmilitaryforcesmuseum.org/texas.htm.

15. Gutierrez, *From the Barrio*, 79.

16. Gutierrez, *From the Barrio*, 87.

17. Gutierrez, *From the Barrio*, 110.

18. Samuel S. Ortega and Arnulfo Hernandez Jr., *The Men of Company E: Toughest Chicano Soldiers of World War II* (CreateSpace, 2015), 60–99.

19. Cindy Ramirez, "New Company E Memorial Raises Questions About Who's Included," *El Paso Matters*, June 27, 2022, https://elpasomatters.org/2022/06/27/el-pasos-new-wwii-company-e-memorial-downtown-raises-questions/.

20. Ramirez, "New Company E."

21. Wolfgang Saxon, "Gen. Mark Clark Dies at 87; Last of World War II Chiefs, Conqueror of Rome," *New York Times*, April 17, 1984, https://www.nytimes.com/1984/04/17/obituaries/gen-mark-clark-dies-at-87-last-of-world-war-ii-chiefs-conqueror-of-rome.html.

22. Gutierrez, *From the Barrio*, 139–48.

23. "Rapido River Disaster," Military.com, accessed July 27, 2022, https://www.military.com/history/rapido-river-disaster.html.

24. Gutierrez, *From the Barrio*, 232.

25. Scott Kuhn, "1st Cavalry Division and the Battle of Manila—75 Years Later," US Army, February 19, 2020, https://www.army.mil/article/232822/1st_cavalry_division_and_the_battle_of_manila_75_years_later.

26. Peter R. Wygle, "Santo Tomas Raid," 1st Cavalry Division Association, accessed August 15, 2022, https://1cda.org/history/santo-tomas-raid/.

27. Wygle, "Santo Tomas Raid."

28. Kuhn, "1st Cavalry Division."

29. Lucy Guevara, "Reynaldo Perez Gallardo," Voces Oral History Center, University of Texas at Austin, March 9, 2000, https://voces.lib.utexas.edu/collections/stories/reynaldo-perez-gallardo.

30. This section is adapted from Richard Parker, "When the Mexican Air Force Went to War Alongside America," *New York Times*, May 27, 2020.

31. This section is adapted from Parker, "When the Mexican Air Force Went to War."

32. This section is adapted from Parker, "When the Mexican Air Force Went to War."

33. US Department of Energy, "Trinity Site—World's First Nuclear Explosion," Office of Legacy Management, accessed August 1, 2022, https://www.energy.gov/lm/doe-history/manhattan-project-background-information-and-preservation-work/manhattan-project-1.

34. Frank Trejo, "Ramon Sr. Villa," Voces Oral History Center, University of Texas at Austin, July 20, 2010, https://voces.lib.utexas.edu/collections/stories/ramon-sr-villa.

35. Susan A. Romano, "Remembering the 'Forgotten Eagles,'" CONR-1AF (AFNORTH and AFSPACE), US Air Force, November 9, 2009, https://www.1af.acc.af.mil/News/Article-Display/Article/289905/remembering-the-forgotten-eagles/.

36. Maggie Rivas-Rodriguez, "Latina/os and World War II," Open Road, accessed August 2, 2022, https://openroadmedia.com/ebook/latinaos-and-world-war-ii/9780292758636.

37. "Research Starters: Worldwide Deaths in World War II," National WWII Museum, accessed August 2, 2022, https://www.nationalww2 museum.org/students-teachers/student-resources/research-starters/research -starters-worldwide-deaths-world-war.

16. CIVIL RIGHTS, 1951–59

1. Malcolm Pirnie, Inc., "Review of ASARCO El Paso Smelting Processes," Texas Custodial Trust (October 2010), http://www.recastingthesmelter .com/wp-content/themes/recastingasarco/downloads/site_documents /Review-of-ASARCO-El-Paso-Smelting-Processes-Report-FINAL.pdf.

2. Hanson W. Baldwin, "Wild V-2 Rocket 'Invades' Mexico; Backtracks in a White Sands Test; Erratic Rocket Falls in Mexico," *New York Times*, May 30, 1947, https://www.nytimes.com/1947/05/30/archives/wild-v2 -rocket-invades-mexico-backtracks-in-a-white-sands-test.html.

3. Perillo, *Educating the Enemy*.

4. "Top 100 Biggest US Cities in the Year 1950," Biggest US Cities, updated May 27, 2022, https://www.biggestuscities.com/1950.

5. Metz, *El Paso Chronicles*, 243–44.

6. Meredith Barnhill, "Juan Martinez," Voces Oral History Center, University of Texas at Austin, August 31, 2005, https://voces.lib.utexas.edu /collections/stories/juan-martinez-0.

7. Edward Kosack, "The Bracero Program and Effects on Human Capital Investments in Mexico, 1942–1964," SSRN (April 2015), http://dx.doi .org/10.2139/ssrn.2603520.

8. Metz, *El Paso Chronicles*, 233–34.

9. Trish Long, "General of the Army Dwight 'Ike' Eisenhower Visited El Paso in 1946, Liked Mexican Food," *El Paso Times*, January 31, 2019, https:// www.elpasotimes.com/story/news/local/el-paso/2019/01/31/general -eisenhower-visited-el-paso-1946-ate-mexican-food-dinner/2709920002/.

10. "The Struggle for Civil Rights," Miller Center, University of Virginia, accessed August 17, 2022, https://millercenter.org/the-presidency /educational-resources/age-of-eisenhower/struggle-civil-rights.

11. Winifred B. Dowling, "The Border at War: World War II Along the United States–Mexico Border," ETD Collection for University of Texas, El Paso (doctoral theses, University of Texas at El Paso, 2010), https:// scholarworks.utep.edu/dissertations/AAI3433544/.

12. "Texas of Truman's Address in El Paso; Truman's Address to El Paso Crowd," *New York Times*, September 26, 1948, https://www.nytimes

.com/1948/09/26/archives/text-of-trumans-address-in-el-paso-trumans
-address-to-el-paso-crowd.html.

13. Trish Long, "Past Presidential Visits: Harry Truman in 1948," *El Paso
Times*, February 6, 2019, https://www.elpasotimes.com/story/archives
/2019/02/06/el-paso-past-presidential-visits-harry-truman-1948
/2796815002/.

14. Associated Press, "Text of Truman's Address in El Paso," *New York Times,*
September 26, 1948, https://timesmachine.nytimes.com/timesmachine
/1948/09/26/96434140.html?pageNumber=66.

15. "Teacher Resource Folder," Truman Library, accessed August 17, 2022,
https://www.trumanlibrary.gov/public/TrumanCivilRights_resources.pdf.

16. Charles H. Martin, "Integrating New Year's Day: The Racial Politics of
College Bowl Games in the American South," *Journal of Sport* 24, no. 3
(Fall 1997): 348–49, https://www.jstor.org/stable/43609500.

17. "Héctor P. García," *Texas Originals*, Humanities Texas, accessed August 17, 2022, https://www.humanitiestexas.org/programs/tx-originals/list
/hector-p-garcia.

18. V. Carl Allsup, "Felix Longoria Affair," Handbook of Texas Online, updated October 22, 2020, https://www.tshaonline.org/handbook/entries
/felix-longoria-affair.

19. George Stith, "Operation Wetback," Digital History, accessed August 17, 2022, https://www.digitalhistory.uh.edu/disp_textbook.cfm
?smtID=3&psid=593.

20. "Joseph M. Swing," Our History, US Citizenship and Immigration Services, updated April 6, 2020, https://www.uscis.gov/about-us/our-history
/commissioners-and-directors/joseph-m-swing.

21. Fred L. Koestler, "Operation Wetback," Handbook of Texas Online, updated March 19, 2016, https://www.tshaonline.org/handbook/entries
/operation-wetback.

22. Matt Ballinger, "From the Archives: How the Times Covered Mass Deportations in the Eisenhower Era," *Los Angeles Times*, accessed August 17,
2022, https://documents.latimes.com/eisenhower-era-deportations/.

23. Wagner, "America's Forgotten History."

24. Trish Long, "1955: Set Integration for Fall Term, First in Texas," *Tales
from the Morgue* (blog), February 5, 2010, https://elpasotimes.typepad.com
/morgue/2010/02/1955-set-integration-for-fall-term-first-in-texas.html.

25. Mario T. García, *The Making of a Mexican American Mayor: Raymond Telles
and the Origins of Latino Political Power* (Tucson: University of Arizona
Press, 2018).

26. "R. E. Thomason Gives Oath of Office to Raymond Telles," *El Paso Times,*
     March 12, 1957, accessed February 28, 2022, https://www.elpasotimes
     .com/story/news/history/blogs/tales-from-the-morgue/2012/07/03/1957
     -re-thomason-gives-oath-of-office-to-raymond-telles/31510175/.

27. Jose Maria Herrera, "Telles, Raymond Lorenzo, Jr. (1915–2013)," Hand-
     book of Texas Online, updated April 28, 2021, https://www.tshaonline
     .org/handbook/entries/telles-raymond-lorenzo-jr.

17. THE NEW FRONTIER, 1960–69

1. "Chavez, Dennis," History, Art & Archives, US House of Representa-
    tives, accessed August 17, 2022, https://history.house.gov/People/Detail
    /10875.

2. Raymond L. Telles, recorded interview by William W. Moss, October 14,
    1970, 6, John F. Kennedy Library Oral History Program.

3. "Remarks of Senator John F. Kennedy, Cortez Hotel Plaza, El Paso, Texas,"
    September 12, 1960, Papers of John F. Kennedy, John F. Kennedy Pres-
    idential Library and Museum, https://www.jfklibrary.org/asset-viewer
    /archives/JFKSEN/0911/JFKSEN-0911-023.

4. Herrera, "Telles, Raymond Lorenzo."

5. "Immigration Under President Kennedy," *Boundless* (blog), September 8,
    2017, https://www.boundless.com/blog/kennedy/.tps://www.boundless
    .com/blog/kennedy/.

6. "Legal Highlight: The Civil Rights Act of 1964," Office of the Assis-
    tant Secretary for Administration & Management, US Department of La-
    bor, accessed August 19, 2022, https://www.dol.gov/agencies/oasam/civil
    -rights-center/statutes/civil-rights-act-of-1964.

7. "Immigration and Nationality Act," LBJ Presidential Library, accessed
    August 19, 2022, https://www.lbjlibrary.org/news-and-press/media-kits
    /immigration-and-nationality-act.

8. *Basketball Defensive Drills: Featuring Coach Don Haskins and the Miners of
    Texas Western,* directed by Thad Horton (Dick Borden Productions, 1967),
    https://www.youtube.com/watch?v=pxHJOAYoD2k.

9. University of Texas at El Paso, "1966. It Was a Landmark Night," *Glory
    Road,* accessed August 19, 2022, https://www.utep.edu/glory-road/the
    -year/index.html.

10. Jeff Berry and Jeff Rice, "Miners—National Champs!" *El Paso Times,*
    accessed March 20, 1966. March 1, 2022. https://www.elpasotimes
    .com/story/life/2016/03/15/1966-el-paso-celebrates-national-championship
    /80815858/.

11. Berry and Rice, "Miners—National Champs!"

12. Berry and Rice, "Miners—National Champs!"

13. Mary Schladen, "How the 1966 NCAA Championship Changed the World," *El Paso Times*, March 19, 2016, https://www.elpasotimes.com /story/sports/college/1966championship/2016/03/19/how-1966-ncaa -championship-changed-world/81882690/.

14. John F. Kennedy, "Remarks at a Luncheon Given in Honor of President López Mateos, 30 June 1962," recorded June 30, 1962, John F. Kennedy Presidential Library and Museum, https://www.jfklibrary.org/asset-viewer /archives/JFKWHA/1962/JFKWHA-111-003/.

15. Jefferson Morley, *Our Man in Mexico: Winston Scott and the Hidden History of the CIA* (Lawrence: University Press of Kansas, 2008).

16. Morley, *Our Man in Mexico.*

17. Lyndon B. Johnson, "Remarks in El Paso at the Inauguration of the New River Channel Completing the Chamizal Boundary Change," December 13, 1968, The American Presidency Project, https://www.presidency .ucsb.edu/documents/remarks-el-paso-the-inauguration-the-new-river -channel-completing-the-chamizal-boundary.

18. Johnson, "Remarks in El Paso."

19. Johnson, "Remarks in El Paso."

20. Herrera, "Telles, Raymond Lorenzo."

21. Paul Kramer, "A Border Crosses," *The New Yorker*, September 20, 2014, https://www.newyorker.com/news/news-desk/moving-mexican-border.

22. Nathan Friedman, "Political Props: Territorial Performance and the Chamizal Dispute," *MAS Context* 27 (Fall 2015), https://www.mascontext .com/issues/27-debate-fall-15/political-props-territorial-performance-and -the-chamizal-dispute/.

18. HELL PASO, 1971–89

1. "El Paso Weather in 1971," Extreme Weather Watch, accessed August 19, 2022, https://www.extremeweatherwatch.com/cities/el-paso/year-1971.

2. "Tombstones and More: Death, Burial, and Cemetery Information, Randolph County, Arkansas," Rootsweb, archived February 9, 2000, https:// web.archive.org/web/20200209032102/http://sites.rootsweb.com /~arrandol/TombstonesCatholic.htm.

3. "Top 100 Biggest US Cities in the Year 1970," Biggest US Cities, accessed August 19, 2022, https://www.biggestuscities.com/1970.

4. Martin Chourre and Stewart Wright, "Population Growth of the Southwest United States, 1900–1990," in *Impact of Climate Change and Land Use*

in the Southwestern United States (US Department of the Interior, US Geological Survey, web conference), last modified December 9, 2016, https://geochange.er.usgs.gov/sw/changes/anthropogenic/population/.

5. Carl Haub, "Changing the Way U.S. Hispanics Are Counted," Population Reference Bureau, November 7, 2012, https://www.prb.org/resources/changing-the-way-u-s-hispanics-are-counted/.

6. Clara Irazábal and Ramzi Farhat, "Historical Overview of Latinos and Planning in the Southwest, 1900 to the Present," in *Diálogos: Placemaking in Latino Communities*, ed. Michael Rios and Leonardo Vazquez (New York: Routledge, 2012), https://www.academia.edu/29831733/HISTORICAL_OVERVIEW_OF_LATINOS_AND_PLANNING_IN_THE_SOUTHWEST_1900_to_the_present.

7. Robert Mogull, "Hispanic-American Poverty," *Journal of Applied Business Research* 21, no. 3 (Summer 2005): 91–101.

8. "Since 1967, a Steady Increase in U.S. Intermarriage," Pew Research Center, May 15, 2017, https://www.pewresearch.org/social-trends/2017/05/18/intermarriage-in-the-u-s-50-years-after-loving-v-virginia/pst_2017-05-15-intermarriage-00-05/.

9. Gretchen Livingston and Anna Brown, "Intermarriage in the U.S. 50 Years After *Loving v. Virginia*," Pew Research Center, May 18, 2017, https://www.pewresearch.org/social-trends/2017/05/18/intermarriage-in-the-u-s-50-years-after-loving-v-virginia/.

10. J. Gordon Melton, "Rosicrucian," Encyclopædia Britannica, updated November 19, 2020, https://www.britannica.com/topic/Rosicrucians.

11. David S. Jones, *A History of Panzer Kaserne, Böblingen, Germany, 1938–2018: 80 Years of German and American Use of Hindenburg und Ludendorff Kaserne and Panzer Kaserne* (Panzer Kaserne: Headquarters, US Marine Corps Forces Europe and Africa, 2018), http://www.usarmygermany.com/Communities/Stuttgart/Unofficial%20History%20of%20Panzer%20Kaserne%20B%C3%B6blingen%20-%20David%20S%20Jones.PDF.

12. "Texas–El Paso's Use of Foreigners Raises Questions," *New York Times*, March 21, 1982, https://www.nytimes.com/1982/03/21/sports/texas-el-paso-s-use-of-foreigners-raises-questions.html.

13. John Burnett, "A Toxic Century: Mining Giant Must Clean Up Mess," NPR, February 4, 2010, https://www.npr.org/2010/02/04/122779177/a-toxic-century-mining-giant-must-clean-up-mess.

14. Martin Donell Kohout, "Smeltertown, TX," Handbook of Texas Online, updated March 5, 2019, https://www.tshaonline.org/handbook/entries/smeltertown-tx.

15. Gilbert Limon, interview by Alejandro Garcia, March 16, 2019, interview no. 1719, transcript, Institute of Oral History, University of Texas at El Paso, https://scholarworks.utep.edu/interviews/1719/.

16. Robert Walker, "Record Earnings Listed by ASARCO," *New York Times*, April 29, 1970, https://www.nytimes.com/1970/04/29/archives/record -earnings-listed-by-asarco-profit-in-quarter-advances-to-107.html.

17. US Department of Justice, "El Paso Intelligence Center," US Drug Enforcement Administration, accessed August 22, 2022, https://www.dea .gov/what-we-do/law-enforcement/epic.

18. US Department of Justice, Office of the Inspector General, Evaluations and Inspections Division, *Review of the Drug Enforcement Administration's El Paso Intelligence Center*, I-2010–005, June 2010, https://oig.justice.gov /reports/DEA/a1005.pdf.

19. Gary Cartwright, "The Black Striker Gets Hit," *Texas Monthly*, December 1981, https://www.texasmonthly.com/news-politics/the-black-striker -gets-hit/.

20. Cartwright, "Black Striker."

21. Cartwright, "Black Striker."

22. Cartwright, "Black Striker."

23. John Purvis, "There Was a Murder at Christmastime 40 Years Ago," KFOX 14, December 6, 2018, https://kfoxtv.com/news/special-assignments /there-was-a-murder-at-christmastime-40-years-ago.

24. Wayne King, "3 Are Found Guilty in Assassination of Federal Judge," *New York Times*, December 15, 1982, https://www.nytimes.com/1982/12/15 /us/3-are-found-guilty-in-assassination-of-federal-judge.html.

25. Robert Moore and Diana Washington Valdez, "Chagra Paroled," *El Paso Times*, December 31, 2003, 1A, https://www.newspapers.com /clip/108103657/; "Chagra," *El Paso Times*, December 31, 2003, 2A, https://www.newspapers.com/clip/108103738/.

19. DRUGS AND MONEY, 1997–2011

1. This section is adapted from Richard Parker and Mike Gallagher, "The Seeds of Narco-Democracy," *Albuquerque Journal*, March 2, 1997, https:// www.abqjournal.com/947764/the-seeds-of-narco-democracy.html.

2. Tim Golden, "To Help Keep Mexico Stable, U.S. Soft-Pedaled Drug War," *New York Times*, July 31, 1995, https://www.nytimes.com/1995/07/31 /world/to-help-keep-mexico-stable-us-soft-pedaled-drug-war.html.

3. Amanda Erickson, "How George H. W. Bush Pushed the United States to Embrace Free Trade," *Washington Post*, December 2, 2018, https://www

.washingtonpost.com/world/2018/12/02/how-george-hw-bush-pushed
-united-states-embrace-free-trade/.

4. Marie-Danielle Smith, "Five Things We Learned About NAFTA from
Secret 1992 Cabinet Documents," *National Post*, July 10, 2018, https://
nationalpost.com/news/politics/five-things-we-learned-about-nafta-from
-secret-1992-cabinet-documents.

5. *The Loewen Group, Inc. and Raymond L. Loewen v. United States of America*, ICSID Case No. ARB(AF)/98/3 (2001), https://nsarchive2.gwu.edu
/NSAEBB/NSAEBB65/claimargument1.pdf.

6. *Loewen v. US.*

7. Thomas Blanton and Michael L. Evans, eds., "Trading Democracy?: Documents from NAFTA's Secret Tribunals," *National Security Archive Electronic Briefing Book* no. 65 (February 2002), https://nsarchive2.gwu.edu
/NSAEBB/NSAEBB65/.

8. Olivia B. Waxman, "4 Things to Know About the History of NAFTA,
as Trump Takes Another Step Toward Replacing It," *Time*, November 30, 2018, https://time.com/5468175/nafta-history/.https://time.com
/5468175/nafta-history/.

9. Alexander Monge-Naranjo, *The Impact of NAFTA on Foreign Direct Investment Flow in Mexico and the Excluded Countries* (Northwestern University, August 2002), The World Bank, https://web.worldbank.org/archive
/website00894A/WEB/PDF/MONGE_NA.PDF.

10. Peter Passell, "International Business; A Payoff for Clinton's Helping
Hand to Mexico," *New York Times*, October 12, 1995, https://www.ny
times.com/1995/10/12/business/international-business-a-payoff-for
-clinton-s-helping-hand-to-mexico.html.

11. Jeff Faux, "NAFTA's Impact on U.S. Workers," *Working Economics Blog*,
Economic Policy Institute, December 9, 2013, https://www.epi.org/blog
/naftas-impact-workers/.

12. James T. Peach and Richard V. Adkisson, "NAFTA and Economic Activity
Along the U.S.-Mexico Border," *Journal of Economic Issues* 34, no. 2 (June
2000): 481–89, https://www.jstor.org/stable/4227577.

13. "Doña Ana County International Jetport Airport," AirNav.com, accessed
August 22, 2022, https://www.airnav.com/airport/KDNA.

14. US Congress, Senate, an Act to Authorize Funds for Federal-Aid Highways,
Highway Safety Programs, and Transit Programs, and for Other Purposes,
108th Cong., 2d sess., 2002, HR Rep 3550, https://www.govinfo.gov
/content/pkg/BILLS-108hr3550pcs/html/BILLS-108hr3550pcs.htm.

15. Ann Saphir, "NAFTA Struck El Paso Hard, an Exit by Trump Could Hurt

More," Reuters, November 13, 2017, https://www.reuters.com/article/us-trade-nafta-elpaso-analysis/nafta-struck-el-paso-hard-an-exit-by-trump-could-hurt-more-idUSKBN1DD1E8.

16. Judith Banister, "Manufacturing Earnings and Compensation in China," *Monthly Labor Review* (August 2005): 22–40, https://www.bls.gov/opub/mlr/2005/08/art3full.pdf.

17. Banister, "Manufacturing Earnings."

18. Jake Ulick, "Dow Snaps Losing Streak," CNN Money, December 12, 2001, https://money.cnn.com/2001/12/12/markets/markets_newyork/.

19. Ulick, "Dow Snaps."

20. *El Sicario: The Autobiography of a Mexican Assassin*, ed. Molly Molloy and Charles Bowden, trans. Molly Molloy (New York: Bold Type Books, 2011).

21. Ramón Gutiérrez, "George W. Bush and Mexican Immigration Policy," *Revue française d'études américaines* 113, no. 3 (2007): 70–76, https://doi.org/10.3917/rfea.113.0070.

22. George W. Bush and Vicente Fox, "The President's News Conference with President Vicente Fox of Mexico in Monterrey," recorded March 22, 2002, The American Presidency Project, https://www.presidency.ucsb.edu/documents/the-presidents-news-conference-with-president-vicente-fox-mexico-monterrey.

23. Jim Rutenberg, "Bush to Unveil Plan to Tighten Border Controls," *New York Times*, May 13, 2006, https://www.nytimes.com/2006/05/13/washington/bush-to-unveil-plan-to-tighten-border-controls.html.

24. Migration Policy Institute, "The Mexican Diaspora in the United States," *RAD Diaspora Profile*, rev. ed. (June 2015), https://www.migrationpolicy.org/sites/default/files/publications/RAD-Mexico.pdf.

25. Gutiérrez, "George W. Bush and Mexican Immigration."

26. Eric Lipton, "Bush Turns to Big Military Contractors to Gain Control of U.S. Borders," *New York Times*, May 18, 2006, https://www.nytimes.com/2006/05/18/world/americas/18iht-bush.html.

27. Lipton, "Bush Turns."

28. "Bush Pushes Immigration Plan on Border Visit," CNN, May 18, 2006, https://www.cnn.com/2006/POLITICS/05/18/bush.border/.

29. Jessica Livingston, "Murder in Juárez: Gender, Sexual Violence, and the Global Assembly Line," *Frontiers: A Journal of Women Studies* 25, no. 1 (2004): 59–76, https://www.jstor.org/stable/3347254.

30. Dudley Althaus, "Mexico's Murdered Women," *Deseret News*, April 20, 2010, https://www.deseret.com/2010/4/20/20109800/mexico-s-murdered-women.

31. Barack Obama, "Transcript of Barack Obama's Victory Speech," NPR, No-

vember 5, 2008, https://www.npr.org/2008/11/05/96624326/transcript
-of-barack-obamas-victory-speech.

32. Will Grant, "Drugs and Security to Top Obama and Pena Nieto Talks in
    Mexico," May 2, 2013, *BBC News*, video, https://www.bbc.com/news/av
    /world-latin-america-22377991.

33. Grant, "Drugs and Security."

34. Devon Duff and Jen Rygler, "Drug Trafficking, Violence, and Mexico's
    Economic Future," *Knowledge at Wharton*, podcast, January 26, 2011,
    https://knowledge.wharton.upenn.edu/article/drug-trafficking-violence
    -and-mexicos-economic-future/.

35. *Fentanyl: The Next Wave of the Opioid Crisis: Hearing Before the Subcommit-
    tee on Oversight and Investigations of the Committee on Energy and Commerce
    House of Representatives*, 115th Cong., 1st sess., March 21, 2017, https://
    www.govinfo.gov/content/pkg/CHRG-115hhrg25507/html/CHRG
    -115hhrg25507.htm.

36. Tim Gaynor, "Obama's Immigration Speech Is No Game Changer,"
    Reuters, May 10, 2011, https://www.reuters.com/article/idINIndia
    -56920520110511.

37. Gaynor, "Obama's Immigration."

38. Zack Budryk, "Deportations Lower Under Trump Administration Than
    Obama: Report," *The Hill*, November 18, 2019, https://docs.house
    .gov/meetings/GO/GO00/20200109/110349/HHRG-116-GO00
    -20200109-SD007.pdf.

20. STRANGERS IN THE LAND OF EGYPT, 2018

1. Amber Phillips, "'They're Rapists.' President Trump's Campaign Launch
   Speech Two Years Later, Annotated," *Washington Post*, June 16, 2017, https://
   www.washingtonpost.com/news/the-fix/wp/2017/06/16/theyre-rapists
   -presidents-trump-campaign-launch-speech-two-years-later-annotated/.

2. Campbell Robertson, Christopher Mele, and Sabrina Travernise, "11
   Killed in Synagogue Massacre; Suspect Charged with 29 Counts," *New
   York Times*, October 27, 2018, https://www.nytimes.com/2018/10/27/us
   /active-shooter-pittsburgh-synagogue-shooting.html.

3. Katharina Buchholz, "U.S. Hate Crimes at New Decade High," *Statista*,
   August 31, 2021, https://www.statista.com/chart/16100/total-number
   -of-hate-crime-incidents-recorded-by-the-fbi/.https://www.statista.com
   /chart/16100/total-number-of-hate-crime-incidents-recorded-by-the-fbi/.

4. Rachel Martin, "Children Heard Crying in Detention Center Audio
   Recording," *Morning Edition*, NPR, June 22, 2018, https://www.npr

.org/2018/06/22/622475099/children-heard-crying-in-detention-center
-audio-recording.

5. This section is adapted from Richard Parker, "After the Pittsburgh Shootings, a Thanksgiving Pilgrimage to the Texas Border," *The Atlantic*, November 22, 2018.

6. Samantha Schmidt, "Trump Judicial Appointee Rules in Favor of Deported
Mexican Mother of Four," *Washington Post*, January 18, 2018, https://www
.washingtonpost.com/news/morning-mix/wp/2018/01/18/a-trump
-judicial-appointee-rules-in-favor-of-deported-mexican-mother-of-four/.

7. Lori Robertson, "Did the Obama Administration Separate Families?"
FactCheck, June 20, 2018, https://www.factcheck.org/2018/06/did-the
-obama-administration-separate-families/.

8. Bradley Jones, "In Republicans' Views of a Border Wall, Proximity to
Mexico Matters," Pew Research Center, March 8, 2017, http://www
.pewresearch.org/fact-tank/2017/03/08/in-republicans-views-of-a-border
-wall-proximity-to-mexico-matters/.

9. This section is adapted from Parker, "After the Pittsburgh Shootings."

21. "EVERYTHING DOWN HERE STICKS, STINGS, OR BITES," 2019

1. This chapter is adapted from Richard Parker, "After the Pittsburgh Shootings, a Thanksgiving Pilgrimage to the Texas Border," *The Atlantic*, November 22, 2018, https://www.theatlantic.com/politics/archive/2018/11
/jews-and-christians-go-border-thanksgiving/576538.

2. Brian Resnick, "White Fear of Demographic Change Is a Powerful
Psychological Force," Vox, January 28, 2017, https://www.vox.com
/science-and-health/2017/1/26/14340542/white-fear-trump-psychology
-minority-majority.

3. Resnick, "White Fear."

4. Tom K. Wong, "Public Opinion About the Border, at the Border" (San
Diego: US Immigration Policy Center, 2015), https://usipc.ucsd.edu
/publications/usipc-border-poll-final.pdf.

5. This section is adapted from Richard Parker, "No Texas Is a Match for
Trump. Not Even Beto," *New York Times*, February 12, 2019, https://www
.nytimes.com/2019/02/12/opinion/el-paso-trump-beto.html.

22. THE DAY HATE CAME TO EL PASO, 2019

1. Brendan Campbell, Angel Mendoza, Tessa Diestel, and News 21 Staff,
"Rising Hate Drives Latinos and Immigrants into Silence," The Center

for Public Integrity, August 22, 2018; accessed June 1, 2022; https://publicintegrity.org/politics/rising-hate-drives-latinos-and-immigrants-into-silence/.

2. Campbell, Mendoza, and Diestel, "Rising Hate."

3. Campbell, Mendoza, and Diestel, "Rising Hate."

4. Campbell, Mendoza, and Diestel, "Rising Hate."

5. Campbell, Mendoza, and Diestel, "Rising Hate."

6. Jim Schaefer and Tresa Baldas, "Inside the El Paso Shooting: A Store Manager, a Frantic Father, Grateful Survivors," *El Paso Times*, August 10, 2019, https://www.elpasotimes.com/in-depth/news/2019/08/10/walmart-el-paso-shooting-survivors-victims-timeline/1962337001/.

7. Victor Ordonez, "Mother of Alleged El Paso Shooter Patrick Crusius Called Police About Son Owning Assault Rifle," *ABC News*, August 8, 2019, https://abcnews.go.com/US/mother-el-paso-shooter-patrick-crusius-called-police/story?id=64846894.

8. Rachel Chason, Annette Nevins, Annie Gowen, and Hailey Fuchs, "As His Environment Changed, Suspect in El Paso Shooting Learned to Hate," *Washington Post*, August 9, 2019, https://www.washingtonpost.com/national/as-his-environment-changed-suspect-in-el-paso-shooting-learned-to-hate/2019/08/09/8ebabf2c-817b-40a3-a79e-e56fbac94cd5_story.html.

9. Renaud Camus, *Abécédaire de l'in-nocence* (Paris: Reinharc, 2011).

10. Josh Alexrod and David Greene, "The Couple Killed Saving Their Baby in El Paso Had Just Found a Future Together," NPR, August 8, 2019, https://www.npr.org/2019/08/08/749099244/the-couple-killed-saving-their-baby-in-el-paso-had-just-found-a-future-together.

11. "Parts of the Manifesto from the White Supremacist El Paso Terrorist Shows Anti-Mexican, Anti-Immigration Radicalization," *Latino Rebels*, August 3, 2019, https://www.latinorebels.com/2019/08/03/manifestoelpasoterrorist/.

12. Joel Angel Juarez, "El Paso Walmart Shooting Victim Dies, Raising Death Toll to 23," NBC News, April 26, 2020, https://www.nbcnews.com/news/us-news/el-paso-walmart-shooting-victim-dies-death-toll-now-23-n1193016.

13. Steve Helling, "3 Years Later, Remembering 23 Fatal Victims of El Paso Mass Shooting," *People*, August 3, 2022, https://people.com/crime/el-paso-mass-shooting-remembering-victims-2-year-later/.

14. Jolie McCullough, "El Paso Shooting Suspect Said He Ordered His AK-47 and Ammo from Overseas," *Texas Tribune*, August 28, 2019, https://www.texastribune.org/2019/08/28/el-paso-shooting-gun-romania/.

15. Bobby Allyn, Dani Matias, Richard Gonzales, and Bill Chappell, "Stories of El Paso Shooting Victims Show Acts of Self-Sacrifice amid Massacre," NPR, August 6, 2019, https://www.npr.org/2019/08/06/748527564 /stories-of-el-paso-shooting-victims-show-acts-of-self-sacrifice-amid -massacre.

16. David Agren, "Mexico to Pursue Legal Action After Seven Citizens Killed in El Paso Shooting," *Guardian*, August 4, 2019, https://www.theguardian .com/us-news/2019/aug/04/mexico-legal-action-us-terrorism-amlo.

17. This section is adapted from Richard Parker, "Was Trump's El Paso Visit a Turning Point?" *New York Times*, August 8, 2019, https://www.nytimes .com/2019/08/08/opinion/el-paso-trump-racism.html.

Index

ABOUT

MARINER BOOKS

MARINER BOOKS traces its beginnings to 1832 when William Ticknor cofounded the Old Corner Bookstore in Boston, from which he would run the legendary firm Ticknor and Fields, publisher of Ralph Waldo Emerson, Harriet Beecher Stowe, Nathaniel Hawthorne, and Henry David Thoreau. Following Ticknor's death, Henry Oscar Houghton acquired Ticknor and Fields and, in 1880, formed Houghton Mifflin, which later merged with venerable Harcourt Publishing to form Houghton Mifflin Harcourt. HarperCollins purchased HMH's trade publishing business in 2021 and reestablished their storied lists and editorial team under the name Mariner Books.

Uniting the legacies of Houghton Mifflin, Harcourt Brace, and Ticknor and Fields, Mariner Books continues one of the great traditions in American bookselling. Our imprints have introduced an incomparable roster of enduring classics, including Hawthorne's *The Scarlet Letter*, Thoreau's *Walden*, Willa Cather's *O Pioneers!*, Virginia Woolf's *To the Lighthouse*, W.E.B. Du Bois's *Black Reconstruction*, J.R.R. Tolkien's *The Lord of the Rings*, Carson McCullers's *The Heart Is a Lonely Hunter*, Ann Petry's *The Narrows*, George Orwell's *Animal Farm* and *Nineteen Eighty-Four*, Rachel Carson's *Silent Spring*, Margaret Walker's *Jubilee*, Italo Calvino's *Invisible Cities*, Alice Walker's *The Color Purple*, Margaret Atwood's *The Handmaid's Tale*, Tim O'Brien's *The Things They Carried*, Philip Roth's *The Plot Against America*, Jhumpa Lahiri's *Interpreter of Maladies,* and many others. Today Mariner Books remains proudly committed to the craft of fine publishing established nearly two centuries ago at the Old Corner Bookstore.